The Ivory Leg in the Ebony Cabinet

The
Ivory Leg
in the
Ebony
Cabinet

Madness, Race,
and Gender
in Victorian America

Thomas Cooley

UNIVERSITY OF MASSACHUSETTS PRESS

Amherst

LC 00-048888
ISBN 1-55849-284-4

Designed by Milenda Nan Ok Lee
Set in Centaur
Printed and bound by Sheridan Books, Inc.

Library of Congress Cataloging-in-Publication Data

Cooley, Thomas
The ivory leg in the ebony cabinet : madness, race, and gender in Victorian America /
Thomas Cooley.
p.   cm.
Includes bibliographical references (p.) and index.
ISBN 1-55849-284-4 (alk. paper)
1. Psychology—United States—History—19th century.   2. United States—
Civilization—19th century.   I. Title.

BF103 .C66 2001
150'.973'09034—dc21
00-048888

British Library Cataloguing in Publication data are available.

For Barbara and Dan

and for

John Crowley

and the other members of

Ed Cady's "German seminar"

"And what is this?" said Middleton; "—a cabinet?
Why do you draw my attention so strongly to it?"

—*Nathaniel Hawthorne*

Few intellectual projects are as important as an archaeology of
racialism, and a successful one requires a sense of the extent to which
cultural practices are (in the anatomical sense) articulated.

—*Henry Louis Gates Jr.*

Contents

Illustrations

Preface

THE "ONE UNSLEEPING, ever-pacing thought" that drives Herman Melville's Captain Ahab as he stumps back and forth on his ivory leg is to lay hold upon the white whale that bit off his member (*M-D*, 963).[1] The equally obsessive but, I hope, not so mad motive of this book is to reconstruct, from primary sources, the chief model of mind by which the nineteenth century, before Freud, defined the human mind (including Ahab's) and, then, to read a wide variety of texts—from the "high literary" productions of Nathaniel Hawthorne and Emily Dickinson to criminal confessions and sideshow specimens—in the light of that model.

Since its thrust is historical, the book does not rely, centrally, on any one of the many recent theories of identity or race or gender or the body as text that might be called upon to support its underlying thesis. Essential studies are cited in the notes; but even here I have had to be highly selective. (A full account of current race theory alone, for example, would require another volume.)

Grounded in metaphor like Melville's, my own account might take as its motto Henry Adams's gloss on his theory of history: "Images are not arguments, rarely lead to proof, but the mind craves them."[2] For this is a book about "the mind" as a cultural construct and about the obsessive images—codified in a system of "scientific" metaphors that actually defined what they were supposed to be describing—by which the nineteenth century grappled with such defining notions as those of gender, race, and madness, especially during times of political and psychological upheaval (such as a slave rebellion or the advent of Freudianism).[3]

My discovery, if I'm right, is just how far-reaching and coherent, not to mention unfounded and wrong-headed, an argument these metaphors actually make, a unity out of multiplicity, as Henry Adams would say, that comes about because the seemingly disconnected fragments of mind and body that one finds lying about in the literature and culture of Victorian America can be traced to what amounts to a national psychology.

That psychology, the dominant paradigm of mind and motive in America before about 1890, I will be arguing, was a "faculty" psychology, which conceived of the human mind as neatly compartmentalized into separate roomlike seats or powers. Each faculty had its proper office or capacity, and each worked together with the others according to predetermined patterns of association in the healthy, balanced mind; the insane mind, in turn, was characterized by dissociation, fragmentation, or distortion among the mind's faculties, often accompanied by physical symptoms that mimicked the mental pathology, such as loss of feeling in a bodily part, or phantom sensations in parts that actually were missing.[4]

Metaphorical association gave the cognitive faculties of the reasoning intellect a "masculine" and "white" valence, whereas the feelings and emotions of the appetitive faculties took on a "feminine" or "black" valence. As these innate sets of capacities vied for "moral" influence over the third principal domain of the mind under faculty psychology—the will or volitional faculty—the intellectual (or "European") part of the mind was expected to dominate over the will so that it would not be overwhelmed or led astray by the instinctual (or "African") part. This was thought to be true in the group as in the individual. Thus a balanced mind, a happy marriage, and a strong nation all drew their legitimacy from the same essentially racist and sexist model, one that posited a union of parts arrayed in a natural hierarchy of authority from head to toe, North to South.

In effect a master/slave psychology, this model prevailed in American thought about the mind until after the Civil War, and it helps to account for the family resemblances not only of the romances and tales of Poe, Hawthorne, and Melville but also of the fiction, essays, speeches, medical and political treatises, exemplary life stories, and other writings of figures as apparently diverse as G. W. F. Hegel, Tom Paine, Thomas Jefferson, "Nat" Turner, Drs. S. Weir Mitchell and Oliver Wendell Holmes, Col. Thomas Wentworth Higginson, Ralph Waldo Emerson, Henry David Thoreau, Frederick Douglass, Harriet Jacobs, Harriet Beecher Stowe, and Walt Whitman.

What unites the works of these, and many other figures from the late eighteenth to the late nineteenth centuries, as I say, is their psychology, which inevitably colored their political and social philosophy. That psychology and its uses are reconstructed in my opening chapters. After a curtain-raising glimpse at some curious vestiges of the old system of thought in an introduction, I explore in chapter 1 the geography of the *sane* mind, particularly the hills and valleys of the brain that represented the various faculties to the mental philosophers and early neurologists such as Dugald Stewart, Thomas Upham, George Combe, and the phrenological Fowlers, who gave the American mind its first map of itself. According to this map, sanity was defined as a balance among the faculties, a union of the different regions of mind analogous (I contend) to the political union of the new nation out of many states, which nonetheless retained their individual powers or "rights." Thus the fundamental American political concept of *e pluribus unum* is, at bottom, a psychological construct.

In chapter 2, I begin the story of the *insane* mind that threads (the story, that is) throughout my larger narrative. If sanity was, literally, mental *balance* to the nineteenth century, insanity stemmed from an imbalance or dissociation among the faculties, the "house divided" that dots the landscape of the American imagination from Poe to Lincoln. A crack in the house could bring the whole structure down, but "mania" and "monomania" (as distinct from "dementia," which I touch on in chapter 7) did not, at least initially, entail a total loss of mind. Madness could be partial in the nineteenth century, a departure from earlier notions of insanity (and bestiality) based on an indivisible mind or soul.

Chapter 3—about "Africanism" in the American mind—turns directly to the racial implications of faculty psychology, particularly in the southern states, including Virginia, seat of the slave rebellion led by Nathaniel ("Nat") Turner in the 1830s. Such revolts, I show here, were to be explained as a kind of social madness, an insurrection of "animal instinct" and blind rage over the powers of right reason that held the more "savage" elements of society in lawful check in the normal state of political affairs. Retaliatory lynchings and bodily mutilations were justifiable in this climate as corrective signs of rational control—a return of authority and order to the body politic—or they were contemnable as "fetishistic" applications of homeopathic medicine, black magic.

As an allopathic corrective or cure for the abiding fear of disruptive "black" powers within its precincts, faculty psychology, I demonstrate in chapter 4, assured the "white" consciousness that the affections as well as the instincts and appetites were also among the "primitive faculties" of the mind, particularly in the "lower" races. Under conditions of proper restraint, "the African," therefore, was said to love his master and naturally wished to do as he was bid, like a genie in a bottle.

The "romancing" of the Nat Turner story, particularly the versions of Thomas R. Gray, Thomas Wentworth Higginson, and William Styron, illustrates this prophylaxis. From the rational sounding male narrator of a Poesque gothic tale who insanely justifies the atrocities he has committed and must be locked up or hanged (Gray's version), the "villainous" Turner (and his responsive reader) is rehabilitated by Higginson and Styron into a "feminine" figure, the fallen damsel in distress of the sentimental novel and the captivity narrative who is not to be feared, or condemned too harshly, because her will was helplessly bound when her feelings got out of control.

Having introduced the racial implications of faculty psychology in chapters 3 and 4, I turn, in the ensuing chapters, to examine more fully its implications for gender. Here and elsewhere, however, I do not mean to suggest that *white, masculine,* and *civilized* or, more especially, *black, feminine,* and *savage* were exact synonyms or antonyms in the nineteenth century, only that they functioned in near relation to one another along culturally predetermined paths of displacement, translation, and substitution.

The chief advocates of the so-called masculine virtues (synonymous with *powers* or *faculties* in the period) whom I discuss in chapter 5, along with their pictures-in-the-mind conception of consciousness, were the Transcendental idealists, particularly Emerson and Thoreau. Exalting (in practice if not in theory) the cognitive powers of the intellect over the appetitive powers of the emotions, these figures feared, and despite their "Romanticism" at times suppressed, their own "feminine" tendencies in ways analogous to the suppression of women and blacks in antebellum society.

By contrast, those abolitionists, feminists, and others who advocated the "feminine" virtues (for example, Poe, Hawthorne, Melville, Stowe, Douglass, and the sculptors Hiram Powers, William Wetmore Story, Erastus D. Palmer, and Harriet Hosmer) distrusted the rule of "whiteness" in America because it rested, they thought, on an imbalance of power among the faculties and the states as they struggled for dominion over the powers of "blackness" in their midst. Thus these radicals subverted the reign of whiteness in ways that nonetheless validated the racist and sexist assumptions implicit in the old psychology.

Stowe, in *Uncle Tom's Cabin, The Minister's Wooing,* and other works discussed in chapter 6, puts forth a neo-Lamarckian view of inherited traits that is at odds with the prevailing notions of heredity (not to mention racial relations) in America at midcentury. As a result, she comes remarkably (though covertly) close to advocating interracial breeding as a program of improvement for white American males and for soothing the growing political tensions in the country. Her Frankenstein creature, Uncle Tom Shelby, is Stowe's ideal manservant with all the "calculating" virtues of the white master *offset* by the "black" virtues of affection and obedience.

Frederick Douglass (chapter 7), though he does not advocate "miscegenation," offers a similar formula or antidote for the barbarities of slavery in antebellum America. A running theme of this and other chapters is that fictional characters, as well as historical ones, in "classic" American literature, particularly "the romance," often exemplify the thought processes, motives, and behavior patterns of faculty psychology. Douglass's Madison Washington of *The Heroic Slave*—a romancing of black history that, like the women's movement, harks back to the rhetoric of the American Revolution, which was also grounded in faculty psychology—is presented as an ideal black man because his "black" virtues (which lead to mutiny on a slave ship) are restrained by his "white" ones (which prevent him from hurting anyone but a slave trader). If Stowe's Uncle Tom is a black white man created in the laboratory of pre-Darwinian eugenics, Douglass's heroic slave is a white black man.

What about a creature such as Donatello, the half man, half beast of Hawthorne's *The Marble Faun*? He and his kind are based, I suggest in chapter 8, upon a conservative interpretation of the theory of heredity imposed upon faculty psychology by the phrenologists, particularly George Combe. Donatello's moral rise can be seen as a fortunate fall into the anxieties of "whiteness" from a blissfully instinctual state of "blackness." A descendant of the amoral beasts of the Tuscan woods, Donatello does not escape his heredity by adopting new traits to fit changes in his environment. He does so by exercising the latent moral potential (or faculty) that he has possessed all along in a dormant state. Thus the Faun's "transformation" into a human being is typical, I argue, of the way characters change in "the romance" as distinct from "the novel."

We enter the house of heredity—and impending madness—in Hawthorne's *House of the Seven Gables* (also discussed in chapter 8). Here any Lamarckian promise that adaptive responses to environment can cause structural changes in the individual capable of being inherited are buried under the inherent "segregationism" of faculty psychology. In a departure from the views of Hegel, whom his wife cited on "the Negro question," Hawthorne held that only a *balance* (not a synthesis) could be achieved in the new generation between warring families, genders, even species—the "incestual" Pyncheons are also comically cannibalistic, since they eat the offspring of the "feathered race" that resides in their henhouse—and, by extension, states and races. To illustrate the conservative, anti-evolutionary bent of faculty psychology in this chapter, I focus on one faculty, Memory (represented by the ebony cabinet of the *American Claimant* manuscripts) as showing the moral and psychological decadence, in Hawthorne's view, of those who dwell in a precognitive past, an "Africa" of the mind.

Had Hawthorne's Donatello failed to balance his animal faculties of Combativeness and Destructiveness with his newfound "moral" feelings of guilt and remorse, he might have slipped into the pit of dementia. To Hawthorne's age this was a total darkness of the mind induced by the loss or atrophy of the faculties, as in Poe's psychological allegory "The Pit and the Pendulum" (which is also an allegory of slavery). Like the rest of the master-slave literature of the period, Poe's tale assumes a pre-Freudian model, based on faculty psychology, of what later would be called "repression." By 1860, however, the old hierarchy of the faculties was being challenged, as indicated by Nathaniel Hawthorne's setting his creature free from his animal nature through the exercise (rather than the restraint) of strong emotions, painful ones in particular. Between 1865 and 1890, in fact, a fundamental shift in mental paradigms took place as faculty psychology gave way to "functional" psychology.

Influenced by Darwinism, this later, but still pre-Freudian model (which I can only sketch in outline in chapter 9) posited an evolutionary or developmental self whose identity was no longer governed by innate capacity but whose inner structure must constantly adapt itself to outer circumstances and events. In place of a mind conceived as a house of many chambers, where thoughts hung like pictures in a gallery, functional psychologists such as William James understood the mind's process as a stream or flow of "consciousness."

The new functional psychology, as I contend by examining Huck Finn's thought processes on the river with Jim, also made the emotions queen, if not master, of the "moral" self. Strictly governed or suppressed under the old model, the affections now came to be seen, potentially, as the individual's (and the state's) best guides to moral behavior. Thus the feeling and instinctual (or "feminine" and "African") parts of the mind were no longer to be disciplined away but cultivated, a return to origins and "the primitive" that persists in modernist models of consciousness. To illustrate the primacy of emotion over intellection in the new psychology, I look also in this chapter at Ursula K. Le Guin's modern allegory of the buried feelings, "The Ones Who Walk Away from Omelas," as a reenactment of William James's "The Moral Philosopher and the Moral Life."

Informed by the Scottish philosophy of "Common Sense," the old view of mind had equated sense with sensation, which was thought to be common to all and thus an indisputable ground of truth. The new model held, rather, that each individual consciousness experienced its sensations of the outside world in a manner that was distinctive and uniquely subjective. In both autobiography and fiction, this new understanding of subjectivity called for a "realistic" (or "situational") narrative about individual, often multiple, selves in place of the "romance" of types that had been one expression of faculty psychology. It also called for a new kind of poetry.

Here (chapter 10) my chief exemplar of the new psychology is Emily Dickinson, whose poetry of the personal consciousness is the work not of a retrograde seventeenth-century sensibility but of a recognizably modernist one. That is, Dickinson's "I" has far more in common, I would argue, however contrary to recent readings, with the speakers of T. S. Eliot's poetry (or Ernest Hemingway's fiction) than of Anne Bradstreet's and Edward Taylor's—or Walt Whitman's.

To show how radically Dickinson broke with the old paradigm of subjectivity and selfhood, I pair her in this chapter with Mrs. E. P. W. Packard, a political and social reformer who nonetheless clung to the old model even when her husband had her legally committed to a state mental institution for disagreeing with his religious ideas. Gendering the faculties as her father did, Mrs. Packard renounced her husband's "mastery" over her intellect only to displace his "lordly" authority upon the keeper of an insane asylum who literally enslaved her. A key mechanism of Dr. McFarland's control and his patient's submission was an incriminating letter, which I liken to that purloined from the queen in Poe's tale.

Emily Dickinson played with the master-slave conventions of the old psychology, too, notably in an exchange of letters. She, however, suffered no one to master her mind but the queenly self. Informed, perhaps, by the psychology of Alexander Bain (who also influenced William James), Dickinson's poems subsume the old faculties of knowing and feeling in a single "white exploit" of consciousness that made her "letters" incomprehensible to minds trained on the old model.

This may help explain why Dickinson, waiting for her readers to catch up with the new sensibility (which I explore further in a brief "epilogue"), buried her poems during her lifetime. Even the generation of Dickinson, Mark Twain, and William, Henry, and Alice James entered the "jungle" (their metaphor) of the new psychology with fear and trembling. It was not until the next generation, the first to feel the full impact of Freudianism, that the Anglo-American psyche began fully to embrace the emotional, instinctive self from which it felt dissociated, in part, by the war.

Thus began a "back to Africa" movement even in the "white" consciousness, which I trace briefly, in the epilogue, from T. S. Eliot to Toni Morrison. Morrison's *Beloved* is a throwback to the old "primitivism." It resurrects much of the imagery and psychology of the nineteenth-century romance of race and gender, except that, in Morrison's narrative, whiteness and masculinity are attributes of "savagery," while blackness and femininity define the precincts of "civilization."

The idea of poking around in the recesses of the mind as the nineteenth-century conceived it has haunted me for a long time. It grows directly out of my earlier work in self-narrative, particularly *Educated Lives: The Rise of Modern Autobiography in America* (1976); but I also owe inspiration to two great minds in the field, those of William Charvat and Terence Martin, whose *Instructed Vision* (1961), taking off from Charvat, linked early ideas of mind in England and America to the origins of American fiction. To this brilliant reader of texts I owe both an intellectual debt and personal one. (In his more recent work, *Parables of Possibility: The American Need for Beginnings* [1995], Martin further establishes that the great tradition of Adamic innocence and the frontier made "a blank slate" of American history and the past. He examines the slate in its positive aspect; I look at the negative.) In recent years, Charvat's pioneering work has opened frontiers for many scholars interested in the profession of authorship and the history of the book; in spirit, however, my debt is to the Charvat of *The Origins of American Critical Thought, 1810–1835* (1936), the foundation study of Common Sense philosophy in America.[5]

Earlier studies of the Common Sense school focus on its metaphysics and theology; my focus is on the broader system of "psychology" of which the philosophy of Common Sense was but one expression. Historians of psychology and science such as Edwin Boring, Stephen Jay Gould, Jenney Bourne Taylor, and Sally Shuttleworth have long been aware of faculty psychology and other models of mind as broad interpretative devices; but that power has yet to be tapped systematically by practitioners of literary and textual studies, in part because the primary materials, as Elaine Showalter has said, are generally scattered and unavailable. I, too, predict that Taylor and Shuttleworth's new anthology of psychological texts from 1830 to 1890, *Embodied Selves* (1998) will transform how we analyze fiction and other forms of narrative from this period and from both sides of the Atlantic.[6] I only wish *this* cabinet of wonderful curiosities had been available earlier.

Readers of Michel Foucault will recognize his ghost here, too, particularly the Foucault of *Madness and Civilization* (1965) and *Discipline and Punish* (1977). The master-slave model of psychology that I uncover—down to such appendages as Ahab's artificial leg, the evil eye of the mad-doctor, and the transparent eyeball of the Transcendentalists—may be seen as an internalized surveillance device akin to Bentham's panopticon. Certainly, it had a similar policing effect, though Hegel is perhaps our best guide here.

My intent in *The Ivory Leg in the Ebony Cabinet*, however, is not to write a sequel to a sequel, though I do bring the mind/body narrative forward in time. It is, rather, to see what can be done with "origins" as a species of critical inquiry.

Where this tack leads is far afield from earlier studies, to a sort of Africa of the Anglo-American mind, or, rather, the nineteenth century's conception of it.

As an "archaeology of racialism" (in Henry Louis Gates's phrase) this book is in part a response to Toni Morrison's call for a closer look at the importance of race and slavery in "classic" American literature. The contemplation of a "black presence," she wrote in *Playing in the Dark: Whiteness and the Literary Imagination* (1992) "is central to any understanding of our national literature and should not be permitted to hover at the margins of the literary imagination" (5).

Morrison's claim was that just as margins imply a center and text, a ground, "white" writing (indeed white experience) in America of the nineteenth century was inevitably produced (and lived) in relation to "blackness" or "Africanism" and can only be understood against that background. Figure and ground in American culture are one and indivisible, Eric Sundquist declared in *To Wake the Nations: Race in the Making of American Literature* (1993), the strongest of many "answers" to Morrison's call.[7] "White" culture in America simply could not have evolved as it has without "black" culture, Sundquist argues; and he makes the case by meticuously examining such conjunctions as slavery and the postcolonial ideology of the American revolution, the legal and political basis of segregation as represented in American literature, and the appropriation of African folklore and oral tradition in American writing.

One of Sundquist's most illuminating examples, for me, of the complexities of authorship arising out of the black presence in American culture is *The Confessions of Nat Turner* (1831). Sundquist's fine treatment of this literal collaboration, in the black-and-white of print, between a rebel slave and his amanuensis, Thomas R. Gray, indicates where my study departs from Sundquist's and related studies of an "integrated," American culture, such as Shelley Fisher Fishkin's *Was Huck Black?* (1993).[8]

Drawing on the work of Sacvan Bercovitch, Sundquist interprets the *Confessions* as an American "jeremiad" that exposed the "fraudulence of the revolutionary paradigm" in postrevolutionary America and cries out eloquently from the published scripture long after the living prophet's voice was choked off in 1831. That, in effect, is the "white" side of the story; mine is the "black." Thomas Gray attempts to neutralize the power of "Turner's" *Confessions*, I argue, not simply by making Turner out to be a madman, a religious fanatic rather than a true prophet, but by presenting him as the embodiment of the perversely seductive "imp" side of the ever-divided self of faculty psychology, precursor to the *ids, others,* and *abjects* of a later day. To tell the full story of that version of an American self (and white writers could no more escape it than black writers could) is the main business of this book.

In one direction, that story works against the larger narrative of an "integrated American literature" (Fishkin) that many critics are telling today. The two sides of the mind could be brought into balance with each other under the faculty psychology model; but, particularly in the version purveyed in the 1830s and forties by the phrenologists and other advocates of physical barriers within the brain, the two halves of the self could never be truly integrated. Thus the many representations in the nineteenth century, in all kinds of writing and oratory and in sculpture and the visual arts, of human motives based on this pervasive model make me wonder with Gates (in *Anatomy of Racism*) and Cornel West (in "Black Critics and the Pitfalls of Canon Formation") whether, at times, current "ideologies of pluralism" (West) may not, with the best of intentions, conceal "irresoluable conflict" even within such conventionally "white" narratives as those of Emerson and Thoreau.[9] As Jared Gardner reminds us in *Master Plots: Race and the Founding of an American Literature, 1787–1845* (1998), "the same period in which American literature arrives at its 'renaissance' is also the period in which race theory in the United States goes through its most profound transformations, giving rise to the 'American school' of scientific racism, whose 'discoveries' would help script the racialized consciousness of the second half of the nineteenth century."[10] It is this same period in which the old psychology reaches its fullest articulation.

In another direction, however, a full understanding of faculty psychology and its implications does contribute to a "desegregated," if not a fully integrated, view of Anglo-American culture, for it demonstrates that racialism (and an accompanying "sexualism") was everywhere in the nineteenth century because it was inherent in the nineteenth-century conception of mind. In making this claim about the ubiquity of racialism in the nineteenth century, my account resembles studies both of disease—such as Sander L. Gilman's *Difference and Pathology: Stereotypes of Sexuality, Race, and Madness* (1985)—and of "the gothic" in Anglo-American culture.[11]

Teresa Goddu, for example, in *Gothic America: Narrative, History, and Nation* (1997), takes to task earlier critics, such as F. O. Matthiessen, who relegated the fiction of Poe, Brown, and John Neal to the back of the bus and who largely ignored works that dealt overtly with race, which Goddu—along with Dana Nelson and Joan Dayan (*Fables of Mind: An Inquiry into Poe's Fiction*)—finds elaborately encoded in American gothicism.[12] The great American "renaissance" tradition marginalized the gothic and other indications of a black presence in American culture, Goddu contends, because the gothic, by symbolically unmasking racial atrocities and the dehumanization of commercialism (as in Hawthorne's stories of veiled ladies on public display), did not square with the "national myth of new-world innocence."[13]

Psychological and formalist critics of the forties, fifties, and sixties defused the gothic, in part, by linking it with the romance and the "world elsewhere" of Richard Poirer, Richard Chase, and Leslie Fiedler. The term "romance" (despite its utility for Susanna Rowson, Poe, Hawthorne, and Henry James) has, therefore, faded somewhat from the critical vocabulary of the last twenty years because a generation of new historicists like Goddu have criticized earlier critics who used the term for being blind to political and social reality. I agree that the "romance" tradition of criticism was often politically naïve and that, as Dennis Berthold has said in a penetrating review of Goddu, "by contrasting the American 'romance' with the British 'novel'" adherents of the romance school perpetuated "the hoary myth of American exceptionalism." [14] However, with Berthold and Edgar Dryden (*The Form of American Romance* [1988]), I would like to rehabilitate the term *romance* as a critical concept by linking it historically with faculty psychology, a model of mind that, while characteristically and ubiquitously American, cut across national borders, as well as those of race and gender. [15] This is not to privilege psychology over politics, as the older tradition did, but to articulate (in the anatomical sense) the intimate and contradictory ties between them that were always there.

Once we see the psychological complications and contradictions beneath the "naïve" fictional veils of the romance, its cultural and political complexities can be seen to inform even such apparent subversions of black authorship as Thomas Gray's "transcription" of *The Confessions of Nat Turner*. Like Gray, Turner's rapt auditor and "confessor," the white reader of Turner's jeremiad takes on the role of the reader-victim of a Poe tale, who succumbs unwillingly, and so is not to be held morally responsible for his or her action, to "the fierceness of the delight of its horror"—as in "The Imp of the Perverse." Leaving the dangerous and prophetic Turner to hover at the margins of his own story, Gray's appropriation of Turner's ghost as his own shadow self is typical of the tricks the "black" or appetitive side of the psyche plays with the "white" or cognitive side under the model of nineteenth-century faculty psychology. This, I take it, is what Toni Morrison means by "romancing the shadow."

Too often, it seems to me, the "new historicism," under which rubric this book probably will be seen to fall, sacrifices text to context, the individual whole to a collection of parts. Articulation, let it be said at the outset, is the aim here; and the test of my back-to-origins approach will be not only how well it turns up family resemblances in apparently disparate types and forms but also how well it captures the colorations of individual specimens. In the end, though, I do hope to establish among the texts examined here something close to Darwin's "propinquity of descent." That is, I hope to show that the similarities I see in my "specimens" derive not from an arbitrary perception of likeness but from a common ancestor, namely faculty psychology, whose parent features are retained by the offspring in some detail. Thus would I escape the fate of the collector in Hawthorne's sketch who is so "addicted" to "queer analogies" that he places "the golden thigh of Phythgagoras ... on the same shelf with Peter Stuyvesant's wooden leg, that was fabled to be of silver." [16]

A number of people have helped me with this book. I wish especially to thank Barbara Cooley for her editorial expertise and for her moral support through thick and thin. Richard D. Altick, Morris Beja, Steven Fink, Barbara Rigney, Arnold Shapiro, and Frances Shapiro of Ohio State; William Cain of Wellesley; John Crowley and Susan Edmunds of Syracuse University; Thomas Wortham of U.C.L.A., and Clark Dougan of the University of Massachusetts Press read the manuscript, in whole or part, and gave me wonderful suggestions. I thank them all but take full credit for any "idiotoid" (Alice James) aspects that remain.

THOMAS COOLEY

Columbus, Ohio

Vestiges

Little Shop of Race and Gender

> Then mark the cloven sphere that holds
> All thought in its mysterious folds.
> That feels sensations faintest thrill,
> And flashes forth the sovereign will.
>
> —*Oliver Wendell Holmes, M.D.*

> In a cabinet of natural history, we become sensible of a certain occult
> recognition and sympathy in regard to the most unwieldly and eccentric
> forms of beast, fish, and insect.
>
> —*Ralph Waldo Emerson*

 THIS BOOK is a study in human remains, as the sociologists call them, the remnants, all too visible still, of an ancient system of beliefs about race and gender, sanity and madness. Most of the relics to be exhumed here are metaphorical; but strewn throughout the narrative are many actual body parts, from Broca's brain and the genitalia of Sartje Bartmann, the so-called Hottentot Venus, to Henry James Sr.'s missing leg.

Whether preserved in bell jars or the living museums of racial prejudice and sexual taboo, these *disjecta membra* bear the caliper marks of an age of measurement. With what it thought to be mathematical precision, the nineteenth century tagged and weighed every physical aspect and organ of human anatomy: the trunk in relation to the extremities, the contours of the brain, the planes of the head and face, even the shape of the nose.[1] Besides the study of healthy specimens, men and women at all levels of society—Dr. Oliver Wendell Holmes as avidly as Jack the Ripper—also assayed the human body in its "morbid" states, particularly of amputation and dismemberment.[2] Why this fascination, to the point of obsession, with the surfaces of the body, especially in bits and pieces?

Any but the most superficial answers to such questions are more likely to lie in the mind rather than the brain, for mind, unlike the physical hemispheres that hold it, is always a figurative construct, a fiction of its times. When Sigmund Freud first lectured here in 1909, for example, the median American mind harbored no recognizably modern notion of the unconscious. Before 1890, it still clung to a "faculty psychology" model that defined mental illness as a dissociation of the mind's constituent parts, or "organs." Madness, in this scheme, was a sign of "moral" decay, thought to be preventable or correctable, in many cases, under rigorous conditions of cultural and political hygiene. Hence the nineteenth century's obsession with bodily disfigurement, whether in the dissecting room or beneath the hanging tree.[3]

Conceiving of the mind (as distinct from the brain) in explicitly physical terms—most notably as a series of interconnecting rooms or chambers—the nineteenth century projected its deepest fears of mental and social disintegration upon the maimed body, a practice indelibly imprinted upon the American consciousness by the amputations, moral and geographical no less than medical, of the Civil War. If a house divided from itself could not stand, neither could the human body when its members were cut off from one another—and from the unionizing head. In a society that defined madness as a literal dissociation of the mental faculties, divisions in the external body or its environs typically signified metaphysical divisions, a severing of the internal parts or chambers of the mind from each other. "Mad" Ahab's obsession with his missing member in *Moby Dick* is a case in point, of course. But so are the physical fragmentations we have come to associate with the wastelands of modernism, which T. S. Eliot, harking back to the faculty psychology model, diagnosed as outward and visible signs of a "dissociation of sensibility" in the modern psyche.[4]

Since this is the model of mind from which those of our own time directly evolve, I propose to take it apart in the following pages, thereby tracing some of American culture's most basic conceptions of itself to their roots in traditional Anglo-American notions of self and society, sanity and madness, race and gender. How else are we to understand the mindsets of the immediate past and their residue in present consciousness, except by trying to understand how an earlier age defined some of its key, culturally-determined terms, such as *right* or *wrong, sane* or *insane, masculine* or *feminine, white* or *black* or *red?*[5]

Drawing on individual case histories—all "true" stories, though some of them are imagined—I am proposing, then, to reconstruct the anatomy of a national mindset that goes to the heart of much of the sexism and racism that still persists in this country. (One motive for such an inquiry would be the same one that inspired Holmes to go after puerperal fever, even though he suspected, correctly, that the infection was often carried by the doctors themselves: the hope of some day eradicating a pestilence.) Consider, for example, the bizarre case of the hastily preserved remains of a gentleman scholar at Harvard.

Holmes and the Parkman Murder

Dr. John Webster, professor of chemistry at the Harvard Medical School, was spending more time than usual behind the locked doors of his laboratory. His behavior might even have been termed "suspicious." Harvard Medical had just taken up its new quarters across from the Massachusetts General Hospital, and Webster's lab was located there, on land donated to the school by the wealthy Boston physician, George Parkman, to whom Webster owed money. At the rear, the new building extended on stilts over the tidal flats of the Charles River, a convenience in those ecologically lax times since bits of human tissue and other small body parts could be dropped into the water at high tide from the dissecting rooms above. On November 23, 1849, however, Dr. Webster found himself with more body parts than the chutes could judiciously handle.

Fees for the upcoming school term had just been collected, and for the moment the penurious professor had a little cash. Just before two o'clock that afternoon, the janitor recalled, an irate gentleman entered the building looking for Dr. Webster. It was Parkman, the school's benefactor, after whom a chaired professorship had been named in gratitude for his gift of the site that was soon to become—at least in part—his last resting place. The Parkman Professorship was currently occupied by Oliver Wendell Holmes, the poet and father of the jurist, who taught human anatomy and maintained a "spacious but obscure and irregular crypt" for preparing specimens beneath the stepped tiers of the lecture theater.[6]

Also dean of the school, Holmes had recently changed the course of medical education in America by signing a five-thousand-dollar bond with the city of Boston for the classroom use of bodies that otherwise would be buried intact at public expense. "Professor Bones," as Holmes addressed himself to students, knew the value of hands-on experience with genuine corporeality from his own student days in France in the 1830s. There the budding anatomist simply paid the police fifty centimes for an unclaimed corpse at the Paris morgue. Here, as in England, human cadavers were still hard to come by at midcentury, even for legitimate scientific purposes.

The difficulty had to do with the traditional Anglo-Protestant reverence for the body as what Holmes, in one of his poems, called "The Living Temple." Though he took it apart in the dissecting room, Holmes, like other men of his time and upbringing, considered the humblest human body to be a place of the sacred mysteries: "O Father!" his anatomist's hymn implores, "make these mystic temples thine!" When the temple's "last tottering pillars fall," he be-

FIG. 1 Massachusetts General Hospital in 1853 and (to the right) Harvard Medical School, where Dr. Oliver Wendell Holmes was dean when Professor Webster murdered Professor Parkman. Courtesy of the Boston Public Library.

seeched the architect, "Take the poor dust thy mercy warms, / And mould it into heavenly forms!"[7] (Note that the doctor anticipates a change in *form*, not in *kind* as the human specimen undergoes its final processing. Transformation, metamorphosis—not development or evolution—is the theme of this literature.) Holmes's contract with the city of Boston, therefore, called for a "decent" burial of the remains once his students finished with their cadavers.

It was Holmes's reverence for the more earthly forms of a privileged class and caste, however, that hindered the search for his patron, the unfortunate Parkman, whose aging pillars were cut from under him before they could crumble of natural causes.

When Parkman had been missing for a week, the school janitor asked three members of the faculty to help him break into the chemistry lab. His plea fell upon ears well-attuned to the nuances of the place. The faculty of Harvard Medical understood perfectly that their dean would never for an instant countenance the incredible accusation that a Harvard professor of twenty years' standing had committed a heinous crime against one of his own. Thus they

instructed the suspicious janitor, Littlefield, who apparently had a lower opinion of Harvard professors, to proceed alone.

Entering the laboratory through an adjoining privy, the janitor came immediately upon a human pelvis, a left leg, and a right thigh. Gold fillings and other
dental work found in the lab furnace soon identified the parts as Parkman's.
Webster never admitted committing the grisly murder, but he was found guilty
and hanged a year later, almost to the day, as the result of a sensational trial
that made legal history for condemning a man to death on the basis of circum-
stantial evidence. Official annals of the Harvard Medical School include this
sentence about the scene of the crime: "Further search of the school revealed a
thorax and a left thigh packed in a tea chest filled with tan and covered with
minerals in the corner of the same laboratory."[8]

Since tan (or tannin or tanbark) was used for tanning hides, the professor
of chemistry apparently intended to preserve at least some of his victim's remains. For what purpose, one wonders: was the chemist simply keeping his
gruesome treasure from spoiling and giving him away before he could dispose
of it? or had he actually turned into a Poesque savage?

And Gentlemen of the Club

Either way, Webster's tea chest had been appropriated to a use that the overseers of Harvard College and the dean of the Medical School could scarcely
credit, even as the evidence piled up, to a gentlemen of their school. Had not
Holmes spoken in "The Living Temple" of "reason's reins" upon "the outward
moving frame"?[9] The uncalloused hand of the scholar might rake among the
ruins of the temple in the pursuit of science and the defeat of quackery—as
practiced in such desecrations of the mind-body relation as phrenology, physiognomy, craniometry, mesmerism, and the host of other schemes for parceling
human nature into the arbitrary categories, both biological and ideological, that
form the background of this book. But to slay a living fellow even in the heat
of passion—preposterous! Surely, "Cain, where is thy brother?" was never
meant to be asked of the Boston aristocrat.

As favorably inclined toward their own class as they could be predisposed
against persons of other castes and colors, even of the other gender (as we shall
see from still more bizarre vestiges of institutionalized prejudice in Victorian
America), the faculty of Harvard Medical continued politely to consult Webster about school matters in his jail cell. At the chemistry professor's trial,
Holmes was called as an expert witness for the prosecution, testifying that
Parkman's remains belonged, in fact, to Parkman. But he also testified for the
defense as a witness to Webster's good character. "It is, of course, understood,"

he wrote to Jared Sparks, president of Harvard and the first professor of history in an American University, "that only a temporary substitute is wished for in the emergency."[10]

Of course. For Holmes was not intentionally covering up his colleague's misdeeds. Nor was he legalistically presuming innocence until guilt had been proved. Holmes and the others believed sincerely that a rational white man of the "better" class could never be guilty of the hideous imposture imputed, unaccountably, to Webster. Like most of the other gross instances of social, sexual, and racial stereotyping to be examined in the following pages, the prejudices of Holmes and his peers were largely unconscious. (And, therefore, perhaps, all the more revealing of their culture's most deeply rooted beliefs.) No wonder, then, that Boston society turned upon Webster with such fury when a jury of his peers concluded that the chemistry professor actually had perpetrated an unspeakable crime—not only against humanity but also against his own kind.

Though Holmes had supported Harriot K. Hunt's application to the school, he did not push it with the overseers, and Harvard Medical in 1850 remained a club for men, if not always gentlemen. For a woman's point of view on the Parkman murder, consequently, we must turn to an outsider, Sophia Hawthorne, wife of the romancer. On September 29 of that year, she voiced a dissenting opinion in the case:

> I am really surprised to hear that Professor Webster is hanged—I find I did not really think he would be. Poor wretch! I do not believe in legal murder any more than in malicious murder—Until we can cause life I think we have no right to take it away—& I suspect that a century or two hence hanging will be looked upon as an unaccountable barbarism, inconceivable of a community calling itself Christian—A murderer forfeits his freedom because he is a dangerous wild beast—but his life! It is a sacred & mysterious gift of GOD & He alone should dispose of it.

As usual with her fonder predictions about humankind, Sophia Hawthorne was wrong again. "I know that wiser & better minds than mine have a different view," she added ironically, as if to check her natural optimism for the future of the race. "Still I must look with my own eyes till I am convinced by superior argument that they are blind."[11]

In his classes, the witty Dr. Holmes liked to parody the sort of arguments to which Sophia Hawthorne referred. Reversing the usual classroom procedure, one of his verses calls upon the professor of anatomy to explain his views

on human reproduction to incredulous male students. "Call Number One—
Professor Bones":

> There, take your place, look in my face,
> Stand up upon your legs
> And tell me why it's all a lie
> that men are hatched from eggs.
> Oh Professor
> Professor, can't you tell?
> I rather guess that you'll confess
> The ovum is a *sell*.[12]

Though childless himself, Oliver Wendell Holmes Jr., the jurist, knew all
about the ovum. A product, in part, of his father's masculinizing humor, the
keen legal mind of the poet-anatomist's son was one of those "better and wiser"
minds to which Sophia Hawthorne sarcastically attributed "superior argument," a capacity routinely assigned without irony in her day to men, even by
many women. The younger Holmes had figured out the basic biological
differences between boys and girls and, growing up in a privileged New England household, a few other distinctions besides. Thus as late as *Buck v. Bell*
(1927) Associate Justice Holmes of the U.S. Supreme Court upheld the steril-
ization of Carrie Buck, an African American woman, on the now infamous
grounds that "three generations of imbeciles are enough" (*MM*, 335). Apparently, if some minds were superior to others, as in the case of the all-male faculty of the Harvard Medical School of 1850, where a member could be disen-
franchised only by turning him into a wild beast, some must be *inferior*—in
their basic architecture.

Back Brain, Front Brain

"A hundred years ago," observe Anne Moire and David Jessel in a more recent
commentary on "brain sex," the notion that men and women are fundamentally
different "in a whole range of aptitudes, skills, and abilities, would have been a
leaden truism, a statement of the yawningly obvious."[13] So would the observation, no longer tenable to living brains, male or female, that "Caucasians"
differed from persons of "Ethiopian" and "American" (that is, Native American) descent in a similar range of aptitudes and capacities. (The racial categories are Samuel G. Morton's in *Crania Americana* of 1839.)

Not so "yawningly obvious" to the twentieth-century mind, however, is that the human mind of a hundred years ago, regardless of gender or color, was organized differently from ours. In the nineteenth century, the mind—as well as the almost virgin territory of the brain—was oriented from front to back, as opposed to the left-right orientation we speak of today. Or so it thought.

Consider the case of Robert Bennett Bean, a poor scientist and a virulent racist, who not so nicely illustrates a common presupposition in the minds of many white males about other minds of a century ago. A physician practicing in Virginia, Bean measured the corpus colossum in brains once attached to "representative" samplings of black and white Americans. His findings: "The Negro is primarily affectionate, immensely emotional, then sensual and under stimulation passionate. . . . [T]here is instability of character incident to lack of self-control, especially in connection with the sexual relation. . . . One would naturally expect some such character for the Negro, because the whole posterior part of the brain is large, and the whole anterior portion is small."[14]

Suspicious of Bean's findings, Franklin P. Mall of Johns Hopkins University repeated Bean's study in 1909. Mall measured 106 brains, including 18 from Bean's original sampling. Mall, however, did his measurements blind: that is, he did not ascertain until afterward whether he had measured a "white" brain or a "black" one. Mall found no differences by race in his brain ratios, and therefore "no difference between the races" in terms of mental function, suggesting that if anyone in this study had a small brain, it was Bean.[15]

The corpus collosum adjoins the left and right hemispheres of the brain; except for his politics, however, Bean's mind, like those of most craniologists of the nineteenth century, operated along a different axis. Bean plotted ratios based on measurements of the front and back of the corpus collosum. In doing so, as Steven Jay Gould points out in *The Mismeasure of Man* (1981), he was simply "following a cardinal tenet of craniometry, that higher mental functions reside in the front of the brain and sensorimotor capacities toward the rear" (77). We may speak today of behaviors that are right-brained or left-brained, but the nineteenth century clove to front-brainedness and back-brainedness. Front-brained people were more intelligent; back-brained people were more instinctual and emotional. Thus blacks, many whites "reasoned," were naturally backward, while they themselves were meant to stand out front.

The nineteenth century did not reify back-brainedness in "inferior" *races* alone. It found this same psychophysical orientation in women of all races, though African women, such as Sartje Bartmann, the "Hottentot Venus," were especially so endowed. "We might ask if the small size of the female brain depends exclusively upon the small size of her body," wrote the French anatomist, Paul Broca. We might ask, but Broca, whose school also placed the higher cognitive functions in the front of the brain and those of sensation and emotion in the back, already knew the answer: "we must not forget that women are, on the average, a little less intelligent thań men."[16]

Broca was a distinguished surgeon and one of the first neurologists to establish that specific parts of the human brain control specific functions of human behavior. "Broca's region" in the inferior frontal convolution is named after him because he correctly identified it as the center of articulate speech. Broca, moreover, was no misogynist; but he could not altogether escape the prejudices of his day even in the field in which he was otherwise a pioneer. Neither could Broca's colleague, Gustave LeBon, who was, it would appear, genuinely misogynistic. LeBon drew this analogy: "All psychologists who have studied the intelligence of women, as well as poets and novelists, recognize today [1879] that they represent the most inferior forms of human evolution and that they are closer to children and savages than to an adult, civilized man."[17]

Women, children, and "savages"—he might have added madmen—on the one hand, and "adult, civilized" males on the other: curious as it seems today, this sort of pigeonholing was typical of the race and gender "science" of the nineteenth century, which chose its specimens to fit its preconceived categories of mental, moral, and other human capacities.

Crude vestiges of social and political prejudice, those categories—and many of the related terms in which Victorian prejudices of race, gender, class, and caste expressed themselves—derive, I believe, from a "faculty" theory of human psychology that conceived of the mind in spacial or geographical terms. Thus it is no accident, as I demonstrate in chapter 3 and later, that the gradual collapse after 1850 of this whole system of classifying human beings and their mental and moral capacities coincided with the West's first systematic exploration of the African subcontinent. (The rigors of actually visiting "the dark continent," instead of merely fantasizing about it, so drastically altered Western notions of "savagery" and "civilization," self and other, that even such pathological repressives as William Dean Howells would come, at the end of the century, to speak of "the black heart's-truth" as more or less normative.)[18]

Under the faculty psychology model, the human mind was divided spatially, first into two, then, in the late eighteenth century, into three basic compartments or mental domains: the faculties or "seats" of Knowing (or cognition), of Feeling (or appetition), and the Will. Knowing and Feeling were further subdivided into as many as thirty or forty smaller compartments that housed the individual faculties (Memory, Imagination, Acquisitiveness, Self-Esteem, Cautiousness, etc.); when an item, or thought, was placed in one bin under the control of one faculty, it was temporarily separated from those in other bins under other faculties, making the human mind a sort of cerebral chest of drawers.

Nathaniel Hawthorne, for example, is working with this analogy when his hero, Middleton, of the "American Claimant" manuscripts returns to the England of his childhood in search of a dimly remembered family mansion. What Middleton finds instead is a wonderful piece of furniture, an ebony cabinet of mirrors, more a piece of "architecture" than of "upholstery," that mocks his grandiose vision of the past and turns his dreams of vast ancestral holdings into "a fairy reality" (*ACM*, 27–28). Such are the tricks that Memory—the mental faculty or "activity" invoked by the darker (and more obscure) image of my title—plays upon the unwary mind, particularly when distorted by greed or desire, as in Middleton's case.

In faculty psychology, memory is that power of cognition by which virtual images of real past experiences are re-presented in present consciousness, as in this passage from Emerson's essay on "Intellect" (king of the faculties, to his mind):

> If you gather apples in the sunshine, or make hay, or hoe corn, and then retire within doors, and shut your eyes . . . you shall still see apples hanging in the bright light, . . . or the tasselled grass, or the corn-flags, and this for five or six hours afterwards. There lie the impressions on the retentive organ, though you knew it not. So lies the whole series of natural images with which your life has made you acquainted in your memory, though you know it not, and a thrill of passion flashes light on their dark chamber, and the active power seizes instantly the fit image, as the word of its momentary thought. (*EEL*, 421–22)

The implications of a passage like this, as a lens through which to examine the nineteenth century mind's understanding of itself, are enormous. Besides mixing science and metaphor with reckless abandon, Emerson begins by assuming that all knowledge is grounded in the senses: his observer must first *see*—sight is the primary sense in this passage as in most of Emerson's writing—the objects of perception in the bright light of day before he can retain them in his mind as subjects of contemplation. Next, sense data must be "impressed" upon the "retentive organ" in the form of images. The analogy is with printing, perhaps, or engraving. And so it is not surprising, when we consider that some versions of faculty psychology located the power of language directly behind or beneath the eyeballs, that Emerson goes on, here as elsewhere, to ground his theory of language in a theory of visual perception. It is not only words that have their source in "natural images," Emerson believes, however. Thought itself arises from visual images, or pictures in the mind, often arranged in linear fashion, like words on the printed page.

Thus, in Emerson's formulation, the eyeball is only the first in a series of perceptive organs that retain or process impressions of sensory experience. Faculty psychology conceived of the entire brain as a collection of organs, each with its distinct neurological function. ("The term Faculty," said the phrenologist George Combe, "is used to denote a particular power of feeling or thinking, connected with a particular part of the brain" [*SP,* 98].) Because the brain was made up of multiple organs with fixed borders or limits to their jurisdiction, the mind as a whole was to be conceived not as an organism but as an architectural or geographic structure divided into regions or "chambers" that housed such distinct mental "powers" as "passion" or "memory." Within these chambers, some of which were "dark" in their normal state, thinking—or at least remembering—took place when one or more mental images was selected from among its fellows and summoned into the light, as from a chest, tomb or dungeon.

The order of precedence here is crucial for our understanding of the origins of much of the racial and gender prejudice that clouded the nineteenth-century's prevailing idea of mind. The cloven or divided "sphere" of the brain may democratically hold "all thought in its mysterious folds," as Dr. Holmes said; but the route by which a thought progresses through the folds and valleys of the *mind,* in this scheme, is tortuously selective. First, in its journey toward conscious expression—even if that expression is only an act of speaking or writing, as in the case of Emerson's observer—the waking thought must pass from the realm of sensation into that of cognition (which the age considered the rightful habitation of "adult, civilized" white men). Here the object of sensory perception is fitted with a mental image of itself analogous to the retained images of physical sight on the retina.[19]

Once it is cast as an idea *of* or *about* something either external to the mind, like Emerson's apples, or internal to it (the idea of forbidden knowledge implied by the apples of Eden, say), the mental impression or image passes into the realm of passion and feeling (the "feminine" and "savage" region of the mind). Here it is embraced or rejected, loved or feared. Only then, after the borning thought has passed as a shadow through the valleys of cognition and appetition, can the will, from its own "sovereign" territory, flash forth the moral, motor, and other commands that translate the thought into action.

Because it retains, potentially, all the mental images or thoughts from a person's past ("the whole series of natural images with which your life has made you acquainted"), memory is a particularly important faculty in this scheme. Within its limits as a repository of actual experience, memory, among all the compartments of the mental cabinet that faculty psychology made of the human mind, was thought by some to serve a function even more vital than that of the imagination, the other cognitive power celebrated and demonized by the nineteenth century for its visionary powers. (Even Coleridge defined the creative power as "half memory, half imagination.") Without memory, one lost not only all direct knowledge of the past—thus dwelling perpetually, according to this racially benighted Western view of history, in the mental darkness of the African subcontinent—one lost personal identity as well. Perhaps this is why, when offered "a draught of Lethe," the visitor to Hawthorne's musem of wonders in "The Virtuoso's Collection," will give up none of his recollections. "As well never to have lived," he says, "as to lose them now" (*MOM*, 490).

In the history of science, "cabinets," before they dwindled into ponderous pieces of furniture, were chambers for housing the oddities—a human skull, a rare shell, an insect in amber, a unicorn's horn—in the collection of an intellectual "virtuoso," a Renaissance gentleman with a particular penchant for "natural history" who, recognizing no limits to the inquiring mind, took all fields of knowledge as his province.[20] A visual model (like the "theaters" of memory in medieval manuals of logic and rhetoric) of the compartmentalized mind of faculty psychology, the cabinet, was debased for profit in the nineteenth century by, among other showmen and charlatans, P. T. Barnum. (Visitors to Barnum's "museums" were invited, by a sign prominently displayed, to view the "egress," which snapped shut behind the less literate patron, requiring another admission fee to reenter.)[21] Moreover, even the honest virtuoso ran the risk of going too far in his quest for knowledge among the artifacts of the mere intellect, as in Hawthorne's tale.

Still, the keeping of cabinets has a compelling intellectual history; and this book, though it makes no claim to virtuosity, is in form, as in content, a cabinet. That is, it offers for the reader's perusal a quaint archaeology of race, gender, and madness based upon a curious collection of cultural and social artifacts that still inform the darker corners of the American consciousness (and that we, therefore, relegate to the dust bins of the past at our peril). Gleaned from a wide range of sources—in fiction, autobiography, diaries, slave narratives, poems, legal documents, treatises in mental and moral philosophy, clinical case histories, anatomical drawings, and more—some of these curiosities may seem only marginally significant at first. As in any good cabinet, however, the value of the collection as cultural signifier lies in whatever web of relation can be seen to obtain among its members by the exhibitor and the willing patron of the collection.

Professor Gould Meets the Hottentot Venus

However willing, even eager, to be enlightened they were, the gentlemen of London and Paris who flocked to view the "Hottentot Venus" early in the nineteenth century were not much interested in the back of her *head*. A member of the Khoi-San peoples, Sartje Bartmann was, as Richard D. Altick puts it in *The Shows of London*, "steatopygic to a fault."[22] At Bartmann's ample buttocks, the men (and women) of "civilized" European society were allowed to gape like savages, but they were not permitted to see the *tablier*, or little curtain of skin formed by the enlarged labia minora in some Khoi-San females. Her *tablier* was not made publicly visible, that is, until Bartmann died and Georges Cuvier, the greatest anatomist in France, dissected her body, preserving the genitalia in a bell jar. "I have the honor, to present to the Academy," he wrote in a monograph on the subject, "the genital organs of this woman prepared in a manner that leaves no doubt about the nature of her *tablier*."[23]

The jar containing Sartje Bartmann's female curtain of shame (the usual English translation of *feminae sinus pudoris*) ended up on a shelf in the back wards of the Musée de L'Homme (*sic*) in Paris, where Steven Jay Gould, the Harvard paleontologist, rediscovered it a few years ago. What makes his find a crude but telling measure of gender and racial bias in the nineteenth century is the other bell jar that resides a shelf or two below Sartje's. It contains the preserved brain of Paul Broca, the craniologist. The Museum of Man in Paris does not house Broca's penis, according to Gould, nor the genitalia of any other eminent men. That would be gauche. But while its shelves groan with numerous "male" brains, Gould discovered no brains of women whatsoever in the collection.[24]

Upon autopsy, Broca's brain was found to weigh 1,424 grams, "a bit above average," Gould notes, "but nothing to crow about" (*MM*, 92).[25] Broca could take comfort in outdoing Franz Josef Gall (1,198 grams), the father of phrenology, the pseudoscience of reading mental capacity from the exterior contours of the cranium; but he would have been chagrined by the prowess of Gall's pupil, Johann Kaspar Spurzheim (1,559 grams), whom Sophia Hawthorne remembered as a kindly hulking man (hence his cranial bulk) with enormous shoulders. Walt Whitman, a great admirer of these and other phrenologists— they "are not poets, but they are the lawgivers of poets"—fell in between Gall and Spurzheim with a brain of 1,282 grams, weighed, presumably, *before* it was dropped on the lab floor of the American Anthropometric Society by a technician.[26] A few years after presenting his prize of female anatomy to the French Academy, Georges Cuvier himself weighed in at an much heftier 1,830 grams, not far short of Ivan Turgenev's record of more than 2,000.

Obviously, the one fact about human intelligence that can be inferred from these numbers is that brain weight does not measure it. Yet if the doctors wanted to study the normal behavior of a woman in the nineteenth century, it is equally clear, they looked to other parts of her anatomy than the head. "Without doubt there exist some distinguished women, very superior to the average man," conceded Gustave LeBon, "but they are as exceptional as the birth of any monstrosity, as, for example, of a gorilla with two heads; consequently, we may neglect them entirely" (*MM*, 105).

LeBon's monster, alas, was no freak. It was precisely as an ape or other sub-human beast in a cage that many "civilized" white men, especially in America, once characterized not only "inferior" races and the "weaker" sex, but also the "feminine" impulses and "savage" instincts lurking within themselves. In the following pages, we will track these beastly (and sadly lingering) images of race and gender to their common lair in faculty psychology. But this study also aspires, in a small way, to stretch the limits of our conventional, either-or thinking about human difference, an enterprise that began for me personally some time ago.

My First Hermaphrodite

The first (and only) time I have ever seen essential male and female body parts conjoined in one living person was in a sideshow at the county fair when I was twelve. In the crowded tent, segregated by gender—but not race, though this was South Carolina before the Civil Rights movement—the dark curtain lifted, and a large white woman was shining a flashlight on the lower half of her loose fitting cotton dress. When the woman raised her skirts, petals of flesh unfolded below, and a short, thick snake poked its head from the fringed garden. Fascinating to a pubescent boy who wanted desperately to learn more, anything about sex.

I was all eyes that night and so I don't remember what "The Hermaphrodite," as she/he was billed, had to say. Since this was the Bible Belt, it must have been something like, "I'm going to show you this and if you laugh, God may strike you the same way," as in Flannery O'Connor's short story, "A Temple of the Holy Ghost," an update in prose of Holmes's "The Living Temple." Because I didn't really know then where the lines were drawn, I found nothing to laugh at in a person who appeared to cross them. But I did notice that the hermaphrodite used outmoded grammar: "God made me thisaway and I don't dispute hit."[27] What most fascinates me now, however, as a cultural historian and literary scholar, is why the adults flocked to that tent.

Such a display of gross anatomies couldn't have titillated them as it did my innocence. More than by idle curiosity, I suspect, the grown-ups were drawn there to reaffirm boundaries. Isn't this why so-called normal people usually stare at "freaks"? ("He could strike you thisaway.... But he has not.") Just for a moment, though, all of us—young and old, male and female, black and white—were drawn together in that heathen temple by our common wonder and relief. We forgot even our contrived differences, as Mr. Head and his grandson (who are constructed, though comically, on the faculty psychology model) do in another O'Connor story, "The Artificial Nigger," when they contemplate one of those obscene lawn ornaments that still grace the posh suburbs of Atlanta.

As an icon of white culture, this plaster figure of a black boy eating watermelon "was meant to look happy because his mouth was stretched up at the corners." The happy child: it is the nineteenth century's most enduring image of the African American, and it still profanes the American landscape, even on the bright green lawns of eastern and midwestern towns, where the figure has been painted a not-so-discrete white. Despite its painted grin, the weather-worn black face in O'Connor's iconoclastic tale takes on "a wild look of misery instead." Staring at the crumbling image together, the old man and the boy, who has never seen a real black person before this day, "both feel it dissolving their differences like an action of mercy."[28]

Up till now in this little racial and family standoff, Mr. Head, as his name implies, has assumed an attitude of pure, benighted front-brained whiteness. Surely, if *he* can learn something from other people's suffering, there's hope for the rest of us. Even mercy.

ONE

A Geography of the Mind

Her intellect is better ordered at present than this mysterious power
called Will. What a strange power it is. In the Reason there is an inevitable
Law. There is no question whether to see truth or not, provided the Reason is
clear to see & of high quality to be able to see. There is no choice.
In the Will alone is Freedom.

—*Sophia Peabody Hawthorne*

 WHEN A FRIEND'S toddler fell head-first from her
crib, Sophia Peabody reported to her mother in a letter of
1841: "Little Alice . . . bruised her intellect sadly. If she had
struck her affections, the consequences might have been
fatal, for she fell with great force, but she came plump
down upon Comparison, Eventuality & Individuality, &
the vast Chimborazo height."[1]

Still unconquered at the time, the Chimborazo, tallest peak in Equador, lent
its name to the region of Alice's brain then supposed to be the seat of the mind's
highest intellectual functions. Little Alice had landed, in other words, upon the
front of her head rather than the crown, a fortunate fall since the vast, unex-
plored territory within the girl's cerebral cortex left plenty of room to cushion
the blow. Satirizing the chief model of mind of her age, Sophia Peabody (soon
to be Hawthorne and the mother of two remarkable daughters) was pre-
tending to find a damaged intellect less debilitating, in females, than faulty
affections.

Sophia Peabody's other names for whole realms of mental activity came not
from physical geography but from phrenology, the pseudoscience of plotting
a person's character and temperament from the natural contours of the head.[2]
Poe refers to this chimerical scheme in "The Imp of the Perverse" when his
narrator pronounces "Perversity"—the dark inner voice that urges us to throw
ourselves from mountain peaks and other heights upon the black forms below—to be a "propensity" overlooked by the phrenologists in their accounts
of mental "faculties and impulses of the *prima mobilia* of the human soul"
(*PPTE*, 826).

Phrenology and the Roots of Human Motives

Poe's narrator, of course, is mad, but many sane people, including Poe himself, once believed that phrenology opened the way to an exact topography of the mind and therefore held the key to human motives. When Johann Kaspar Spurzheim, disciple of Franz Joseph Gall, the father of phrenology, died suddenly while lecturing in America in 1832, the Massachusetts Medical Association called his passing "a calamity to mankind." (*"Phrenologize our nation,"* had been Spurzheim's fervent teaching, "for thereby it will *reform the world."*)[3]

Characteristically, Sophia Peabody's oldest sister, Elizabeth, wondered "if phrenology be true." But even she lamented that Spurzheim "left a great work unfinished."[4] And a few years later, Mary Peabody Mann, middle sister of the three Peabody sisters of Salem, and her husband Horace Mann, the congressman and college president, would name their second son after the Scottish phrenologist, George Combe, author of *The Constitution of Man* (1828). Meant for a textbook in the "Common Schools," an abridged American edition of Combe's influential work carried "An Appendix Describing the Five Principal Races." The "faithful study" of its lessons, reported the *Journal of Education* in the 1850s, "would save many a promising youth from a premature grave."[5]

Among the many people who took phrenology seriously in the nineteenth century was George H. Crosby who, on October 14, 1864, entered the Boston studio of A. O'Leary, phrenologist, to have his head read or, in the parlance of practitioners, his character "delineated." Crosby paid a fee, of course, and like countless others before him, he also bought a little book. On the title page were a blank line, above which the "examiner" penned the subject's name, then the printed words "As Given By," and another blank line awaiting the examiner's signature when the session was completed. The purpose of this manual, O'Leary wrote, was to "assist the examiner in describing and recording the traits of character of the person examined."[6] In it was represented by name and number each region of the brain where a particular trait was thought to lodge, thereby forming a sort of geography of human character in general. On the individual head of the person examined, highly developed traits were said to show up as ridges or bumps; undersized faculties appeared as dips or valleys. (A skeptical Oliver Wendell Holmes objected that reading a person's inner character from the bumps on the head was like trying to count the money in a safe by feeling the knobs on the door.)[7]

In the case of George Crosby—and anyone else who walked through O'Leary's door—the exact number of character traits to be examined was thirty seven, including Philoprogenitiveness (love of offspring), Adhesiveness,

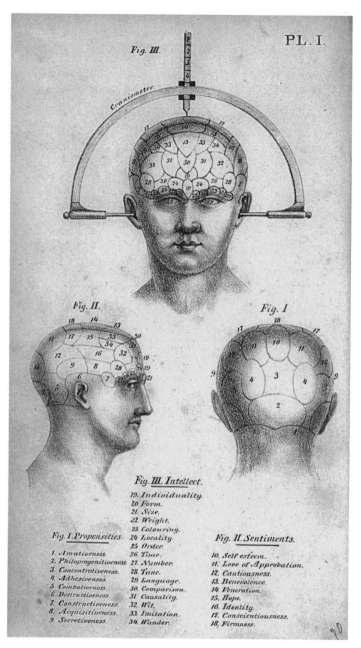

PL. I.

Fig. III.

Craniometer.

Fig. II.

Fig. I

Fig. III. Intellect.

19. Individuality.
20. Form.
21. Size.
22. Weight.
23. Colouring.
24. Locality.
25. Order.
26. Time.
27. Number.
28. Tune.
29. Language.
30. Comparison.
31. Causality.
32. Wit.
33. Imitation.
34. Wonder.

Fig. I. Propensities.

1. Amativeness.
2. Philoprogenitiveness.
3. Concentrotiveness.
4. Adhesiveness.
5. Combativeness.
6. Destructiveness.
7. Constructiveness.
8. Acquisitiveness.
9. Secretiveness.

Fig. II. Sentiments.

10. Self esteem.
11. Love of Approbation.
12. Cautiousness.
13. Benevolence.
14. Veneration.
15. Hope.
16. Ideality.
17. Conscientiousness.
18. Firmness.

FIG. 2 A finely drawn phrenological head, showing the seats of the faculties and encompassed by a "craniometer," the principal instrument for measuring the volume of the brain in the early nineteenth century. In *An Examination of Phrenology* (1837), source of this illustration, Thomas Sewall, M.D., described the device and its operation: "It consists of a brass semicircle, connected at the extremities, with two horizontal bars, terminating in a small knob to be placed in the external opening of each ear. By this means, while the semicircle remains fixed at its extremities, its circumference moves freely backward and forward. Attached to this, is a sliding graduated scale, which is easily brought in contact with any part of the surface of the head."

Inhabitiveness, Amativeness, and the other "domestic propensities." Among the "selfish propensities and sentiments" to be gauged were Combativeness, Destructiveness, Alimentiveness (fondness for food), Acquisitiveness, Secretiveness, Cautiousness, Self-Esteem, Firmness, and Mirthfulness.[8] (Mark Twain had his head read at least twice, at wide intervals, by phrenologists who found no trace of a sense of Mirth.)

Then there were "moral sentiments" such as Hope, Veneration, and Benevolence; such "intellectual" and "perceptive faculties" as Individuality, and the sense of Form, Size, Weight, Color, Order, Locality, Time, and Language. And, finally, among the "reasoning organs," were Causality and Comparison. On O'Leary's charts, each of these thirty-seven traits ranged through twenty-one degrees of development from "small" to "average" (2d, 3d, and 4th degree) to "very large."

O'Leary's character manual (entered in the District Court of Massachusetts in 1860) followed the formula established by the most successful of them all, *Practical Phrenology* (1846), by Orson Squire Fowler, A.B., who often collaborated with his brother, Lorenzo Fowler, and with Samuel R. Wells, who was married to their sister Charlotte ("the Mother of Phrenology"). Walt Whitman remembered "the 'Phrenological Cabinet' of Fowler & Wells, Nassau street near Beekman" as "one of the choice places of New York to me." "Here," he said, "were all the busts, examples, curios, and books of that study obtainable. I went there often, and once for myself had a very elaborate and leisurely examination and 'chart of bumps' written out (I have it yet)." The date on which Whitman had his head examined by the establishment of Fowler & Wells was July 16, 1849; for this service, he paid three dollars.[9]

The subtitle of Fowler's phrenology reads in full: "Giving a Concise Elementary View of Phrenology; Presenting Some New and Important Remarks upon the Temperaments; and Describing the Primary Mental Powers in Seven Different Degrees of Development; the Mental Phenomena Produced by Their Combined Action; and the Location of the Organs [bold type], Amply Illustrated by Cuts. Also the Phrenological Developments, together with the Character and Talents, of" [and then the blank for the client's name].

By no strange coincidence, Fowler's book also lists thirty-seven basic character traits, most of them named exactly as in O'Leary's manual, so influential were the Fowlers and so wholesale O'Leary's borrowings. The "cuts" (or illustrations) to which Fowler refers include the usual generic heads with their numbered seats. The domestic propensities are located in the occipital lobe, the selfish ones in the temporal. The sentiments (selfish and moral) occupy the parietal lobe and that portion of the frontal that rounds the top, or crown, of the head. The intellectual faculties are seated in the rest of the frontal lobe, the faculties of reason immediately behind the brow and those of perception a little lower—all in keeping with the higher-functions-in-the-front, lower-ones-in-the-back alignment of the nineteenth-century mind.

Besides generic heads, some of the profiles in Fowler's *Practical Phrenology* are those of recognizable historical figures, notably George Washington and Ben Franklin.[10] Fowler's "cut" of Washington is just the sort of conventional likeness that pops into Ishmael's mind in *Moby-Dick* when he sees Queequeg for the first time. Queequeg's shaved head reminds him "of General Washington's head, as seen in the popular busts of him." It was, he says, "phrenologically an excellent one." In Melville's dark "Pagan," the "very projecting" brows and long slope above them, like two "promontories thickly wooded on top," indicate both highly developed intellectual and moral faculties. Despite the tattoos that mar the outer man in western eyes, Queequeg's inner character is as noble as any that a "civilized," white upbringing could inscribe. "Queequeg," says Ishmael, "was George Washington cannibalistically developed" (*M-D*, 846–47).[11]

After sleeping together—"You had almost thought I had been his wife"— Ishmael and Queequeg fast become "bosom friends" in Melville's romance (*M-D*, 820, 849). More conventional persons, the George Crosbys of the day, tended to proceed more cautiously and with benefit of professional counsel. How was one to know whether an intended spouse would be compatible? To check the alignment of their proclivities, a nervous couple of the first half of the nineteenth century could turn to dual character charts in such guides as *Marriage: Its History and Ceremonies; with a Phrenological and Physiological Exposition of the Functions and Qualifications for Happy Marriages* by L. N. Fowler. In its twenty-second edition by 1853, this best-selling forerunner of modern self-help manuals carried the liberating motto, "Be Ye Not Unequally Yoked Together."

According to the ink marks on his personal chart, George Crosby was not the most promising of marriage partners. An amorous man of the twentieth degree of Amativeness who liked to contemplate women's bodies, in particular "those parts that lie beneath the chin," he had an equally strong desire for property (Acquisitiveness) and a strong Intellect, though "wanting, a little," said the examiner, in "Discipline." His Philoprogenitiveness, however, seemed only middling: on the whole Crosby was thought to prefer animals to children. And his memory of daily events (Eventuality), as of people's names, ranked so near the bottom that he was advised to study history and biography and to keep a journal.

The examiner was not sure whether his client could carry a tune, a specific, localized function in this scheme and, therefore, like the others, ultimately a faculty, or capacity, of the brain. For phrenology was nothing more than a physiology worked out by scientists, philosophers, and charlatans of the eighteenth and nineteenth centuries to accompany the faculty psychology that had been the dominant model of mind and human nature in Europe and America from ancient times. (The "humour" psychology of the middle ages was incorporated in faculty psychology's notion of temperament, of which, in the early nineteenth century, there were still thought to be four basic types: Bilious, Nervous, Sanguine, and Lymphatic.)

Psych 101 in 1825: The Scots Bring Common Sense to America

In American colleges of the eighteenth and early nineteenth centuries, "Mental and Moral Philosophy" were usually taught by the president, often a man of Scottish descent like the slave-owner William Dunbar (profiled in chapter 3), since the Scots, on the whole, were more willing than the English to invest in the intellectual wasteland of the colonies and the new republic.

The Scots had long venerated education, particularly of the mental and moral faculties, about which they theorized with scholastic thoroughness and zeal. The Vienna of this earlier psychological ferment was Edinburgh, and the most learned treatises in the field were written in the great Scottish universities and taught there in textbook form. Those textbooks poured into America in large numbers.

They were also copied by dozens of professors in American schools, such as Thomas Upham, Hawthorne's teacher at Bowdoin, whose *Elements of Mental Philosophy* appeared in 1831. When Hawthorne took Upham's equivalent of Psych 101 as a college senior in the 1820s, his text (the model for Upham's own book later) was Dugald Stewart's *Elements of the Philosophy of the Human Mind* (1792), a book that Thomas Jefferson called, when he received his copy from the author in 1824, "the text book of most of our colleges and academies."[12]

Stewart, like Upham and the others, divided the mind into three basic parts—the Intellect, the Feelings, and the Will. Or, in the words of Edgar Allan Poe in "The Poetic Principle": "Dividing the world of mind into its three most immediately obvious distinctions, we have the Pure Intellect, Taste, and the Moral Sense" (*PPTE*, 1436).Though intimately related, each of the three divisions of mind was thought to address its own distinct phenomena. According to Sir William Hamilton, Stewart's editor, these were: "the phenomena of Knowledge or Cognition," "the phenomena of Feeling or of Pleasure and Pain," and "the phenomena of Conation or of Will and Desire."[13] Again Poe, whose fictional characters are drawn precisely on this scheme, was technically explicit: "Nevertheless, we find the *offices* of the trio [of mental departments] marked with a sufficient distinction. Just as the Intellect concerns itself with

Truth, so Taste informs us of the Beautiful while the Moral sense is regardful of Duty" (*PPTE*, 1436).

The "Scottish Realists," as they were called, further divided the faculties of the intellect into Sensation, Perception, Conception, Abstraction, Intuition, Consciousness, Reasoning, Imagination, and their "Auxiliary powers" of Habit, Attention, Association, and Memory (Upham's formulation [*UEMP,* vol. 1, 449–50]). Among the feelings or sensibilities, were placed the Natural Emotions (such as the sense of Beauty), the Desires (including Instincts, Appetites, Propensities, and Affections), and the Moral Emotions and Feelings of Obligation (*UEMP,* vol. 2, 29–36). The Will was considered to be an indivisible faculty.

The names and precise number of the faculties varied according to who was doing the counting and naming, but it was generally held that all the phenomena of thought in the healthy mind moved in train from the intellect to the feelings to the will, or from cognition to appetition to volition. In this fashion: I *sense* the oaken cask in the cellar. Informed by my physical senses, particularly taste and smell, I *conceive* that it is a cask of wine. (The italicized terms are Upham's names for the intellectual powers.) I *abstract* the qualities of the wine from one another and *attend* to them. (This is fine old sherry, a cask of Amontillado!) *Conscious* of my thoughts now, I *remember* other wines I have sipped. I *reason* that this one is like the others—delicious and intoxicating. I *imagine* myself drinking the wine; but before I actually consume it, I *judge* my sensual, imbibing self to be overly indulgent. I pass these "intellections" along to my Sensibilities, of which, by Upham's count, there are two general classes, "Natural" and "Moral."

My "natural desires" or "animal propensities" include "instincts" (respiration, swallowing, instinctive acts of self-preservation) and "appetites" (hunger, thirst); they urge me to drink the wine, as Thoreau's natural instincts urged him to eat a woodchuck raw at Walden. My "moral emotions" include approval, disapproval, and feelings of moral beauty and sublimity. They tell me not to drink the cask of wine because gluttony is unsightly—an offense to the aesthetic sense—and, more seriously, because it is morally wrong.

Guided by my sensual desires alone—which are closest in order of precedence to the will—I would not hesitate to consume the wine (or drunkenly let down my guard and be lured to my grave in the wine cellar, as in Poe's "Cask of Amontillado"). However, informed of the consequence of my actions by my intellect, I am urged by my higher emotions and feelings (or the moral sense) to abstain. I resolve on balance (as Ahab does not when he resolves to avenge himself upon the whale) to drink water instead of wine.

For modern readers, the hardest part of this antique system to swallow, perhaps, is the moral aspect of mental philosophy, especially the idea of "moral liberty" as self-control. (Mark Twain, who deplored it, identified the old-fashioned "moral sense," with its finicky sensibilities and pale passions, as a tapeworm.) In his *First Principles* (1824), however, Asa Burton, a country preacher from Connecticut who independently came up with the idea of a tripartite mind, lucidly explained the moral sense by analogy with the physical sense of Taste. (*Taste*, the favored term among the Scottish philosophers who had such a profound influence upon America psychology, was an alternative name for the Sensibilities, a blanket designation for the emotions, affections, desires, passions, appetites, and all other classes of feelings.) If we had no physical sense of taste, Burton analogized, "food would neither please or disgust us. By a mental taste, the mind is pleased or displeased with all objects with which it is conversant." Such is the moral sense: virtue appeals to it; vice rises in its gorge. Thus Burton proclaimed "the faculty of taste" to be "the most important property of the mind."[14]

About the centrality of taste in the operations of the mind, the aesthete Poe agreed: "I place Taste in the middle," he wrote in "The Poetic Principle, "because it is just this position, which, in the mind, it occupies. It holds intimate relations with either extreme; but from the Moral Sense is separated by so faint a difference that Aristotle has not hesitated to place some of its operations among the virtues themselves" (*PPTE*, 1436).

Thomas Upham, Hawthorne's psychology professor, called the faculty of Taste a "theatre" in which human motives "mingle in perpetual conflict" (*UEMP*, vol. 2, 26–26). And many years after he graduated from college, Hawthorne was still defining his kind of fiction as "a theatre, a little removed from the highway of ordinary traffic," where the "creatures" of his brain could "play out their phantasmagorical antics," enabling the romance writer, along with the moral philosopher, to study "the truth of the human heart."[15]

Like the physical appetites, the appetitive (or emotional) faculties could be especially treacherous in this psychology, however, because their appeal to action is so immediate, verging as they do, in the normal train of thought, more directly than the intellectual faculties upon the will. Upham's *Elements of Mental Philosophy* (1831; new edition, 1869) gives this account of the mind's proper order of precedent or chain of command: "The natural progress of the mind, in bringing the Will into action, is from intellections to emotions ... and then from emotions to desires. ... It is in Desires ... that we find a class of immediate antecedents to the acts of the Will. ... Volition is the great result, to which [all the compartments of the mind] contribute, and with which they all, therefore, sustain an established connection, though not with the same degree of nearness" (*UEMP*, vol. 1, 474–78).

As the nearest faculties to it in this scheme, the base desires excite the will—
"only an executive faculty," said Asa Burton—most immediately and force-
fully.[16] As the most remote, the higher intellectual faculties address the will
with the greatest calm and restraint. Thus under faculty psychology it was imperative to mental and moral health—if not social and political hygiene—
that, as the bard observed, "The will of man is by his reason swayed."

It was emphatically the will of *man*, especially one of Anglo-European descent, however, that the psychology of common sense expected to be truly
swayed by the intellect.

The Scots' three-part division of the mind departed in a crucial way from
earlier views. The Puritans and their heirs in America had divided the mind
into only two parts: for Jonathan Edwards, as for the scholastic philosophers
before him, feelings were scarcely to be distinguished from volitions. ("A man
never, in any instance, wills anything contrary to his desires, or desires anything
contrary to his will. . . . The thing which he wills, the very same he desires; and
he does not will a thing and desire the contrary in any particular.") Thus Edwards's *Freedom of the Will* (1754), one of the earlier treatises in mental and moral
philosophy written in the New World, determined, in effect, that we do not
have it.[17]

By splitting off the will from the feelings and from the intellect, the Scots
and their contemporaries (notably Immanuel Kant) opened the way to a secular
freedom of the will. An early twentieth-century reviewer of Upham's *Elements*
made the key point about what this freedom entails: "He means by freedom a
true power of causality."[18]

Coming to this same understanding of free will after three months of inten-
sive study, as he said, upon three words, "free-moral-agency," Asa Burton in
America had arrived independently at the crux of Thomas Reid's philosophical
inquiry in Scotland. A "material world does exist distinct from the mind," said
Burton, declaring "that all objects, of which we obtain a knowledge through
the medium of our bodily senses, are real existences."[19] Hence the "realism" of
a philosophy that grew out of opposition to the theories of Locke, Berkeley,
and Hume.

The founder of Scottish realism, Reid had charged that "all philosophers
from Plato to Mr. Hume, agree in this, that we do not perceive external objects
immediately; and that the immediate object of perception must be some image
present to the mind." Reid's most original contribution to metaphysics was to
deny "the existence of something intermediate" between thought and the external objects of perception, whether such intermediaries were called "ideas, species, forms, shadows, phantasms, images" (*WDS*, vol. 1, 48–51).

It followed from Reid's theories, said Dugald Stewart, his most admiring follower and effective opponent, "that it is the external objects themselves, and not any species or images of these objects, that the mind perceives" (*WDS*, vol. 1, 68). Instead of pale Platonic ghosts that play upon the spume of things, in other words, the mind's most fleeting shadows, to the realist, were potentially substantial. How does the mind know which of its perceptions are really real? Again Burton had the answer: "through the medium of our bodily senses."[20]

Before the American Revolution, most moral philosophers in American schools taught (as did Johann Daniel Gros at Columbia as late as 1795) that "man is not to follow sense." Innate reason and understanding were "to direct the steps of his feet, the desires of his heart—not to obey but to regulate sense and passion."[21] Hence the ancient metaphor of reason as king of the faculties and of madness as usurpation, the toppling of the king upon his throne.

Scottish realism (or "Common Sense" philosophy) did not dethrone reason, but it elevated the senses to the rank of prime minister. "That our senses are to be trusted in the information they give us, seems to me a first principle," said John Witherspoon in the lectures on moral philosophy that introduced Scottish realism to America, "because they [the senses] are the foundation of all our reasonings."[22] Samuel Stanhope Smith, who succeeded Witherspoon at the little Presbyterian seminary that would one day become Princeton, agreed with his father-in-law: "The testimony of our senses, and of all our simple perceptions," he wrote in *Lectures on Moral and Political Philosophy* (1812), "ought to be admitted as true, and no ulterior evidence required of the reality, or of the nature of the facts which they confirm." And in 1819 Levi Hedge of Harvard defined human perception as precisely "the knowledge, that we gain by sensation, of some quality in the object."[23] Such a view of human perception (a common sensing) was the foundation of the doctrine of common sense (a common knowing).

In a burgeoning democracy, the idea of a common sense appealed both to the masses—on the eve of the Revolution, when the population of America was only about 2.5 million, Tom Paine sold almost a half million copies of his pamphlet by that title—and to the ruling class. The framers of the Declaration of Independence, for example, founding *fathers* all, could tell themselves that they knew what was best for the country because any mind capable of governing itself—a class that did not necessarily include, in their opinion, the minds of women and black men—was capable of governing the minds of others. Declaring their own views to be "self-evident," they could "logically" mount a popular uprising to enforce them. (Though no surgeon has ever located its organ, many Americans long after the Revolution—and surgeons and scientists, especially, perhaps—still cling to the idea of a common sense without realizing where it comes from, or that it is a metaphysical construct, like the notion of an all-pervading ether or William James's jack of spades.)

This faith in self-evident truths derives from a distinctively American solution to an old conundrum (in the formulation of Ralph Waldo Emerson): "whether nature enjoy a substantial existence without, or is only in the apocalypse of the mind." Emerson was a philosophical idealist, but so great was the appeal of realism in America that Emerson solved this puzzle for himself in a way that anticipates the "pragmatism" of William James, Charles Sanders Peirce, John Dewey and others: "In my utter impotence to test the authenticity of the report of my senses, to know whether the impressions they make on me correspond with outlying objects, what difference does it make, whether Orion is up there in heaven, or some god paints the image in the firmament of the soul?" (*EEL*, 32).

That the ultimate test of a perceived truth is whether or not it works for most people was Scottish realism's greatest legacy to American thought and culture. The end and purpose of this pragmatic approach, a characteristically American doctrine, perhaps our only native philosophy, was the regulation of human behavior, what Emerson called "The Conduct of Life" (*EEL*, 937).

As I indicate in chapters 3 and 4, however, the very division of the faculties by which the Scots conferred free will and common sense upon the nation about the time of the American Revolution only widened the psychological gulf between the races and genders in the textbook American mind as it contemplated the specters that would break out of their prisons to erupt, eventually, in civil war.

TWO

The House of Madness

Shivering, Denver approached the house, regarding it, as she always did,
as a person rather than a structure.

— *Toni Morrison*

THOUGH FACULTY psychology addressed the normative Human Mind (in capital letters), it left room for speculation about those flawed minds, such as Roderick Usher's of "The Fall of the House of Usher," that dwelt in the house of madness. A poet as well as a maniac, Usher inserts a sample of his verse into Poe's tale. Entitled "The Haunted Palace," it develops a psychological theme:

> In the greenest of our valleys,
> By good angels tenanted,
> Once a fair and stately palace—
> Radiant palace—raised its head.
> In the monarch Thought's dominion—
> It stood there!
> Never seraph spread a pinion
> Over fabric half so fair. (*PPTE*, 325–26)

At first, all is well in this happy valley. Golden banners crown the roof of the stately palace; two luminous windows reveal the monarch on his throne, attended by noble spirits dancing in harmony to the ordered measures of a lute; and from the palace door, lined with pearl and ruby, issue sweet echoes that attest to "the wit and wisdom of the king" (*PPTE*, 326).

It's an old conceit. We see it in Edmund Spenser, for example, whose psychology in the sixteenth century was essentially the same as Poe's in the nineteenth. And of course we see it in the works of Hawthorne, who got his architectural metaphors, in part, from Spenser. The golden banners are the yellow locks of a human head; the pearl and ruby of the door are the teeth and lips of a mouth that sings sweetly of the harmony within; and the two luminous windows represent the eyes, which traditionally open into the soul or mind.

The orderly dance within Poe's happy palace is soon disrupted, however. "Evil things in robes of sorrow" assail the monarch's "high estate," toppling him from his seat, as Usher soon will be toppled from his (*PPTE*, 326). Now when travelers peer within the once luminous windows, they see fantastic figures bathed in red light and moving in discord; and in place of sweet voices at the palace door, they are greeted by a rush of hideous laughter. This grim, unsmiling laugh is the cackle of madness that echoes through the corridors of many a Poe tale. In Usher's poem, the palace of reason, monarch of the head, has been usurped.

By whom or what, Poe explained in a letter of 1841: "By The Haunted Palace I mean to imply a mind haunted by phantoms—a disordered brain."[1] The "evil things" that topple the king in Usher's poem—where revolution or insurrection in the state is a metaphor for revolution in the mind—are not physical assailants, then, but ghastly visions.

The Collocation of the Stones: Sanity as Mental Balance

Though solitary, Roderick Usher's crumbling mansion, a favorite stop on everybody's tour of the show places of the nineteenth-century psyche, hardly stands alone. From Clara Wieland's closet and other haunted nooks in the fiction of Charles Brockden Brown at the beginning of the century to Henry James's "Jolly Corner" around the far bend, the parade of (once) better homes, decaying gardens, and claustral chambers is almost endless—not merely as places for stories to happen in, but also as central symbols, unifying narrative principles, almost as chief characters.

Besides all the other decaying houses, closed chambers, curtained beds, and pits and graves in the works of Poe, there are, to name only a few: Captain Ahab's cabin aboard Melville's *Pequod* (itself a mobile home); Hawthorne's Custom House with its ghosts in the attic where the scarlet letter is found; his claustral house of the seven gables (to be aired in chapter 8); the little compound of the socialists in *The Blithedale Romance*; and the towers and caves in *Fanshawe* and *The Marble Faun*; Holmes's chambered nautilus, with its ever more stately mansions of the soul; Thoreau's hut; Huck Finn's raft and the two-story frame house that floats down the river carrying Pap's body among the treasure; Charlotte Perkins Gilman's ancestral mansion papered with yellow, bulging eyeballs; the shifting portals of Madeline Yale Wynne's "Little Room" (a less well-known site that deserves to be reopened); and the "pigeon house" to which Edna Pontillier retreats before committing suicide; not to mention all the stately homes with skeletons in the closet in the works of Henry James and Edith Wharton, chief realtors and estate agents of the lot. (Harriet Jacobs's attic in *Incidents in the Life of a Slave Girl* [1861] is an especially complicated case.)[2]

The reason, fundamentally, for so many shaky structures in classic American literature, I would say, is that they are underpinned by faculty psychology, which conceived of the mind as a congeries of seats or chambers, interconnected in the healthy mind, cut off from each other in the labyrinth of a house divided from itself by mental disorder. "But the house!" exclaims William Wilson in Poe's most obvious tale of mental dissociation and a divided will. "There was really no end to its windings—to its incomprehensible subdivisions" (*PPTE*, 340).

Central to all of these narratives, as Jared Gardner has observed of Poe's tales, "is the question of whether there is some ultimate interior thing that can survive the calamities that befall exteriors. Ships capsize, houses collapse, bodies decay, nations divide: does there remain something primal—something buried—that can survive these calamities? The soul, the race—the 'whiteness'?"[3] To such an inquiry, faculty psychology, as I understand it, says, yes, a human power or faculty "therein lieth, which dieth not" (in the words of Poe's "Ligeia" [*PPTE*, 263]): it is the human will; and in its physical representations, it is to be colored white if driven primarily by intellect and reason, black if driven primarily by feeling and desire. As faculty psychology crumbled in the second half of the nineteenth century, however, the cracks that Poe perceived in this ancient system for explaining human motivation and belief opened so wide that emotion would come to be seen not only as the strongest but also the best of the enduring moral powers.

Clinging to his reason even as he is overcome by mad visions, Roderick Usher is a fragile image of sanity as the age defined it. Usher is obsessed with "the gray stones of the home of his forefathers," which, though darkened with age, retain the color of the gray matter of the human brain. It is the "method of collocation of these stones," that particularly fascinates him, "the order of their arrangement." Above all, Usher seems absorbed in "the long undisturbed endurance of this arrangement, and in its reduplication in the still waters of the tarn." Long undisturbed, that is, until now (*PPTE*, 340).

As the matching facades of Usher and his dilapidated house suggest, Poe and his age defined sanity as, literally, mental balance—the collocation of the mind's parts, or powers, in harmonious equilibrium. Insanity, consequently, was imbalance, disjuncture, the collapse of the mind's system of organization. In this psychology, the building blocks of the mind were the faculties, and when individual faculties fell into decay through disease or madness, like the crumbling stones of Usher's mansion, the stability of the entire mind was threatened.

Thus when Usher "trespasses" upon the "kingdom of inorganization," the "barely perceptible fissure" in the façade of his house widens, the scene is bathed in moonlight (signifying lunacy), and the entire structure comes tumbling down (*PPTE*, 320).

Likewise, the balance of the whole could be upset when a single faculty or cluster of faculties was exercised at the expense of the others. Thus Emerson was pleading for mental health in "The Over-Soul" when he said that "the multitude of scholars and authors" have talent rather than genius. Their "talent is some exaggerated faculty, some overgrown member, so that their strength is a disease." In "the *divided* state," Emerson anatomized on another occasion, the American scholar is but the "delegated intellect" of society (and, therefore, essentially insane); in a state of social and mental sanity, he would be a whole "Man Thinking" (*EEL*, 396, 54). (One of the convictions I have been led to by going back to such old-fashioned notions of human psychology as these is just how many familiar narratives—*The Scarlet Letter*, for example, or *Walden*, or *Adventures of Huckleberry Finn*, or, more recently, Toni Morrison's *Beloved*—are really, if read in the context of older models of mind, about people who are threatened by madness or who actually go mad.)

It was, no doubt, the host of looney visions like Usher's in Poe's tales that led Dr. David Skae, physician to the Royal Asylum in Edinburgh, to declare in 1857 that Edgar Allan Poe's "whole life evinced that he laboured under moral insanity" (*MD*, 533). In the mid-nineteenth century, seeing visions was still the chief test of madness. "Almost all attempts at a definition of insanity, both by medical writers and legal authorities," wrote Dr. Skae, "have been founded on the same idea which occurred to Locke,—namely, that in every case of insanity there was some delusion, and that delusion was, in fact, an essential feature of insanity. This continues to be generally believed even at the present day" (*MD*, 526).[4]

Breaking the mind down according to the fundamental divisions of faculty psychology, Skae and other authorities formally recognized "two great classes" of insanity: "moral" (or "emotional," the kind he ascribed to Poe) and "intelligential" (or "notional"). In moral insanity, said Skae, "the emotions, passions, or desires alone are affected." In cases of intellectual insanity, it is "the ideas or understanding." Either kind could be "general" or "partial." If there is "general perversion of the emotions and passions" or a "perturbation of the ideas or understanding, general excitement, and incoherent raving on a variety of subjects," the condition "is called mania, or general madness" (*MD*, 526–33). When, however, the patient exhibits "a morbid excitement" of only "one particular emotion or passion," or "a perversion only in particular trains of thought, or in reference to one object" (for instance, Nat Turner's white serpent or Ahab's white whale), the condition is called "monomania or partial insanity." In all cases of insanity, whether moral or emotional, general or partial, the will is affected (*MD*, 526).

Diagnosed in these terms, Poe's Roderick Usher would be a case of "general mania" of the "intellectual" sort: in a moment of hysteria at the end of Poe's tale, he is scared to death not by substantial horrors but by the mere shadow of "the terrors he had anticipated." Those terrors, which take the form of his pale sister Madeline returned from the grave in a scarlet-stained shroud, are most directly anticipated in his feeling "that the period will sooner or later arrive when I must abandon life and reason together, in some struggle with the grim phantasm, Fear" (*PPTE*, 335, 322).[5]

In the lexicon of nineteenth-century psychology, "phantasms" were images arising in the mind without necessary, direct correspondence to objects or stimuli in the outside world. Vapors in the brain, they rose as Usher's house seems to rise from the tarn into which it subsides when he abandons life as well as reason at the end of the tale. The mad vision of the lady Madeline of Usher in her shroud, surely a robe of sorrow, is an hallucination, another "ghastly vision" of the disordered brain as in "The Haunted Palace."[6]

Usher loses his mental balance and his life when he thinks his dead (or at least buried) sister returns from the grave in which he has so hastily lain her. Whatever else Usher may have done to his sister, the atmosphere in the household is unhealthfully close. There is more than a whiff of incest in the House of Usher, for the family tree has no collateral branches, and Usher's madness may be the inheritance of long inbreeding, just the sort of "sin against purity of character" that Louis Agassiz, the Harvard biologist, feared from an intermingling of the races. Has he "ushered" his sister prematurely to her grave in order to bury his guilt in the basement of the old house? Or is he placing temptation at arm's length, an eminently rational man's fierce struggle against the family malady?

Whether or not Usher desires his sister, he clearly fears her, and for good reason from the point of view of his "masculine" faculties of reason. Usher's psychological as well as his biological twin, Lady Madeline embodies the female presence in the house. When Usher confines his sister's body at the bottom of the mansion in a copper-clad dungeon once reserved for munitions, he is attempting to put the volatile "feminine" passions of the place under lock and key. And to Poe himself, of course, the suppressing of passion and feeling was a prelude to insurrection, if not resurrection, in "Thought's Dominion."

If Usher's mental and physical collapse indicate a general intellectual mania brought about by the failure of the rational mind to keep the emotions under control, a good example in fiction of emotional monomania would be that of

Roger Chillingworth, the demonic physician of *The Scarlet Letter*, who makes revenge—the "one particular emotion or passion" cited by his colleague Dr. Skae—the guiding principle of his life. The climax of Chillingworth's hot pursuit of *his* psychological twin, the passive minister Arthur Dimmesdale, comes when the now mad doctor drugs his trusting patient and enters his private chamber in broad daylight to look for the telltale letter he expects to find on Dimmesdale's breast: "The physician advanced directly in front of his patient, laid his hand upon his bosom, and thrust aside the vestment, that, hitherto, had always covered it even from the professional eye. Then, indeed, Mr. Dimmesdale shuddered, and slightly stirred" (*SL*, 138).

In this scene of psychic rape, Chillingworth probes, as a chapter title tells us, "The Interior of a Heart." And, as at the climax of "The Fall of the House of Usher," the victim is male.[7]

Notice that it is with "the professional eye," a psychological instrument, rather than with medical bleedings, blisters, setons, or even more drugs, that Hawthorne's physician masters his patient's inner depths. Among the Indians in the forest Chillingworth has studied the medicinal effects of herbs (and perhaps black magic as well), but his methods are more those of the physician of the eighteenth and early nineteenth centuries than of 1640. The eye, in particular, was a highly touted remedy in the mind doctor's professional bag of tricks as he made the transition from physical to "moral" forms of restraint in the treatment of mental disease.

Foucault's Beast

Perhaps the most celebrated use of the eye in psychomedical history was that of Francis Willis, royal physician to George III. When King George recovered in 1788 from one of his attacks of mania, a parliamentary committee learned that the patient had been allowed to shave himself during treatment with a cutthroat razor. "If the Royal patient had become outrageous at the moment," inquired Lord Burke of Dr. Willis, what power did the doctor possess "of instantaneously terrifying him into obedience"? Willis replied authoritatively, "Place the candles between us, Mr. Burke, and I'll give you an answer. There Sir! by the EYE! I should have looked at him *thus*, Sir—*thus!*" In the glare of Willis's "basiliskan" stare, Burke is said to have averted his head and made no reply.[8]

Dr. Willis's withering stare was the "moral" equivalent of the whips and chains by which physicians and keepers of asylums before 1800 had routinely beaten their charges, even royal ones, into submission. The British sovereign was used to command; but deprived of his reason, said Dr. Willis, he was no longer fit to rule even himself. His diseased will would have to be so "sub-jugated" to the will of the mad-doctor as to brook "no idea of resistence." (Though their critics weren't always so sure, it was not the doctors themselves who were supposed to be mad, of course, but the patients in whom these early psychiatrists, or "alienists," specialized.) Thus Dr. Willis's first principle was "to make himself formidable—to inspire awe," and even the queen capitulated (as in a Poe tale) when a physician demanded "unlimited powers" in the treatment of her husband's mental illness.[9]

Accordingly, George III, King of England, underwent the following harsh treatment for mania, as reported by Countess Harcourt: "The unhappy patient . . . was no longer treated as a human being. His body was immediately encased in a machine which left no liberty of motion. He was sometimes chained to a stake. He was frequently beaten and starved, and at best he was kept in subjection by menacing and violent language."[10] An adaptation of the sort of machine—the dunking stool, Guislain's Chinese Temple, Cox's swing—that encased the British sovereign was a curious chair invented in 1810 by Benjamin Rush of Philadelphia, one of the leading mad-doctors of his day in America. Rush described the contraption gleefully in a letter to his son:

> I have lately contrived a chair and introduced it to our Hospital to assist in curing madness. It binds and confines every part of the body. By keeping the trunk erect, it lessens the impetus of the blood toward the brain. By preventing the muscles from acting, it reduces the force and frequency of the pulse, and by the position of the head and feet favors the easy application of cold water or ice to the former, and warm water to the latter. Its effects have been truly delightful to me. It acts as a sedative to the tongue and temper as well as to the blood vessels. In 24, 12, 6, and in some cases in 4 hours, the most refractory patients have been composed. I have called it a *Tranquillizer.*

Rush was so pleased with his invention that he planned shortly, he told his son, to "add to it a box in which all the above effects will I hope be produced more promptly by keeping the patients in a standing posture."[11]

The rationale behind such engines of torture in the beastly treatment of mental patients of the eighteenth and early nineteenth centuries, whether paupers or kings, was that madness entailed the complete overthrow of sovereign reason, and without reason madmen were no longer men but beasts. "Has he the comfort of a fire?" inquired Dorothea Dix, a leading advocate of asylum reform in early nineteenth-century America, when compiling one of her case studies. "Fire? Fire indeed!" the uncle of the "maniac" responded. "What does a crazy man need of fire? Red-hot iron wants fire as much as he!"[12]

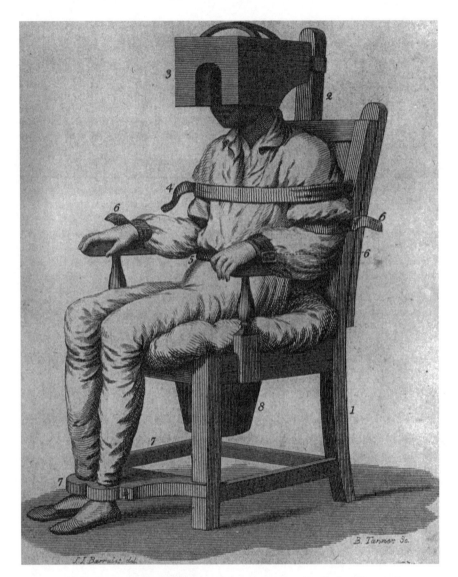

FIG. 3 Benjamin Rush's "Tranquillizer" of 1810 reduced the chambers of the mind to their absolute physical limits. The race and sex of the doctor's patient-prisoner in this illustration are as ambiguous as his or her mental condition.

The Protestant church had long ago voiced its official opinion on the brute nature of mental disease in such edicts as the Reverend Andrew Snape's "Sermon Preach'd Before the Lord Mayor, the Alderman, Sheriffs and Gouvenours of the Several Hospitals of the City of London," April 16, 1718: "Distraction ... divests the rational soul of all its noble and distinguishing Endowments, and sinks unhappy Man below the mute and senseless Part of Creation: even brutal Instinct being a surer and safer guide than disturb'd Reason, and every tame Species of Animals more sociable and less hurtful than humanity thus unmann'd." [13] It was in this sense that madmen and "savages" (whether red or black) were thought, as late as the first half of the nineteenth century, to be "effeminate." If reason was the mark of man, then creatures deficient in reason—such as madmen, nonwhite males, and women—were "unmann'd," the back-brained thralls of their animal natures: women, of their unbridled passions; savages, of their brute instincts. This was why anti-Darwinian biologists such as Louis Agassiz were so disturbed by the "emasculating" prospect of "miscegenation" in America.

Even the evolutionary biologist E. D. Cope, writing in 1890, saw no inconsistency in pacing racial "devolution" at a rate far more rapid than that of the evolution of species. "The highest race of man" (by which he meant "the white race"), said Cope, "cannot afford to lose or even to compromise the advantages it has acquired by hundreds of centuries of toil and hardship, by mingling its blood with the lowest." Cope feared most for the purity of the mental faculties of those whites who came into physical contact with blacks: "We cannot cloud or extinguish the fine nervous susceptibility, and the mental force, which cultivation develops in the constitution of the Indo-European, by the fleshly instincts, and dark mind of the African." [14]

Dark minds versus light ones, fine sensibilities versus animal instincts: the black and white divide between the races in the minds of "Indo-European" males at the end of the nineteenth century may seem to have closed little since the beginning of the eighteenth, when absolute difference was thought to separate reason and unreason, sanity and madness, man and beast. The subtext of Cope's and Agassiz's remarks on difference in race, however, is that the borders of one are dangerously close, in their minds, to intersecting with those of the other.

Michel Foucault has remarked a similar perception of diminishing difference between sane persons and madmen in the treatment of insanity. In *Madness and Civilization*, Foucault argues that the "negative fact that the madman [was] not treated like a 'human being'" once had "a very positive meaning": that he was a brute meant that he *"was not a sick man."* The day was to come, however, Foucault observed, when "this presence of animality in madness would be considered as the sign—indeed the very essence—of disease." [15]

That day dawned at the beginning of the nineteenth century with the rise of the so-called moral treatment of insanity at such institutions as "The Retreat" near York, England, an asylum for disturbed members of the Society of Friends (like Melville's Captain Ahab). Under the direction of William Tuke, "neither chains nor corporeal punishment [were] tolerated in this establishment." By the time John Conolly imposed "non-restraint" even for paupers at Hanwell Asylum in the 1840s, the asylum reform movement was well under way.[16]

Psychologically and ethically liberating as the new moral treatment of mental illness promised to be, however, lawmakers and physicians of the nineteenth century were not inclined to abandon altogether their authority as "guardians of the moral order and agents of social control" (the phrase is Vieda Skultans's).[17] The fearful image of the doctor with the burning eye as master and keeper licensed to "protect" society from the madman (or woman) through physical force would simply be transferred to the patient and internalized (as in the strange case of Mrs. E. P. W. Packard, outlined in chapter 10). During the course of the century, *she* was to become her own social monitor on a model defined by her physician, who was almost invariably white and male. Thus the "new woman" of the 1880s and '90s who replaced the "true woman" of the 1840s might no longer be pronounced "hysterical," but she would still be diagnosed as "neurasthenic."

The inverse of Usher's (and Uncle Tom Shelby's) "hyper-feminized" condition, this enforced masculinizing is the focus of much of the imaginative literature in English by and about women in the nineteenth and early twentieth centuries. (Charlotte Perkins Gilman's "The Yellow Wallpaper," 1899, is but one brilliant example.) At a time when mental disease no longer protected anyone, as Foucault said, from "whatever might be fragile, precarious, or sickly in man," a woman's back-brained susceptibility to the emotions and other sensibilities could mark her (in the conventionally male eye) as potentially unstable and therefore in need of having "manly" restraint instilled within her. Likewise in men, the conservative social order could require, at the first signs of emergent "feminine" impulses, however seductive, that they be kept under lock and key (like Usher's female twin in her deep vault) lest they break out and wrest control of the psyche and the state.

This is why Hester Prynne in *The Scarlet Letter* must be publicly subjected to that Foucault-like instrument of discipline, the pillory, or scaffold. "In fact," writes Hawthorne, mindful of his culture's comparatively recent shift from physical engines of torture and surveillance to symbolic ones, "this scaffold constituted a portion of a penal machine, which now, for two or three generations past, has been merely historical and traditionary among us, but was held, in the old time, to be as effectual an agent in the promotion of good citizenship as ever was the guillotine among the terrorists of France" (*SL*, 55). When Hester is driven like a slave girl from the prison to the pillory, she steps forth bravely "as if by her own free-will"; but Hawthorne's staunchest heroine is on the verge of madness. "At moments," we are told, she felt "as if she must needs shriek out with the full power of her lungs, and cast herself . . . down upon the ground, or else go mad at once" (*SL*, 57).[18]

A precipitous collapse—a swoon, madness, or suicide—is the usual choice of the heroine of romance when faced with irreconcilable psychic conflict. Hester, however, is too strong-willed to let herself be cast down without a struggle. She "was not of the order," says Hawthorne, "that escapes from too intense suffering by a swoon" (*SL*, 69). Public emblem of the precipice Hester did not resist, the raised platform at the center of Hawthorne's narrative has been erected by the Puritan fathers, who have her in mind as an object lesson in "woman's frailty and sinful passion." Hester on the scaffold, therefore, is the living embodiment, as Hawthorne's psychology conceived them, of the "feminine" will (directed primarily by the heart) threatened by the "masculine" will (directed primarily by the head).

The executive of the public will who drives Hester from her prison to be put on display in the marketplace, as if she were mounting the stage in Thomas Upham's "theatre" of the mind, is the town beadle. Laying one hand upon Hester's shoulder, this grim embodiment of masculine authority extends his "official staff" toward her with the other. Hester shoves it away, but she cannot evade the piercing gaze of the male eye. For looming above her on a balcony overlooking the scaffold, as if detached from their bodies, are the faces of "the Governor" and the other head men he rules over, including Arthur Dimmesdale, her lover, whose Bunyanesque name tells us where his faint heart lands him. In their tall hats, "steeple-crowned" like Hawthorne's chilliest dreams in his sketches, these "sages of rigid aspect," represent the Puritan patriarchy, whose will is law. It would be difficult, says Hawthorne, to choose from the whole community "the same number of wise and virtuous persons, who should be less capable of sitting in judgment on an erring woman's heart" (*SL*, 64).[19]

On the verge of fainting, Hester cannot control her train of thought because her moral proctors have siphoned away the volition by which the normal, waking mind chooses what thoughts it will entertain, and in what order. When, willy nilly, they do come, as in Hawthorne's sketch of "The Haunted Mind," the figures in Hester's reverie appear each "precisely as vivid as another" (*SL*, 57). We do not enter Hester's "stream of consciousness" (as William James would later call it) on the scaffold, however, because the techniques of the modern novel, which are based on a different psychology from Hawthorne's, were not yet available to the writer of fiction in 1851. Faculty psychology's model of consciousness was spatial and architectural, like pictures at an exhibition: "Next rose before her, in memory's picture-gallery, the intricate and narrow thoroughfares, the tall, gray houses, the huge cathedrals, and the public edifices, ancient in date and quaint in architecture, of a Continental city; where a new life had awaited her, still in connection with the misshapen scholar; a new life, but feeding itself on time-worn materials, like a tuft of green moss on a crumbling wall" (*SL*, 58).

The "misshapen scholar," of course, is Roger Chillingworth, Hester's husband, a man old enough to be her father. When his image takes its place in the mossy chamber of her memories, Hester fixates upon the eyes: "His "bleared optics," she recalls, "had a strange, penetrating power"(*SL*, 58). Hester has started her inevitable mental journey back to the present; and Hawthorne, in this remarkable "interior" scene, has taken us so deeply into the antique workings of his character's mind that we, too, are brought up with a start. When the shadowy figure from Hester's past proves to be the ugly reality she must now face, says Hawthorne, he "took possession of her thoughts."

Besides the scaffold, the other outward and visible emblem of Hester's moral and psychological fall, of course, is the scarlet *A* on her breast, which Hawthorne reduced from the historic double-cipher, *AD* (for "adultery"), in order, perhaps, to emphasize its steep sides. This has not been Hester's story or Dimmesdale's or Chillingworth's, but the story of the letter, the precipice in miniature, from which Hawthorne's greatest romance takes its title. All the chief characters of the tale approach the apex of mental and moral crisis signified by it, teeter on the brink for a time, and then come down the other side transformed.

Hester alone among the adults is changed for the better. Whereas the men, Dimmesdale and Chillingworth, slowly deteriorate into madness, Hester begins in a kind of madness and comes out as sane and balanced as a darkling tale will allow. At the end of the romance, when Hester returns to New England and takes up the letter again—this time of her own volition—the narrator will drop the qualifying "as if" from his explanation of her motives: "She had returned, therefore, and resumed,—of her own free will, for not the sternest magistrate of that iron period would have imposed it,—resumed the symbol of which we have related so dark a tale" (*SL*, 236). Between the first scaffold scene and Hester's last appearance on stage, her dream of free will has become a reality.

In the meantime, Hester Prynne has been living in a "lonesome cottage by the sea-shore" where her body has taken on a "marble coldness" of aspect owing to "the circumstance that her life had turned, in a great measure, from passion and feeling, to thought" (*SL*, 164).[20] Though many readers of *The Scarlet Letter* never realize that it is haunted, Hester's cottage by the sea is the "haunted palace" of "The Fall of the House of Usher" in miniature. Here Hawthorne's scarlet woman entertains "shadowy guests," "demons" that would make her a witch in the eyes of the Puritan fathers "could they have been seen so much as knocking at her door" (SL, 164).

Hester's nightly visitors reside only in her head, but they are nonetheless real. In Hester's lonely hut, "thoughts visited her, such as dared to enter no other dwelling in New England." These wild visions are the radical political and religious ideas of the Renaissance. By harboring them, Hester trespasses upon a region of thought's dominion usually reserved for men, an infraction, says Hawthorne, "which our forefathers, had they known of it, would have held to be a deadlier crime than that stigmatized by the scarlet letter" (SL, 164).

Instead of going mad—as Roderic Usher does when he gives in to the fears, real or imagined, that take shape in the house of a mind at war with itself— Hester, in her isolation, assumes a "freedom of speculation" that develops her intellectual part. Exercising her "newly emancipated" faculties to the full, the liberated Hester throws off the chains imposed upon her mind by the Puritan fathers: The "world's law," says Hawthorne, "was no law for her mind" (SL, 164). He might have said the same of another New England female recluse of the period, Emily Dickinson, who had read Thomas Upham and whose intellectual life, could almost have been modeled after Hester's. Dickinson's theory of the psychological effects of pain, however, was more sanguine than Hawthorne's because informed by the mental philosophy that would replace Stewart's and Upham's in the American model of mind of the 1860s.

In Hawthorne's stock of metaphor, white marble, like moonlight, signifies intellect without feeling, art without life. The "marble coldness" of Hester's face and body—which contrast starkly with her dark hair, this being no shrinking blond heroine—would indicate that she has suffered a loss of feeling concomitant to the growth of her intellect. Is the asthenia permanent? The "Forest Interlude" chapters toward the close of *The Scarlet Letter* confirm what we have suspected all along: forced to submit to the collective masculine will of the village, and denied contact with her lover, Hester has buried her feelings beneath a stony countenance; but they have not been snuffed out.

Alone in the woods with Dimmesdale and little Pearl, their daughter, Hester unpins the letter from her breast and, taking off the drab Puritan cap that has covered it for so long, lets down her "rich and luxuriant" hair (SL, 202). The passions that caused Hester to stray from the straight and narrow (probably on some mossy mound in this same darkling wood), this intimate, exterior-as-interior scene tells us, have only smoldered these seven years; and the scarlet letter from Hester's breast will still be warm to the romancer's touch when Hawthorne "finds" it two centuries later in the attic (the chamber of memory where relics of the past are usually stored) of the Salem Custom House.

Thus in "the neutral territory" of romance, as Hawthorne called it, the writer of fiction has imbued his fantasies with both masculine and feminine faculties. By combining an expanded intellect with her reawakened feelings, Hawthorne has mimicked in Hester Prynne a sane (in the sense of mentally balanced) adult, the only one in his narrative. The others are all "moral maniacs," or *monomaniacs*, as Dr. Skae might say.

The Second Test of Madness: Ahab's Ivory Obsession

Asylum reform in Britain and America in the first half of the nineteenth century had been helped along by phrenology. As J. Q. Rumball, an itinerant lecturer and practical reader of bumps, pointed out to the British Parliament in 1843, "most of the Superintendents of our Public Asylums are Phrenologists." (Though he kept a private, apparently unlicensed, madhouse, "yet Rumball," says Roger Cooter, "should not be dismissed too quickly.")[21]

Even the worst quacks among the phrenologists subscribed to Franz Josef Gall's principle, as stated in his treatise *On the Functions of the Brain and of Each of Its Parts*, that "each particular cerebral part, according to its development, may modify, in some degree, the manifestation of a particular moral quality, or intellectual faculty."[22] To Gall and his followers, mind was a function of the brain, and since the brain comprised many organs, or faculties, mind was no longer to be considered indivisible like the soul.

The notion of a divisible mind linked to physical organs made a "*rupture épistemologique*" (Foucault) between the old conception of insanity and the moralists' new conception.[23] In a Cartesian universe, mental disturbances, paradoxically, had been ascribed to physical causes treatable by physical means because the mind, or spirit, was not itself subject to disease. Madness, therefore, was to be understood not as a disease of the human mind but as a total loss of mind that turned humans into beasts fit only to be caged and whipped.

Under the new conception, it did not appear, as Sydney Smith noted in his "Account of the York Retreat" (1814), "that because a man is mad upon one subject, that he is to be considered in a state of complete mental degradation."[24] It was possible to be only partially mad. Consequently, partial insanity, or *monomania*—the term was coined in France in 1820 by Jean Étienne Dominique Esquirol—soon became the most popular diagnosis for mental disease in England, Scotland, and America.

The most grandly raving case of monomania of which I am aware in the annals of fictive American madness is Melville's Captain Ahab. Like Arthur Dimmesdale with his scarlet stigma or Roderick Usher with his sister's bloody shroud, Ahab fixates upon the white whale, thus exhibiting Dr. Skae's "perver-

THE HOUSE OF MADNESS   41

sion only in particular trains of thought, or in reference to one object." He also betrays the main physical symptom by which physicians and the keepers of asylums identified the loss of self-control that was thought to enslave the human will in acute cases. "The most essential and characteristic feature of acute mania," said Dr. Skae, "appears to be the loss of self-control . . . resulting in violent and excessive restlessness, walking to and fro" (*MD*, 530). Like his uneven walk, to which it contributes, Ahab's artificial leg is an outward sign that one or more of his inward faculties are maimed—or hardened, like ivory.

In the early nineteenth century, lawyers and physicians in America and Britain such as Thomas Gray, who took down the confession of Nat Turner, were confident that they knew a maniac when they saw one. After such trials as the Nancy Farrer case (next chapter), however, the courts were no longer so sure that all people who are mad suffer from delusions. Or, conversely, that all people who suffer from delusions are mad: they may be under the temporary influence of alcohol or other drugs, or they may be coming down with a fever, or walking in their sleep. If seeing visions was not, alone, a sufficient measure of madness, then a more stringent test was needed. To the delusion test should be added, said such physicians as John Haslam, medical officer of Bethlem-Royal Hospital, London—or "Bedlam," as it had long come to be called, both locally and generically—"the impossibility of convincing the insane that this false judgment, error, or delusion, was a delusion."[25] By the middle of the century, such stiffer tests were routine.

To be declared insane under the twofold test for madness, a person had not only to be haunted by visions: he or she also had to cling to those visions (as the mad governess sticks to her story of the "ghosts" in Henry James's "The Turn of the Screw"). Instead of the madman's taking hold of his obsession, or mania, it took possession of him or her. Thus freedom of the will became the ultimate measure of sanity in nineteenth-century America. "More recent authorities," said Dr. Skae in 1857, "have introduced another element into their definitions of insanity,—namely, the loss of self control—of moral liberty" (*MD*, 526).

When we first see Captain Ahab on his quarterdeck, he is standing still, his ivory leg inserted in an auger hole that keeps him artificially erect as he looks out to sea for the beast that "dismasted" more than his leg. Ahab's posture is the outward and visible sign of his iron will: there was, says Melville, "a determinate, unsurrenderable willfulness in the fixed and fearless, forward dedication of that glance." When next we see him, Ahab has begun to pace. The planks on the deck outside his cabin, we soon learn, are so accustomed to his "ivory stride," that "they were all over dented, like geological stones, with the peculiar mark of his walk." So is Ahab's forehead: his heavy brow is "ribbed and dented" with "still stranger foot-prints—the foot-prints of his one un-sleeping, ever-pacing thought" (*M-D*, 963).

That the forehead of the whale is marked with these same indentations does not mean that Ahab has translated the hieroglyphics of the universe any more accurately than Nat Turner did when he saw a serpent in the sky and strange figures on the leaves of the trees; it means only that the malevolent purpose that Ahab ascribes to the whale—the cosmic design of whiteness to appall—springs from within his own head. Pursuing his quarry with a madman's fixity of purpose, Captain Ahab has stumped off the deep end. "It is not probable," however, says Melville, "that this monomania in him took its instant rise at the precise time of his bodily dismemberment" (*M-D*, 989).

Mental illness steals upon Ahab *after* his dismemberment, on the homeward voyage, as he lies alone in his cabin raving. Ahab's lonely cabin on the high seas, from which he excludes even the black cabin boy Pip, is his haunted palace; here it is that the wild vision of punishing the whale first swims into Ahab's deranged thoughts. Sleeping or waking, Ahab cannot escape the grip of this phantasm, even though his "soul" has "dissociated" itself from "the character-izing mind" that gave birth to his monstrous obsession (*M-D*, 1007).

In the nineteenth century, mental "dissociation" occurred when one faculty or set of faculties broke off from the others; in extreme cases, the split took place without the victim's knowledge. Captain Ahab is not so far gone as Wil-liam Wilson or Dr. Jekyll; he has an inkling of his true state of mind: "my means are sane, my motive and my object mad." But Ahab is "without power to kill, or change, or shun" his obsession. The madness of chasing the whale, says Melville, "was only subject to his perceptibility, not to his will determi-nate" (*M-D*, 991).

Perceptibility is a faculty of the intellect. Ahab's loss of free will, however, does not mean that he has lost his "higher" cognitive, or knowing, powers and thus turned himself into a mere beast utterly devoid of reason. "Not one jot of his great natural intellect had perished," Melville tells us, in Ahab's "special" (that is, partial) madness. Instead, Ahab's thinking organs have been enslaved by his feeling organs: "Yielding up all his thoughts and fancies to his one su-preme purpose," Ahab has let his mind's guiding and directing power be usurped by the "sheer inveteracy" of a will driven by "one unachieved revenge-ful desire" (*M-D*, 990, 1007).

Ahab's monomania is thus "emotional" or "moral" rather than "notional" or "intellectual." In this decaying hulk of humanity, as in Emerson's analogy defining the sexes, the rudder has given way to the sail, and the *Pequod*—Cap-tain Ahab having mistaken some other part of his anatomy for the front of his head—plunges headlong in pursuit of her master's relentless longing, taking the entire crew, except for Ishmael, down with the ship.

Mad with (or *at*) the universe's largest living embodiment of whiteness, yet exerting absolute dominion over the will of the crew with his iron lance, Melville's dark old white man has reversed the chain of command in the normal mind, and his power of causality has been maimed. Thereby upsetting his mental balance: rooted in the black deck of his "cannibal of a craft," Captain Ahab's artificial leg is constructed of whalebone, a token of the beast that bit him. Ahab can pursue his "revengeful desire" from no other vantage than this ivory "stand-point," as Melville calls it (*M-D*, 964). This is the sympathetic magic of Africa; evidently, the captain of the *Pequod* has reverted to a savagery darker than any that drives his blackest harpooner. Why then, I wonder, does Melville (like Poe and Hawthorne) figure this deranged mental state as a haze of whiteness rather than a cloud of blackness?

THREE

American Africanism

These are all forgotten now; and this poor negro, who did not even possess a
name, beyond one abrupt monosyllable,—for even the name of Turner was
the master's property,—still lives, a memory of terror, and a symbol of
wild retribution.

—*Thomas Wentworth Higginson*

I could cut off everything else, but not their hands. What else but their hands
do I really need in the Congo?

—*Leopold II*

 SOME TIME BEFORE Sartie Bartmann's death, after
which Georges Cuvier dissected her body, preserving some
parts for science, Cuvier had, in life, scrutinized *la Vénus
Hottentotte* with the comparative anatomist's eye for physical detail: "She had a way of pouting her lips exactly like
what we have observed in the orang-utan. Her movements
had something abrupt and fantastical about them, reminding one of those of
the ape. Her lips were monstrously large. Her ear was like that of many apes,
being small, the tragus weak, and the external border almost obliterated behind.
These are animal characters. I have never seen a human head more like an ape
than that of this woman."[1] Perhaps this caricature of an African woman by a
European male can be accounted for, in its brutality and physical inaccuracy—
great apes have thin lips, more like those of some Caucasians, as Georges Cuvier
surely knew—by the fear of "miscegenation."

Certainly this would have been the case in slave-holding America. "What
unhappiness for the white race—to have tied their existence so closely with
that of negroes in certain countries! God preserve us from such contact!" So
wrote Louis Agassiz (brain size: 1,514 grams), premier natural historian of his
time in America, to his mother back in Europe when he first arrived in Philadelphia in 1846.[2]

Questioned during the Civil War by a member of Lincoln's commission to
study just what degree of "equality" should be accorded to emancipated slaves,

Agassiz advocated equality before the law; but like many white abolitionists, he deemed social equality to be "a natural impossibility flowing from the very character of the negro race." "Miscegenation" or, in Agassiz's phrase, "the production of halfbreeds" was, therefore, to him "as much a sin against nature, as incest in a civilized community is a sin against purity of character" (*MM*, 48). (From the Latin *miscere genus*, the term *miscegenation* merely denotes a "mixing" of race. I retain the quotation marks, however, because only an etymologist can distinguish when the prefix is being used in this neutral sense and when, in the words of my unabridged *Webster's International*, it is placed "before words meaning something wrong or bad.")

Here is a description from the period of a "half-breed" man of color, in this case red, just the sort of human "monstrosity" Agassiz and many other whites feared that "miscegenation" would spawn:

> He was short in stature—not more than four feet eight inches high—but his limbs were of the most Herculean mould. His hands, especially, were so enormously thick and broad as hardly to retain a human shape. . . . His head was equally deformed, being of immense size, with an indentation on the crown (like that of most negroes). . . . The mouth extended nearly from ear to ear; the lips were thin, and seemed, like some other portions of his frame, to be devoid of natural pliancy. (*PPTE*, 1043)

This grotesque image of human animality in an ape-like man is even more exaggerated than Cuvier's caricature of an ape-like woman, though his lips are authentically thin, where Sartje Bartmann's were said to be un-apeishly thick.

The fictional creation of Edgar Allan Poe, this creature's name is Dirk Peters (no less), and he hails from the Black Hills, the son of a fur trader and "an Indian woman of the tribe of Upsarokas" (*PPTE*, 1043). A version of the ravishing brute of Poe's detective tales, especially "Murders in the Rue Morgue," where the murderer actually turns out to be an orangutan, Peters is as close to one as a man can get. He is also, in a narrative long recognized as a submerged allegory of slavery, a study in the white Southerner's anxiety toward an alien, "colored" presence in his midst, a grotesque embodiment, though red, of what Toni Morrison has called "American Africanism." "No early American writer is more important to the concept of American Africanism," says Morrison, "than Poe" (*PD*, 32).

"Africanism," in the mind of white America of the nineteenth century, Morrison reminds us, is an idea closely akin to Herman Melville's notion of "the power of blackness"; and like Melville she believes that the very idea of whiteness in the American imagination could only have been worked out, historically, by contrast with blackness. Morrison's chief real-life example of the phenomenon is William Dunbar, youngest son of Sir Archibald Dunbar of Morayshire, Scotland, who came to America in 1771 at the age of twenty-two. Educated at the University of Aberdeen, Dunbar established a plantation in Mississippi that rivaled the fictional one of William Faulkner's Thomas Sutpen in *Absalom, Absalom!* (1936), to whom Bernard Bailyn has compared him in *Voyage to the West* (1986).

Like a number of the other historical figures in the pages to come, Dunbar was a product of the Scottish enlightenment. In school, he had studied moral philosophy, the inquiry, as he put it, into what makes the "virtuous and happy life" (*PD*, 41). (Moral philosophy was simply the ethical component of mental philosophy; among the Scots, both of these branches of learning were based firmly on faculty psychology.) Recommended by Thomas Jefferson for membership in the American Philosophical Society, Dunbar frequently contributed notes from his plantation in Mississippi on such subjects as geography, linguistics, archaeology, hydrostatics, and climatology. For all his enlightened rationalism, however, like Sutpen wrestling with his slaves—or like Joseph Conrad's Mr. Kurtz of *The Heart of Darkness*, the impeccable European gentleman who stakes out his business headquarters in Africa with human heads—Dunbar epitomizes the white man gone "native" in the wild.

Of the darker side of this white colonial's psyche, Bailyn writes in a passage quoted by Morrison:

> Dunbar, the young *erudit*, the Scottish scientist and man of letters was no sadist. His plantation regime was, by the standards of the time, mild; he clothed and fed his slaves decently, and frequently relented in his more severe punishments. But 4,000 miles from the sources of culture, alone on the far periphery of British civilization where physical survival was a daily struggle, where ruthless exploitation was a way of life, and where disorder, violence, and human degradation were commonplace, he had triumphed by successful adaptation. Endlessly enterprising and resourceful, his finer sensibilities dulled by the abrasions of frontier life, and feeling within himself a sense of authority and autonomy he had not known before, a force that flowed from his absolute control over the lives of others, he emerged a distinctive new man, a borderland gentleman, a man of property in a raw, half-savage world. (*PD*, 41–42)

On July 12, 1776, Dunbar's "property" revolted. Dunbar was astonished and pained, like the naive Yankee sea captain in Melville's "Benito Cereno" (1855) when it dawns upon him at last that a slave mutiny has been going on under his nose. "Judge my surprise," he wrote of this unwonted rebellion against his benevolent dictatorship: "Of what avail is kindness & good usage when rewarded by such ingratitude?" Deeply stung, Dunbar pursued the rebels, captured two, and "condemned them to receive 500 lashes each at five different times, and to carry a chain & log fixt to the ancle" (*PD*, 41). Toni Morrison interprets Dunbar's sentence to mean five hundred lashes each time instead of one hundred each for five times—a total of twenty five hundred lashes per man! "I take this to be a succinct portrait," she writes, "of the process by which the American as new, white, and male was constituted. . . . The site of his transformation is within rawness: he is backgrounded by savagery" (*PD*, 44).

In his bewilderment, Dunbar, "the American as new, white, male," responded to a direct challenge to his authority in the only way by which he could make "sense" of his claim to absolute dominion over those beings of darkness who resisted it: *their* behavior, not his, was lawless, savage, incomprehensible, mad. White men of authority in the republic were still responding to black men in these terms when one of the most notorious slave rebellions in American history broke out in Southampton County, Virginia, in 1831. This was the uprising led by Nathaniel ("Nat") Turner that resulted in the death of fifty-five whites and the trial and immediate execution of more than fifteen slaves, including Turner himself.

The Black Messiah of Jerusalem, Va.

Turner was represented at his trial by self-appointed legal counsel in the person of a lawyer named Thomas R. Gray, who also served as Turner's amanuensis and "confessor." Turner begins "his" *Confessions*, an extraordinary document, no matter who authored it, as if he were speaking to a psychological case worker:

> You have asked me to give a history of the motives which induced me to undertake the late insurrection, as you call it—To do so I must go back to the days of my infancy and even before I was born. I was thirty-one years of age the 2nd of October last, and born the property of Benj. Turner, of this county. In my childhood a circumstance occurred which made an indelible impression on my mind, and laid the ground work of that enthusiasm, which has terminated so fatally to many, both white and black and for which I am about to atone at the gallows. (*CNT*, 99)

One wonders how much this passage, particularly the frank reference to "enthusiasm," was doctored by Gray; the next part, however, has the ring of authenticity:

Being at play with other children, when three or four years old, I was telling them something, which my mother overhearing, said it had happened before I was born—I stuck to my story, however, and related somethings which went, in her opinion, to confirm it—others being called on were greatly astonished, knowing that these things had happened, and caused them to say in my hearing, I surely would be a prophet, as the Lord had shown me things that had happened before my birth. And my father and mother strengthened me in this my first impression, saying in my presence, I was intended for some great purpose, which they had always thought from certain marks on my head and breast. (*CNT*, 99)

At this early point in the *Confessions,* Thomas Gray breaks in with a cosmetological note about Turner's "marks": "a parcel of excrescences [he calls them] which I believe are not at all uncommon, particularly among negroes, as I have seen several with the same" (*CNT,* 99–100).

If Gray had been responding to Turner's account of his calling even a hundred years earlier (still more so if he had passed judgment on Turner during the time of Hawthorne's Puritans), he would have taken the "excrescences" on Turner's skin as marks of the Devil. Being an enlightened borderland gentleman of the nineteenth century, however, Gray reads the birthmarks of this "son of Ham" as racial blemishes, physical signs (to the white eye) of moral disease, of which Gray editorializes that Turner "has either cut them off or they have nearly disappeared" (*CNT,* 100).[3]

Here, as elsewhere in *The Confessions of Nat Turner,* the two principals interpret the same physical objects and events in terms as divergent as black and white. Turner himself, like Hawthorne's Arthur Dimmesdale of *The Scarlet Letter,* gave the marks on his skin a religious significance. His birthmarks, which may or may not be the same "excrescences" Gray refers to, he took to be the sign of a holy prophet, a chosen one. And it was in the character of an Old Testament angel of doom that Turner led his disciples (Henry, Hark, Nelson, and Sam) to wreak vengeance upon the whites, including some people they had never seen before—their skin alone having marked them for destruction.

To a black slave in Virginia before the Civil War, white may well have seemed the color of the serpent of evil, as it does to Melville's Captain Ahab. Moreover, on May 12, 1828, Nathaniel Turner had "heard a loud noise in the heavens, and the Spirit [he reported] instantly appeared to me and said the Serpent was loosened, and Christ had laid down the yoke he had borne for the sins of men, and that I should take it on and fight against the Serpent, for the time was fast approaching when the first should be last and the last should be first" (*CNT,* 104).

This revelation was a heavenly gloss on mysterious signs and symbols that

Turner had seen still earlier: "While laboring in the field, I discovered drops of blood on the corn as though it were dew from heaven—and I communicated it to many, both white and black, in the neighborhood—and I then found on the leaves in the woods hieroglyphic characters, and numbers, with the forms of men in different attitudes, portrayed in blood, and representing the figures I had seen before in the heavens" (*CNT*, 103).

Such figures are open to interpretation. One of the white men to whom Turner confided them, Etheldred T. Brantley, interpreted these hieroglyphics (as the demented Reverend Arthur Dimmesdale does a meteor in the sky) to be signs of his own depravity. They had a "wonderful effect" upon Brantley, says the Reverend Turner, and straight away he "ceased from his wickedness," a white man who could easily take a black man's point of view when it chimed in with his own notion of his personal place in the divine order of things. God, however, seems to have read a more ambiguous purpose in Brantley's conversion, for (according to Turner) this spiritually purified white man "was attacked immediately with a cutaneous eruption, and blood oozed from the pores of his skin." After "praying and fasting nine days," however, Turner reported, "he was healed" (*CNT*, 103).

Turner's own interpretation of these bloody signs and wonders was generally at odds with that of his white masters: "And now the Holy Ghost had revealed itself to me, and made plain the miracles it had shown me— For as the blood of Christ had been shed on this earth, and had ascended to heaven for the salvation of sinners, and was now returning to earth again in the form of dew—and as the leaves on the trees bore the impression of the figures I had seen in the heavens, it was plain to me that the Savior was about to lay down the yoke he had borne for the sins of men and the great day of judgment was at hand" (*CNT*, 103). Thomas Gray interrupted Turner's *Confessions* again at this point to ask for a clarification: "Do you not find yourself mistaken now?" Turner's answer came like a terrible swift sword: "Was not Christ crucified? And by signs in the heavens that it would make known to me when I should commence the great work—and until the first sign appeared, I should conceal it from the knowledge of men— And on the appearance of the sign, (the eclipse of the sun last February) I should arise and prepare myself, and slay my enemies with their own weapons" (*CNT*, 104).

Using the psychological language of his day with some precision, Thomas Gray diagnosed Nat Turner as a case of religious "enthusiasm," setting aside for a time the crudest elements of his age's psychological stereotyping of "inferior" races. Though it troubled Gray that Turner had hardly exhibited the childlike loyalty and devotion usually assigned to Uncle Toms by the polygenisists, he dismissed the rumors of "cowardice" on Turner's part: "As to his

being a coward, his reason as given for not resisting Mr. Phipps [who apprehended Turner in his hiding hole], shews the decision of his character. When
he saw Mr. Phipps present his gun, he said he knew it was impossible for him
to escape as the woods were full of men; he therefore thought it was better to
surrender, and trust to fortune for his escape" (*CNT,* 113).

That Turner had the good judgment, under the circumstances, not to resist
arrest, Gray took as a sign of his superior intelligence: "As to his ignorance"
(which Gray assumed readers would otherwise take for granted in a slave), "he
certainly never had the advantages of education, but he can read and write, (it
was taught him by his parents), and for natural intelligence and quickness of
apprehension, is surpassed by few men I have ever seen." Turner's fine intelligence, however, Gray found perverted in one direction—his obsessive conviction that he was a holy prophet, acting under authority from Christ to slay the
serpent of evil, his white "enemies." "On other subjects," said Gray, Turner
"possesses an uncommon share of intelligence, with a mind capable of attaining
any thing." On the subject of his monomania, his messianic call, however, "He
is a complete fanatic, or plays his part most admirably" (*CNT,* 113).

In the end, Gray "explained" Turner's motives for the rebellion in the same
terms William Dunbar had applied to his runaway slaves more than fifty years
before: "It will thus appear [Gray writes in "To the Public"], that whilst every
thing upon the surface of society wore a calm and peaceful aspect; whilst not
one note of preparation was heard to warn the devoted inhabitants of woe
and death, a gloomy fanatic was revolving in the recesses of his own dark, bewildered, and over-wrought mind, schemes of indiscriminate massacre to the
whites" (*CNT,* 96).

Though Turner, a literate man, commanded a band that swelled by his account to "fifty or sixty, all mounted and armed with guns, axes, swords and
clubs," and though Turner managed to elude his captors for more than six
weeks after the massacre, his confession was submitted to the public as proof
of the mental incompetence of any black man who would do violence to the
people and institutions that enslaved him. Upon a document that might be
interpreted otherwise, Thomas Gray imposed a layer of whitewash: "It reads
an awful, and it is to be hoped, a useful lesson, as to the operations of a mind
like his, endeavoring to grapple with things beyond its reach. How it first became bewildered and confounded, and finally corrupted" (*CNT,* 97).

Gray hastened to reassure the white public, moreover, that Turner's was an
isolated revolt. "If Nat's statements can be relied on, the insurrection in this
county was entirely local," said Gray, "and his designs confided but to a few,
and these in his immediate vicinity." Such violent acts of reprisal, it would
seem, though the "results of long deliberations and a settled purpose of mind"

(*CNT*, 97), were inexplicable, from a white, slave-holding perspective, as wide-spread social and political phenomena. They could only be explained as aberrations, like Nat Turner's highly developed intelligence or a two-headed gorilla, and so Gray ends his part of the record by tallying the "morbid" effects of Turner's monomania upon his passions and will, thereby offsetting the manly intelligence he has previously assigned to his "patient."

The Polygenetic Hypothesis and the Mind of the Savage

To the white, Southern consciousness in America in 1831, a rebellion of the magnitude of the Southampton uprising, willfully directed by a commanding black consciousness, might "reasonably" be accounted for as "the offspring," in Thomas Gray's words, "of a gloomy fanaticism, acting upon materials but too well prepared for such impressions." Not only their leader was a madman, however: Nat Turner's followers were also less than human. "Never," said Gray, "did a band of savages do their work of death more unsparingly" (*CNT*, 96). To many "white minds" of the nineteenth century, the link between madness and savagery in the "black mind" was plain. So also, to the "masculine mind" informed by the stereotypes of faculty psychology, was the tie between savagery and the "feminine mind."[4]

Take, for example, the metaphor of the boat, by which Emerson in his lecture on "Woman" (1855) distinguished the "female" psyche from the "male." Without the intellect and the affections, said the faculty psychology of Emerson's age, the human will is like a vessel in a storm without rudder or sail. As the boat must harness the wind if it is to move purposefully in one direction, the will must be controlled by the other faculties. The intellect, like the rudder, guides the will; the affections drive it, like the sail. "In this ship of humanity," said Emerson, "Man is the will, and Woman the sentiment." The human will (which is restrained by the intellect in the male) "is the rudder, and Sentiment the sail: when Woman affects to steer, the rudder is only a masked sail."[5] (Though I think Emerson was, at times, paternalistic, I'm not insinuating here that he was a misogynist—far from it. Even a "radical" feminist such as Margaret Fuller purported to believe that men predominated in intellect and women in affection, no more than Emerson could she escape the culture's standard paraphernalia for thinking about the mind.)

Men could exhibit "feminine" characteristics in the nineteenth century, of course; and women, "masculine" ones. Thus Longfellow could say of Hawthorne: his spirit "is characterized by a large proportion of feminine elements, depth and tenderness of feeling, exceeding purity of mind."[6] Many men of Longfellow's time believed, however, that the mental faculties of women were genetically distinct from theirs; many women, apparently, concurred. Such was simply human nature as anatomized according to the psychological models of the day, and to ignore the terms of those models would be like dissecting the Freudian psyche without reference to an "unconscious."

Historically, human nature had not always been so divided, however. Classical philosophy, for example, as interpreted by Emerson himself, did not always assign separate faculties to men and women: "Plato said, Women are the same as men in faculty, only less in degree." But Emerson's age insisted, by and large, on a difference in kind: women were creatures of the feelings; men of the intellect. "Man represents Intellect," said Emerson, "and Woman, Love."[7] The twain met in marriage, but otherwise they were psychologically disjunct. By this logic, the age implied, a woman without a good man to restrain her was basically insane.

In the absence of bloody rebellion, infanticide, miscegenation, incest, and other overt forms of savage behavior, one link with the beast was never to be missed in any man or woman of the nineteenth century who failed to conform with the dominant society's standards of "civilized" conduct. This was the physical body: in the female, such "animal characters" as the extended buttocks and vaginal curtain of Sartje Bartmann. Or, in either sex, the mark of the caged beast within could be read in the color and texture of the skin and hair, the size and shape of the head, the flair of the nostrils and lips, the form of the ear ("the tragus weak, and the external border almost obliterated behind"), or any other external stigmata that "disfigured" the body, such as a withered hand, a tatoo, or a crudely fashioned artificial limb.

When Louis Agassiz spoke of the Native American as "indominable, courageous, proud," therefore, it was not because the red man stood, in Agassiz's estimation, on the same intellectual and moral footing as his white cousin. It was rather that this noblest race of "savages" stood out (in his mind) by contrast with men whose skin had a black or yellow hue: "In how very different a light he stands by the side of the submissive, obsequious, imitative negro, or by the side of the tricky, cunning, and cowardly Mongolian!"[8]

At the time (1850) of this racist effusion in *The Christian Examiner*, America's leading biologist was also the country's chief apologist for polygeny (or polygenism), the theory that the principle races of the world belong not to the same human biological class but to separate and distinct species. Were not the very "facts" that peoples of different colors had different temperaments, Agassiz wanted to know, "indications that the different races do not rank upon one level in nature"?[9] So ably did Agassiz and other racially biased scientists in America make the case for polygeny, it became known in Europe as the "American school" of anthropology.

Despite his appeal to facts, Agassiz collected little hard data to buttress his polygenetic hypothesis. His real expertise lay with fishes. The man who seemed most to do so in America was the Philadelphia physician and craniologist Samuel George Morton, author of *Crania Americana*, who held a medical degree from Edinburgh, most fashionable of the Scottish universities from which America derived, in part, a "national" view of human nature and political freedom that could be fundamentally both racist and sexist. Morton began collecting skulls of "the five races of men" in 1830 because, needing them for an anatomy course he was teaching, he could "neither buy nor borrow a cranium of each of these races." Within a few years, however, as Robert E. Beider has said, "the collecting of Indian crania seems to have become a cottage industry on the frontier."[10] By the time Morton's own skull was eligible for collection in 1851, Morton had amassed more than a thousand human specimens, including those of many Native Americans, in "the American Golgotha" as his collection was known.

Morton ranked his skulls, and the races of the people once attached to them, according to cranial capacity. By studying the size of the brain, he purported to address the question that George Combe, the Scottish phrenologist, raised in his review of the *Crania* in 1840. Noting that throughout American history "the aboriginal races" had perished or withdrawn before the "Anglo-Saxon" tides, and arguing, incontrovertibly, that such phenomena "must have a cause," Combe was inspired by Morton to ask "whether that cause be connected with a difference in the brain between the native American race, and their conquering invaders."[11]

Morton himself had argued in favor of such a difference—persuasively so to large-headed Caucasians. And not only did he claim that superior brain size meant a superior brain, he argued that a big brain meant a superior mind, as well. Of the Native American, said Morton, in *Crania Americana*, "the structure of his mind appears to be different from that of the white man." As compared to whites, Morton believed, Native Americans "are not only adverse to the restraints of education, but for the most part are incapable of a continued process of reasoning on abstract subjects." By studying what was left of their heads, the great collector had identified the two principal *internal* earmarks by which persons of his caste and color in the nineteenth century thought they recognized "the savage" in those human beings whom they considered lower down on the family tree: a deficiency in the reasoning faculties and a consequent lack of emotional restraint.[12]

To "prove" that whites were more intelligent and moral than people of other races, Morton measured "representative" skulls of "Caucasians" that were larger than the skulls by which he chose to represent "Americans," "Ethiopians," "Mongolians," and "Malays" (again, the categories are from the *Crania*).

Moreover, like other craniologists of the nineteenth century, Morton simply ignored the fact that brain size in humans is largely a function of body size (hence the diminutive Khoi-San peoples of South Africa have, on average, smaller brains than Northern Europeans; and women, on average, have smaller brains than men).[13]

What should not surprise us about these mismeasures of man and woman, as more recent scientists have shown by recalculating the "statistics" of Morton and other polygenisists, is that most of the fudging of data in support of their racist theories was unintentional. So deeply imprinted upon the old model of mind were these and other demeaning psychological stereotypes of race and gender that even distinguished scientists who took accurate physical measurements, like Paul Broca and Georges Cuvier did in France, unconsciously interpreted their "facts" to fit their presuppositions.[14]

Instead of dying out with the Civil War and the early women's movement, such quaint notions of race and gender inscribed themselves even more deeply in twentieth-century American culture. It was not only the antebellum Southerner—a William Dunbar or an Edgar Allan Poe or a Thomas Gray—who presumed any slave who attempted to overthrow his master to be insane. Thomas A. Bailey, a twentieth-century historian whose textbook, *The American Pageant: A History of the Republic,* was long a staple in American high schools and colleges also wrote of "fanatical Nat Turner, a semi-educated Negro preacher who had visions, organized a conspiracy which resulted in the butchering of about sixty white Virginians, mostly women and children. The outburst was speedily crushed, but an understandable wave of hysteria swept over the South." Bailey, a professor at Stanford, was not known for unusually racist sentiment. He was simply purveying received images of American history that had been long-established by white historians, as when he wrote, "The revolutionists [of 1776] were blessed with outstanding leadership. Washington was a giant among men; Benjamin Franklin was a master among diplomats. . . . The Americans, in addition, enjoyed the moral advantage that came from what they regarded as a just cause."[15]

By such valorizing accounts, even such distinguished historians as Richard Hofstadter (in another standard textbook, *The American Republic*) long perpetuated the myth of the reluctant slaveholder who was forced to serve the demon of institutionalized slavery against his will: "The kindliest slaveholder, either as a buyer or seller, was sometimes forced to break up Negro families. In short, the slaveholder was frequently victimized by the system." Or the myth of the affectionate slave, who willingly kissed his shackles because, like the American woman, he was more a creature of feeling than intellect: "It seems true enough that many white southerners treated their slaves affectionately and that many slaves responded to this treatment with loyalty and devotion." [16]

Hegel's Africa

With the discovery of quinine, first extracted from the bark of the cinchona shrub of South America around 1850, slave-traders and other fortune hunters soon began to swarm into central and eastern Africa as never before, hoping to survive the return trip with their bounty.[17] Quinine also opened the way for travelers and missionaries, such as David Livingstone, another Scot, who reported to churches and newspapers in the West the atrocities he came upon in these once-remote parts. "Besides those actually captured," Livingstone wrote in 1868, "thousands are killed, or die of their wounds and famine, driven from their homes by the slave-raider. Thousands perish in internecine wars, waged for slaves with their own clansmen or neighbors.... The many skeletons amongst the rocks and woods, by the pools, and along the paths of the wilderness, all testify to the awful sacrifice of human life which must be attributed directly or indirectly to this trade of hell" (*OTA*, 32).

Less legendary than Dr. Livingstone, one presumes, but perhaps even more remarkable among the missionaries in darkest Africa of the last half of the nineteenth century, was a minister from Virginia named William Henry Sheppard, cofounder of the American Presbyterian Congo Mission. Though he wore a pith helmet and carried a rifle, Sheppard had the advantage over his white colleagues in the bush of being black. He had not gone to the land of the dead and returned without his skin, like most *muzungu*.

Besides discovering a fabulous kingdom in the heart of Africa that he thought could only have been a fragment of the ancient Egyptian empire, Sheppard was one of the first outsiders to witness what was actually going on in the Congo under Western rule after the slave trade had supposedly ceased in the region. With the Berlin Act of 1885, Germany, France, England, and ten other signatories had ceded the vast "Congo Free State" to King Leopold II of Belgium. The Act charged Leopold "to watch over the preservation of the natives, and to care for the improvement of the conditions of their moral and material well-being, and to help in suppressing slavery, and especially the Slave Trade" (*OTA*, 34). When, however, Sheppard's first report came back from the "Free State," now "secured" by the *Force Publique*, it tallied in one village alone three hundred human skeletons and eighty-one severed right hands, some from the arms of children. Many of the bodies had been prepared as food.[18]

Although native Africans composed most of the *Force Publique*, they reported

FIG. 4 Dr. William Henry Sheppard, cofounder of the American Presbyterian Congo Mission. For his discovery in 1892 of the forbidden land of the Kuba in the central Congo, Sheppard was elected to Britain's Royal Geographic Society.

to King Leopold, an absentee colonial landlord who, through them, bled the country on a scale that made the William Dunbars of colonial America look like emissaries of light. Increasingly, as reports of colonial rule reached "civilization," the heart of darkness seemed to be white.

Unburdened, somewhat, of their sense of racial superiority by Darwin and King Leopold—Freud was yet to come—writers as diverse as Mark Twain, Joseph Conrad, and Arthur Conan Doyle would soon open Western eyes, in the words of Conan Doyle's *Crime of the Congo*, to "the greatest crime in all history, the greater for having been carried out under an odious pretence of philanthropy" (*OTA*, 50). Thus Africa, toward the turn of the century, came to signify the savagery that white men like Conrad's Mr. Kurtz were discovering, with the horror, the horror of self-recognition and self-loathing, in the new Anglo-American conceptions of mind.

Before it opened to the West a rich new field of metaphor as well as rubber and diamonds in the late nineteenth century, however, central Africa was still so physically remote to most Europeans and Americans of European origin as to represent a totally alien "dark continent" halfway around the globe. In America, where the regional tensions that would soon explode in civil war were as much psychological as political or economic, white Americans, far from uncovering a moral "Africa" in their own interiors, had more pressing reasons than ever to locate their feelings of guilt and terror upon the displaced Africans and other "savages" they found so close to home.

About the time Col. Thomas Wentworth Higginson was recruiting the Civil War's first black soldiers on the sea islands of South Carolina, therefore, Sophia Hawthorne wrote to her husband: "You know Hegel says in his Philosophy of History that this is the nature of the nigger—They will lie and sleep and eat and grin for half a century perhaps in Africa and then if any thing rouse them, they are like raging devils and carry all before them. They are a kind of Boa Constrictor. If they taste blood they are like their own Lions, and proceed to devour their masters *whom they love.*"[19] Sophia Hawthorne, who put her faith in feeling and emotion, who sympathized with the oppressed of all races, and who watched the war approach from the relative safety of Concord, had been listening to Gen. Ethan Allen Hitchcock, chairman of Lincoln's Army Board and a specialist in Indian affairs whose official report on the condition of Native Americans was suppressed in the 1830s because it criticized the federal government. In August 1862 Hitchcock told Mrs. Hawthorne in Concord "that if the negroes, who now hold back from fighting, once take fire, that the fire will sweep the south"; she was reporting this expert opinion, which confirmed her own and that of many abolitionists, to her absent husband. "He says the negro is a child and that it will take eons for him to grow to the stature of a man," she wrote. "What to do with him is the question. He says he has no providence, a quality lacking in *all* savages—that he will not work except he is compelled by force."[20]

Sophia Hawthorne's reference to G. W. F. Hegel's *Philosophy of History* fell upon receptive ears. Margaret Fuller, Emerson, Theodore Parker, George Ripley, Sophia Hawthorne's sister Elizabeth Peabody, and many of the Hawthornes' other friends and acquaintances, including General Hitchcock, had all read the Germans, believing that Kant, Herder, Hegel, and Goethe were part of a basic education. Nathaniel Hawthorne himself had studied the language; and though none of Hawthorne's recent biographies mentions Hegel (1770–1831), the architect of *The House of the Seven Gables* had absorbed Hegel's gradualist theory of history, including the notion that "the gradual abolition of slavery" [is] wiser and more equitable than its sudden removal" (*PH*, 199).

What Hegel had actually written about the natives of Africa was that "these people continue long at rest, but suddenly their passions ferment, and then they are quite beside themselves. The destruction which is the consequence of their excitement, is caused by the fact that it is no positive idea, no thought which produces these commotions; a physical rather than a spiritual enthusiasm" (*PH*, 199). An "enthusiasm" (like Nat Turner's) fermented by the passions rather than the intellect, a tendency toward emotional or "physical" monomania rather than the notional or "spiritual" kind: as applied to Africa, the great Hegelian dialetic theory of history would seem to be little more than a conscious grafting of faculty psychology upon a benighted theory of race.

Though Hegel considered Africans who had been transported to America "far more susceptible of European culture than the Indians," he thought of their homeland, Africa itself, as forming "no historical part of the world" for the reason that "it has no movement or development to exhibit." Africa had made no cultural advance in its long non-history because it had developed no dialectic, no tension of opposing principles, to drive it forward. Thus in 1800 Africa embodied for Hegel the single motive force that all of human history would still display to Henry Adams in 1900—pure sensuousness, savagery, the utter license, in Hegel's phrase, of "arbitrary subjective choice" (*PH*, 199).

Any choice that the Native African made concerning his destiny would be "arbitrary," Hegel reasoned, because the African was a slave to his passions. "The standpoint of humanity at this grade," he said, in the language of faculty psychology, is "mere sensuous volition with energy of will" (*PH*, 199). Civilization, moral progress in human affairs, Hegel thought, resulted only from dialectic, and no dialectical tension could be set going where a single principle, unopposed, ruled the psyche (and thus the state). For any advance, or synthesis, to take place, according to the Hegelian view, passion had to be counterbalanced by intellect in the race as in the individual.

To Hegel, the mind of Africa remained essentially the mind of the child because it had been violated by "no positive idea," not even "that of the morality of the family." Reading the "various traits" of African mental geography like a phrenologist, the great philosopher of history concluded "that want of self-control distinguishes the character of the Negroes. This condition is capable of no development or culture, and as we see them at this day, such have they always been" (*PH*, 198).

As Frederick Douglass's biographer, William S. McFeely, has observed, even abolitionist rhetoric in America required slaves to appear as the cloddish beasts that slaveholders had made them.[21] Hegel's psychoracial theory of history comported perfectly, therefore, with the racial stereotypes that had long stamped themselves even upon such "liberal" branches of American thought as the Transcendentalism of Boston and Concord. At times, in fact, Hegel's philosophical idealism is scarcely distinguishable from Emerson's, as when, for example, Hegel writes: "Man is not free, when he is not thinking; for except when thus engaged he sustains a relation to the world around him as to another, an alien, form of being" (*PH*, 361). Before 1860, consequently, Hegel's Africa, the land of perpetual childhood, was white America's Africa, too—with one distinctly American coloration. Hegel had attributed no sense of loyalty or affection to the African: despite his passionate nature, Hegel contended, the African would betray members of his own family into slavery, feeling remorse only because he had no more relations to sell.

Whereas Hegel had hardly seen an African, white Americans, especially in the South, were often outnumbered by them. Terrified that the slouching lion might spring at any moment in their own backyards, they allayed their fears of insurrection and reprisal by telling themselves that "the Negro" was naturally docile, that he was prone, under the judicious lash, to kiss the hand that applied it and, consequently, that such outbreaks of violence as Nat Turner's "enthusiasm" bespoke rare fits of insanity in the black mind. In effect, like the Duke and the King in *Huck Finn*, white, antebellum America hung a sign on "Nigger Jim" proclaiming him "harmless," even kind and gentle, "when not out of his head" (*HF*, 171). (Though the African lions threaten to devour their masters in Sophia Hawthorne's letter, they still "love" them.)

The saving stereotype of the affectionate slave was so essential to an economy based on forced labor that even black Americans of the mid-nineteenth century professed to believe in it: "Truly, the colored race are the most cheerful and forgiving people on the face of the earth," Harriet Jacobs is supposed to have written in *Incidents in the Life of a Slave Girl*. "That their masters sleep in safety is owing to their superabundance of heart; and yet they [the masters] look upon their sufferings with less pity than they would bestow on those of a horse or a dog."[22]

Mount Prognathous

About the shape of Nathaniel Turner's head, either before or after his execution, we are never told in the *Confessions*. Was it "indented at the top," as in Poe's profile of Dirk Peters, "like that of most Negroes"? (Marking the region where the higher "moral sentiments" should be, this dip in the crown, according to phrenology and the polygenisists, was a sure sign of unbridled savagery.) We do learn, however, that Turner exhibited "the true negro face" (*CNT*, 113).

What that might be, exactly, Gray does not say. He asserts only that the "African" character of Turner's physiognomy was "strongly marked" in "every feature" (*CNT*, 113).[23] For an explanation of the standard marks on the physical body, particularly the head, that indicated (to many white supremacists of the period) a lurking Africanism within, we can look to illustrations such as those in O. S. and L. N. Fowler's 1849 *Illustrated Self-Instructor in Phrenology and Physiology*. To the physiognomist of the nineteenth century, the firm, jutting chin of the Fowlers' "African Head" betokened Self-Esteem, a faculty, when strong, said the Fowlers, that "throws the head upward and backward toward the seat of its organ." The African looks out steadfastly upon the world, moreover, because his clear eye draws on the "full perceptives" that lie within his prominent lower brow, a "formation," as Poe might say, thought to be typical of his race (*IS-I*, 32, 41). This could be the face of Stowe's Uncle Tom in his prime, or of Frederick Douglass's Madison Washington, the "heroic slave" in his romance of that title. "Your head is the type of your mentality," claimed the *Self-Instructor*, but however noble, even heroic, might be the physical and corresponding mental characteristics of the model African pictured there, he and his race are represented, nonetheless, by a plainly prognathous face that slopes gradually backward from the jutting chin.

To the practical phrenologist, the backward slope of the African's forehead meant that he was "deficient in reasoning capacity," and the *Self-Instructor* duly places the "African Head" (No. 38) next to that of an "Orang-outang" (No. 37), whose chin juts only slightly further and whose forehead, if anything, appears more rounded. Caucasian faces, by contrast, observed the Fowlers, "have higher and bolder foreheads" because "the Caucasian race is superior in reasoning power . . . to all the other races" (*IS-I*, 41).

Paul Broca went further than the Fowlers. "A group with black skin, woolly

FIG. 5 In the iconography of nineteenth-century race science, the sloping face of the African signified a deficiency in reasoning power. Illustration from O. S. and L. N. Fowler, *Illustrated Self-Instructor in Phrenology and Physiology* (1849), which proclaimed on the front cover: "Self-knowledge is the essence of all knowledge."

hair and a prognathous face," he wrote in the 1860s, "has never been able to raise itself spontaneously to civilization." As their "ordinary equipment," said the renowned French anthropologist, those who ascend to the highest rungs of the human ladder carry along "more or less white skin, straight hair and an orthognathous [vertical] face."[24] To those who squinted down upon it from the frontal Olympus in their own heads, it would seem, lowly Mount Prognathous—as mythical a promontory in the Africa of the American mind as Hemingway's Mt. Kilimanjaro—appeared, through the fog, to be inhabited by a race of intellectual pygmies.

To be sure, the superior Caucasian intellect of the nineteenth century recognized degrees of savagery in the dark minds that ranged downward, in its view, from the mental and moral eminence represented up front in whites by an *orthogonous* face. "The skull of the Negro," wrote George Combe in his *System of Phrenology*, "evidently rises in the scale of development of the moral and intellectual organs: the forehead is higher, and the organs of the sentiments bear a larger proportion to those of the propensities" (*SP*, 577). President of the Phrenological Society of Edinburgh, and one of the most respected mental philosophers

of his day, Combe was not comparing the "higher" forehead of the Negro with
his own capacious cranium, however, but with that of the native American,
particularly the "ferocious" Charib Indians of South America and the Carrib-
bean. The Phrenological Society possessed casts of five Charib heads procured
by Johann Kaspar Spurzheim himself (so "their genuineness may be relied
on"). The society officially judged "the reflecting organs" of these peoples to
be "the most deficient of any human beings whose skulls have come under our
notice." It was not only his intelligence that, from the shape of the head, was
to be adjudged "deficient" in the native American; so were his "sentiments"
and "propensities" (*SP*, 568–69).

Cheek by jowl with an orangutan's head on one side, the African head in the
Fowlers' phrenology is flanked on the other side by that of an "Indian Chief."
Totally bald, he looks like a plump mummy who has undergone radiation therapy (*IS-I*, 41). It would be hard to find a better (or worse) illustration of a racial or ethnic stereotype than this crude, and crudely printed, image from the
Fowlers' *Self-Instructor* in bigotry. As subtle as the cries of a barker selling snake
oil, the Fowlers' many popular manuals, most of them costing less than a dollar,
were widely circulated by mail, and they give a fair, if hardly a pretty, picture
of the images of race and gender to which the mail-order mind of the Anglo-
American consumer was exposed in many forms of print in the nineteenth
century.

With his low forehead, seat of the powers of physical perception, the Fowlers' Indian chief can see and hear "extraordinarily well," a crafty hunter in the
woods like the Indians of James Fenimore Cooper's romances; but his faculties
of reason shrink from the towering heights that awaken the higher intellect of
his pale-faced cousin because they are crammed in the space *above* his low-
bulging brow, where his head slopes steeply backward in front. On the sides,
this head Indian's head tapers to such a point as virtually to eliminate the "organs" located in the crown. It was this sidewise slippery slope that distinguished the mind and character of the red man not only from those of the
white man but also from the mind and character of other men of color, such as
the African. Even by comparison with the prognathous African, whose head
sloped up more gradually, the cone-headed native American was deficient in
the "moral sentiments"—housed in the coronal, or upper (and slightly to the
rear) "lobes" of the brain, as the anterior lobes were thought to be the seat of
the intellectual faculties and the posterior, of the "animal propensities."

Besides prominent foreheads, indicating their greater reasoning powers, or-
thognathos Caucasians, said the Fowlers, also enjoyed "more elevated and
elongated top heads" than other races, indicating that they were superior in
"moral elevation" as well as intellectual prowess (*IS-I*, 41). It was these dual

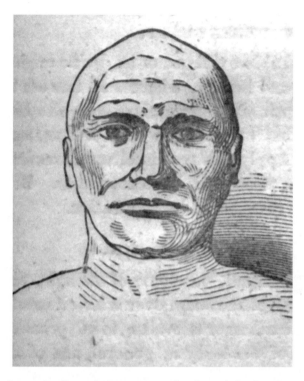

FIG. 6 According to the *Illustrated Self-Instructor in Phrenology and Physiology*, the pointed head of this stereotypical Native American signified his (and his race's) moral and emotional deficiency.

counterweights of highly developed moral *and* intellectual "organs" that, at moments of psychic conflict, kept the better balanced white mind, especially in cerebral males, safely poised on the brink, while weaker, darker minds—including, too often, those of females of all races—slid over the edge into rank sensuality and madness, the helpless victims of their base inclinations.

Courage is a moral sentiment, and everyone in the nineteenth century knew that Indians were brave in battle down to the last Mohican.[25] The courage of the native American, however, like all the other higher emotions and sentiments in persons with depressed frontal and temporal lobes, was thought to be "blind." The Charib Indians, according to Combe, rushed with "unbridled violence on present gratification, blind to every consequence, and incapable of tracing the shortest links in the chain of causation." The reason was their extreme prognathism: "by far the largest quantity of the brain is situated behind the ear; or, in other words, . . . the organs of the animal propensities greatly preponderate over those of the intellectual faculties" (*SP*, 568).

Paul Broca cited Tahitian warriors whose heads had been purposely deformed in childhood: "Frontal deformation produced blind passions, ferocious instincts, and animal courage, all of which I would willingly call occipital courage. We must not confound it with true courage, frontal courage, which we may call Caucasian courage" (1861).[26] The Charibs were all the more savage, Combe "determined" from the skull casts, because the regions of Combativeness and Destructiveness were "prodigiously developed" in "the Charib brain" (*SP*, 568). It did not trouble the phrenologists of Edinburgh and Boston, however, to note that these same "animal" propensities were also highly developed in the brains of Europeans. The European, says Combe approvingly, "lives to a great extent upon animal food, is fierce in his anger, and is characterized by great combative and destructive vigor." That "vigor" had enabled the hardy European to tame a continent, and Combe freely acknowledges that the work of "civilization" required "subduing" the natives by hunting them down "like wild beasts" and nearly "extirpating" them (*SP*, 567–68).

Yet Combe and many of his contemporaries in America, where his *Constitution of Man* was warmly received, saw no occasion for irony in a statement like the following about Native Americans from the chapter, "On the Coincidence between the Natural Talents and Dispositions of Nations, and the Development of their Brains":

> It might naturally have been expected, that, ... during the long period that the Europeans have been settled amongst them, and taught them, by such striking examples, the benefits of industry and social order, they would have been tempted to endeavor to participate in blessings thus providentially brought within their reach. But all has been unavailing; and it now seems certain that the North American Indians, like the bears and wolves, are destined to flee at the approach of civilized man. (*SP*, 564)[27]

Since the brain of the European male was thought to be the most highly developed of any people's in the 1840s and fifties, it might have been expected to recognize more than a tinge of savagery in itself. Combe's representative European brain was so disposed, however, that the idea of the savage seldom coincided in it with the idea of civilization, especially when transplanted to America. As on William Dunbar's plantation, where the borders between savagery and civilization scarcely extended beyond the mind that conceived them, these two estates continued to occupy distinctly separate territories in the odd corners of the Anglo-American psyche.

Such psychological distancing was especially necessary in America, perhaps, because here Europeans found themselves much closer than Hegel's theoretical

Africa to cultures genuinely alien to them, and because the natives, as late as the 1880s, were still fleeing in violent horror at "striking examples" of the "civilized" mind at work.[28] Among the Apaches, for example, rumors lingered until well into the twentieth century that the white man was cannibalistic. Thus Chief Geronimo, a featured attraction in 1904 along with several African Pygmies at the "anthropology" exhibit of the St. Louis World's Fair, warned the Pygmies not to stand too close to "White Eyes": his tribesmen had seen images of human beings on cans of meat handed out by the U.S. Cavalry.[29]

Habeas Corpus: Rutherford B. Hayes and the Case of Nancy Farrer

In the *Confessions of Nat Turner*, Thomas Gray was profiling a genuinely troubled psyche—inspired by Turner, the insurrectionists killed more than twenty-five children, including, by his own admission, "a little infant sleeping in a cradle" (*CNT*, 106). Yet there seems never to have been a moment in Turner's case when a plea of not guilty by reason of insanity might have been entered on his behalf, even though there is nothing in the *Confessions* to indicate that Turner ever realized he had done anything wrong.

"I consider that insane persons *generally* know the difference between right and wrong," wrote a young attorney in Cincinnati, Rutherford Birchard Hayes, who copied this sentiment in his notebook for 1851, attributing it to "Dr. Bell, of the McLean Asylum."[30] (Luther V. Bell had been appointed superintendent of the McLean Asylum outside Boston in 1826. Ralph Waldo Emerson's brother Bulkeley, his son Edward, and the poet Jones Very all came under Bell's care there.) Bell's dictum was the heart of an argument that Hayes was to use later that year in the case of Nancy Farrer, a servant girl who fatally poisoned four persons.

Nancy Farrer was white, though she seemed marked like Nathaniel Turner for sure destruction, "the object of a horror that prejudged her from the first," as William Dean Howells described her in his *Life and Character of Rutherford B. Hayes* (1876). Less kindly sources called Farrer, who was plainly incompetent, "the ugliest girl ever known in Cincinnati."[31] Like Turner, she was a child of religious fanaticism, the daughter of a Mormon prophetess who claimed to be "the bride of Christ."[32] Her upbringing, however, seems to have been psychologically even more destructive than his. Nancy Farrer's "origin, training, and associations," said Howells, "were all of the worst sort; her father had died a sot in the hospital, her mother was insane; with such parentage, what must her life, her mind be?"[33]

Nancy Farrer had been induced to commit her crimes by a man—"the really responsible author of her act," Howells called him—who skipped town to

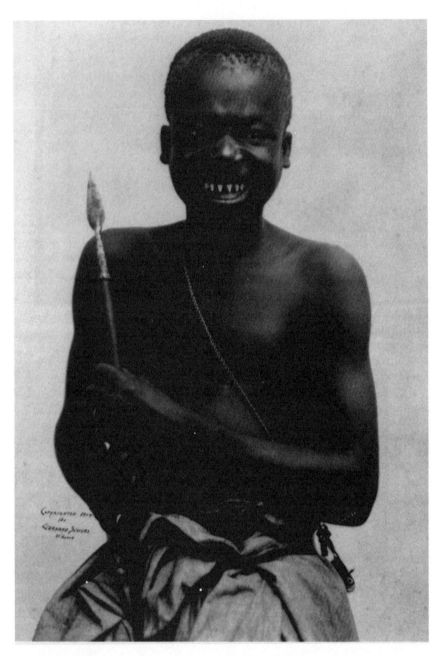

FIG. 7 Ota Benga, his teeth filed to points in imitation of the crocodile, feigns ferocity for professional photographers at the St. Louis World's Fair of 1904. After the fair closed, this star of the "anthropology" exhibit was moved to the Bronx Zoo.

escape prosecution, leaving Farrer to assume sole blame for the murders. Until her charity case was assigned to Hayes by the court (when her earlier court-appointed attorney showed up drunk), Farrer hadn't a prayer of escaping execution, even though she was female, largely because of her looks. Popular feeling was heightened against her, said Howells, because "of the repulsive plainness and brutality [he might almost have said the savagery] of her face." Yet Hayes was convinced that Farrer was not a "morally free agent," even though she knew the difference between right and wrong.[34]

So was Howells, who recounted the story twenty-five years later in terms that might have come from his *Heroines of Fiction*. Nancy Farrer, said Howells, was "wholly in the power of the man who instigated her crimes." "Once under the sway of the real murderer, who had won the wretched creature's love in order the better to enslave her will, she had no volition of her own."[35] At an inquest of lunacy, Hayes managed to persuade the court that Farrer was not responsible for her actions, even though she knew they were wrong, because she could not help herself, a precedent that made legal history in the sentencing of the criminally insane in America and helped to launch a political career that led, eventually, to the White House.

A passage in Hayes's pleadings before the court carried a slightly veiled reference to his own sister's mental illness:

> The calamity of insanity is one which may touch very nearly the happiness of the best of our citizens. We all know that in some of its thousand forms it has carried grief and agony unspeakable into many a happy home; and we must all wish to see such rules in regard to it established as would satisfy an intelligent man if, instead of this friendless girl, his own sister or his own daughter were on trial. And surely to establish such rules will be a most noble achievement of that intelligence and reason which God has given to you, but denied to her whose fate is in your hands."

Howells, whose household as a child included an idiot brother who suffered a bone spur to the brain, was moved by the "sober eloquence and logic" of these words.[36] And so, after an intitial verdict of guilty, was the court. Instead of going to the gallows, therefore, Nancy Farrer, upon appeal to the Ohio Supreme Court, went to an insane asylum.

It is not hard to see why the American legal system hanged Nat Turner at once, even as it spared Nancy Farrer. The legal climate in America was less hostile by the 1850s to pleas of not guilty by reason of insanity, and Farrer was tried in Ohio while Turner was sentenced in Virginia, soon-to-be capital of the wartime confederacy. Furthermore, Nancy Farrer was a woman, however homely, a "friendless girl" whom the (male) juror was admonished to judge as if "his own sister or his own daughter were on trial." Obviously she posed no real threat to a society dominated by white men; after all, her criminal behavior had been dictated by one.[37]

Turner, on the other hand, a physically powerful man (though "below the ordinary stature," like Poe's Dirk Peters) struck the public as capable of doing them harm, despite his apparent ignorance of wrongdoing. The real reason for Turner's summary execution upon capture, it would seem, was his blackness. A newspaper editorial published soon after the uprising made this point: "Was it the fear of Nat Turner, and his deluded, drunken handful of followers, which produced such effects? . . . No, sir: it was the suspicion eternally attached to the slave himself,—the suspicion that a Nat Turner might be in every family; that the same bloody deed might be acted over at any time and any place" (*TO*, 324–25).

Not Turner's actual deeds, however bloody, said the editorialist, but this "withering apprehension"—the mere idea of a hostile black presence in their midst— caused the white community "to have quailed and trembled by the paralyzing and deadening weight with which it falls upon and prostrates the heart of every man who has helpless dependents to protect" (*TO*, 325). What is being described here in the psychological terms of the day is a case of mass hysteria: an idea or image in the mind, a mere cognition, whether grounded in reality or groundless, causes the emotions to quail, and the will is momentarily paralyzed with fear. Then a psychological reaction (which Thomas Wentworth Higginson compared to "the enthusiasm" for the Polish revolution gripping the nation at the same time) sets in, and a frenzy of irrational behavior ensues, as in a dream or nightmare, before the will can regain control.

Among the mad "effects" attributable to the frenzied reaction of the white community to the Turner uprising, Higginson cites "one hundred and twenty negroes" killed in retaliation in little more than a day: "Men were tortured to death, burned, maimed, and subjected to nameless atrocities" (*TO*, 300, 325). One of the atrocities that Higginson does name appears in a horror "story" (his word), involving a slave called Antonio who was forced to "confess" at gunpoint: "He told 'em he didn't know any thing about any insurrection. They shot several balls through him, quartered him, and put his head on a pole at the fork of the road leading to the court."[38]

Antonio's fate is assigned, almost verbatim, by Herman Melville to his fictional Babo, leader of the slave mutiny in "Benito Cereno." After Babo is captured, he is returned in irons to Lima, his master's home port, where he is tried and "dragged to the gibbet at the tail of a mule." Babo's body is then burned— in North America, the lynch mob would have used coal oil—"but for many days," writes Melville, "the head, that hive of subtlety, fixed on a pole in the Plaza, met, unabashed, the gaze of the whites."[39] By the time of Babo's execution, such "Blackhead signposts" had become almost conventional in the annals of slavery, "the spot living on in memory, as Eric Sundquist has said, "long after the head itself was gone."[40]

Nat Turner was not decapitated publicly after he was hanged. But Higginson offers this grim footnote on the final disposition of Turner's remains: "His body, after his death, was given over to the surgeons for dissection," presumably so they could look for internal abnormalities, especially within the hemispheres of that "hive of subtlety" with which Turner had plotted the insurrection (*TO*, 319).

Such decapitations and other public reminders of torture and death, as Robyn Wiegman observes in his "anatomy of lynching," are always "about the law."[41] Thus Thomas Gray, Nat Turner's "confessor," admonished history to record Turner's execution as a necessary prescription for restoring the white social order. Turner's written confession was submitted to the public as proof of "the policy of our laws in restraint of this class of our population, and to induce all those entrusted with their execution, as well as our citizens generally, to see that they are strictly and rigidly enforced" (*CNT*, 97). The bodily part that Gray assigns, as a token of their authority and function, to the enforcers of the white penal code is, predictably, the eye: "Each particular community should look to its own safety," he writes in "To the Public, "whilst the general guardians of the laws, keep a watchful eye over all" (*CNT*, 97).

For all his moralizing, then, Gray was yet another case of the white doctor (or lawyer or magistrate or minister) as scourge rather than "moral" healer. Justice may be blind and a woman; but, as I will be arguing throughout these pages, the eye in Gray's day, like the law, was thought to be fundamentally a "masculine" agent of "rational" surveillance over the "irrational," "feminine," "black"—in short, African—elements of society and of the human mind. Instead of the actions of a partially deranged mind, therefore, Turner's deeds, in Gray's estimation, amount to the savage acts of a black mind wholly other than the "normal" white mind that struggles (and fails) to comprehend them. No longer a man, Turner has become, to Gray's black and white understanding, the "beast" that madness made of even the once kingly mind in the eighteenth century, before the advent of "moral" reforms in the treatment of mental disease at the beginning of the nineteenth.

It would be wrong to deduce, however, that by treating Nat Turner as a madman Thomas Gray and the white community successfully neutralized the effect of his revolt or his power as a propagandist. I can only agree with Eric Sundquist that "although Gray's text serves to contain and suppress Turner's revolt by situating it within a description of fanaticism, it does not obliterate the meaning of the revolt as an event or as a textual reflection on religious and political principles of liberation." Whether we think of Gray or Turner as the primary author of *The Confessions*—and surely Sundquist is right to say that though we read it "as if it were Gray's text . . . it is never possible *not* to read it also as Turner's"—Turner's narrative (or the narrative of Turner) kept the fact of the rebellion alive in the cabinets of memory and history long after his death and was thus, as a "sign of power" (Sundquist), as valid and true as the "saner" writings of Frederick Douglass.[42]

FOUR

Romancing the Shadow

The girl's splendor dazzled him ... and the remote taint of her servile and savage origin gave her a kind of fascination which refuses to let itself be put in words: it was like the grace of a limp, the occult, indefinable loveableness of a deformity, but transcending these by its allurement in infinite degree, and going for the reason of its effect deep into the mysterious places of being where the spirit and the animal meet and part in us.

—*William Dean Howells*

 THE SHAPE of their heads aside, the facial feature that more than any other links Thomas Gray's Nat Turner with other representations, such as Melville's Babo and Poe's Dirk Peters, of the savage man of color in white folklore and popular fiction is its stony indifference to human feelings.

Peters' mouth, you may recall, stretches from ear to ear; but his facial expression, the grin of the human ape, "never varied under the influence of any emotion whatever." And in Melville's story, Babo's face is "unabashed" by the gaze of the whites even before he is decapitated; for once he is caught, the cunning slave clamps his mouth shut and never again utters a human sound. So terrifyingly inhuman is his "aspect," says Melville, that when forced to look at it by the court, Don Benito Cereno, the Spanish ship captain whose slave vessel Babo has commandeered, faints dead away.

"You are saved," cries Amasa ("a mas'a"?) Delano, the whiter captain of Melville's tale to his darker, Hispanic counterpart; "what has cast such a shadow upon you?" Taking these lines as an epigraph for *Invisible Man* (1952), Ralph Ellison left the reader to seek out Don Benito's reply: "the negro." [1]

Melville's Yankee sea captain, a man of "good nature, compassion, and charity," would never dream of trafficking in human cargo; but neither can his understanding grasp the idea that a slave might hate his master, no matter how "charitable," just because he was master. "So far," says the Spanish captain, who *is* conversant with the power of blackness, "may even the best man err in judging the conduct of one with the recesses of whose condition he is not acquainted."[2]

Even one as steeped in the nineteenth century as Ralph Waldo Ellison, whose fiction stains the white radiance of the earlier Ralph Waldo's Yankee idealism on every page, could not altogether escape the preoccupations of his times. Asked by an interviewer if he considered "the search for identity" to be "primarily an American theme," Ellison replied, "It is *the* American theme." The book under immediate discussion: *Adventures of Huckleberry Finn.*[3]

Huck Finn, however, is not primarily about the search for identity (Huck's, Jim's, nor the country's). And neither, I think, is most of the rest of classic American literature. If there is *an* American theme before about 1920, it is freedom, especially freedom of the will.

Ellison's invisible black man is invested with a transparently post-Freudian id. To such politically and psychologically "repressed" persons of the twentieth century, freedom is self-expression, self-release, the loss of inhibition—what most people white *or* black in early nineteenth-century America took to be lawlessness, savagery, the power of darkness. Why, then, instead of recoiling, as George Cuvier professed to do when he encountered a black woman whom he imagined to be ape-like, does Poe's Arthur Gordon Pym (who is, of course, white and whose name has the same rhythms as Poe's own) repeatedly swoon into the hairy arms of the half breed, Dirk Peters?

The answer is again "the negro," this time in his, or more often (except in the pages of the exquisitely perverse Poe) *her* capacity as object of forbidden desire in the white imagination. This impulse to embrace what we now call "the Other" Poe called the "imp of the perverse." Toni Morrison calls it "romancing the shadow," and she defines the shadow—what an earlier age would have referred to as the "animal propensities"—in the dominant white culture of the nineteenth century as "a fabricated brew of darkness, otherness, alarm, and desire that is uniquely American" (*PD*, 32).

Colonel Higginson to the Rescue

Any freedom, including religious freedom, that this country afforded to the early white settlers of New England and the Carolinas had to be realized against the background of a vast wilderness inhabited, as they believed, by "wild" men and women of color who were joined very early in American history by still darker "savages" from Africa. Thus it was perhaps inevitable that the whites who showed their pale faces on the dark continent of America would define themselves and their centers of culture by contrast with blackness.

There are sound linguistic reasons for this. Given the narrow range of physical difference in human beings—only about 20 percent by some estimates, far less than in many other species—if one has "white features," one has to stretch to identify them by contrast with "black features." When, however, we read the human body as a culturally inscribed text in black and white, red and yellow on the differences of mind and spirit *within* the living temple, we have little recourse, linguistically, but to proceed by contrasting our principal terms.

Lerone Bennett, author of *Confrontation Black and White* (1965), does just this when he takes novelist William Styron to task for his "biased" account of the Turner uprising. (In his fictional *Confessions of Nat Turner* [1967] Styron avers, erroneously, that Nat Turner's revolt was the only significant rebellion led by a slave in American history. Even white apologists for Turner's dark deeds, it would appear, still feel obliged to explain them away as a rare anomaly, like Gustave LeBon's woman of superior intelligence.)[4] Then a senior editor of *Ebony* magazine, Bennett was denigrating, in the root sense of "to blacken," Styron's white version of the Turner uprising in order to establish the validity of his own "historical" version:

> According to the historical data, the real Nat Turner was a virile, commanding, courageous figure. Styron rejects history by rejecting this image of Nat Turner. In fact, he wages literary war on this image, substituting an impotent, cowardly, irresolute creature of his own imagination for the real black man who killed or ordered killed real white people for real historical reasons. The man Styron substitutes for Nat Turner is not only the antithesis of Nat Turner; he is the antithesis of blackness. In fact, he is a standard Styron type: a neurasthenic, Hamlet-like white intellectual in blackface." (*CNT,* 5)

The issue here is not who the living Nathaniel Turner—about whom little is known—actually might or might not have been; it is the arguably more important one of how we construct those images of ourselves in the black and white of the written word that we call *history* or *(auto)biography* or *fiction* or *the law.*[5] Bennett himself touches on the key difference between writing or thinking about human history and actually living it when he asserts, "We are not quibbling here over footnotes in scholarly journals. We are objecting to something more insidious, more dangerous. *We are objecting to a deliberate attempt to steal the meaning of a man's life*" (*CNT,* 5).

The jury and executioner took Nathaniel Turner's life, but no one, not even William Styron or Thomas Gray, has the power to give or take, in any absolute sense, the meaning of a human life. Since all forms of writing are acts of interpretation in a particular cultural moment, anybody's account of Turner's (or any other) life is colored more than a shade by the prejudices of his time and place, and by his language. It is but a rendering, like Turner's own reading of the hieroglyphs counseling him to revolt that he thought he saw on the leaves in the forest. Or, as Maurice Merleau-Ponty puts the matter in a line that Bennett quotes, "History never confesses" (*CNT,* 3).[6]

No more (or less) historically accurate than Styron's, Bennett's rendering of the Turner rebellion was, however, a more authoritatively "black" rendering. "No event in recent years has touched and stirred the black intellectual community more," wrote John Henrik Clarke in 1968, than the publication of Styron's version of *The Confessions of Nat Turner* the year before. "With a few notable exceptions," as Clarke observed, most black readers saw Styron's "meditation on history" as a romance, like Poe's narrative of Pym at the South Pole, "of the perfect whiteness of the snow." Many, including the novelists John O. Killens and John A. Williams, felt that "their" black history had been betrayed. This benighted white man's version of a black man's story, they charged, in Bennett's words, "tells us little about the historical Nat Turner and a great deal about William Styron and the white culture structure which made the book a modern literary happening" (*CNT,* vii, 4).

To African American historians, teachers, writers, editors and other intellectuals of the 1960s, Styron's brand of whiteness-masquerading-as-blackness must have seemed especially offensive—just one more instance of Southern guilt still unwilling to face the historical "facts"—if for no other reason than because his book attracted so much attention.

Many preferred the much earlier account of the Turner rebellion by Thomas Wentworth Higginson, white colonel of the First South Carolina Volunteers, the first black regiment to enter the Civil War, who wrote in 1861: "Thus, for instance, we know that Nat Turner's young wife was a slave; we know that she belonged to a different master from himself; we know little more than this, but this is much. For this is equivalent to saying that, by day or by night, her husband had no more power to protect her than the man who lies bound upon a plundered vessel's deck has power to protect his wife on board the pirate schooner disappearing in the horizon" (*TO,* 280).

How much of this brief account is fiction and how much is "history"? Is the historical part, moreover, "white" or "black"? It is a historical fact, apparently, that Nathaniel Turner had a wife and that she lived apart from him on a separate plantation under a different master. This we "know," as Higginson said; though new evidence might prove us mistaken, facts are knowable—in the sense of being verifiable—whether or not they are known. It is not quite so certain that Turner's young wife (in Higginson's words) "was tortured under the lash, after her husband's execution, to make her produce his papers," information that Higginson attributes in *Travellers and Outlaws* (1889) to newspaper reports of the Turner uprising (*TO*, 281).

What actually happened to Nat Turner's wife may well have been intimidating, more likely terrifying, perhaps physically brutal. "Tortured under the lash," however, is the language of derring-do, like the metaphor of plundering pirates in Higginson's account of Turner's psychological state. The moment that Higginson starts to interpret his data, the moment he says of the limited facts, "but this is much," he has launched into history, a story that inevitably varies, as mere facts do not, according to the ideological complexion of the teller and the kind of language he or she uses. (That Higginson himself expected history to imitate fiction and drama is suggested by his assessment of Harriet Beecher Stowe's novel based on the Dred Scott case: "Mrs. Stowe's 'Dred' seems dim and melodramatic beside the actual Nat Turner," writes Higginson, "and DeQuincey's 'Avenger' is his only parallel in imaginative literature" [*TO*, 321].)

Higginson's status as the colonel (though white) of a "colored" regiment under fire in the Civil War gave him an authority that might well make his account of Turner's history more palatable to African American readers than that of William Styron, who not only lacked such authority for his account but, as a white southern male with no black "credentials," might have seemed positively suspect (a skepticism that has been leveled at Styron's fictional treatment of Jews). Moreover, Higginson's language of adventure and historical romance can seem racially neutral, whereas Styron's language sounded false to the ear of many African American readers—"Back with the Wind," said Mike Thelwell—when they first heard it in Nat Turner's mouth, a mixture of the King James Bible and, said Lerone Bennett, the "vocabulary of U. B. Phillips," to Bennett's mind "the classic apologist for slavery" (*CNT*, 7, 79).

Styron announced that he was crossing the border between fiction and history by subtitling his book "a meditation on history." Bennett accuses Styron of "trying to escape history" altogether: his meditation is "a record of the hallucinatory silence of our history, of 350 years" (quoting Styron's Nat) "of talk buried deep in dreams" (*CNT*, 3). And well it may be. But because history deals with meaning(s) and not just facts, all history is "meditation," if not the "dream" to which Bennett relegates Styron's fiction.

By attributing to *his* Nat Turner the motives and feelings of a man bound by pirates who steal away with his wife, Colonel Higginson's "white" account of the history of the Turner uprising may be more easily assimilated by black readers than Styron's because it establishes a plot remote from the literal experience of any American reader in the twentieth century, black or white. This launching into "neutral territory," as Hawthorne called it, is the fundamental strategy of the romance, and not only of the historical romance but also of the more psychological kind practiced by Hawthorne, Melville, Poe, and, more recently, Saul Bellow, Bernard Malamud, William Styron, Ralph Ellison, and Toni Morrison.

Bellow's modern romance, *Henderson the Rain King* (1959), for example, reverses the black diaspora by sending its naïve white hero to Africa to purge himself of the evils of modern civilization and get in touch with his emotional roots. On his way back home, Henderson stops off in "Newfoundland," a land of whiteness at the top of the globe that is similar to that of Poe's Pym at the bottom. Here, against a background of dazzling snow and ice, Henderson engages in an African fertility ritual that brings renewed vitality to the wasteland, and Bellow fantasizes about placing black–white, male–female relations in America upon a new basis of mutual regard and sympathy.

An escape from history, perhaps. But like Morrison, I am "more persuaded by arguments that find in [the romance] the head-on encounter with very real, pressing historical forces and the contradictions inherent in them." I agree with Morrison's eloquent argument that "Romance offered writers not less but more; not a narrow ahistorical canvas but a wide historical one; not escape but entanglement" (*PD*, 36–37).

The first avowedly fictional form of extended prose narrative written in America, the romance, as Morrison recognizes, is an "exploration of anxiety" (*PD*, 36). But it is also, I would argue, the place where, in fear and trembling, the poles of the American psyche—North and South, white and black, masculine and feminine—first came together. By casting them in exotic disguises, the romance invited the nineteenth-century reader to flirt with those subversive elements—not only in the body politic but also in the physical body and in the mind—from which he or she had been officially schooled to recoil with alarm.[7]

Thus I suspect that Colonel Higginson's romanticized history of the Turner rebellion had its way with the white reader in 1861 for the same reason that the image (or one of its variants) of pirates stealing away with their hostage bride still calls out to the reader from the cover of today's "true" romance in the paperback section of any mass-market bookstore. A thinly disguised parable of psychosexual slavery, Higginson's account—not just of the events themselves, but also of the motives behind the events—recapitulated the essential plot of all romances: entrapment, whether physical or psychological, and the lure of escape into strange territory.

To the nineteenth-century reader, Higginson's exotic pirate schooner was but a version of Emerson's familiar "ship of humanity" run amok. Like Ahab's whale, its marauding savages "plundered" the delicately trimmed vessel of normal commerce among the genders, mental faculties, and races—pirates are traditionally "swarthy" in romances—leaving the normal (usually white and male) authorities that are supposed to arrest them helplessly "bound." A conceit of male impotence and female servitude, Higginson's account, though explicitly about human bondage, was implicitly liberating: deprived of free will, the "masculine" half of this broken union, represented by the physically restrained husband in Higginson's psychological parable, can no longer be held responsible for failing to keep the "feminine" half under lock and key.

Meanwhile, the defenseless young wife, with equal license, finds herself exposed to a host of dark-skinned "savages" who carry her toward new horizons of depravity that the duly (but covertly) initiated reader of Higginson's little romance can easily imagine. Here—but especially in the longer psychological romance (of which Toni Morrison is a modern master)—is where even the whitest sensibility's feelings of "otherness" and "alarm" could come together to release its suppressed feelings of "desire" for the shadow self. For in the romance, the psychological writers of the nineteenth century had found a medium capable of rendering, through images and parables, those "recesses" of human mind and motive that, even late in the nineteenth century, Howells (and Mark Twain and Henry James) still shuddered to put directly into words.

In Higginson's historical romancing of the Turner legend in 1861, it is Nathaniel Turner, the wronged husband, who is locked in chains when he tries to save himself and his wife from the degradations of slavery. In the gothic romance devised by Thomas Gray and others closer to the actual events of 1831, black Nat is the marauding pirate and the white community is the hostage bride.

The title page alone of *The Confessions of Nat Turner* suggests that Thomas Gray, the opportunist who implored Turner's jailer to let him take down the prisoner's oral history and "voluntary" confession, was well aware that the gallows biography (of which the criminal confession is a subspecies) had the same mesmeric power over some readers as the penny dreadful and other forms of pulp fiction. (In *Billy Budd*, for example, Melville satirizes the public appetite for sensationalized "history" when he commemorates the hanging of Billy Budd with a street ballad entitled "Billy in the Darbies.")

Printed off in black and white and circulated for a price, Thomas Gray's tale of Turner in the darbies (or chains) of the Jerusalem jailhouse promised not only an "authentic account of the whole insurrection" but also a menu of juicy details about "the prison where he was confined" and "LISTS OF THE WHITES WHO WERE MURDERED, AND OF THE NEGROES BROUGHT BEFORE THE COURT OF SOUTHAMPTON AND THERE SENTENCED, &c" (*CNT,* 92).

It is the ending of Gray's narrative, however, as period builds upon period, that most artfully imposes the gothic shapes of the fiction of his day upon the bare bones of fact: "The calm, deliberate composure with which he spoke of his late deeds and intentions, the expression of his fiend-like face when excited by enthusiasm, still bearing the stains of the blood of helpless innocence about him; clothed with rags and covered with chains; yet daring to raise his manacled hands to heaven, with a spirit soaring above the attributes of man; I looked on him and my blood curdled in my veins" (*CNT*, 113).

Here, I would argue, is a first-rate specimen of romancing the shadow. Just how conscious Gray is of what he is doing is difficult, and finally unnecessary, to say; just as it is hard to say how consciously William Styron understood what he was doing when, in the era of Kwame Ture (a.k.a. Stokely Carmichael) and the Black Panthers, he made his fictional black revolutionary an ineffectual creature whose "effeminacy" even Lerone Bennett does not sufficiently put into words. (Styron, contends Henry Louis Gates, must have been at least dimly aware that he was offering himself up, a willing white victim, for the critical slaughter.)

At the climax of "Turner's" narrative, Thomas Gray, however unknowingly, is surely manipulating the facts (and his audience) for dramatic effect, much as did the authors, most of them female, of the romances and sentimental novels of his day. Thus we half expect Gray's "narrator" to swoon upon the narrow jailhouse floor, like the tender consumer of a gothic romance whose sensibilities have overcome her sense, as Jane Austen said they shouldn't, at the sight of Turner's dark, now "fiend-like" but strangely fascinating face.[8]

The horror stories that passed into folklore after the Turner uprising show only one side of the white psyche, the obviously brutal one motivated by the fear that the shadow might someday prevail. The gothic endings of many a Poe tale, as of *The Confessions of Nat Turner*, however, imply a far more complicated and ambiguous attitude toward the black presence in antebellum America, North and South, on the part of many whites, male and female.

The Black Imp in White America

The most technically detailed treatise on the swoon of which I am aware in the nineteenth century is Poe's "The Imp of the Perverse" (1845). The narrator of this strange tale assumes a position characteristic of period: "We stand on the brink of a precipice. We peer into the abyss—we grow sick and dizzy. Our first impulse is to shrink from the danger. Unaccountably we remain. By slow degrees our sickness, and dizziness, and horror, become merged in a cloud of unnameable feeling. By gradations, still more imperceptible, this cloud assumes shape, as did the vapor from the bottle out of which arose the genius in the

Arabian Nights" (*PPTE*, 829). At such a moment, says Poe's narrator, we engage in an internal "conflict" of "the substance with the shadow" wherein "it is the shadow which prevails," words, though spoken of the individual psyche, that would soon apply all too mournfully well to a nation divided by the madness of civil war (*PPTE*, 828).

In American slang of the nineteenth century, *shadow* was an epithet for persons of color, as in the title of Frances Ellen Watkins Harper's *Iola Leroy; or Shadows Uplifted* (1892), one of the first novels written by an African American woman in America. Even when dissected and bottled, the Hottentot Venus would call to the nineteenth-century mind a black female essence, so strong was the image of "the negro" in the white (and especially southern, as in Poe's case) consciousness of the nineteenth century. Poe's genie, trapped in a bottle until its "master" or "mistress" calls it forth to do his or her bidding, augurs the rise, however, of a dark *male* form. This presence, says Poe's trembling narrator, "chills the very marrow of our bones with the fierceness of the delight of its horror" (*PPTE*, 829).

In the nineteenth century, the chilling of the very marrow of one's bones was the psychosexual condition that followed immediately upon the curdling of the blood in one's veins. Like the shuddering narrator on the brink of swooning helplessly at the end of Thomas Gray's version of the Turner confessions, Poe's male narrator has been radically "feminized" in accordance with the stereotypes of his culture. So, like Gray's, has his intended reader.

On the surface, Poe's critical commentary on the short story reassured readers that they were in good hands when they submitted themselves to the prose tales of a master romancer. However, the subtext, it seems to me, of Poe's reviews of Hawthorne's *Twice-Told Tales*, his classic definition of the tale form, is that the chivalric Poe, a southern gentleman writing about the borderlands of the mind, covertly considered the tale to be a form of psychological mastery, even rape. To a writer of "ambitious genius," says Poe, the tale offers an "advantageous field of exertion." It is "a far finer field than the essay" (Emerson's preferred form). The prose tale, Poe rhapsodized, "has even points of superiority over the poem" (*PER*, 585, 568).

Given Poe's passion for poetry, this comes as a surprise. Poe's aesthetic, however, is founded on faculty psychology; and it presumes that prose and poetry speak to different capacities, the intellect and the feelings, respectively. Since the sensibilities of few people are sufficiently developed, by Poe's exacting standard, to appreciate poetry, prose exerts a far greater sway over "the mass of mankind" (*PER*, 573).

Again, Poe's metaphors of mind evoke mountains and plateaus: "Thus the field of this species of composition [the tale], if not in so elevated a region on the mountain of Mind, is a table-land of far vaster extent than the domain of the mere poem" (*PER*, 573). As in the tales themselves, psychic possession, the power of one will over another, is Poe's theme in his literary criticism. Only now *we* are his unsuspecting victims. The fiction writer, says Poe, tricks the reader of a horrific story into a false sense of intimacy. To the reader, the tale appears to be a collaboration between equals, a marriage of the minds: "He feels and intensely enjoys the seeming novelty of the thought, enjoys it as really novel, as absolutely original with the writer—*and* himself. They two, he fancies, have, alone . . . thought thus. They two have, together, created this thing" (*PER*, 581).

At the moment of their apparently mutual conception, however, the author takes the reader into his power: "During the hour of perusal," says Poe, "the soul of the reader is at the writer's control" (*PER*, 586). The tale as Poe conceives it, then, is a psychological trap. It lures the reader to the brink of self-abandonment, as in "The Imp of The Perverse," which, with its maddening exegesis on circumlocution, can be read as a parody of the experience of reading a psychological tale or romance.[9]

The chains in which the romancer's mesmeric powers bind the reader's will are the same as those that enslave the mind "of him, who shuddering upon the edge of a precipice, thus meditates a plunge" in "The Imp of the Perverse." It is the usual mental chain or train from thought to feeling to volition, except that now, under the romancer's influence, the reader cannot break it: "That single thought is enough. The impulse increases to a wish, the wish to a desire, the desire to an uncontrollable longing, and the longing . . . is indulged" (*PPTE*, 828).

Poe's psychological precipice, as I have said, is one of the most haunting and haunted spots in the landscape of the nineteenth-century imagination. It is the craggy slope (to name but a few) where Carwin the ventriloquist tempts Clara Wieland to plunge into madness in the fiction of Charles Brockden Brown; it is grimly figured in the scaffold where Hester Prynne is forced to stand before the crowd in *The Scarlet Letter*; though less familiar to most readers, it is the rock where Fanshawe and the Angler struggle to the death in Hawthorne's first romance and the cliff from which Donatello, the Faun, throws the Monk in his last. (In *The Blithedale Romance*, Hawthorne even gives the rock a name, Eliot's Pulpit.) It is the "precipice others must resist" (i.e., "sin") in Emily Dickinson's satiric poems; the "close place" where Huck Finn decides to go to hell for stealing Jim; the tower upon which Henry James's governess first sees the ghosts; the stairway in the "Jolly Corner" where Spencer Brydon faints at the sight of his alter self.

It is, in short—this recurring crisis in representations of the American psyche—the moment at which the human will makes a choice, wittingly or unwittingly, that determines henceforth whether it is to be master or slave of the other faculties of the mind, especially its "animal propensities."

Using the densely technical language of phrenology and mental philosophy, the narrator of "the Imp of the Perverse" explains the internal mechanism by which (he thinks) the mind, in moments of crisis and temptation, loses its free will and allows itself to be drawn, against all reason, over the edge to mental and moral destruction. It is a "passion" so "demoniacally impatient" that its presence can only be explained by positing an organ, or faculty, of "Perverseness," one that "the phrenologists have failed to make room for" and which was "over-looked by all the moralists who preceded them" (*PPTE*, 826).

Poe's narrator does not throw himself physically over a precipice; he does, however, against all reason and the conscious will, submit to the one (verbal) impulse that will put him in chains. In a nightmare of guilty passion, he confesses to committing a murder: "The long-imprisoned secret burst forth from my soul," he says. And having spilled enough of his guilty secret to the authorities to ensure his conviction, he immediately "fell prostrate in a swoon." Tomorrow he is to be hanged, the "consummation" of his fate, like Nat Turner's (*PPTE*, 831–832).

Poe's narrator, of course, is mad, his secret guilt having long ago enslaved his reason, so that he can no longer understand, much less control, his own motives. Poe, himself, however, was not mad (Dr. Skae of the Royal Asylum notwithstanding); and he gives a correct diagnosis, in the vocabulary of the clinical psychology of his day, of his character's mental condition. Poe's narrator is the victim of his own "propensities," those "radical, primitive, irreducible sentiment[s]" that constitute, says Poe, "the *prima mobilia* of the human soul" along with the fairer "moral sentiment[s]" and the still paler faculties "of the pure intellect" (*PPTE*, 826).

In "The Imp of the Perverse," in other words, Poe was addressing the suppressed motives and feelings of the dominant culture in nineteenth-century America, an aspect of history for which the fiction of a period is perhaps always the most complete record. "Perverse" only to his mad narrator, the idea of a black "imp" or demon that put such psychological pressure upon the guilty mind that its prisoners would break out, even against its will, was making more and more sense to Poe and his countrymen as the slavery issue intensified in the decades before the Civil War.

What Poe realizes that his logically minded, but mad, narrator does not, is that the "propensities," especially the dark or "animal" ones, are stronger in this psychology than the other, he might have said "whiter," powers of the mind and heart. So strong are these buried desires and impulses, in fact, that they refuse to stay buried.

The Haunted Mind

In "The Haunted Mind" (1835), a sketch written about the same time as "The Imp of the Perverse," Nathaniel Hawthorne explicitly refers to the mind's buried impulses as slaves or "prisoners." The psychological edge, or jumping-off place, in his sketch is the borderland between sleep and waking:

> In the depths of every heart, there is a tomb and a dungeon, though the lights, the music, and revelry above may cause us to forget their existence, and the buried ones, or prisoners, whom they hide. But sometimes, and oftenest at midnight, these dark receptacles are flung wide open. In an hour like this, when the mind has a passive sensibility, but no active strength; when the imagination is a mirror, imparting vividness to all ideas, without the power of selecting or controlling them; then pray that your griefs may slumber, and the brotherhood of remorse not break their chain. (*T-TT*, 306)

Hawthorne is here describing the psychological mechanism we now call "repression," the unconscious exclusion of painful desires or fears from the waking mind. The buried thoughts that startle his slumbering consciousness, moreover, have been shoved into their "dark receptacles" by "remorse," a constant theme in Freud's works as in Hawthorne's. Banished from those regions of the mind that do not wish to recall them—whether on the principle of pleasure or pain—the prisoners in Hawthorne's sketch break their chains nonetheless; and they come swarming forth in an act of psychological rebellion analogous to the insurrection of Nat Turner and *his* dark "brotherhood."

No ardent abolitionist, young Hawthorne quickly transforms his most deeply suppressed feelings of remorse from dark brothers into pale sisters. By his bed glides a "pale young mourner, wearing a sister's likeness to first love." Calling his first love a "sister" may be simply a turn of phrase or, conceivably, a veiled reference to incestuous longings that young Hawthorne himself might once have felt—and deeply feared. Whoever she is, this sad young woman recalls the dreamer's "earliest Sorrow." In her train follows another "shade of ruined lovliness." Says Hawthorne, "she was your fondest Hope, but a delusive one; so call her Disappointment now" (*T-TT*, 307). Poe calls her Lenore or Madeline or Ulalume; and when his slumbering males reach for her, they go mad.

That these images of pent-up feeling assume visible shape in the waking consciousness, however faint or drowsy, introduces a problem with the use of a Freudian model of psychological repression to analyze Hawthorne's and Poe's understanding of the human mind haunted by guilt and desire. In Freudian psychology, the dungeons of the mind may be thrown open in the study of dreams by psychoanalysis; but once repressed impulses rise to the surface, they cease to be part of the unconscious, a region, especially in Freud's early, spatial formulations, completely walled off from the conscious mind. Tried and found guilty, the prisoners that burst from Hawthorne's dungeons once stood before a tribunal of the knowing and reflecting faculties (as in Poe's scarifying tale of the buried consciousness, "The Pit and the Pendulum").

Hawthorne's specters are forgotten memories—his psychology recognized no oxymoron here—*intentionally* kept under lock and key by the will. Thus besides dungeons and caves, Hawthorne also figured the "dark receptacles" in which the mind stored its most haunting memories as an ebony chest of drawers, a sort of compartmentalized Africa of the mind where the thoughts and desires were segregated into black and white, fair and foul by the colonializing will.

By contrast with the involuntarily buried shadows of the Freudian unconscious, the dark longings and aversions of the "heart" in Hawthorne's sketch spring from their depths only because the conscious mind has temporarily lost its normal power to hold them back. In the neutral state between sleeping and waking, the dreamer's consciousness "has a passive sensibility, but no active strength" (*T-TT*, 306). His most powerful intellectual faculty, the imagination, can impart "vividness" to the mind's pictures. But it has lost "the power of selecting or controlling" them because, as explained by Dugald Stewart, the mental philosopher whose works Hawthorne studied in college, "in sleep those operations of the mind are suspended, which depend on our volition" (*WDS*, vol. 1, 241). These images of remorse, that is, come willy nilly (will-I, nil-I) to the slumbering consciousness because the will to restrain them is slumbering, too.

In the psychology that Poe and Hawthorne grew up with, this was a condition akin to madness, rather than a normal condition of the nether mind, sleeping or waking, as in Freudian psychology. "Madness," said Stewart, "in many cases arises entirely from a suspension of the influence of the will over the succession of our thoughts; in consequence of which the objects of the imagination appear to have an existence independent of our volition and are therefore mistaken for realities" (*WDS*, vol. 1, 109). (This would be precisely the case of the mad narrator of "The Imp of the Perverse.")

When Stewart advanced this theory of madness at the end of the eighteenth century, seeing "unrealities"—visions, ghosts, shadows—was the chief test of insanity in the mad-house and in the courtroom. By the middle of the nineteenth century, the second test of madness, based on free will or "moral liberty," had become well established; but Dr. Skae of the Scottish asylum was still citing Dugald Stewart among his authorities in 1857: "As was remarked by Dugald Stewart, the insane are very much like persons asleep, by whom the objects of reverie, and the conceptions which pass through their minds, are believed at the time to have a real existence, because they cannot correct their judgment regarding them by voluntarily referring to the objects by which they are surrounded, as persons do when awake" (*MD*, 526–27).

The key word here is *voluntarily*. The insane person, in the "Common Sense" view, can not help himself any more than Nancy Farrer could. His will is a slave to the "objects" of his (or, perhaps more often in this literature, her) imagination and reverie, especially when those imaginary objects, or phantasms, are born of fear and desire. "Is it not," Dr. Skae asked, "the suspension of some power of volition, self-direction, or judgment which makes the insane the sport of their passions and desires, and gives rise in them to the belief in the extraordinary delusions which fill them with ecstasy, terror, or despair?" (*MD*, 526–27).

In the psychological romances of the nineteenth century, however, the most extraordinary delusions of ecstasy or terror sometimes turn out to be real, and rational self-control and self-direction prove illusory. Emotion, that is, appears to the "Romantic" (and early modernist) sensibility, if not superior to intellect, then equally to be contended with—as "female" psychological impulses with "male" ones, "black" impulses with "white."

When Poe's alter self swoons into the arms of the savage on the dark mountain in *Pym*, therefore, the "shadow" of escape that wanders into Pym's mind turns out to be the reality, and pale death, the illusion. The dusky figure in Pym's reverie is his half-breed companion, the ape-like Peters, whose massive arms catch Pym/Poe in his fall. The rational man has only swooned, and it is the animal man who saves him. In the psychology of the nineteenth century, then, the swoon is a "little death," like orgasm, of the knowing and reflecting faculties, a temporary giving-in to the "savage" instinct and unbridled passion that the age associated with the physical body and the more "primitive" impulses, or "propensities," of the mind.

What could be more terrifying (or perversely desirable) in a swooning white man's dreams than an able-bodied man of color? The drift of *Pym*, with its cataclysmic ending upon yet another precipice, suggests it might be a disembodied white one.

Approaching the bottom of the earth in a canoe, his will completely abandoned to the currents that draw his little boat inexorably toward the South Pole, Pym encounters a horror of such magnitude that he might reasonably be expected to topple over the edge and never return. We hear the din announcing that a sensory overload is just around the bend, to be followed immediately by a swoon. Then Pym sees the definitive figure of whiteness in Poe's fiction: "And now we rushed into the embraces of the cataract, where a chasm threw itself open to receive us. But there arose in our pathway a shrouded human figure, very far larger in its proportions than any dweller among men. And the hue of the skin of the figure was of the perfect whiteness of the snow" (PPTE, 1179).

This is the passage with which Toni Morrison begins her study of American Africanism, or the idea of Africa in the conventional models of mind of the nineteenth century. One aspect of the white romanticizing of black history that even she does not delve into, however, is why, in the collective imagination of this country, the most profoundly terrifying images, those designs of darkness most calculated to appall—as in Robert Frost's poem, "Design"—are so often images of pure whiteness.[10] Where does this white fright come from, this aversion to its own, even in the mind of white America? My contention is that it comes from a suppressed disgust for "pure" intellect, which the nineteenth-century mind regarded as basically "masculine."[11]

The Whale: Male or Female?

The great white figure at the end of Pym's journey, I would hazard, is simply another form of Ahab's whale, which is also "hooded," and which pulls down the ship and its crew against their will. To Ahab's disturbed mind and the other organs that direct it, there is little doubt about the gender of that deity whose unbending will, Ahab thinks, is embodied in the whale and in the dark waters churned into white foam by its mighty back and forth motions: "I will dismember my dismemberer" (M-D, 971).

During a typhoon, when tongues of lightning tip the masts of the *Pequod* with fire, Ahab strikes a characteristic pose, one of the many "furious tropes," including that of the title, by which Melville characterizes Ahab's obsession as grotesquely male: "he stood erect before the lofty tri-pointed trinity of flames." Suddenly the fire glints upon Ahab's harpoon, which "remained firmly lashed in its conspicuous crotch, so that it projected beyond his whale-boat's bow." In this remarkable scene, Ahab grabs "the keen steel barb" and uses this "fiery dart" to whip the mutinous crew into submission. Then, like a gunslinger puffing the smoke from his barrel, he extinguishes the flame with "one blast of his breath" (M-D, 1333–35).

Ahab wields his flaming lance so masterfully because he is "a true child" of the lightning in the night sky: "thou art my fiery father; my sweet mother, I know not. . . . I read my sire." It is the apparent indifference of the father ("the personified impersonal") to the son that moves Ahab to defy him. "Come in thy lowest form of love, and I will kneel and kiss thee," says Ahab; but in the highest, as pure, indifferent power, "thy right worship is defiance." Ahab has approached this stern father before and has gotten so burned "that to this hour I bear the scar." Like the fissure that runs from the roof of Roderick Usher's house to the foundation, Ahab's birthmark as a child of lightning marks him as a man maddened from top to toe, perhaps by hereditary tendencies (*M-D*, 1333–34).

The child will not spare himself the father's chastening rod. Standing up to his sire, Ahab clutches the chains that run to the lightning rods at the top of each mast. "Javelins" of light pierce his brain: "The lightning flashes through my skull; mine eye-balls ache and ache; my whole beaten brain seems as beheaded, and rolling on some stunning ground" (*M-D*, 1334).

During this strange ecstasy—an "original relation" with the universe by any standard, even Emerson's—Ahab has had his eyes closed. When he opens them again, he fears that the light of his mind has been blinded: "The javelins cease; open eyes; see, or not? There burn the flames" (*M-D*, 1334). Ahab's eyes have been spared; but in its fiery brush with the supernatural, the transparent eyeball of Emerson's essays has been scorched by a searing vision of the towering indifference of the universe. In the eye of this beholder, the whiteness of the whale represents the color of evil because it reflects the light of a divine intellect so blind to human suffering or affection as to deny the paternity of its dark Ahabs and Ishmaels. "The reason the mass of men fear God, and *at bottom dislike* Him," Melville wrote in a letter to Hawthorne as *Moby-Dick* was going through the press, "is because they rather distrust His heart, and fancy Him all brain like a watch."[12]

Ahab sees his clash with the white whale as a battle of wits, "the most brain-battering fight" between his own "steel skull" and that of a hard-headed God. Administering what he thinks is a dose of his own medicine to the great, white, male embodiment of pure cognition at the head of the universe, Ahab has gone overboard on the appetitive side, as I have said: "Vengeance on a dumb brute! that simply smote thee from blindest instinct!" cries Starbuck, the first mate, when Ahab broaches his purpose to the crew: "Madness!" (*M-D*, 961).

Pacing the quarterdeck of his "cannibal" craft like a man in a trance, Ahab is in a perpetual state of sleep walking. Having lost his free will—which depends upon a balance among the faculties—Ahab's mind, like the dreamer's in Hawthorne's sketch, "has a passive sensibility, but no active strength." Still capable of "imparting vividness to all ideas" (such as the notion that whiteness embodies the evil of the universe), his intellect is "without the power of selecting or controlling" those ideas (*T-TT*, 306). The master's reason has become enslaved by his emotion, thereby "emasculating" him in the nineteenth-century sense of depriving his mind of the controlling and directing power of reason.

When Starbuck questions Ahab's sanity, the mad captain replies with a defensive jab at the mate's masculinity. Surely "the best lance out of all Nantucket," Ahab taunts, will not hold back when all the other harpooners are honing theirs. "Something" seminal shoots from Ahab's "dilated nostrils" and enters Starbuck's lungs. "Starbuck now is mine," Ahab gloats (M-D, 968). More than "matched" and mated by Ahab's fervor, says Starbuck of his soul, "she's overmanned." The mate's assailant is too strong for him. "But he drilled deep down and blasted all my reason" (M-D, 973).

Starbuck's intellect, like Ahab's, can still perceive his master's purpose to be "heaven-insulting," but it can no longer incite his will to act on that knowledge. Captain Ahab has deprived his literal second in command of *his* free will, too: "I see his impious end; but feel," Starbuck laments, "that I must help him to it. Will I, nil I!" (M-D, 973).

During *this* psychic rape scene, Ahab hears a "low laugh in the hole" from the dark crew, and he feels "the presaging vibrations of the winds in the cordage" of the sails (M-D, 968). Ahab does not heed these premonitions of disaster, but Melville does, and he describes them as the "shadows" of Ahab's inner motives: "But rather are ye predictions than warnings, ye shadows! Yet not so much predictions from without, as verifications of . . . things within. For with little external to constrain us, the innermost necessities in our being, these still drive us on" (M-D, 968). These dark omens signal that the savage hunt for the totemic whale has begun; they are also a measure of the boundless "Africanism" in Ahab's haunted mind.

Emotional rather than notional, the "necessities" that drive Ahab are the "feminine" and "savage" impulses, the "powers of blackness," that have been building up in his "innermost" being. Unleashed by his mad rage, they direct the master of the *Pequod* to revolt against the powers (or faculties) of whiteness that once kept them in chains.

Melville would seem to be acknowledging, with Hawthorne, that "a tomb and a dungeon" are among the chambers "of every heart" and that the dark "prisoners," or thoughts and feelings, "buried" in them ("ye shadows") *will* out. All auguries are ambiguous, but these "presaging vibrations" would also seem to suggest that Melville divined an analogy for racial repression in his age's model of mental repression and that he posited a psychological cause of the coming turmoil in a nation divided by its attitudes toward slavery.

If so, the shadows in Ahab's mind may be taken not only as "warnings" but also as "predictions," in 1851, of the social and political upheaval that was soon to grip the country in a sort of waking nightmare. For the motives that drive Ahab to slay the serpent of whiteness are "verifications" of "things within"; and in 1851, the anti-slavery movement, led by the feminists, such as Harriet Beecher Stowe, was exerting such pressure on the national conscience, or moral sense, that "little external" could keep its feelings of anger and remorse bottled up much longer.[13]

Ultimately, however, the figurations of race that float through Melville's works from their lodgings in faculty psychology are "overmanned," in their ambiguity, by Melville's (and his psychology's) ambivalence toward gender. Though a mighty scourge of whiteness in its incarnation as "masculine" indifference to feeling, Ahab, once he has broken Starbuck's will, has no room in his cabin or his heart for a mate.[14] Obsessed with vengeance, Ahab stands upon his ivory leg ever "ready to sacrifice all mortal interests to that one passion." He will not even admit Pip, the black cabin boy who, "true" to his race, loves his master more than he fears him. Thrusting his harpoon into the devouring cavity that has "dismasted" him, Ahab blindly assaults the whale in what may be seen as yet another psychological rape of a male "victim." If, that is, Moby-Dick is to be conceived as unambiguously male.

When Ahab butts heads with the whale, he thinks he is confronting the mastermind of a heartless universe. Instead of conforming to the contours of the godhead's limitless brain, as Ahab supposes in his monomania, however, the whale's brain turns out to be, intellectually, its puniest organ.

Leslie Fiedler has spoken of Ahab's whale as that supreme bugbear of male homoeroticism, a "castrating penis."[15] The external body of the whale would appear amply phallic, to be sure; on the inside, however, the whale looks deeply vaginal. In the chapter on the sperm whale's head, Ishmael takes us on a tour.

Beneath the whale's enormous head spreads the mouth, and the gateway to this mighty opening, like the pearl and ruby doorway of the castle in Usher's poem, is lined with teeth, a menacing "portcullis" that has impaled many a poor wight who tried to breach it. Once we enter the whale, however, the interior is "beautiful" and "chaste-looking," for the whale's mouth is "papered" like a bridal chamber from floor to ceiling with "a glistening white membrane, glossy as bridal satins" (M-D, 1148).

Immediately above this virginal orifice, in the cranial cavity of the sperm whale, lies its reservoir of oil. Ishmael speaks of "all that apparent effeminacy" in this great cavity, protected by the tough hide of the whale that "so impregnably invests" it (M-D, 1153). So effectively does that tough membrane guard the soft inner parts of the whale that no man can penetrate them: "the sharpest lance," he reports, "impotently rebounds from it" (M-D, 1154).

The effeminacy of the whale's interior, however, says Ishmael, can be read from the exterior of the whale by using the techniques of "sensible physiology" (specifically physiognomy, or "phizmahogany," as Hawthorne disparagingly called the "science" in a letter to his wife in 1862).[16] What we discover, under Ishmael's tutelage, is that the mighty sperm whale (like women, children, and "savages," according to the readers of bumps and humps of the nineteenth century) is a back-brained creature.[17]

Purveying "practical cetology," as the Fowlers taught "practical" phrenology, Ishmael organizes his discourse like one of the Fowler's "illustrated self-instructors" in the science of the head: "The Sperm Whale's Head—Contrasted View"; "The Right Whale's Head—Contrasted View" (M-D, 1145, 1149). What Professor Ishmael says about the eyes is especially noteworthy. They are located far down and back on the sides, near the angle of the jaw. Thus "the position of the whale's eyes," he observes, "corresponds to that of a man's ears" (M-D, 1145–46). The whale's "opposite powers of vision," Ishmael conjectures, may lead to a "helpless perplexity of volition," for a whale will appear to vacillate when beset by several whaleboats at once from different directions (M-D, 1147).

Now, it is the eyes that define the front of the head, reasons Ishmael; and since the whale's eyes are to the sides, the front of the whale's head must be another back. Thus, he anatomizes, the whale's head has "two backs, so to speak; but, at the same time, two fronts (side fronts)" (M-D, 1146). By Ishmael's logic, the double-backs of the sperm whale's head, when added to the great slope of its forehead, would indicate that behind the battering ram power of the whale's great brow lies an intellect not much bigger, proportionately, than a sparrow's. Instead of a cosmic battle of wits, therefore, Ahab's monomaniacal pursuit of the whale represents the blind clash of passion (Ahab's) and instinct (the whale's), the "feminine" and the "savage." The ivory leg has taken over from the transparent eyeball, as it were, and drives the once neatly trimmed ship of Ahab's psyche to destruction.

If Ahab's emotional monomania is intended to show the havoc that the wounded heart can wreak as the unfettered guide of human conduct, Ishmael, in a comic counterpoint to his master's tragic vision, shows us the limits of the head. Though he scientifically dissects the whale, Ishmael, try as he might, cannot penetrate the deep mystery of him/her. Ishmael's commonsense way of owning the whale is to heap up surface details concerning the Leviathan as if the inner meaning of the whale, like its outer bulk, is "only to be estimated as piled wood is—by the cord" (M-D, 1154). Ishmael has consumed more fish than meat, however, for in his cetology mode he sounds like a learned blockhead. ("But I have always eaten meat & have not created a rugged brain with it, & so has he," Sophia Hawthorne once wrote her mother in a letter about the makeup of her husband's "exquisitely delicate brain." "The organization of genius is finer & more susceptible than that of blockheads, you know.")

In his *Essay on Human Understanding*, John Locke located objective reality in such primary qualities as bulk, figure, number, situation, motion, or rest. Knowing these, according to the great empiricist, we know something as it really exists apart from the mind perceiving it. To Melville's perception, however, the whale is more than the sum of its parts. Ishmael is the object of Melville's satire when he claims to know the whole truth of the whale by reciting its visible surfaces and qualities.

At times Ishmael sounds like a good Lockeian. Melville almost never. The qualities of the whale do not explain the meaning of the whale. The interior is not to be comprehended by the exterior. When Ishmael pompously rehearses facts and figures to explain the whale, Melville is laughing up his sleeve. Melville's own position, I would guess, is closer to the one Ishmael falls into when he says of both the "speculative" Kantian and the "practical" Lockian heads that weigh down the *Pequod*, "throw all these thunder-heads overboard, and then you will float light and right" (*M-D*, 1143–1144). As an essay on the *limits* of human understanding, *Moby-Dick* probably teaches the perspective that Ishmael adopts as he approaches the Right Whale's head: "But as you come nearer to this great head it begins to assume different aspects, according to your point of view" (*M-D*, 1149).

And such, I take it, is the significance of the doubloon, the Spanish gold piece that Ahab tacks to the mast of the *Pequod*. Each man reads this "talisman" of the whale and "image of the rounder globe" according to his own lights (*M-D*, 1254). Ahab sees only himself in the flame, the tower, and the crowing cock atop the Chimborazo peaks of a mental and moral Equator on the coin. Starbuck, the Christian, sees the Holy Trinity. Stubb sees the precarious life cycle of man, but the "jollity" of his temperament causes him to laugh at it. Flask, least imaginative of the mates, comprehends but "a round thing of gold"—it will buy 960 cigars (*M-D*, 1257). "I look, you look, he looks; we look, ye look, they look," says mad Pip, the sage grammatologist, of this deconstructionist exercise (*M-D*, 1258). It is Queequeg, however, the wise primitive, who best knows how to deal with a mystery: after comparing the markings on the coin with the tattoos on his legs, he walks away shaking his head—perhaps over the inadequacy of the physical body or other outward signs and symbols to body forth the dim shapes of the inner landscapes of the mind and heart.

The Steeple

Though not so furious as Melville's and Poe's, Hawthorne's tropes of whiteness were no less monstrous or rigid; they loom, in fact, as Huck Finn might say, big as a church. Perhaps Hawthorne's languid dreamer fears the pale maidens who come to him in "The Haunted Mind" because they are dead. But elsewhere he welcomes the women of his dreams with open arms. In another sketch of the period, "Sunday at Home" (1837), about the sleepiest day of the New England week, Hawthorne's bachelor self gazes lazily from his window in this same haunted "chamber under the eaves" of his mother's and sisters' house in Salem. Among the congregation filing into the church on the corner, the daydreamer spies a young woman with shoes laced "pretty high above the ankles" (*T-TT,* 23). Reflecting that a "white stocking is infinitely more effective than a black one," young Hawthorne lapses into voyeurism: "were I the minister himself I must needs look" (*T-TT,* 22–23). So long as it is relieved by a tinge of living scarlet at the cheek, white, the paler the better, is ever the color of choice for this reclusive gentleman; and the eye, the best instrument for savoring it from afar.

Pure white, however, terrified Hawthorne almost as much as it did Melville and Poe. Consequently, his dreamer is even more appalled by what he sees in the night sky outside his chamber window, etched with frost like "a frozen dream," than by the pale figures in his nightmares within (*T-TT,* 305). Outside his window stands the corner church, deserted now that sunlight and the young woman in white stockings have departed. "What a moral loneliness, on weekdays, broods round about its stately height!" says the dreamer, an utterance we can not translate accurately today without understanding that by *moral* the nineteenth century was coming to mean *emotional* (*T-TT,* 20). In the moonlight, the snow-laden spire of the church points upward toward the stars. As the dreamer's gaze follows it, he shivers even under "four blankets and a woolen comforter" (*T-TT,* 306).

It is not the physical cold of a New England winter's eve without central heating that is so chilling to the mind in Hawthorne's sketch, however, but "the bare idea of a polar atmosphere" (*T-TT,* 306). Hawthorne's night thoughts have carried him to the polar reaches of Poe's psychological journey in *Pym.* In the sharp steeple pointing toward "the wintry lustre of the firmament," Hawthorne erects his own stark image of the mind in the grip of pure whiteness, as Pym's mind is stilled at the other pole when he penetrates the great veil of whiteness with the prow of his canoe, or as Ahab's mind is gripped by the obsessive idea of planting his lance in the white whale (*T-TT,* 306). To Hawthorne's stargazer as to Pym, or Captain Ahab, or Ishmael atop the masthead of the *Pequod,* the

white radiance of eternity lends but cold comfort because, again, it is an unfeel-
ingly "masculine" essence.

In the "furious tropes" of *Moby-Dick*, the greatest threat to Ishmael's sanity
comes not from "miscegenation" or other deviations from the psychosexual
norms of his time but from clinging to the cold speculations of the mainmast
when, like Hawthorne's church steeple, it thrusts its barren tip into the clouds.
In "The Whiteness of the Whale" chapter, Ishmael explains why he finds the
"phenomenon of whiteness" so appalling: it is the "great colorless all-color."
Either white is the absolute of all colors rolled into one; or, if "we consider that
other theory of the natural philosophers, that all other earthly hues . . . are but
subtile deceits, not actually inherent in substances, but only laid on from without," it is the total absence of color (*M-D*, 1001).[18]

The "other theory" to which Ishmael refers here would seem to be the "phe-
nomenalism" of David Hume, since it locates the perceived phenomena of nature, including color, not in substances themselves but in the eye of the beholder.[19] Instead of leaving this "unreal" theory out of account, however—as
Husserl would one day advise and as Emerson did by declaring substances to
be, in effect, inherent in mind—"mad" Captain Ahab obsessively challenges
it. For if whiteness, as a "positive" value, whether of good or evil, is merely a
phenomenon of the mind, then the perception of white as the supreme color
in the order of nature is false. The natural supremacy of white is a cosmic joke.

"Pondering all this," as Melville says, Ishmael has cast off into strange latitudes of mind and heart, like the romancer dreaming by his fireside (*M-D*, 1001).
But that way lies madness. To escape the siren call of his Platonic daydreams,
Ishmael descends from the lonely crow's nest to "squeeze sperm" with the
Pequod's "dusky crew" and to marry up with that "comely Cannibal" Queequeg,
a man of color whose body is covered with the ritualistic markings of the
savage.

Young Hawthorne's response to the "bare idea" of polar whiteness at the
heart of the universe was more conventional. Shortly after he graduated from
Bowdoin in 1825, Hawthorne had checked out of the Salem library a book by
Chandler Robbins entitled *Remarks on the Disorders of Literary Men*. It was preventa-
tive medicine young Hawthorne sought, for Robbins's book inquires into "the
Means of preventing the Evils usually incident to Sedentary and Studious Habits."[20] Robbins offered a realist's commonsense prescription for banishing the
terrors of the night: to embrace the material world of the senses rather than the
phantoms of lonely contemplation and reflection, so easily mistaken for realities by the dreamy "literary" mind.

As if following Robbins to the letter, the dreamer in "The Haunted Mind"
looks with "eager minuteness" at the domestic scene around him. He takes

"note of the table near the fire-place, the book with an ivory knife between its leaves, the unfolded letter, the hat and the fallen glove"—all familiar objects of ordinary perception (*T-TT,* 308). One "object," however is missing from this scheme. How pleasant it would be, reflects Hawthorne's bachelor (soon to marry Sophia Amelia Peabody of Salem) not to dream alone. What if "the quiet throb of a purer heart" broke the dreamer's solitude "as if the fond sleeper were involving you in her dream"? (*T-TT,* 308). After a restless night, the haunted mind has come home to the usual solution to its metaphysical dilemmas that Common Sense offered the budding romancer as an alternative to madness—a tempering marriage of the stark "masculine" powers of the head with the softer "feminine" virtues of the heart.

FIVE

Bachelor's Bower

The Fearful Female

> Woman's nature was stamped and sealed by the Almighty, and there is no
> danger of her unsexing herself while his eye watches her.
>
> —*Lucy Stone*

 ON THE COVER of Orson Fowler's *American Phreno-logical Journal* there regularly appeared in profile a stylized human head, crammed like an overstuffed attic with frameless visual allegories of the mind's faculties and propensities. "Cautiousness," for example, was represented by a crude illustration, in Fowler's words, of a "hen surprised by a hawk; her chickens having been warned, are fleeing for safety."[1] Fowler's diagram solves the riddle with which Walt Whitman began a rough draft of a poem called "Pictures" around 1854:

> In a little house pictures I keep, many pictures
>   hanging suspended—
> It is not a fixed house,
> It is round—it is but a few inches from one side of it
>   to the other side.[2]

Drawn, like Fowler's and Poe's, upon the model of faculty psychology, Whitman's "little house," of course, was the head, and the pictures in this small but infinitely expansive chamber represented not only the capacities of the mind but also thoughts themselves, which faculty psychology conceived as visual images "hanging suspended" in the mind, and which Common Sense philosophy took to represent a more than virtual reality.

Since thoughts were to be conceived as mental pictures, on this model, the process of thinking constituted a sign or picture language to be deciphered by the mind's eye—like Queequeg's tattoos or the emblems on the Spanish

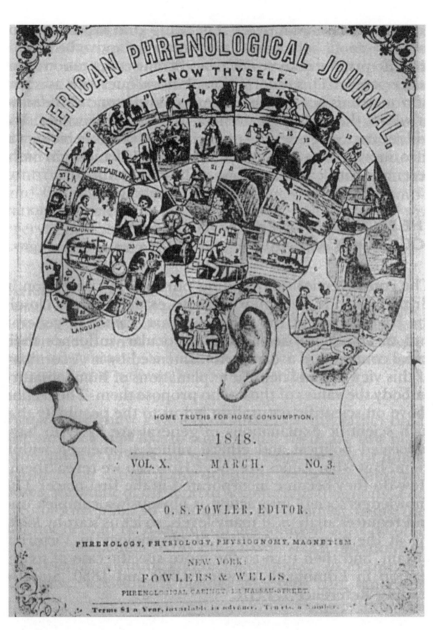

FIG. 8 This crude illustration of the human head, representing the operation of each mental faculty by a visual allegory, appeared regularly in the 1840s on the cover of Orson Squire Fowler's *American Phrenological Journal*. Such pictures in the mind assumed a "segregated" model of human consciousness.

doubloon that Captain Ahab tacks to the mast as a reward to the first sailor who spies the white whale. Before Paul Broca discovered the center of articulate speech in the inferior frontal convolution of the brain, therefore, the nineteenth century located the power of "Language" (faculty #35 on the Phrenological Fowlers' plaster busts) just behind the eyeballs, physical organs of sight and insight more highly developed in the heads of white males, according to the Germanic *Naturphilosophie* underlying American Transcendentalism (to which Poe, Hawthorne, and Melville were philosophically opposed), than in the heads of any other race or gender.

Emerson explained, in technically precise terms, how thinking takes place on this model at the snow-crowned summits of the mind's highest brows: "A man conversing in earnest, if he watch his intellectual processes, will find that a material image more or less luminous arises in his mind, contemporaneous with every thought, which furnishes the vestment of the thought." An "enraged man," for example, said Emerson, represents himself to the mind as "a lion, a cunning man is a fox, a firm man is a rock, a learned man is a torch" (*EEL*, 23, 20).[3] And a contemplative man?

Might not his serene state of mind be perfectly comprehended by a man peering into a deep, clear pond, just as a once luminous intellect overshadowed by dark premonitions might be pictured by a raven perched atop a pallid marble bust similar to those found in the phrenologist's cabinet?

Informed by Scottish Common Sense philosophy, with its emphasis on sensation as a trustworthy guide to reality, faculty psychology assumed that nature supplies the mind not only with the phenomena of consciousness but, as in the Fowlers' diagrams, with an iconography of itself in the act of processing those phenomena.

Not only is Melville's whale, then, what Emerson in *Nature* calls "a natural fact" to be "read" by the faculties of the intellect. Ahab's *pursuit* of the whale presents a verbal picture of the mind of a deranged man chasing mental phantoms. In Ahab's case, those phantoms or "phantasms"—mental images detached from physical reality—body forth his "irrational" (but nonetheless "real," to the anti-Transcendentalists) fears of the intellectual powers of the mind when divorced from feeling.

These were precisely the mental faculties that Emerson and, to a lesser degree, the other Transcendentalists held in highest esteem. In their figurations of the mind at work in its picture-making capacity, I would suggest, it is the emotional, or "feminine," capacities of the mind that threaten its serenity and must be (imperfectly) suppressed by the masterful intellect. So if the heroes and heroines of the romance tend to slip into emotional or "moral" monomania when the normal balance of their mental faculties is disturbed, the speakers of the philosophical essay, lecture, and poem (the veriest "prose," according to Poe) tend to go overboard on the intellectual or "notional" side.

Asylum in the Woods

Emerson's "American Scholar" address, delivered to the Phi Beta Kappa society at Harvard in 1837, is usually celebrated as the American declaration of intellectual independence. ("We have listened too long to the courtly muses of Europe.") It might better be seen as a call for sanity, a diagnosis of national mania: "The mind of this country, taught to aim at low objects, eats upon itself" (*EEL*, 70).

Addressing Harvard's best and brightest—including Henry David Thoreau if he did not take an assembly cut that day—Emerson predicted for these young men a harsher trial than that foreseen by most real-world speeches on such academic occasions: they were, he said, soon to be dismembered. In the savage world of business and commerce, where every worker is "a good finger, a stomach, a neck, an elbow, but never a man," they would be hired heads only. Sickened by the materialism of American culture, the best young minds of the country, he feared, would retreat from the world into their books and ivory towers. Brooding in solitary confinement—the discomfiting idea, he might have added, of reunion with a lost Lenore or Annabel Lee having never even entered their celibate minds—many would "die of disgust, some of them suicides." "What," he asked, "is the remedy?" (*EEL*, 70).

To the disturbed young masculine mind of the 1830s, Emerson prescribed a nature cure that countermanded the earlier formulas of Common Sense. In "The Art of Preserving Health" (1744), the poet-physician John Armstrong had advised:

> Go, soft enthusiast! quit the cypress groves,
> Nor to the rivulet's lonely moanings tune
> Your sad complaint.
> Go, seek the cheerful haunts
> Of men, and mingle with the bustling crowd;
> Lay schemes for wealth, or power, or fame, the wish
> Of nobler minds, and push them night and day (*WDS*, vol. 1, 382)

Quit the cypress groves of morbid reflection, said the voice of Common Sense, and go into business in town. Quit town, said *Nature* (1836), a mental health manual of sorts like *Walden* or Margaret Fuller's *Summer on the Lakes* (1844); go into the groves of New England oak, pine, and alder and meditate upon the sylvan scene. Reflect beside still waters: a deep, clear pond is ideal. Take, in short, what Sophia Hawthorne called "an air bath." Then, said Emerson, the over-stuffed "head bathed by the blithe air" will be transformed into a "transparent eye-ball," the material image, to Emerson's way of thinking, of the healthy intellect exercising its supreme powers (*EEL*, 10). Never mind that, technically, such an organ would be blind and, without a lens, would cease to braid "yon beam of seeming white . . . out of seven-hued light," the greatest marvel of the sighted eye according to Dr. Holmes's anatomical poem, "The Living Temple."[4]

But then Holmes cured his patients with "allopathic" methods, while Emerson's nature cure was fundamentally "homeopathic," the other main division of physical medicine in their day and the basic principle behind the "fetishism" of the "savage." Just as Sophia Peabody took strychnine for her nervous headaches and Ahab stumped after the whale on a whale bone leg, Emerson believed the best remedies to be natural remedies and that like cured like.

Allopathic physicians such as Holmes dismissed homeopathy's hair-of-the dog (or bone-of-the-whale) cures as mere superstition, black magic. (From the Greek *allos*, meaning "other," allopathy employed remedies causing effects different from those of the diseases they were meant to treat, as do most modern medical practices except for immunizations.) At the very time young Holmes was studying allopathic medicine in France, however, homeopathy was flourishing in Germany, bastion of the idealistic philosophy limned by Emerson's eye/I.

Transcendentalism, in fact, was a brilliant grafting of German Idealism—with an admixture of Oriental philosophy—on Scottish Realism. To the Scottish influence, in particular, the Transcendentalists owed their faith in the organs of sense as avenues of knowledge. There is no calamity "which nature cannot repair," said Emerson, "leaving me my eyes" (*EEL*, 10). Instead of bringing "the ideal philosophy" down to earth as the Scottish realists did, however, Emerson and the other Transcendentalists tended to drag mother nature into the sky.

Only by studying nature instead of books, said Emerson and Thoreau, does the contemplative mind escape the malaise of the American scholar or such stay-at-homes as the speaker of "The Raven," who is napping over many an ancient tome when the bird enters his study. Emerson's "Each and All," shows what happens, to the studious mind when it tears a natural object, such as a bird, from its context: the integrity of the whole collapses like Usher's mansion, and the speaker falls into despondency. As usual here, Emerson is relying mainly upon his eyes:

> I thought the sparrow's note from heaven,
> Singing at dawn on the alder bough;
> I brought him home, in his nest, at even;
> He sings the song, but it pleases not now,
> For I did not bring home the river and sky;—
> He sang to my ear,—they sang to my eye.[5]

In what sense do objects in nature—whether real or just the painted charms of Hume's phenomenology—"sing" to the eye? Phrenology offers a clue to the root causes of Emerson's synesthesia. To the person whose organ of "Comparison" was very large, O'Leary's *Delineation of Character* had this to say: "You are remarkable for your aptitude ... in tracing similarities and dissimilarities, agreements and disagreements, harmonies and contrasts."[6] Located in the front of the brain just above the power of language, Comparison was one of the mind's chief intellectual faculties. Drawing upon the material images provided to the mind by "Observation" (depicted in the phrenological heads by a man peering through a telescope), Comparison constituted the faculty of "inductive reasoning," the very power that Emerson assigned to the transparent eyeball.

Though we tend nowadays to use the single term, *metonomy*, for both tropes, Emerson's and Thoreau's classical rhetoric distinguished more rigorously between *metonymy*—words that stand for each other—and *synecdoche*—objects that stand for each other. Or as Emerson put it in *Nature:* "It is not words only that are emblematic; it is things which are emblematic" (*EEL*, 20). In the synecdoches of Transcendentalism, the eye is both a metaphor for the human head, of which it is physically a part, and for the human mind to which it is attached metaphorically or by analogy. Instead of another dismemberment, like Ahab's leg, therefore, the transparent eyeball of *Nature* is meant to signify a mind of the highest integrity, since Transcendentalism assumed that the part may be taken for the whole in human psychology as in "natural history" (and other fields of exploration from the tropics to the poles).

Transcendentalism inherited its analogic method, in part, from the *Naturphilosophie* of Germany. The embryologist Lorenz Oken, for example, whom his admiring student, Louis Agassiz, described as "constructing the universe out of his own brain," had written a series of aphorisms in his *Lehrbuch* (1809–11): "The animal kingdom is only one animal"; "The animal kingdom is only a dismemberment of the highest animal, that is, of Man"; "Animals become nobler in rank, the greater the number of organs that are collectively liberated or severed from the Grand Animal, and that enter into combination. An animal that, for example, lived only as intestine, would be, doubtless, inferior to one that with the intestine were to combine a skin."[7]

By this logic a man who lived primarily as skin—that is, in Oken's system of bio-racial analogies, one in whom feeling or the tactile sense dominated, as among black Africans—would be inferior to the man in whom tongue, or speech, was the primary sense, such as the brown Australian-Malayan. And the tongue man would be inferior to the nose man (the Native American); the nose man, to the ear man (the yellow Asiatic-Mongolian); and the ear man would yield to that pinnacle of evolution, the Caucasian, or eye man. Just why he assigned the five senses in exactly this order to the five traditional races, Oken neglected to say, though in lower animals, which he also divided into five classes, Oken assayed a natural history of linear descent in which individual organs stand for whole creatures, from fishes to mammals.

With the following words, Charles Darwin was forever to dissever (as Poe might say) from any connection with reality all theories of natural history, race, gender, and psychology based solely on the perception of analogy, the phrenologists' power of Comparison: "Something more is included in our classification than mere resemblance. I believe that something more is . . . propinquity of descent,—the only known cause of the similarity of organic beings."[8] To the American Transcendentalists, however, as to the German natural philosophers and the British quinarians (such as William Swainson, who, in the decades before Darwin, wrote paeans, as Emerson did, to the circle as the perfect image of nature) mere resemblance in the mind's eye was enough to certify that nature rose in spires of form, like Holmes's chambered nautilus, to ever higher pinnacles of intelligence.

The chief lesson to be learned from disturbing the organic unity of nature, therefore (as in "Each and All") is: "All are needed by each one; / Nothing is fair or good alone."[9] When Emerson's speaker returns the bird to its natural place in the woods, not only is integrity restored to the physical scene, but the mind that perceives nature as an emblem of oneness and harmony also is made whole again. Using only his nose at first, the speaker inhales the violets that surround his reinstated bird in the bough, but soon this grosser sense, like his sense of hearing in the earlier stanza, yields to the higher sense of sight: looking around him, he sees the oaks and firs that adjoin the bird's bough; then, looking down, the pinecones and acorns from which they sprang; and, finally, as Emerson's material images body forth his speaker's intellectual processes, he looks up into "the eternal sky, / Full of light and of deity" that mirrors all overhead: "Again I saw, again I heard, / The rolling river, the morning bird;— / Beauty through my senses stole; / I yielded myself to the perfect whole."

Beginning high on a precipice ("Little thinks, in the field, yon red-cloaked clown / Of thee from the hill-top looking down"), "Each and All" ends in a swoon. Instead of the spectral figures to whom so many men succumb in the works of Poe and Hawthorne, however, the Emersonian "I," we are advised, yields itself to a real beauty, one attested by the senses rather than the hallucinations of madness. Will this vision in the heady clouds upon the precipice's edge take, ultimately, a feminine or a masculine shape?

The phrenologist's account of the intellectual processes could apply to the metaphor-making heads of most Transcendentalists, but one line in O'Leary's description of the faculty of Comparison might have been meant for Emerson in particular, or for the author of *Walden:* "Indeed, to compare one thing with another, and to discern between them, to illustrate by comparisons, metaphors, parables, is a passion with you, and one that gives its entire tone to your intellect." [10]

An *intellectual* passion: perhaps this oxymoronical notion can help to "explain" one of the more curious extirpations in "Each and All":

> The lover watched his graceful maid,
> As 'mid the virgin train she strayed,
> Nor knew her beauty's best attire
> Was woven still by the snow-white choir.
> At last she came to his hermitage,
> Like the bird from the woodlands to the cage;—
> The gay enchantment was undone,
> A gentle wife, but fairy none.

Emerson would not be the first philosopher to entertain visions of nymphs in the wood, but to lump the fairy bride of his poem with sparrows and seashells is shamelessly to objectify her.

A twice-married man with one of the finer houses in Concord, Emerson believed that home is the proper place for women. "They should be found," said his essay "Woman" (1855), "in fit surroundings—with fair approaches, with agreeable architecture, and with all advantages which the means of man collect." [11] Yet when the bride of "Each and All" comes home with her bridegroom, it is to a gilded "cage," where she is divested of the enchantment that suffuses her in the wood.

Thus the bride of "Each and All" is most beautiful to the masculine mind when she is most etherialized, a vision in white, part of the "snow-white choir" of fairy-tale maidens who compose the "train" of sister visions that pass through the speaker's reflections. She is most to be treasured, that is, when placed upon a pedestal to be contemplated by the groom's idealizing eye, Transcendentalism's chief metaphor for the intellect. The fairest "aspect under which the beauty of the world may be viewed," says *Nature*, is as "an object of the intellect." Such perfect "objects" are characteristically white because the intellect, according to Emerson, is devoid of the coloration of passion and feeling. "The intellect," he exults, "searches out the absolute order of things as they stand in the mind of God, and without the colors of affection" (*EEL*, 18).

Though Emerson called physical nature, including the human body, "my beautiful mother," his natural religion idealized her into thin air, the godly region of pure cognition. Conceiving of the deity as a disembodied Power, a potency or capacity—like the unsummoned genie in a lamp, or like a faculty of the mind—Unitarianism had already divested God not only of his three persons (one of whom, the Holy Ghost, by some accounts, was female) but also of his robe and long white beard, even his right hand. ("That hand is amputated now," wrote Emily Dickinson in 1862, "And God Cannot be Found.")[12]

A Unitarian minister before he gave up the cloth, Emerson, in his New England Brahminism, desexed the deity even more radically. God became for him an "Oversoul," a great disembodied mind in the sky. Here was the patriarch of the Old Testament shorn of his ill temper: a commanding will informed by pure intellect uncolored by passion; but a patriarch still.

When Emerson extends his transparent eyeball skyward upon its phallic stalk, he is immersing his head in a masculine element (as is Thoreau when he bathes in the pond, which reflects the sky). For in the cosmology of Transcendentalism, the sky is male: "the sky with its eternal calm, and full of everlasting orbs [like eyes?], is the type of Reason. That which intellectually considered we call Reason, considered in relation to nature we call Spirit. . . . And man in all ages and countries, embodies it in his language as the FATHER" (*EEL*, 21).

As a "sensualist," Emerson relied upon the organs of sense, particularly his eyes, more as aids to reflection than portals of ecstasy. (The work of Coleridge that most attracted him: *Aids to Reflection.*) Thus Emerson was perhaps more deeply influenced by Carlyle, a Scot, than by the more visionary English Romantics. For Emerson, as for Wordsworth, Coleridge, and even Dugald Stewart, the most creative faculty of the mind was the imagination. Emerson, however, defined "Imagination" in *Nature* "to be the use which the Reason makes of the material world" (*EEL*, 34).

In Emerson's scheme, *Reason* is the mind's metaphor-making power; it works by "perceiving the analogy that marries Mind and Matter" (*EEL*, 26). That marriage required a divorce: the material object—a bird in the bough, for example—had first to be detached "from the life like a ripe fruit" if it was ever truly "to become a thought of the mind." Unlike the perishable Madelines and

Lenores of Poe's fiction who turn into specters when they become mere objects of the disintegrating masculine consciousness, Emerson's fair beauties are "raised, transfigured; the corruptible has put on incorruption" (*EEL*, 61).

Another of Emerson's encounters with nymphs in the wood is instructive here. Meeting up with Hawthorne and Margaret Fuller at Brook Farm one day, Emerson watched two women—a Swiss and a Native American—cavorting in the forest with men. As Hawthorne's journal recorded the scene: "It has left a fantastic impression on my memory, this intermingling of wild and fabulous characters with real and homely ones, in the secluded nook of the woods . . . as if the every day laws of Nature were suspended." As Emerson's journal recorded what appears to have been the same scene: "strange that we should so value the wild man, the Ishmaelite . . . and yet every step we take, everything we do, is to tame him."[13]

In many "primitive" religions, mother earth must join with father sky to insure fertility. Emerson, however, wedded the two in the all-pervading ether of pure thought so as to *tame* the Ishmaelite within him. There is a curiously onanistic quality about Transcendentalism. Emerson, Thoreau, Alcott, even the crusty, almost avuncular Elizabeth Palmer Peabody, Hawthorne's sister-in-law, go off into the woods alone to spill their intellectual seed. They are joined there by no fair companions, female or male, such as haunt the reveries of Poe, Hawthorne, and Melville. Or if for a moment they should be, as in "Each and All," they are reluctant to bring them home. The rightful issue of the Transcendentalist's "marriage of thought with nature" in the woods, as Emerson observed in "Intellect," was "the generation of the mind." In their intercourse with nature, the Transcendentalists impregnated themselves—with disembodied ideas. This was the "occult relation" with the vegetable that Emerson so fervently recommended as a tonic to the troubled male psyche (*EEL*, 422, 11).

Depriving God the Father of the other marks of his manhood and of a potentially feminine gender, the Oversoul nonetheless left him his eye. God became for Emerson a great eye in the sky—the Dr. T. J. Eckleburg of *The Great Gatsby* with sight—but it was the cold masculine eye of the mad-doctor, guardian of moral order and agent of social control, that presided over Emerson's asylum in the woods.

Recognizing, as Hawthorne did, that the "feminine" and the "savage" intermingled synonymously in his culture's notion of the natural state, Emerson etherialized mother nature, translating her into father sky in order to tame not only the "wild man" within him but, also—what he feared more, perhaps—the wild woman. Hawthorne may only have flirted with the licentiousness of nature and a fallen Eve in the darkling forests of his fiction, but Emerson resisted the spell of the wilderness almost entirely. An emissary of whiteness who explored the woods and waters as long as they were within sight of the New England village, he sought evidence in nature of the dispassionate intellect's lordly mastery—not to defy its laws as Captain Ahab does—but to *impose* them upon "every step we take, everything we do."

A Refined Disgust

Politically liberal for its time, Emerson's essay on "Woman" conceded that women "have an unquestionable right to their own property. And if a woman demand votes, offices and political equality with men, . . . it must not be refused." The psychology underlying his generation's notions of gender, however, was inherently paternalistic. Women may engage in trades and careers as a "resource," Emerson said. But there is no employment that women will not "quit for a suitable marriage." For "the life of the affections is primary to them." [14] This, I think, is why Emerson's ideal of "Beauty" turns out to be so cerebrally "masculine": like many of his contemporaries, male and female, he seems to have harbored the same doubts about the affections as trustworthy guides to conduct as the Scottish Realists did.

To the pale recluse who retreated into the woods and groves of pure intellect and contemplation, Dugald Stewart offered this warning:

> Removed to a distance from society, and from the pursuits of life, when we have been long accustomed to converse with our own thoughts, . . . without exposing us to the inconveniences resulting from the bustle of the world, we are apt to contract an unnatural predilection for meditation, and to lose all interest in external occurrences. In such a situation too, the mind gradually loses the command, which education, when properly conducted, gives it over the train of its ideas; till at length the most extravagant dreams of imagination acquire as powerful an influence in exciting all its passions, as if they were realities. (*WDS*, vol. 1, 381–82)

It was the loss of self-control, the mind's "command" over "the train of its ideas," that really frightened Dugald Stewart, who cautioned against "the effect of novels, in misleading the passions of youth." So long as the imagination stayed within bounds, said Stewart, it could inspire "heroic actions" and "exalted characters," words that may have stirred young Hawthorne in his garret in Salem. When "ill-regulated," however, the imagination became, even to Stewart, a "fruitful" source of error and disappointment because it affected "the passions too deeply to leave us at all times the cool exercise of reason." When the imagination habitually disrupted the passions, there followed, he said, "that state of mind which is commonly known by the name of *enthusiasm*." Here, in sum, is Common Sense's case against the contemplative life (*WDS*, vol. 1, 381–90).[15]

These are not simply the words of a dour Calvinist who feared that young men and women, their lust kindled by "the scenes into which the Novelist introduces us," might fling their books aside and incline to carnal zeal (*WDS*, vol. 1, 389). Dugald Stewart's argument against the passions is far more subtle than this, and like Thomas Jefferson's (and Emerson's in the "American Scholar") it centers on "disgust." The "inordinate passion prevalent for novels," said Jefferson, was a threat to education in this country not only because it fed "a bloated imagination" but also because it led to "sickly judgment," resulting in "disgust towards all the real business of life."[16]

"Disgust," or "moral" revulsion, in this scheme, is a function of the sentiments and sensibilities. Normally, said Common Sense, the sensibilities of civilized human beings find vice repulsive and attempt to correct it. The "Taste" or "Moral Sense" of the habitual reader of fiction, however, grows finicky. Fiction presents us, according to Stewart "with histories of elegant and dignified distress." In real life "we have to act, not with refined and elegant characters, but with the mean, the illiterate, the vulgar, and the profligate." Thus the "perusal of fictitious history," violates the social contract because it "has a tendency to increase that disgust, which we naturally feel at the concomitants of distress, and to cultivate a false refinement of taste, inconsistent with our condition as members of society" (*WDS*, vol. 1, 389).

In short, too much excitement of the passions unchecked by social contact can develop in susceptible minds the rarefied taste and refined sensibility of Emerson's American scholar or the effete gentlemen in Poe who dream themselves out of the world. In this twilight realm of heavy draperies, incense, and indirect lighting, the active powers are lost in thought, women become objects of supersensible desire, and men become women.

The sort of women they become, Emily Dickinson was to satirize in lines that consider doing violence to these overly "feminine" females:

> What Soft—Cherubic Creatures—
> These Gentlewomen are—
> One would as soon assault a Plush—
> Or violate a Star— (#401)

Dickinson's plush *dames* suffer from a lack of mental exercise. They are creatures of "Dimity Convictions," learned in part, no doubt, from those fashionable clergymen whom Emerson found celibate and "mincing" in his Divinity

School address. Stirred by no deep feelings, either of remorse or desire, they are "Of Deity—ashamed." They have developed (as Stewart warned they would) "A Horror so refined / Of freckled Human Nature" that they shun redemption as a glory too "common" for their discriminating taste (#401). Never far from their fainting couches, these soft creatures lose the power to think when they give up their womanly power to feel, thereby becoming easy prey to the "masculine" gaze of the speaker who contemplates raping them.

Well before Dickinson's day, good taste and refined sensibilities were standard upholstery of the stereotypical gentlewoman in America. Edward Dickinson, the poet's father, for example, seems to have married Emily Norcross, whom he appears otherwise scarcely to have known at the time, primarily because she figured in his mind to be the genteel mistress of a respectable household with himself at the head.

Emerson did not wish to deny the power of woman in her proper sphere—namely, the home. But the metaphor of the boat—which assigns the office of the sail to women and that of the rudder to men—argues that Emerson considered a woman's will to be the wind's will. (The word *spirit*, says *Nature*, "means primarily wind.") Though his essay on "Woman" celebrates the "spontaneity" and force of the gender, Emerson was afraid of a will driven (as he saw it) more by the affections than the intellect. The reason: "All that is spontaneous is irresistible." Thus the manly intellect must stand guard over womanly affections, ever ready to grab the tiller, he concluded in "Woman," because "whatever the woman's heart is prompted to desire, the man's mind is simultaneously prompted to accomplish."[17]

Men had always gripped the tiller—too tightly, said Emerson's fellow Transcendentalist, Margaret Fuller. In *Woman in the Nineteenth Century* (1845), Fuller conceded that men displayed "a preponderance" of intellect; women, of affection. Setting the terms for a "Great Lawsuit" between the genders, she assigned Energy, Power, and Intellect to the male and Harmony, Beauty, and Love to the female. Where Emerson found these differences to be in-born, a difference in kind between the genders (as between the races), however, Fuller attributed them to socialization, a strategy of the women's movement in America from its first meeting in Seneca Falls, New York, in 1848. "What is the cause of this?" Fuller asked of the dissociation of faculties she saw between men and women. Since, by nature, "the faculties have not been given pure to either," she determined, it must be "Man" himself who brought about such an imbalance. Coming before Woman "in the order of time," said Fuller, Man used his superior force to enslave her. "He educated Woman more as a servant than a daughter, and found himself a king without a queen," the fate from which Monsieur

Dupin saves the kingdom in "The Purloined Letter," Poe's finest tale of what Fuller called "Femality" subjugated by men.)[18]

The children of this unequal union were the degenerate sons that the polygenisists feared from the interbreeding of the races. "More and more," according to Fuller's feminist anthropology, "men seemed sons of the hand-maid, rather than the princess." Soon "there were so many Ishmaelites that the rest grew frightened and indignant." When a son was born at last to Abraham's legal wife, Sarah, the blame for the dark blemishes of Abraham's illegitimate son Ishmael, said Fuller, fell not upon the father, the patriarch, but upon his concubine; and Hagar was driven into the wilderness as if she alone were the mother of savagery in the race.

The Pond in the Eye of the Mind

Though Emerson was the married man of property and Thoreau the perennial bachelor who squatted on his patron's lands, the bachelor would seem, of the two, the more inclined to balance his intellectual prospects with passion, and the more domestically inclined in his choice of metaphors and parables. If a person would know beans about himself, *Walden* advises, he must cultivate a bean patch in his own backyard. Under such homely schooling, he may be reborn, like the "beautiful bug which came out of the dry leaf"—pun always intended in Thoreau—"of an old table of apple-tree wood, which had stood in a farmer's kitchen for sixty years . . . from an egg deposited in the living tree many years earlier" (*WAL*, 333). So may the buried life be resurrected, says this parable of transformation—*Walden* in miniature—while the "astonished family of man" sit round the most "trivial and handselled" of furniture, rapt (like Poe's Usher) as new life gnaws from its "well-seasoned tomb" (*WAL*, 333).

Endowed with an acute sense of hearing, Thoreau was more likely than Emerson to listen, rather than watch, as new life gnaws forth in the springtime of the mind. The conceit that most clearly sets the intellectual tone of *Walden*, however, is Thoreau's comparison of the pond to "earth's eye," a limpid pool fringed by "fluviatile" trees and overhung like brows by the vegetation along its curving shoreline. Looking into it, says Thoreau, "the beholder measures the depth of his own nature" (*WAL*, 186).

He also beholds the eye of God staring back at him. "Intermediate in its nature between land and sky," the pond is "sky water," and it bears the imprint of a masculine mind. "It is the work of a brave man surely," says Thoreau, "in whom there was no guile! He rounded this water with his hand, deepened and clarified it in his thought, and in his will bequeathed it to Concord." Thoreau derives this idea of the mind of God from gazing at his own image in the pond, and he can see by its "face" that the pond "is visited by the same reflection" (*WAL*, 188–89, 193).[19]

One blustery day, however, the smooth, reflecting surface of the pond is disturbed by a bird: "Having looked in vain over the pond for a loon, suddenly one, sailing out from the shore toward the middle a few rods in front of me, set up his wild laugh and betrayed himself. I pursued with a paddle and he dived, but when he came up I was nearer than before. He dived again, but I miscalculated the direction he would take, and we were fifty rods apart when he came to the surface this time, for I had helped to widen the interval; and again he laughed long and loud, and with more reason than before" (*WAL*, 234). Like Poe's detective putting himself in mental concert with his adversary, or like Ahab plotting the whale's probable course, Thoreau tries to read the bird's thoughts: "While he was thinking one thing in his brain, I was endeavoring to divine his thought in mine" (*WAL*, 235). Once it dips beneath the surface of the pond, however, the bird eludes human insight, despite a white breast that stands out like the whiteness of the whale against the dark water: "no wit could divine where in the deep pond, beneath the smooth surface, he might be speeding his way like a fish" (*WAL*, 235). If seen as a "natural fact" in the Emersonian sense, the white whale that Captain Ahab chases across the face of the deep is the loon of Walden Pond grown to monstrous proportions. In Melville's grand critique of the pure reason of the Transcendentalists, Captain Ahab's Transcendentalism differs chiefly from Concord's in this detail: it presumes, as Poe did, that divine will is antagonistic to human will, whereas Concord assumed concord between the two.

If an enraged man is a lion and a cunning man is a fox, then a man chasing a loon must be a looney man. Thoreau's great loon chase represents an interval of madness in *Walden*, the temporary insanity that Thoreau finds exemplified in nature side by side with the cool exercise of reason. As an allegory of the intellectual process, the loon chase pictures a mind feverishly pursuing ideas that lie just beyond its reach. When the bird disappears into the mist, the mind of the loon chaser has grown as murky as the "tumultuous surface" of the pond (*WAL*, 236). The transparent eyeball can see no further beyond the immediate evidence of the senses than can the bloodshot eye of grief and dissipation. Pantheism makes as much sense as Unitarianism. The real madness, suggests Thoreau's mild parody of Transcendentalist thinking, would be to persist in the quest for absolute knowledge anyway (as Ahab does).

Thoreau's bird does not talk to his lonely man, who wisely gives up the chase before he is carried past the brink of the pond, and sanity, by phantoms. But by matching wits with a bird's brain in *Walden*—and losing the contest—Thoreau capitulates for a time to the wildness in nature and the brute in man. As a reversion to the primitive, Thoreau's romance of the woods calls into question not only the Romantic idea that the natural state is less savage than the civilized state, but also the primacy of intellect over instinct. Instead of an instrument for scanning the heavens, Thoreau's head, his "instinct" tells him, becomes "an organ for burrowing, as some creatures use their snout and fore-paws, and with it I would mine and burrow my way through these hills" (*WAL*, 98).[20]

A source of reassuring parables to the dispassionate intellect, unhanseled nature can seem numbing or even hostile to a will encumbered by human feelings and appetites. When the pond ices over in winter, the once transparent surfaces of nature become the very medium in which Thoreau appears divided from himself: "Sometimes . . . when the ice was covered with shallow puddles, I saw a double shadow of myself, one standing on the head of the other, one on the ice, the other on the trees or hill-side" (*WAL*, 293). His vision distorted by this wintry whiteness, as in a fun-house mirror, the reflective man of Thoreau's narrative must yield to the animal man, who is driven instinctively back inside his burrow by the sight of his own twin shadows.

When a double shadow standing out against a polar background of ice and snow is the only positive image of the self that nature can provide the mind, it is time to seek food and shelter in one's inner haunts: in the "genial atmosphere of my house," says Thoreau, "I soon recovered my faculties and prolonged my life" (*WAL*, 254).

Thoreau's Old Flame

Seat of the affections in *Walden*, as the pond is the seat of the intellect, Thoreau's hut lies midway between the wintry poles of sky and water in the bumps and valleys of this psychological landscape. In the spring, before it is finished, the hut is so open to the elements as to be almost a part of nature: "When I first took up my abode in the woods, . . . " Thoreau writes, "my house was not finished for winter, but was merely a defense against the rain, without plastering or chimney, the walls being of rough weather-stained boards, with wide chinks, which made it cool at night." Caging neither a bird nor a bride in his hermitage, Thoreau has made himself "neighbor to birds," he says, by "having caged myself near them" (*WAL*, 84–85).

In the early morning, when its timbers are still saturated with dew, the hut resembles the pond itself, throwing off its morning mists "like ghosts" stealing into the woods "at the breaking up of some nocturnal conventicle" (*WAL*, 86).

Or like the vapors rising from Usher's tarn. On the pond, focal point of Thoreau's daylight visions, the vapors begin to lift at dawn, but in his hut they linger on because it is the scene of Thoreau's "night-thoughts."

Situated on the edge of the village, between the woods and the water, not far from Hester Prynne's cottage, the hut is haunted by shadowy forms that take up their abode in Thoreau's "attic" once he builds a fireplace and chimney in preparation for the oncoming winter (exposure to which may have hastened Thoreau's early death from tuberculosis). "When I began to have a fire at evening, before I plastered my house," he writes, "the chimney carried smoke particularly well, because of the numerous chinks between the boards." Once he plasters his house and chimney, however, the vapors from Thoreau's fireplace collect under the peak of the roof, where they blend pleasingly with his meditations: "Should not every apartment in which man dwells be lofty enough to create some obscurity overhead, where flickering shadows may play at evening about the rafters? These forms are more agreeable to the fancy and imagination than fresco paintings or other the most expensive furniture" (*WAL*, 242).

In "Smoke," a little poem set into the "House-Warming" chapter, Thoreau gives more definite outlines to these airy forms as they take shape in the upper reaches of the imagination. First they rise in his mind as a bird, then as a spectral woman gathering up her skirts as she departs in the night. Encoded as smoke signals or skywriting, Thoreau's "midnight visions" waft from his chimney toward heaven, turning day into night and carrying a message: "Go thou my incense upward from this hearth, / And ask the gods to pardon this clear flame" (*WAL*, 252). In this example of the metonymies of Transcendentalism, the flame is both the life-giving fire on Thoreau's hearth and the flame in his heart.

To illustrate "Comparison" (faculty #37), the iconographic heads of the phrenologists pictured a man (sometimes with a child on his lap) gazing into the flames of an open hearth. "The Wood-Fire" by Ellen Sturgis Hooper (1812–48) suggests why a fireplace might be the fitting icon of a mind engaged in "life imaging," or drawing comparisons:

> Never bright flame, may be denied to me
> Thy dear, life imaging, close sympathy.
> What but my hopes shot upward e'er so bright?
> What but my fortunes sunk so low in night? (*WAL*, 254)

To the mind musing before an open fire in "close sympathy" with the flames, they seem to replicate in visual form its hopes and desires—as in Poe's cloud on the precipice's edge, but without the dark dangers of the abyss below.

Hooper's poem, which Thoreau quotes in part, laments the passing of the open fire with the advent of the Franklin stove in most New England households by the second quarter of the nineteenth century. No longer, she observes, do we converse with ghosts by the fire's "unequal light." Was it "banished from our hearth and hall," she wonders, because the flames rose "then too fanciful / For our life's common light, who are so dull?" Did the fire, holding converse with "our congenial souls," convey "secrets too bold" (*WAL*, 254–55)?

Thoreau's fire-lit hut by the pond is the haunted palace of his dreams, but it is not his dream house. In that structure, as described in *Walden*, there is not only a "mistress" but also a great company of inmates: some of them "live in the fireplace, some in the recess of a window, and some on settles, some at one end of the hall, some at another, and some aloft on rafters with the spiders." This "larger and more populous house" stands "in a golden age"; built "of enduring materials, and without gingerbread work," it consists of the single room of "a vast, rude, substantial, primitive hall." The bare rafters of this house support "a sort of lower heaven," and the household god here is Saturn without his gloomier aspects, the deity of festivals and agriculture. It is a house "whose inside is as open and manifest as a bird's nest, and you cannot go in at the front door and out at the back without seeing some of its inhabitants" (*WAL*, 244).

Thoreau's idea of a heavenly house of many mansions is remarkably down to earth and cozy, "such a shelter as you would be glad to reach in a tempestuous night" and thus a fine place to be snowbound (as in Whittier's poem where the inmates, in the tradition of fireside poetry, domesticate the dangers of the savage weather outside as Thoreau domesticates an arrowhead by examining it in the firelight of his hut). It contains "all the essentials of a house," and in it "the weary traveller may wash, and eat, and converse, and sleep, without further journey" (*WAL*, 243).

Such a rude chamber is a distant cry from the mountaintops of "Man Thinking's" loftiest aspirations. To the mind that would hitch its wagon to a star, Emerson had recommended as objects of study the "meal in the firkin, the meat in the pan" only because "the near reveals the far." Thoreau, however, attended to the affairs of pot and kettle because they offered him an enlightenment usually reserved for women in the nineteenth century. Otherwise, he wanted to know, "How can the scholar, who dwells away in the North West Territory of the Isle of Man tell what is parliamentary in the kitchen?" (*WAL*, 245).

Though rooted on Emerson's ground, the earthy domesticity of Thoreau's hut (even in heaven) is more like the "attainable felicity" that Ishmael embraces in *Moby-Dick* and from which Captain Ahab, having shut his cabin to all companionship, male or female, is forever barred. "Not placing it anywhere in the intellect or fancy," Ishmael (and probably Melville himself) had located this "conceit" of happiness "in the wife, the heart, the bed, the table, the saddle, the fire-side, the country" (*M-D*, 1239).

Whatever the preferred conceit in this literature—whether heart and bed or head and bachelor's bower—it was the mind's "eye" that fixed upon these thought "pictures" in an orderly linear sequence guided by the will in the balanced mind or (in a mind disturbed like that of the whale under attack) a "vascillation" back and forth, will-I nil-I, between conflicting mental images.

Uncle Tom's Wagon

Consider this sequence from *Uncle Tom's Cabin* as an illustration of the normal (and deviant) progress of thought in the reflective mind of the nineteenth century. Tom is jogging along to market on the wagon seat beside the slave trader, Mr. Haley. I quote the passage at some length because it captures not only what the characters are thinking, but also how they think, as conveyed on the model of faculty psychology:

> Mr. Haley and Tom jogged onward in their wagon, each, for a time, absorbed in his own reflections. Now, the reflections of two men sitting side by side are a curious thing,—seated on the same seat, having the same eyes, ears, hands and organs of all sorts, and having pass before their eyes the same objects,—it is wonderful [Common Sense having failed, in Stowe's view, to yield a solution to "the slavery question"] what a variety we shall find in these same reflections!
>
> As, for example, Mr. Haley: he thought first of Tom's length, and breadth, and height, and what he would sell for, if he was kept fat and in good case till he got him into market. He thought of how he should make out his gang; he thought of the respective market value of certain suppositious men and women and children who were to compose it, and other kindred topics of the business; then he thought of himself, and how humane he was, that whereas other men chained their "niggers" hand and foot both, he only put fetters on the feet, and left Tom the use of his hands, as long as he behaved well; and he sighed to think how ungrateful human nature was, so that there was even room to doubt whether Tom appreciated his mercies. He had been taken in so by "niggers" whom he had favoured; but still he was astonished to consider how good-natured he yet remained!
>
> As to Tom, he was thinking over some words of an unfashionable old book, which kept running through his head, again and again, as follows: "We have here no continuing city, but we seek one to come; wherefore God himself is not ashamed to be called our God; for he hath prepared for us a city." These words

of an ancient volume, got up principally by "ignorant and unlearned men," have, through all time, kept up, somehow, a strange sort of power over the minds of poor, simple fellows, like Tom. They stir up the soul from its depths, and rouse, as with trumpet call, courage, energy, and enthusiasm, where before was only the blackness of despair. (*UTC*, 100–101)

At first, the mind of each character in this passage seems stuck in its own amber, the static "passages of thought" that Gordon Taylor has found characteristic of nineteenth-century fiction.[21] By comparison with the fluid states of consciousness that define the modern novel, the thought processes depicted in older American fiction may appear static initially; but they lurch along, often without a hitch, by a logic of their own, though it is a different logic from the one we have grown accustomed to in fiction, which more closely resembles the slow progress G. W. F. Hegel ascribed to human history in general, particularly in Uncle Tom's African homeland.

We do not enter the stream of Tom's or Mr. Haley's consciousness, that is, because the mid-nineteenth century did not yet conceive of human consciousness as flowing in a continuous stream. It was more like a wagon ride. It jerked along, sometimes at a frantic pace, shifting from thought to thought, feeling to feeling as one faculty took over the reins from another.

Thus when Tom and Mr. Haley—each occupied with his own musings, as if in a solitary chamber—slowly turn their thoughts toward a conclusion, their feelings intensify, and each moves a step closer to a "moral" choice among the ideas pictured alternately to their minds. Mr. Haley's lust for material gain, however, drives his mind back along in the same old rut that it has always followed. Tom's more "spiritual" longings, on the other hand, give his a new direction, one more in line with the transformation that is being worked out in his character. Yet the process of association—swaying now toward this mental image, now that—by which their thoughts move along gradually to their separate destinations is said to be less under control in Tom's mind than in the mind of his keeper.[22]

By comparison with the predictable sequence of Mr. Haley's, Tom's thoughts follow upon the train of a benign madness: his newfound mental energy and courage (like Nat Turner's) are the offspring of "enthusiasm." Unleashed like the bosom prisoners in the nightmares of Hawthorne and Poe, they rise "somehow" to the surface of Tom's dark mind "from its depths." Just how these specters of hope well up from the "blackness of despair" imposed upon it by the white mind, however, Tom cannot conceive because he is still a half-formed creature struggling toward heaven, like Hawthorne's Donatello in *The Marble Faun*. Even Stowe herself professes not to fathom the depths of superstition in Tom's mind. She hazards only that he must yield his will to a "strange" external power embodied in an old book.

Now the reflections of two great abolitionists—one male, the other female, one black, the other white—are a curious thing. Both committed fervently to the emancipation of the slave and believing as they do that common sense demands the freedom of all men and women, both pretend to be surprised that two men with the "same eyes, ears, hands, and organs of all sorts, and having pass before their eyes the same objects" would reach, by the same corridors of thought, such wondrously different conclusions.

Yet in *The Heroic Slave* the black abolitionist, Frederick Douglass reflects as follows upon the differences of mind and heart between an Uncle Tom and his master when the ship of humanity is in danger of being overrun by pirates at sea: "It may do very well for an overseer, a contemptible hireling, to take advantage of fears already in existence, and which his presence has no power to inspire; to swagger about whip in hand, and discourse on the timidity and cowardice of negroes; for they have a smooth sea and a fair wind. It is one thing to manage a company of slaves on a Virginia plantation, and quite another thing to quell an insurrection on the lonely billows of the Atlantic, where every breeze speaks of courage and liberty. For the negro to act cowardly on shore, may be to act wisely" (*HS,* 62).

As to the white abolitionist, Mrs. Stowe, she concurs in pronouncing the overseer of slaves to be a contemptible human being. (Surely the most widely despised villain in this line of work in all the annals of American slavery is Stowe's Simon Legree). And she readily admits that black men and women have feelings, same as other folks, even "courage" and Christian "charity."

Yet for all their good intentions, many white abolitionists—such as Stowe, whose popular books worked far more practical good for the abolitionist cause than Douglass's little-known fiction, especially among whites—still saw the ideal black man in their collective mind's eye as a childlike Uncle Tom, a "poor simple fellow," incapable of reasoned revolt, whose back-brained mind, even when more advanced than his fellows' minds in intellect and moral sentiment, could still be mesmerized into plodding along for eons more down the same interminable rows of thought by a dark old fetish.

SIX

Mrs. Stowe's Fantasy of the White Black Man

For example: if all the animal organs are large, and all the organs of the moral sentiments and intellect are small, the individual will be naturally prone to animal indulgence in the highest degree.

—*Thomas Sewall, M.D.*

A nation is composed of individuals, and what is true of all the parts (which in a nation preserve their individuality,) must hold good of the whole.

—*George Combe*

 WHEN SIMON LEGREE'S eyes and hands probe Uncle Tom Shelby's body on the auction block, Tom reacts precisely as Thomas Gray purported, in the *Confessions*, to react to Nat Turner's "fiend-like" physiognomy: "he felt," we are told, "an immediate and revolting horror at him" (*UTC*, 197).[1]

Harriet Beecher Stowe is romancing the shadow in *Uncle Tom's Cabin*, drawing her reader, more or less unawares, like the mesmerized "victim" of a Poe tale, into a territory where the usual black and white polarities of race and gender in the nineteenth-century mind are reversed. For if the reader's blood could be made to curdle at the sight of the brutish Simon Legree, it might be induced to warm, correspondingly, to the image of black Tom shivering helplessly before this looming white terror.[2]

It was a strategy that Mrs. Stowe (as she was usually called) borrowed, in part, from the women's movement, whose first convention at Seneca Falls in 1848 grew out of a meeting of abolitionists. Perceiving (as Sigmund Freud would one day disparagingly put it) "an analogy for the oppression of women in that of the Negro," many feminists such as Margaret Fuller and Elizabeth Cady Stanton professed to see in marriage a form of institutionalized "white" slavery. The Seneca Falls "Declaration of Sentiments," for example, cited "repeated injuries and usurpations on the part of man toward woman," compelling the wife "to promise obedience to her husband, he becoming, to all intents and purposes, her master."[3]

As indicated by their "revolutionary" language—"We hold these truths to be self-evident: that all men and women are created equal"—the one hundred signers of the "Declaration" had adopted their tactics from earlier separatists, such as Tom Paine, whose "Occasional Letter on the Female Sex" (1775) discovered barbary pirates in the heart of North America long before Colonel Higginson did.

"More than one half of the globe is covered with savages," Paine had told readers of the *Pennsylvania Magazine* in what was soon to become the home state of Lucretia Mott, the Quaker minister who founded the Philadelphia Female Anti-Slavery Society; "and among all these people women are completely wretched." It was not only "in a state of barbarity" such as obtained in Asia (Paine) or Africa (Hegel) that "beauty in bondage waits the caprices of a master," however. Said Paine, "Man . . . in all climates, and in all ages, has been either an insensible husband or an oppressor."[4]

In this early commentary on gender in America, Paine was not seeking the total divorce of "sensibility" from "brutality" that his "Common Sense" would call for a year later (in more or less the same terms) when promoting the colonies' break with Great Britain. Nor was his argument, or that of the Seneca Falls revolutionaries inspired by it and other political documents of the late eighteenth century, really based on the "rationalism" to which the ideals of the American Revolution are often said to appeal. An exercise in applied faculty psychology, "An Occasional Letter on the Female Sex" appealed far more to emotion than to reason (as did both the American Declaration of Independence and the Seneca Falls "Declaration of Sentiments"); and it promoted a "union" of man and woman—his "savage rudeness" to be softened by her "moral ideas"—on the assumption that the sexes were born with different faculties and needed each other to achieve mental and political balance (as opposed to a Hegelian "synthesis").

Those feminists of the 1840s and fifties, such as Stanton and Mott, who sought equal rights for women on the grounds that they were born with the same faculties as men, were not opposed to the union of the sexes in marriage (though they questioned existing divorce laws based "upon a false supposition of the supremacy of man"); but they stoutly maintained that separate was not equal, in politics as in mental and moral philosophy. In particular, they deplored what they saw as a double standard of moral and sexual conduct: the physically dominant sex "has created a false public sentiment," the Seneca Falls convention declared, "by giving the world a different code of morals for men and women, by which moral delinquencies which exclude women from society, are not only to be tolerated, but deemed of little account in man."[5]

The signers of the Seneca Falls "Declaration" expected their ideas to meet with "ridicule" and "misconception"; but Stanton, in *Eighty Years and More* (1898) remembered the public reaction to "our Declaration of Rights and Resolutions" as more negative than it actually was: "so pronounced was the popular voice against us in the parlor, press, and pulpit," she wrote, long after the fact, "that most of the ladies who had attended the convention and signed the declaration, one by one, withdrew their names and influence and joined our persecutors."[6]

Actually, many people of both sexes who did not attend the Seneca Falls convention conceded that there was an imbalance of power between men and women in America and that it needed to be redressed. Horace Greeley, for example, responded in the influential *New York Tribune* that "the demand of women to equal participation with men in political" affairs was "a natural right." Stanton herself recalled that the anti-slavery newspapers "stood by us manfully"; and so "did Frederick Douglass, both at the convention and in his paper, *The North Star.*"[7] (It might be going too far to say that Douglass, the only person of color known to have attended the Seneca Falls meetings, got a lesson in tactics from the feminists, which he then adapted to the antislavery campaign; but soon after the convention, Douglass's writings, most notably *The Heroic Slave* of 1853, would hark back directly to the radical Common Sense psychology of the American revolution.)

Where these radical republicans of the mind and heart came into greatest conflict with the moderates, such as Sophia Hawthorne, then, was on an issue roughly equivalent, in the psychological sphere, to the debate raging over states' rights in the political sphere—the separation of powers.

By the time the Hawthornes united in 1842, American culture accorded an unprecedented importance (as Nancy F. Cott has remarked in *The Bonds of Womanhood*) "to women's roles as wives, mothers, and mistresses of household."[8] This emphasis upon the distinctive roles of women bred a paradox: by widening the traditional separation of powers between the sexes, it tended (theoretically) to offset the imbalance between them.

As their spheres of influence drew further apart, the public world of business and politics dominated by men became increasingly dependent upon the private household (dominated more and more by women) for, in Cott's words, "the transmission of culture, the maintenance of social stability, and the pursuit of happiness" (in short, for "moral" balance).[9] One result of this amicable separation was to lend even greater importance to the family as a social institu-tion in its own right, as in *Uncle Tom's Cabin*, where domestic values are presented as the country's best hope for eliminating slavery.

Less radical than Stanton and Margaret Fuller in that they did not strike at the root distinction between inborn "masculine" and "feminine" traits were those feminists who sought a union of the contending parties precisely because they recognized a "natural" division of mind between the genders, as between the races, and thus promoted the separation of "male" and "female" powers in the so-called cults of domesticity and in "the true woman." [10]

As the recently married Sophia Peabody Hawthorne seemed to do when she wrote to her mother: "no one who has ever become one with another being, as true husband & wife must become if really united, will ever, can ever say that each is wholly independent of the other." To this ancient faith of newlyweds—that in marriage "Heart & spirit are forever, indissolubly one"—the new Mrs. Hawthorne, however, added a qualifier: "except intellectually." [11] Like many other new wives of the period, Hawthorne was not insisting that her mental powers be regarded as identical with her husband's, rather that they be seen as independently effectual: "No two minds were ever more completely indepen-dent & individual than Mr Hawthorne's & mine. It would be impossible to have any intercourse with one another, if our minds ran into one another." It was an ideal of marriage (and of human heredity) that many, as late as 1855, were still trying to apply to the nation as a whole: a "union" that was "indissol-ubly one" while the constituent states remained "completely independent & individual."

Harriet Beecher Stowe seems to have agreed with the feminists that marriage as traditionally defined (in part by faculty psychology) enforced a master-slave relationship in which the "female" powers of the emotions were subjugated to the "masculine" powers of the intellect. Her solution to the dilemma posed by "slavery"—in marriage and in society at large—was far from conventional, however. Taking us deep into forbidden latitudes, as the romance alone was free to do in the nineteenth century, *Uncle Tom's Cabin* comes close to offering, as a solution to the psychological ills dividing the country, a biological com-mingling not only of the gendered faculties, but also those conventionally ap-portioned by race. Whereas Poe and Hawthorne went so far, in their fiction, as to contemplate the hereditary evils (and forbidden attractions?) of incest in the American house and home, Stowe went further: *Uncle Tom's Cabin* (another haunting American literary house, albeit in the lower rent district) goes so far as to entertain, on some shadowy level, the *salutary* effects of "miscegenation."

A More Perfect Union

The mind of George Combe's "civilized" white man could imagine the mind of "the savage" to lie outside its kin because, in faculty psychology, the animal propensities were thought to be separate and distinct from the moral sentiments even in the same mind. What distinguished the European from "less civilized" races in this system was not that he displayed no "animal" tendencies whatsoever but that they were held in check by the powerful moral sentiments and faculties of reflection he had developed in the upper reaches of his European brain as it scrabbled grayly up the evolutionary ladder.

There are no biologically bad faculties in faculty psychology, only imbalances among them. "All the faculties, when active in a due degree," said Combe in the *System*, "produce actions good, proper, or necessary. It is excess of activity that occasions abuses...." The mere fact that a particular organ is small, he cautioned, "is not the cause of a faculty producing abuses." For example, the organ of "Benevolence" (small in savages, naturally) will not make for cruelty simply because it is puny. However, said Combe, when "one organ is small, abuses may result from another being left without proper restraint." Thus powerfully developed animal propensities, such as Combativeness and Destructiveness, produce "cruel and ferocious actions" in the savage because his countervailing Benevolence and other moral sentiments are "weak." In the Caucasian mind, where the moral sentiments are proportionally larger, they produce "force of character" (*SP*, 459).[12]

The worst moral deficiency in the character of Native Americans, it was generally imagined by whites in the early nineteenth century, was, in George Combe's words, "their want of natural affection," even for their children (*SP*, 575). Coupled with his great destructive powers, this lack of fellow-feeling made the Indian bloodthirsty and morose—like Poe's Dirk Peters.

The character of the imported African, by contrast, though "primitive," was not marked by so deep a dye of savagery as stained the hand of the red Indian. The back-brained African retained "powerful animal propensities," said the Fowlers, as indicated by the thick, furlike crest of hair so prominent in their crude sketch of the African head. (In this he resembled the biblical Samson, a favorite name among slave-holders, along with Mars and Jupiter, for their choicest male properties.) But because his prognathous forehead sloped more gently backward, the African's moral sentiments were not so drastically sheared, in the polygenists' view, as those of the native American.

By contrast with the bald Indian who took scalps, the worst deficiencies of moral character, besides petty stealing, that the unreasoning faculties of the nineteenth-century Caucasian head could lay upon the battered head of "the

Negro" were his "shiftlessness"—even when working outdoors, said the Fowlers, a person with coarse hair and dark skin "needs perpetual telling and showing"—and his, or more especially her, sexual promiscuity (*IS-I*, 31–32). A child himself in the myopic white eye, "the Negro" loved children, said the polygenisists, even when he could not tell which were his own (a condition, before DNA testing, to which some white men on the plantations were also curiously prone).

"To the Indian, stern, silent, moody, ruminating," according to Timothy Flint, one of Combe's "authorities" in the strange land of the Mississippi, "existence seems a burden." Not so the African, he professed to think. "To the Negro, remove only pain and hunger, it is naturally a state of enjoyment. As soon as his toils are for a moment suspended [that it was only for a moment is assumed] he sings, he seizes his fiddle, he dances." A natural-born bachelor "uncle" with no sense of responsibility, the fun-loving Toms and Remuses and (when not engaged in revolution) Nats found life generally satisfactual, the polygenisists told themselves, because, though "easily excitable, in the highest degree susceptible of all the passions," they were "more especially so of the . . . gentle affections." If treated kindly, therefore—and slaveholders in particular must have been greatly relieved to hear it—"the Negro" could not help being fond of his master; and though incapable of profound affection, he was also— a still greater comfort to "ole massa" perhaps—mentally and morally incapable of sustained revolt.[13]

What seems most unusual at first, then, about Harriet Beecher Stowe's profoundly appealing (to the reader of fiction in the 1850s, who was almost exclusively white) embodiment of the African American in Uncle Tom Shelby is not his affectionate good nature, but his intelligence: "Look at his head; them high forrads allays shows calculatin niggers, that'll do any kind o'thing," boasts Mr. Haley, the slave trader who calculates Tom's value during their slow wagon ride to market (*UTC*, 129).

Might he, for example, mastermind an armed rebellion among his fellow slaves? Like Nat Turner, Stowe's Tom has both the physical strength and the intelligence to do so. But not to worry, Stowe reassures the apprehensive reader, reinforcing the stereotypes even as she aims to smash them: it's against his nature. "Wal, there might be something in that ar," says Haley, "if it warnt for his character" (*UTC*, 129).

In a crude parody of the Christian argument that the physical body is a temple of the Holy Ghost, worthy of veneration because of the indwelling spirit it symbolizes, Haley tries to get more money for Tom because of his "oncommon" intelligence: "Now, a nigger of that ar heft and build is worth considerable, just, as you may say, for his body, supposin he's stupid; but come to put in his calculatin faculties, and them which I can show he has oncommon, why, of course, it makes him come higher" (*UTC*, 129).

Stowe's satire is intended to fix the limits of the "calculatin faculties" of the intellect as sole guides to moral behavior, especially in the masculine mind; but it requires the reader to accept many aspects of the period's stereotypes of race as well as gender. (Mentally, Stowe's Tom towers above her "Sambo"—"a full black, of great size, very lively, voluble, and full of trick and grimace"—and most of the other male slaves in *Uncle Tom's Cabin*, who are fit to work in the fields, she implies, but not in the big house [*UTC*, 285].)

Tom's unusual intelligence, Stowe insinuates, does make him a more valuable servant because, often intractable in white men, it is restrained by his naturally docile character as a black man! "I can show recommends," says Haley, "from his master and others" (including, he might have added, Mrs. Stowe herself) "to prove he is . . . the most humble, prayin, pious crittur ye ever did see" (*UTC*, 285).

Tom Shelby is Stowe's answer to the vexing question (in the minds of many whites at war with themselves) of what to do with "the Negro." In the inversions of her romance, it is the decent, but ineffectual, white master, Mr. Shelby, who lacks the "providence" that Hegel and General Hitchcock denied to the African. And it is the black slave, Tom, a model of Christian stewardship, who proves so faithful and trustworthy that he lets himself be sold away from his own wife and children—when he might have fled back to Africa, as Eliza Harris does—in order to provide economic security for the improvident whites.

To the hard-working and often financially hard-pressed Mrs. Stowe—wife, daughter, and, seven times over, sister of ministers and theologians who often had trouble making ends meet—providence in a man was next to godliness. A working woman's ideal servant, the dark genie of her fondest dreams, Tom, the perfect male domestic, makes the ultimate sacrifice of the working class *white* husband and father, a martyrdom denied even to the "true woman" and mother of the period: he pays out his body in honest toil to keep the family together. (Hardly indiscriminate in matters so close to home, George Combe devotes most of a chapter of the *System* to choosing a superior house servant by the shape of the head and other externals.)

In the harsh bio-economics of the period, for which slavery in Stowe's book (as in *Huck Finn*) is often little more than a metaphor, Uncle Tom's body is his only marketable asset. "What shall I pay for the body?" asks George Shelby of Simon Legree, Tom's last earthly owner. In a grotesque parody of moral and commercial rectitude, the animalistic Simon rises "doggedly" to his full height: "I don't sell dead niggers . . . " (*UTC*, 363).

This is the truest romancing of black history in *Uncle Tom's Cabin*, a racial morality tale that more than any other work of fiction, history, or law, except for Lincoln's Emancipation Proclamation, helped to nudge the northern, "whiter" region of a nation on the brink of coming apart toward a desperate resolution of its moral dilemma by demonizing the "blacker" southern region.

If Tom's bad "white" traits (his calculating intellectual faculties) are offset by his good "black" ones (his powers of emotion and affection), the reverse is also true. Though Tom has "been called a preacher in them parts he came from," as Nat Turner was, there is no danger, Stowe hastens to inform the reader of *Uncle Tom's Cabin*, that Tom's religious enthusiasm will degenerate into monomania. Tom's piety, says Haley, is not of the "roarin'" kind; "them ar an't no account, in black or white." Rather, Tom is "your rail softly, quiet, stiddy, honest, pious [person], that the hull world couldn't temp 'em to do nothing that they thinks is wrong" (*UTC*, 130).[14]

Tom's lower passions and animal propensities, that is, are not to be feared any more than his higher intelligence because they, too, are offset by the refined "moral sentiments" that have had more room to develop in his rounded "Caucasian" head than in the more sloping head of "the African." If the degenerate Haley and Simon Legree are throwbacks to the brute in the white man, Uncle Tom Shelby is the African savage tamed, converted—one might even say knighted—by the missionizing power of the Christian home.

The Black Knight

Whereas Hegel and Emerson looked to the "masculine" province of pure intellect for moral progress and the defeat of superstition, Mrs. Stowe directed her readers to pure feeling, the special province of the "feminine" mind. "Give my love to Mas'r, and dear good Missis, and everybody in the place," the dying Tom charges before turning, with his last breath, to forgive Simon Legree, "—it's nothing *but* love" (*UTC*, 363).

What made the feelings and emotions—such "propensities and sentiments" as "Fear, Compassion, and Veneration" (the terms are George Combe's)—so powerful as weapons in this psychopolitical battle was not just their primal force as human motives but also their involuntary flow, like figures in a dream. We fear Simon Legree even though he is white, and we feel compassion and veneration for Tom, even though he is black, because, under this scheme, we are naturally equipped with emotional faculties that are always excited by their proper objects, no matter how unlikely the guise in which they may appear.

"When an object in distress is presented," said Combe in his *System*, "the faculty of Benevolence starts into activity, and produces the feelings which depend upon it. When an object threatening danger is perceived, Cautiousness gives an instantaneous emotion of fear" (*SP,* 460).

We may act on those emotions, or not, as we choose, if they are counterbalanced and illuminated by cognitions; but, said Combe, the "activities" of the feeling faculties themselves, unlike those of the "intellectual and reflecting" faculties, are not subject to the will. That is, Combe observed, "We have it in our power to permit or restrain the manifestation of it in action; but we have no option, if the organ be excited, to experience, or not to experience, the feeling itself" (*SP,* 460).

Hence Stowe's and the antislavery movement's flirtation, as in *Uncle Tom's Cabin,* with the romance of sentiment, a kissing-cousin of Hawthorne's more psychological kind. In the romance, where contradictory impulses of mind and heart were brought together to marry, like opposing families joined in a new generation, Stowe had found a perfect vehicle for her psychopolitical argument: that only the "moral sentiments" can assure emancipation in the mind and state, and that the curse of slavery soon would be lifted from the land if those men of property who sought to divide the country would allow the Christian home to take its rightful place instead of the countinghouse as the culture's focal institution.[15]

To a generation taught since childhood that mental balance required the faculties to stay in their separate compartments and that social order depended upon keeping "the Negro" in his place, the romance made possible a sort of "benign miscegenation." Here the stark blacks and whites of custom and the law could intermingle with impunity in the reader's mind because, in the neutral territory of romance, the cognitive powers had long been challenged, and often overwhelmed, by the appetitive faculties. Instead of a two-headed gorilla, then, Stowe insinuated, the white reader of *Uncle Tom's Cabin* who did not always judge a book by its cover would find in her hybrid hero "all the moral and Christian virtues bound in black morocco" (*UTC,* 129).

Only mildly ironic, these are the words of the enlightened Southerner, Augustine St. Clare, whose name suggests that no false virtue clouds his clear head and true heart. As he ponders the bill of sale for Tom, St. Clare wonders "if I was divided up and inventoried how much I might bring. Say so much for the shape of my head, so much for a high forehead, so much for arms, and hands, and legs, and then so much for education, learning, talent, honesty, religion! Bless me! there would be small charge on that last, I'm thinking" (*UTC,* 131).

This unflattering self-appraisal by one of Stowe's most chivalric characters is nonetheless built on a theory of human nature that "divided up and inventoried" the mind into black and white classes of mental powers and moral virtues as rigidly segregated from each other as the social and racial classes of the day. Stowe does not call her heroes the Black Knight or the Knight of the Red Cross, but her romance of Christian charity replicates the virtue-defeats-vice plot of medieval chivalric romance because Stowe's psychology in the nineteenth century was essentially the same as Spenser's in the sixteenth. (In a different age, with a different model of mind, we can speculate that the nineteenth century's obsessive dwelling upon parts of the physical body at moments of self-examination and moral crisis was symptomatic of its unconscious fears of mental dissociation as a literal pulling-apart of the normal equilibrium of the faculties, as if drawn and quartered at the tail of a mule.)

The great chivalric romance of national unity upon which *Uncle Tom's Cabin* explicitly builds is that of the triumph of St. George, patron saint of England, over the dragon. "The old satan!" cries George Shelby as the remorseless Simon Legree saunters over to the dying "Martyr," Uncle Tom. When this "young master" George—soon to pledge himself to drive the "curse" of slavery from the land—knocks Simon Legree to the ground, says Stowe, "he would have formed no bad personification of his great namesake triumphing over the dragon" (*UTC*, 364).

George's symbolic slaying of the Southern dragon is just the sort of triumph of good over evil that Nat Turner had in mind when he went forth to scotch "the Serpent" of white oppression—not with the ax or tomahawk of the savage but with a sword, the consecrated weapon of the Christian knight marching as to war.

Yet it was also as a serpent of evil from Southern climes, namely a boa constrictor, that Sophia Hawthorne gave form to the fears unleashed in the minds of many white Americans, even in the North, by the prospect of arming newly emancipated slaves to fight on the side of right in the Civil War. So pervasive was this imagery in the dominant culture of North America, even among those whites who fought for emancipation, that Hegel's entire commentary on Africa incorporated fewer concrete metaphors of bestiality than the single brief paragraph about lions, snakes, and "raging devils" in Hawthorne's letter to her husband.

Such black-and-white demonizing of "alien" aspects of the self (and a perceived other) Hegel attributed, as Nathaniel Hawthorne did, to the Protestant ethos: "In the Protestant theology ... on the one side," said *The Philosophy of History*, "we have the will of the individual—the spirit of man—I myself, and, on the other, the grace of God, the Holy Ghost; and so in the wicked, the Devil" (*PH*, 360).

Here again, as in the ancient psychomachy of Latin poetry and the medieval morality play, religious conversion is to be explained as a battle of wills for control of the spirit. ("Grace," even in most Protestant theologies, is the action of God's will without regard to the wishes of the individual.) Hegel, however, perceived—despite his racism and without a Freudian vocabulary—that the old Protestant theology of conversion was fundamentally a dramatized psychology of opposing or divided mental faculties.

The idea of external powers of good and evil to be contended with—the basic plot of the drama, or romance, of salvation as interpreted by traditional Protestantism—made the human will a potentially heroic (or demonic) force, a St. George slaying or succumbing to dragons. However, in its zeal such a narrative, Hegel argued, did not recognize (as Poe clearly did) that both its saints and Satans, like those of other fictions, originated in the mind.

If, as Hegel said, the only real combatant in this holy war was "I myself," then the contending spiritual powers that the Protestant mind figured to itself as embodiments of God, self, and the Devil were actually but the figments of mental faculties (especially the fragments of a divided will) unknowingly at odds with one another. By the time of Hegel's death in 1831, this would be the age's very definition of insanity.

What makes Hegel's analysis of the psychology of early Protestantism especially instructive now, however, is that, by his account, whether the Protestant mind thought it was contending with God or the Devil, it engaged in the struggle because it believed *its* own deepest subjectivity to be inherently "evil" (*PH,* 360). As does that model Protestant, Huckleberry Finn, when he thinks he is going to hell for stealing Jim from slavery: that Huck saves himself from John Bunyan's heaven by listening to the "degenerate" side of his moral sense and deciding to steal Jim anyway is not only an Hegelian act of "arbitrary subjective choice" but also a morally insane act (in a "civilization" based on commercialism) that, in the end, lands Huck happily in Indian territory, as close to the blissfully savage state of Hegel's Africa as a backsliding Sam Clemens could get him and still be within firing range of Arkansas and Mississippi.

In the realm of pure cognition, said Hegel, the mature mind realizes that it is "with itself alone." No longer fearing its own subjectivity, it is serenely aware that "that which is diverse from itself, sensuous or spiritual, no longer presents an object of dread, for in contemplating such diversity it is inwardly free and can freely confront it." Again Hegel sounds like Emerson: "A practical interest makes use of, consumes the objects offered to it; a theoretical interest calmly contemplates them, assured that in themselves they present no alien element" (*PH,* 360).[16]

If, however, on the Hegelian summits of pure mind, the knowing and reflecting faculties—particularly Memory—would no longer mistake for realities such apparently dreadful (but actually fictitious) objects as white whales, black insurrectionists, marauding Indians, and incestuous forefathers whose sins sow madness to the seventh generation, the sentiments and propensities would also be emancipated from the childish need to cling to objects of sentiment and affection, such as a humble log cabin or a homey raft occupied by a motherly black "uncle."

Between these extremes of mind and heart, as in the ideal marriage, the romance seemed to offer a compromise. The great therapeutic value of the romance to the beleaguered American conscience lay in its ambiguous power to induce the divided mind of the reader to embrace, for a time, its own worst demons without having, necessarily, to recognize them as phantoms of its own making. Or, to put it most cynically, the ambiguities of the romance allowed the crafty romancer to exploit any latent guilt his or her reader might feel for secretly harboring ideas and appetites that ran counter to those inscribed by the dominant culture.

Inevitably, Harriet Beecher Stowe's ambitions as an abolitionist, if not a feminist—Lincoln's "little woman/big war" remark is well known—required Stowe to bend her era's stereotypes of negritude, both sexual and racial, rather than to break them. The profound effect of *Uncle Tom's Cabin* in unifying the Northern white knight against the Southern dragon (as if she had been studying the imagery of both Nat Turner and Sophia Hawthorne) may perhaps be attributed to the fact that it permitted the reader to confront thorny questions of race in the guise of more familiar (and less threatening?) categories of gender.

Since the "immediate and revolting horror" that Stowe's Tom feels when he first encounters the apelike Simon Legree was a sure sign of the refined taste and sensibilities of the "true woman" of the period, Stowe's design would seem to be, in the psychological terms of her day, to "feminize" the reader of *Uncle Tom's Cabin*, male as well as female. ("Man is not free," Stowe was, in effect, rewriting Hegel to say, "when he is not feeling.") Only so much latitude was granted to even the most daring romancer, however. She could mingle the blacks and whites of the mind but not (overtly) those of the body. How Tom got his "white" traits, therefore, remains a mystery; like Topsy, presumably, they just "growed."

For *Uncle Tom's Cabin* to work its moral transformation in the consumer's mind, Stowe must spare the white, particularly male, reader the "sickness, and dizziness, and horror" of physical "miscegenation" that "mad" Poe called up from the alluring brinks and abysses of the the nineteenth century's understanding of mental processes and pitfalls. Thus when Evangeline St. Clare suddenly loses her balance and falls "sheer over the side" of the steamboat carrying Tom to New Orleans, the perfect servant is "standing just under her on the lower deck" like a powerful genie waiting patiently at the foot of a precipice for his lamp to be stroked (*UTC*, 128). The ethereal blond heroine of romance in miniature, Little Eva, though a child, is without a child's "usual chubbiness and squareness of outline." Her body has "an undulating and aerial grace, such as one might dream of for some mythic and allegorical being," or such as a virile black man, a "broad-chested, strong-armed fellow" like Tom, might dream of for the ideal companion of his reverie in the absence of a darker mate (such as Poe's Ligeia) (*UTC*, 126, 128).[17]

But never fear: though an adult in body, Tom has the "impressible nature of his kindly race, ever yearning toward the simple and childlike" (*UTC*, 127). Thus, as the very image of white, feminine beauty topples from her pedestal, black Tom may be allowed to plunge to the rescue without a moment's "moral" hesitation on the reader's part.

Instead of carrying the golden damsel in distress off to his lair and devouring or marrying her, Stowe's Sir Tom "caught her in his arms, and swimming with her to the boat-side, handed her up, all dripping, to the grasp of hundreds of hands, which, as if they had all belonged to one man, were stretched eagerly out to receive her." Tom has served the white social order with even "more efficient aid" than the noble St. Clair, who, standing on a higher deck than the lowly slave, must be restrained from leaping blindly over the railing after his daughter like a savage (*UTC*, 128).

As a reward for returning the lily maiden—a child like Poe's Annabel Lee and soon to lie in a sepulchre by the sea—safely into white, male hands, we might at least expect Tom to be given his freedom. Instead, little lady Evangeline St. Clare offers her dark knight the best reward he can hope for in Stowe's fantasy of limitless male providence in the Christian home: she begs her princely father to buy him for her.

The White Captive

For a more robust, if less "pure," ideal of maidenhood (and America) than Little Eva or Annabel Lee, we need only look to the astonishing display of the white female body in the sculpture of the day—and, in Mrs. Stowe's fiction, to *The Minister's Wooing* (1859).

A love story of the faculties, *The Minister's Wooing* is set in New England soon after the revolution, thus taking us back to the origins of an American family bred *before* the decline of the Frenchified St. Clares, who parent the doomed Little Eva, enfeebled daughter of the degenerate South. A refined lady of leisure, Marie St. Clare, Eva's mother, represents the woman, described in Stowe's *Household Papers and Stories* (1864), "who enfeebles her muscular system by sedentary occupation, and over-stimulates her brain and nervous system," acquired traits in the individual that, in Mrs. Stowe's mind, would seem to be heritable. By contrast, Katy Scudder, mother of Mary Scudder in *The Minister's Wooing*, is Stowe's sturdy "Yankee woman" of old with her "steady nerves" and "healthy digestion" who is said "to have 'Faculty.'" [18]

Both of these American women—one from the extreme northern region of the country, the other from the extreme southern region, one giving birth when the federal union is born, the other giving birth on the eve of civil war, as the union it is being pulled apart by factionalism—pass on their essential character traits to their daughters by the "laws of descent." (Mrs. Stowe, like Walt Whitman, was a neo-Lamarckian.) [19]

Under these laws, the high-strung, ludicrously blond Little Eva, as an ideal of American beauty and potential womanhood, must soon depart. Mary Scudder, however, is primed to bequeath to her offspring traits or combinations of traits superior even to those of her parents. Whereas Mrs. Scudder is a practical woman without a "particle of ideality," Mary inherits her father's "sublime" moral faculties along with her mother's talent for housework. [20] (George Scudder is an unworldly man who abhors the slave trade that is making Newport wealthy at the end of the eighteenth century.)

Were Mary to wed Samuel Hopkins, the minister who woos her, she would be making a mismatch similar to that of the overly refined St. Clares, whose mentalities are too much alike, for the minister's "ideality had dealt only with the intellectual and invisible." Their combined intellectual and aesthetic tendencies—the Fowlers defined "Ideality," faculty #23 on their plaster busts, as "*Taste*, love of beauty, poetry"—would be too rarefied and angular, like the minister's forehead, where "squareness of ideality" has lent a "marked effect to its outline." Consequently, Mary is more happily paired, once the minister relinquishes his claim, with the youthful James Marvyn, whose lofty intellect, indicated by his "high forehead," is balanced and tempered, like Ishmael's, by his experience aboard a whaling ship of "all the races of men and their ways." The head of *their* child, Stowe insinuates, would be "as rounded and full in its sphere of faculties, as that of Da Vinci or Michel Angelo." [21]

Stowe, you will notice, compares the ideal head that houses the combined faculties from a healthy marriage to those of the great Renaissance artists themselves, rather than to the heads they painted and sculpted. It was in the rendering of the head, in particular, that Stowe's ideals of health and beauty, especially in women, departed most drastically from classical models, as did those of many American sculptors of her day. [22]

Like Mrs. Stowe, Hiram Powers, William Wetmore Story, Erastus D. Palmer, Harriet Hosmer, Joseph Mozier, Joel Hart and other workers in marble and bronze lamented the unnatural attitudes in which the "modern" woman's body had been "compressed" (Stowe) by the dictates of fashion (and thus commercialism) in dress and beauty since the beginning of the century. Asked about the plaster limbs strewn throughout his studio, Hart, for example, whose *Woman Triumphant* was destroyed in 1877, replied, "Yes, I am making them all the time. It is very hard to find good models among women, for their forms are usually ruined by the vicious customs of pinching and squeezing, and tightly binding what nature intended to be free."[23]

Like her sisters of antiquity and the Renaissance, the American Venus of the mid–nineteenth century was meant, her Pygmalions agreed, to display the natural female form without binding drapery, or at least free of entangling alliances with the corset and bustle. "In her day women were never seen with such enormous developments in their rear below the waist, and she wonders if it be real or fictitious," said Hiram Powers, defending his *Eve* from the encumbrance even of a fig leaf (*AMP,* 284). (Hosmer's *Zenobia in Chains,* 1859, which resembles various statues of "America" or "Liberty" of the period, is covered from neck to toe, but loosely so; and Hosmer's heroine is hearty enough to carry her heavy gold chains with ease.) Unlike her daughters in America, the Eve of old, said Powers, "will not allow her waist to be reduced by bandaging because she is far more comfortable as she is and besides, she has some regard for her health, which might suffer from such restraint, upon her lungs, heart, liver" (*AMP,* 284).

It is when Palmer and his contemporaries in the plastic arts get to the hair and heads of their Eves and Venuses and Americas, however, that they break even with classical ideals of female form and beauty—in one particular, what they regarded as a disproportionately small head. "The world is tired of looking at small-headed Venuses, which belong, like the De Medici, to a voluptuous rather than to an intellectual age," an admirer of Palmer's wrote in 1859 about the artist's new ideals of American beauty (*AMP,* 83).

The modern American Venus to which the reviewer referred was Palmer's *The White Captive,* displayed publicly in 1859, the same year as the publication of *The Minister's Wooing.* Modern art historians tend to regard this full-length nude in white marble, arms bound to a tree trunk by the only bit of drapery in the composition, as innocuous and unoriginal; but Charles Colbert makes a convincing case for rereading Palmer's work, and that of other master sculptors of this "naïve" period, as sophisticated examples of Hiram Powers's phrenological dictum that "mind forms the features" in art as in life (*AMP,* 289). Seen in this light, the bare, white images of these female slaves not only conform with the stereotypes of race and gender that I have been examining in other media, they also confirm that the human form, particularly the head, was often a metaphor for the nation or its parts in antebellum America and that mental balance, or a happy marriage of the faculties, was a common emblem in the period for a strong federal union of the states.

Powers's *America* or *Liberty* (1848–50), for example, sports a head that Mrs. Stowe would have approved of. It is almost as "rounded and full in its sphere of faculties" as the bulging bronze orb of his *Daniel Webster* (1858), whose high, rounded forehead, betokening huge "reflectives," was a matter of national pride with the phrenologists. In *America's* case, the rounded effect of the head, despite hints of a "Greek" nose, is enhanced by the arrangement of her hair, which is pulled back in a bun, revealing an intelligent forehead and bulging temples and accentuating the "domestic propensities"—including "Inhabitiveness" or "Love of home, patriotism"—located on the crown of the head.[24]

The head of Powers's *Webster* displays far less hair than that of his idealized female; but the same wide range of faculties—the intellectual offset by the affective—indicates that these two ideals of American vigor have their heads together. Clearest proof of the union of complementary faculties in their mental spheres, however, is that symbol of national unity in the political sphere to which they point. The imposing figures in both of Powers's compositions, whether male or female, are supported by a fasces, the bundle of sticks that, in the form of a torch, still accompanies the motto *e pluribus unum* on a dime, though Miss Liberty's image has been displaced by the rounded profile of FDR.

Were we to call upon Walt Whitman to decode this scarcely veiled iconography, he would, no doubt, reply (as in the 1855 *Preface* to *Leaves of Grass*): "These American states strong and healthy and accomplished shall receive no pleasure from violations of natural models and must not permit them," whether in art or "human physiology" or nationhood. "The human form," Whitman and many of his contemporaries took for granted, was the model of a healthy organization in all three: disunion in any of these spheres (except race) was a sign of degradation and disease in the others.[25]

Thus even before passage of the Kansas-Nebraska Act of 1854 made him an abolitionist, Hiram Powers hoped his *America* might help allay "the fever of secession that had gripped some quarters of the republic." (Powers was speaking, of course, of the "southern" quarters, those "regions" of "Insanity" and "Hate," anterior and posterior, that constitute trouble spots in the drawings of the female body in Joseph Rhodes Buchanan's *System of Anthropology*, which took the bare body of Powers's *Greek Slave* as a template for Buchanan's fantasy of the mind/body topos [*AMP*, 20].)[26]

At the time of its execution, however, not even *The Greek Slave*, which was admired as much in New Orleans as in Boston, carried the explicitly antislavery sentiment that has since been attributed to it. ("The warm reception accorded

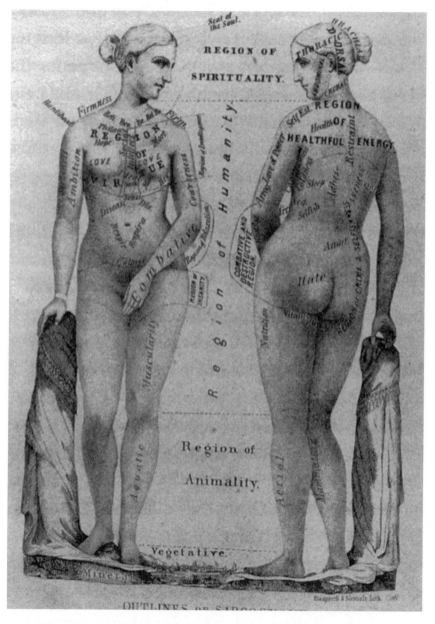

FIG. 9 Hiram Powers's *Greek Slave* provides the template for Joseph R. Buchanan's "Outlines of Sarcognomy." From his *System of Anthropology* (1854).

The Greek Slave during her nationwide tour in the late 1840s," argues Charles Colbert in his study of phrenology and the fine arts before 1865, "marks a watershed in American culture" [*AMP*, 282]).[27] The slave's national identity seems not to have been altogether fixed even in mind of the sculptor, who sometimes regarded her as "Circassian," a species of Caucasian favored in "enslavement" fantasies of the period (*AMP*, 302–04). One aspect of the "Greek" slave's racial identity was crystal clear from the beginning, however: she was not to be regarded as a Turk or other person of color.

That the physical union of white and black (or red) was considered "unnatural," and that America (to draw another implication from Whitman's words) "shall receive no pleasure from violations of natural models and must not permit them," is the racial subtext to be read in the pristine bodies of these white slaves and most of the other marble men and maidens in the studios of Americans at home and abroad in the mid–nineteenth century. (Even in Whitman's poems, "Ethopia" is represented as an old woman rather than the robust Eve upon whom "clean and vigorous children are jetted and conceived" by the American Adam.)[28]

Thus no fasces—it is supplanted by a stump—rises from the base of Erastus Dow Palmer's *White Captive*, for no union of opposites is contemplated here (overtly). From the obligatory thick ankles of the *Venus de' Medici*—a strong form requires a strong pedestal, as Harriet Hosmer told her critics—the body of Palmer's captive expands fulsomely, especially in the stomach, thighs, and hips. Only the nubile breasts imply late adolescence.

And then we see the head. It is so large in proportion to the body as to suggest a preadolescent stage of development and a Victorian fantasy of the child-woman that might have caused a Nathaniel Hawthorne to blush, if not a Lewis Carroll. But to a viewer schooled in faculty psychology, the ostensible message of Palmer's maiden in distress was that her head—with an assist from her touch-me-not posture (a variation on *contrapposto*)—was sufficient armor to shield this pure white virgin—at least morally—from the red "savages" who have carried her off into the forest primeval. "Palmer has . . . given us the broad brow of a large-brained and cultivated woman," said the reviewer who was so tired of small heads on his Venuses. "Her head and face bespeak not only intellectual superiority, but high moral culture" (*AMP*, 82).

If the puerile but ethereal Evangeline St. Clare cannot be allowed to grow up and wed her black knight—her only acceptable lover being her father in Stowe's fantasy of a naive mingling of the races—Palmer's white captive must face her captors, in the words of another contemporary viewer, with "imperious disgust" (*AMP*, 83). (Antebellum gentlemen flocked to see *The White Captive*, to be sure; but many of her admirers, as of Powers's *Greek Slave*, were women.)

Still, there is nothing in the Captive's demeanor to suggest that she is going to faint dead away anytime soon. Meanwhile, as in Higginson's little white captivity narrative, the observer, having entered the fevered latitudes of the romance, is permitted to imagine whatever forbidden union of contraries he or she might dread to witness. (Again, I mean to insinuate, the romance narrative as the nineteenth century understood and practiced it in whatever medium *was* a captivity narrative and vice versa.)

So where does this white romancing of race and gender boundaries leave little Eva's black "neighbor" girl, Topsy? The answer is in a sort of evolutionary limbo: "There stood the two children representatives of the two extremes of society. The fair, high-bred child, with her golden head, her deep eyes, her spiritual, noble brow, and prince-like movements; and her black, keen, subtle, cringing, yet acute neighbor. They stood the representatives of their races. The Saxon, born of ages of cultivation, command, education, physical and moral eminence; the Afric, born of ages of oppression, submission, ignorance, toil and vice!" (*UTC*, 213).

If only the two races could interbreed, Stowe seems on the very verge of crying out from the hilltops: what a blessing of "improvement" (the phrenologist's goal) for both! It is probably no slip of the pen that the little white princess in Stowe's description evinces "prince-like movements," for Evangeline St. Clare, though her mother's daughter, also embodies the physical and moral traits of her father, who has blue eyes, golden hair, a "Greek outline" of features and "a fair complexion." His twin brother, by contrast has "black fiery eyes, coal-black hair," a "strong, fine Roman profile and rich brown complexion" (*UTC*, 195).

Augustine St. Clare and his brother, Alfred, are representatives, respectively, of the "Mental" and the "Motive" temperaments; and so, it seems to me, are little Eva and Topsy.[29] What if their opposing traits could be "married" in the offspring of a single set of parents?

St. Clare, the effete southern gentleman whose "abstract ideality" prevents him from efficiently managing his plantation, lacks the "calculating firmness" of his more worldly brother (*UTC*, 195). (Located on the crown of the head, "Firmness," the prime male faculty attributed by Ishmael to the sperm whale, is defined by the Fowlers as "Stability, perseverance, willfulness.")[30] Consequently, St. Clare, the Southerner, though kind to his slaves, is afraid that the sons of illicit black-white unions will rise up one day (or night) and lead their pure black half-brothers in revolt. Stowe, however, would appear to have a different view of the psychological and physical mingling of the races, though she was probably afraid to admit it, even to herself.

Standing on the brink of a social and sexual abyss, Stowe was drawn to the idea that "the Afric" might no longer "cringe" (as Topsy does) if his or her motive powers were combined with the mental and moral powers of "the Saxon" (embodied in little Eva and Augustine St. Clare, as in the white, female captives of Palmer and Powers). If Uncle Tom Shelby is (covertly) Stowe's ideal white black man, George Harris, offspring of an illicit interracial liaison who can pass for a "Spanish" don, is her even more potent fantasy of the ideal black white man.

In 1852, however, the overt espousal by a white woman of "breeding" of widespread interracial marriage as a cure, however modestly proposed, for the nation's political divisions would have been looked upon as sheer madness, even in New England. This dizzying prospect could be approached only in the charmed (and veiled) latitudes of the romance of sentiments. Even here, poor Topsy, the captive black child of Stowe's narrative, must be left to develop into a woman of no definite form, for her past, her parentage, and even her prior physical development are clouded: "Never was born, . . . never had no father, nor mother, nor nothin'. . . . I spect I growed" (*UTC*, 209–10).[31]

SEVEN

Frederick Douglass and the Whiteness of Blackness

The first step towards lightening The White Man's Burden is through teaching the virtues of cleanliness. Pears' Soap is a potent factor in brightening the dark corners of the earth as civilization advances.

—*Advertisement in* McClure's *magazine* (1899)

 HARRIET BEECHER STOWE'S raven-hued Topsy is a rare bird in nineteenth-century literature: a curious case of spontaneous generation—not to be confused with spontaneous combustion, the even rarer malady that apparently besets the elder Wieland in Charles Brockden Brown's romance of that title—and one that perhaps reflects Stowe's own ambivalence toward the competing notions of heredity that threaten to break out in her fiction. A girl who "just growed" is a unique individual, metaphorically without parents and origins and thus without inherited family traits. As a representative "Afric," however, Topsy is assigned characteristics ("subtle, cringing, yet acute") supposed by the polygenists to be *racial* in origin. Is Stowe herself suggesting, after all, that racial characteristics dominate family ones, and that type or species determines the "character" of the individual? Is she, in short, giving in to the racial determinism that asked, rhetorically, with Jeremiah, "Can the Ethopian change his skin, or the leopard his spots?" Or is this near-advocate of "miscegenation" insinuating that only the individual stands a chance of breaking the mold of race by some Lamarckian mechanism for acquiring new traits, and that Topsy has simply failed to do so? Or none of the above?

Although *The Minister's Wooing* came out in 1859 along with Charles Darwin's *On the Origin of Species*, it is probably safe to say that Stowe did not fully comprehend Darwin's work in all its complexity, a daunting task for the nonspecialist even today.[1] To Darwin, of course, the strictly hereditarian argument of "the American school" of anthropology put the trait before the mate. Even Darwin's theory of speciation could be twisted to "prove" that the male (or white)

member of the species (or human race) had more up front than the female (or black or red) member. "I have always maintained that ... men did not differ much in intellect, only in zeal and hard work," Darwin once told his cousin Francis Galton, author of *Heredity Genius* (1869). "The rejoinder that might be made to his remark about hard work," said Sir Francis, who misunderstood Darwin's theory of natural selection, "is that character, including the aptitude for work, is heritable like every other faculty."[2] Galton, who coined the term *eugenics*, was no amateur in the pre-Darwinian laboratories of race and gender; he was a trained biologist; and as late as 1909, he was still defending his hereditarian position against Darwinian's revolutionary idea that environment alters heredity over time.

Though Stowe may not have understood Darwin in every detail, the likes of Topsy and Little Eva suggest that it had occurred to their creator, along with the other Lamarckians and proto-Darwinians of her day, that some aspects of human behavior may have more to do with nurture than with nature (a debate that was beginning to come into sharp focus in the late 1850s). Besides being children of different races, Topsy and Little Eva, says Stowe, are offspring of entirely different environments: her little blond goddess is not just a "Saxon," she is "born of ages of cultivation, command, education, physical and moral eminence." Stowe's little black imp, Topsy, by contrast, is "born of ages of oppression, submission, ignorance, toil and vice" (*UTC*, 213). Change that environment, their "master" insinuates (in an underlying racial argument similar to Margaret Fuller's feminist one), and white America will discover, to their amazement, that the black "savages" in their midst will be transformed—and transformation is probably the concept here, rather than evolution—into the "civilized" creatures they have always been, potentially, especially during the childhood of the individual.

Stowe's adult characters, however, are a different matter. Her Uncle Tom, like Douglass's heroic slave, is *born* with his good character traits, both "black" and "white" (though Stowe heretically implies that such traits must not be strictly heritable by race, since Tom is "pure" African). And the mulatto George Harris has *inherited* the best of both races as well, though perhaps from his black and white ancestors, respectively. To the extent that Stowe (and Frederick Douglass) merely assigned typically "white" (to the nineteenth-century way of thinking) traits to their black characters and "black" traits to their white ones, these emissaries of cultural enlightment were challenging the racial stereotypes of their day but not the psychological imperatives upon which those stereotypes rested.

As late as 1899, illustrated advertisements for Pears' soap in popular American magazines such as *McClure's* showed Admiral George Dewey and his fellow

The first step towards lightening

The White Man's Burden

is through teaching the virtues of cleanliness.

Pears' Soap

is a potent factor in brightening the dark corners of the earth as civilization advances, while amongst the cultured of all nations it holds the highest place—it is the ideal toilet soap.

FIG. 10 Advertisement in *McClure's* magazine for October 1899.

missionaries scrubbing away at the skin of native Africans with little blocks of pure, imported whiteness. In that antique corner of the North American mind where color (black, red, yellow) denoted savagery, white was still the perceived tincture of civilization. It marked the man or woman as something other than a beast; and carrying the essence of whiteness to the ends of the earth was the highest mission of the nineteenth-century soldier missionary. (Clad in immaculate white from chin to toe in the Pears' soap ads, Admiral Dewey had to wash his hands first, however.)

Thus Frederick Douglass, who was so far from being an Uncle Tom that he made his white relatives and overseers out to be even meaner than they were, probably had no choice, rhetorically, in *The Heroic Slave* (1853)—the first extended "black" historical romance, or romance of black history, produced in this country by an African American—but to argue that the "best" black men were actually white on the inside.[3] (In *Uncle Tom's Cabin*, Stowe, by contrast, had argued, in effect, that the best white men were black, a "feminine" position on gender that the culturally "masculinized" Douglass, who was writing his narrative in direct response to Stowe's, could not accept even in the service of his position on race.)[4] Drawing on the all-men-are-equal rhetoric of 1776, Douglass attacked what Eric Sundquist has called the "fradulence" of applying "the revolutionary paradigm" to whites only in postrevolutionary America. The psychology on which that rhetoric was based, however, assumed that the individual is a composite of contending faculties, some of them inferior by nature to others; and like everyone else in the new republic, Douglass had no viable alternative model of the self to draw on. He could contest the value of placing reason before affection, or vice versa; but he and his age did not yet have a popular scientific or philosophical basis for exposing the fraudulence of a paradigm of mental parts that held some parts of the equally created self to be more equal than others.

The Heroic Slave: White Rhetoric, Black Revolution

Based on the *Creole* incident of ten years before, Douglass's fictional account of the escape of 134 human commodities from a North American cargo ship begins with a question addressed to the leader of the near-bloodless mutiny, one Madison Washington: "Why is thy look so like despair?" (*HS*, 25).[5] This is Douglass's equivalent of "What has cast such a shadow upon you," the rhetorical query with which Melville, who was familiar with the *Creole* incident, would end his subversive story of a mutiny in which slaves are the real masters and the apparent masters are enslaved by their own prejudices. In Melville's narrative, "the negro" is the answer. In Douglass's, conversely, it is the white system of social and political authority that has cast the shadow of despair upon the black psyche in America.[6]

Upon gaining his freedom, Madison Washington dropped from the records (though not the folklore) of American slavery. Little is known about him or his state of mind during the mutiny, except that he had earlier escaped to Canada, then been sold back into bondage when he returned to Virginia hoping to free his wife.[7]

So little is known about the historical Washington, in fact, that this obscure black man with a name "ominous of greatness" eluded the historian like a runaway slave hidden by his own darkness. The author of *The Heroic Slave* could only come before the reader, he said, "speaking of marks, traces, possibles, and probabilities." Washington seemed to Douglass at once a "guiding star" glimpsed through the parted clouds on a stormy night and the "peak" of a dangerous rock revealed to the sailor by lightning. To capture this shadowy figure on the blank white page of history, his chronicler must read him in the signs, as Mark Twain's Jim reads the night sky to Huck Finn. Voodoo biography soon gives way in Douglass's narrative, however, to more conventional modes of telling a life (*HS*, 26).

Since Douglass is reading the fugitive signs of American history from a black perspective, *The Heroic Slave* finds in Madison Washington and the *Creole* mutiny none of the excrescences, physical and political, that Thomas Gray and other white historians read into the Nat Turner revolt. Instead, Douglass tells the story of a natural nobleman's struggle for life, liberty, and the pursuit of happiness, a classically "white" tale, which Douglass romances from the scant historical facts in much the same way the American colonists justified their mutiny from Britain by using the rhetoric of Common Sense philosophy.

Douglass identified his nearly anonymous black hero, whose name, though more substantial than Nat Turner's abrupt monosyllable, still was not entirely his own, with his illustrious white namesakes, men whose names rang synonymously with liberty in America and who had presumed to sign themselves, "We, the people." "Let those account for it who can," says the narrator of *The Heroic Slave*, "but there stands the fact, that a man who loved liberty as well as did Patrick Henry,—who deserved it as much as Thomas Jefferson,—and who fought for it with a valor as high, an arm as strong, and against odds as great, as he who led all the armies of the American colonies through the great war for freedom and independence, lives now only in the chattel records of his native State" (*HS*, 25).

The irony of Madison Washington's name had not escaped the proslavery press, who reported the *Creole* mutiny in language similar to the demonizing rhetoric they accorded Turner's rebellion a few years before. They "branded" him, Douglass told an assemblage of abolitionists in Ireland, as "a thief, robber and murderer."[8] They "blackened," in other words, Madison Washington's doubly white name.

In the name of liberty, the great patriots of 1776 had tarred the (sometimes certifiably maniacal) king of England with this same brush. That "barbarous and hellish power, which hath stirred up the Indians and the Negroes to destroy us": so Paine's "Common Sense" painted the British monarchy on the eve of the American Revolution. He did not mean "to exhibit horror for the purpose of provoking revenge," said Paine, only (as in Hawthorne's sketch of the passive mind) "to awaken us from fatal and unmanly slumbers, that we may pursue determinately some fixed object."[9]

Paine had asked the reader of "Common Sense" to "divest himself of prejudice and prepossession."[10] Douglass asked no less of the reader of *The Heroic Slave*. His narrative concludes with a debate between two white sailors, Williams and Grant, in the Marine Coffee-house in Richmond; it is intended to show that a keen intelligence and other virtues of the cool head are hardly the exclusive property of white Americans. Williams represents the voice of prejudice, the "white" view of history: "'Well, betwixt you and me,' said Williams, "that whole affair on board of the Creole was miserably and disgracefully managed. Those black rascals got the upper hand of ye altogether; and, in my opinion, the whole disaster was the result of ignorance of the real character of *darkies* in general. . . . All that is needed in dealing with a set of rebellious *darkies*, is to show that yer not afraid of 'em'" (*HS*, 61).

Grant, who actually witnessed the mutiny, represents the voice of common sense: "'I will state the facts precisely as they came under my own observation. Mr. Williams speaks of 'ignorant negroes,' . . . but had he been on board the *Creole* as I was, he would have seen cause to admit that there are exceptions to this general rule. The leader of the mutiny in question was just as shrewd a fellow as ever I met in my life, and was as well fitted to lead in a dangerous enterprise as any one white man in ten thousand'" (*HS*, 65).

Looked at without "prejudice and prepossession," the facts will appear the same to one man's "observation" as to another's: this is the commonsense basis of "Common Sense," a phrase with such a complicated pedigree that Sir William Hamilton devotes a sixty-page footnote to its history and etymology in his edition of Thomas Reid's works.

Even in its most arcane applications, however, common sense consistently referred to the mind's ability to perceive reality *extra mentem* with the aid of the senses, equally reliable in all persons who are not physically impaired or mentally ill. Perhaps because it referred truth to a consensus drawn from common experience, this "realism" appealed greatly to the budding democracy in

America. One legacy of Common Sense philosophy so conceived, in fact, is the notion of "self-evident" truths from which derive the "unalienable" rights of the Declaration of Independence and, subsequently, of *The Heroic Slave.*

Here is Douglass's black hero, no meek child-man of the white imagination, at the moment when his struggle with the shadow—the desire, long smoldering within him, to escape the tyranny of slavery—has reached its "high resolution": "'Liberty, the inalienable birth-right of every man, precious and priceless, will be mine. My resolution is fixed, *I shall be free*'" (*HS*, 28). The heroic slave's personal "declaration of his purpose" (and his equivalent of Huck Finn's resolution to go to hell), this speech directly echoes the "unalienable" rights of the national "Declaration" by which the Continental Congress of 1776 signified in black and white its resolve to break with the "barbarities" (Paine and Jefferson) of the old order.

The basic argument of *The Heroic Slave* is an argument by analogy: what was true psychologically—and, therefore, morally—of the revolutionaries of 1776, Douglass contends, is true of the mutineers of 1841. "God is my witness," declares Washington to the white crew upon taking over the *Creole*, "that LIBERTY, not *malice,* is the motive for this night's work. . . . We have struck for our freedom, and if a true man's heart be in you, you will honor us for the deed. We have done that which you applaud your fathers for doing, and if we are murderers, *so were they*" (*HS*, 66).

The "fathers" of Douglass's black-or-white rhetoric had argued in a similar if-then fashion. The Declaration of 1776 consists of two interlocking logical arguments, an inductive one "proving" King George to be a "tyrant" and a deductive argument that goes: If, in the eyes of the people, a government is ruled by tyrants, then "it is their right, it is their duty, to throw off such government." As Douglass would after them, the architects of this earlier mutiny battered the true man's heart with more than reason, however.

Inspired by Tom Paine's "Common Sense," Jefferson and the other signers were asking the reader of the "Declaration," in Paine's words, to "suffer his reason *and* his feelings to determine for themselves" (italics added) the proper course of human events. This was a radical departure from the Common Sense philosophy of Thomas Reid, its founder. Though they referred truth to common experience (a *consensus gentium*), the Scottish realists, particularly Reid, had in mind a consensus drawn primarily from the exercise of the intellectual faculties. The revolutionaries in America, however, having scant legal basis for their actions, rallied support for their cause by equating political freedom with *moral liberty,* or freedom of the will based upon the free exercise of the sentiments. A democratizing of the faculties for pragmatic purposes, their appeal to *emotion* as well as reason was more in keeping with the views of Reid's adversary,

Dugald Stewart. This was a distinctly American appropriation of the philosophy of Common Sense; and it would have the effect, over the next century, of emancipating the passions and feelings from their long subservience to the intellect.

For all its apparent rationalism, the American declaration of divorce from Great Britain is a gothic tale of the horrors visited upon the colonists by King George III, who, in this version of the essential romance plot, plays the marauding pirate (or "the Negro"), while the colonists take the role of the shackled victims. Approximately thirty in number, these alarms and terrors of the night include "Merciless Indian Savages," "large Armies of foreign mercenaries," and "circumstances of Cruelty & perfidy scarcely paralleled in the most barbarous ages." (Come one, come all; see these impostures of British rule with your own eyes!)

Most of the barbarous acts of "perfidy" enumerated in the Declaration, a veritable cabinet of mental and moral outrages, are cast in psychosexual terms: King George is a "Prince," the signers concede, but a prince of darkness whose "invasions" and "ravages" the people of America have endured with "patient sufferance." Having violated "the consent of the governed" by "repeated injury," he is now to be resisted "with manly firmness." Fearing "invasion from without, and convulsions within," the signers of the Declaration put before the reader's observation as indisputable facts the British sovereign's "long train of abuses and usurpations." Recalling these barbarisms, "totally unworthy the Head of a civilized nation," to the public mind and heart, common sense demands—*revolt!*

Thus did the founding fathers rewrite American history in the only way, according to Dugald Stewart (and Hawthorne), that history ever changes: by imposing imagination upon memory to form a "new creation," the true romance of democracy.

Frederick Douglass could be more bold in his fiction than in his speeches to white audiences, where he sometimes seemed almost to concede "the inferiority of our race." ("What if we are inferior? Is it a valid argument for making slaves of us?") Douglass wanted to abolish slavery in America; he could not wait to abolish racial prejudice first, and Douglass knew that the prejudice against color in this country was endemic among whites, even those who opposed slavery on moral grounds and who suspected that "biologically inferior" races might actually walk upright if given an education. "The people of America deprive us of every privilege," Douglass declared in the "American Prejudice Against Color" (1845); "they turn round and taunt us with our inferiority!—they stand upon our necks, they impudently taunt us, and ask the question, why we don't stand up erect? they tie our feet, and ask us why we don't run?"[11]

The cadences could almost be Tom Paine's. Indeed, Douglass had devel-

oped his oratorical skills, in part, by studying Caleb Bingham's extracts of political speeches in *The Columbian Orator*, 1797, which raised a familiar cry: "'Tis the
old argument on the part of tyrants," as Douglass declared. "Tyrants have ever
justified their tyranny by arguing on the inferiority of their victims." [12]

Even when Douglass seemed to grant "that the Negroes in America are inferior to the Whites," the point at issue, for him, was that the dominant white
social order actually caused the "inferiority" it purported to discover in "the
negro" by depriving African Americans, especially slaves, of the means of bet-
tering themselves. In many southern states before the Civil War, not only were
slaves forbidden to learn to read and write, teaching them to do so also was
punishable by law. In Louisiana, Douglass claimed, the legal penalty for a second offense was death—to the teacher.

Taking a page from the women's movement, particularly the Seneca Falls
"Declaration of Sentiments" of 1848, which borrowed its rhetoric from the
earlier Declaration of Independence, Douglass set out in his narrative to prove
that a grown-up black man, fully developed in every faculty and capable of
balanced thinking on the most abstract of subjects, was no aberration. Once he
takes over the slave ship, therefore, instead of cannibalizing the crew like a
proper savage, Douglass's Madison Washington conducts himself with such
pristine civility that Tom Grant, the sensible sailor, grants him to be, as Douglass urges all his white readers to do, "a superior man."

The prejudice against color was so indelibly imprinted in the white mind in
the nineteenth century, however, Douglass realized, that even the Tom Grants
of America, especially in the South, could not always be counted on to believe
the testimony of their own eyes and ears. "It was not that his principles were
wrong in the abstract," says Grant of the heroic fugitive's subversive motives,
"for they were the principles of 1776. But I could not bring myself to recognize
their application to one whom I deemed my inferior" (*HS*, 68). To close the
debate between prejudice and common sense in his narrative, Douglass must
introduce a perspective totally untainted by whiteness, except for a mocking
trace of ivory framed by ebony portals.

The *Creole* has landed safely in Nassau, and a company of black soldiers
come aboard to protect the ship's property; to a man they exhibit Dugald Stewart's (or Thomas Gray's) refined sense of moral disgust in the face of "conclusions at which our nature revolts": "I told them by the laws of Virginia and the
laws of the United States," says Grant, that "the slaves on board were as much
property as the barrels of flour in the hold. At this the stupid blockheads
showed their *ivory*, [and] rolled up their white eyes in horror, as if the idea of
putting men on a footing with merchandise were revolting to their humanity"
(*HS*, 69).

The Abolitionist from Ohio: Huck Finn Grows Up

Douglass published *The Heroic Slave* in direct protest of the Fugitive Slave Act of 1850, which put white citizens of free states, such as Mr. Listwell, Madison Washington's fictional "confessor," under heavy legal penalties for harboring runaway slaves. A farmer in the border state of Ohio and a convert to abolitionism, Mr. Listwell, whose Bunyanesque name told white readers how Douglass wanted them to respond to his narrative, is the inverse of Nat Turner's Thomas Gray.

In a set of coincidences worthy of a Dickens novel, Mr. Listwell, traveling through Virginia on horseback, happens to overhear Madison Washington's cry for freedom in the wilderness. Five years later, when Washington, acting upon his resolve at last, reaches Ohio on the underground railroad, he turns up at Mr. Listwell's door. The scene is a fire-lit chamber, very like the one in the "Custom House" sketch where Hawthorne conceived *The Scarlet Letter*, and thus the neutral territory of romance, though on a stormy night more befitting a Poe tale:

> A single lamp burnt brightly on the centre-table. All was still and comfortable within; but the night was cold and dark.... It was a night for strange noises and for strange fancies. A whole wilderness of thought might pass through one's mind during such an evening. The smouldering embers, partaking of the spirit of the restless night, became fruitful of varied and fantastic pictures, and revived many bygone scenes and old impressions.... [T]here are certain seasons when the slightest sound sends a jar through all the subtle chambers of the mind; and such a season was this. (*HS*, 31)

Dozing by the fire, Mr. and Mrs. Listwell, hear a noise outside the door. "What can it mean? certainly no one can be out on such a night as this." The startled wife's question is essentially the one that Poe's narrator puts to Roderic Usher when that curious couple think they hear the deceased Madeline bursting from her tomb. Mr. Listwell, however, refuses to believe that the sound means spirits or other horrors. It is "but the wind," he says, and gets up to investigate (*HS*, 32).

A commonsensical Midwesterner, Mr. Listwell is confronting things that go bump in the night as James Beattie advised in his *Dissertations Moral and Critical* (1783). Setting forth common sense's usual way of dealing with "imaginary terrors," Beattie writes: "By the glimmerings of the moon, I have once and again beheld, at midnight the exact form of a man or woman, sitting silent and motionless by my bedside. Had I hid my head, without daring to look the appari tion in the face, I should have passed the night in horror, and risen in the morning with the persuasion of having seen a ghost. But, rousing myself, and resolving to find out the truth, I discovered, that it was nothing more than the accidental disposition of my clothes upon a chair." [13]

Likewise, a coffin that once appeared at his bedside, says Beattie, turned out to be "only a stream of yellowish light, falling in a particular manner upon the floor." When confronted with this vision, the slumberer refused to be terrified but "started up, and recollecting, that I had heard of such things having been seen by others, I set myself to examine it." [14]

When Mr. Listwell sets about to examine his superstitious fears in common-sense fashion, his chamber door opens to admit, not a raven of darkness but Monte, the family's faithful dog. Monte is accompanied by a black stranger; but even "canine instinct" has enough common sense to know that this apparition of darkness is "a friend, not an enemy of the family." The stranger asks for "a resting place," though not a final one, for he is on his way to Canada (*HS*, 32–33).

By an involuntary thought process typical of faculty psychology, Mr. Listwell recognizes Madison Washington—"the recollection of the Virginia forest scene flashed upon him"—and he and his wife feed the fugitive and turn over their own bed to this tall, powerfully built black man, who threatens neither their sanity nor their sexual relations. "It was the first time in his life," says Douglass, that the slave had met so humane and friendly a greeting at the hands of persons whose color was unlike his own" (*HS*, 33–34).

Though he lives in a remote house in the woods, Frederick Douglass's Mr. Listwell is no pale recluse who withdraws from the affairs of the world in moral disgust. When he and Madison Washington meet again after that stormy evening by the fireside, Mr. Listwell has passed another bad night. Returning to Virginia on business, he has taken refuge in a dilapidated tavern, a metaphor for the old South: "Its fine old portico looks well at a distance, and gives the building an air of grandeur," Douglass writes. "A nearer view, however, does little to sustain this pretension" (*HS*, 47).

With a slight shift in visual perspective, as at the beginning of "The Fall of the House of Usher," Douglass's traveler (who, in contrast to Poe's, trusts the evidence of his senses) perceives at once that he is entering a house of madness, the Jeffersonian dream turned to nightmare because constructed, like the porticos of Monticello, on slave labor.

The state of decay is further advanced here than at the beginning of Poe's tale, however, since darker deeds than any transgressions of the Usher twins have been perpetrated within. Again, the narrator draws the analogy between the decaying structure and a human head. Like the vacant, eye-like windows of

Usher's mansion, those of Douglass's tavern stare blankly at the approaching traveler because the "places in the upper windows once occupied with large panes of glass" are now stuffed with old hats and rags. The side of the building, as if from the discharge of some hideous eyewash, is "much discolored in sundry places by slops poured from the upper windows." And over all is cast a "gloomy mantle of ruin," reminding the narrator of "a human skull, after the flesh has mingled with the earth" (HS, 47–48).

Douglass does not mention fungi growing like hair at the eaves as Poe does; but from this crumbling edifice of the Old Dominion, "the moulding boards along the roofing have dropped off" and, in falling from the crown, have left "holes and crevices in the rented wall for bats and swallows to build their nests in" (HS, 47). (In his romance of the old South, Swallow Barn [1832], John Pendleton Kennedy had tried to make the structures of slavery, from the humble cabin to the manor house, seem cozy and sustaining.)

We might compare Douglass's tavern of once-grand pretensions to the Grangerford mansion that Huck Finn encountered about this same time on the border between Tennessee and Kentucky. Like Usher's, the Grangerford's house has a crack in it, the inherited system of false chivalry that justifies the family's ancient feud with the Shepherdsons and that, in Clemens's view, fostered slavery in the South and helped to justify the war.

In his innocence, Huck admires the "genteel" appointments of this borderland gentleman's domain, especially the "lovely" basket of fake fruit in the parlor that, to Huck, seems "much redder and yellower and prettier than real ones is, but they warn't real because you could see where pieces had got chipped off and showed the white chalk or whatever it was, underneath" (HF, 120). A house built on white chalk, Clemens belatedly insinuates through the eyes of his junior realist—or is he a sentimentalist?— cannot stand.

The antithesis of Pap Finn, who rails at any "gov'ment" that would give the vote to blacks, Douglass's Mr. Listwell is the socially responsible adult white male that Clemens, by 1885, said he could no longer dream up for young Huck to grow into. Douglass, however, in 1851 had no difficulty imagining the ideal white man; and he sends him across the threshold of the mind's darkling chambers to pass the night in the enemy's camp.

As we might expect from such evil haunts, "what snatches of sleep" Mr. Listwell got, says Douglass, "were interrupted by dreams which were anything than pleasant." Hundreds of dark figures seem to crowd his resting place, and he hears a "loud and confused clamour, cursing and cracking of whips, and the noise of chains. . . . This uproar was kept up with undulating course, till near morning. There was loud laughing,—loud singing,—loud cursing,—and yet there seemed to be weeping and mourning in the midst of all" (HS, 52).

Suddenly the hellish clamor startles Mr. Listwell from his bed. Simply exam-ining these night visions in the light of common sense, like James Beattie with his ghost and coffin, will not dispel them, however, for the spirits that trouble Mr. Listwell's slumbers are real. During the night, a gang of slaves—men, women, and children on their way to the Richmond market—have been driven in chains to the tavern. Tethered among them is Madison Washington, caught when he came back to liberate his wife. "It was madness to have returned," Mr. Listwell tells him (*HS*, 57).

In order to avoid suspicion, Mr. Listwell pretends to be a buyer of slaves. Merely putting on this evil robe of sorrow, however, prompts in him a crisis of conscience similar to Huck Finn's when he decides to send the letter to Tom Sawyer revealing where Miss Watson's runaway Jim can be found.

Huck's internal tug-of-war is typical of the mental processes, as faculty psy-chology once understood them, gone awry at moments of psychic conflict: "It was a close place. I took it up, and held it [the letter to Tom] in my hand. I was a trembling, because I'd got to decide, forever, betwixt two things, and I knowed it" (*HF*, 223). Here, floating along on Clemens's Mississippi with the other debris of romance, is the old notion of the mind as a "close place" where thoughts become "things" presented alternately to the faculties in visible form—like a ghost or shadow but one (to the sentimental realist) with sub-stance—as Huck's letter to Tom gives shape and form to his moral dilemma, or as any letter takes the place of the author's thoughts or physical person.[15]

When Huck first leans toward Miss Watson's heaven by "deciding" to send the letter, he is, of course, Clemens's irony tells us, being pushed in the wrong direction. Huck's sound heart soon triumphs, however, over his "deformed conscience." (In the dualities of faculty psychology, which were being redefined as Clemens wrote, it would be technically more accurate to say that Huck re-solves the dilemma of a divided conscience, or moral sense, by listening to his emotions rather than his intellect.) Quickened by a surge of sentiment for Jim, Huck's will overturns the cold dictates of reason with only a cursory glance at the precipice over which he expects to plummet: "I studied a minute, sort of holding my breath, and then says to myself: 'All right, then, I'll *go* to hell'—and tore it up" (*HF*, 223).[16]

Mr. Listwell vacillates, too, before deciding betwixt two warring courses of action: it would be foolish "to impart a knowledge of his real character and sentiments" to the denizens of the tavern, he reasons, since this would "be im-parting intelligence with the certainty of seeing it and himself both abused." Such reflections, however, Mr. Listwell confesses, do not "altogether satisfy his conscience, for, hating slavery as he did, and regarding it to be the immediate duty of every man to cry out against it . . . it was hard for him to admit to himself the possibility of circumstances wherein a man might, properly, hold his tongue on the subject" (*HS*, 53).

Hold it he does for a time, however, in moral disgust, as Huck holds his breath before taking the plunge. "All right, then, I'll go to hell," Mr. Listwell says to himself, in effect; and he joins the procession of fantastic figures that issue from the old tavern at daybreak. Accompanying this remorseful train to Richmond, where Madison Washington is driven aboard the *Creole*, bound for New Orleans, Mr. Listwell slips "three strong *files*" into his shackled hands (*HS*, 59). The files will enable the heroic slave to break his bonds and lead one of the most successful slave insurrections in American history—without taking a single white wife, mother, or child beyond forbidden horizons.

Uncle Tom and Aunt Jim

Frederick Douglass was first an orator and rhetorician and only incidentally a writer of fiction. His Mr. Listwell, consequently, is barely credible as a "real" character (even in a romance, where characters tend to be types), so transparently does he represent an ideological point of view. The debate in Mr. Listwell's mind, which Douglass hoped to bring to a crisis in the reader's, is simply the debate between Williams and Grant internalized—that is, placed, or staged, in the mind of a single character—and more fully resolved.

Neither an overly idealistic New Englander like Melville's Captain Delano, nor a Southerner whose pride gets in the way of his common sense as Tom Grant's does, Mr. Listwell embodies what Douglass perceived to be a new social mind, that of the Westerner, the man of the border states soon to be personified for many by President Lincoln. If this new regional mind—more democratic in its virtues and vices, less inclined than that of older settlers in the wilderness, such as William Dunbar on his Mississippi plantation, to draw absolute distinctions between savagery and civilization, black and white—could be shaped and directed to the cause of abolition, Douglass calculated, the rest of the country might be obliged to follow.

It was this new borderland gentleman, the person sitting on the fence, ideologically, between slave state and free—whether in Ohio and Illinois or in New York—that Douglass hoped to tip over the edge with Mr. Listwell's psychological tug-of-war. In 1853, four years before the Dred Scott decision, this did not yet mean a literal call to arms; but Douglass sought to arouse in his uncommitted readers a sense of the imperative duty to cry out against the slave system, particularly as shored up by the Fugitive Slave Act, which made all citizens, willy nilly, legal accomplices of the slave owners.

In the exemplary mind of Mr. Listwell, man of the middle states, the old boundaries between knowing and feeling, white and black, male and female have not been dissolved, however. Douglass has simply moved them around, assigning to Mr. Listwell a superior "black" mind in which the legal sophistries upholding the slave system are undercut by simple feelings and plain virtue, as he assigns to Madison Washington a superior "white" mind whose anger and enthusiasm are offset by right reason. A specimen black man with the intellectual capacity of "one white man in ten thousand," Madison Washington has also developed, in the upper reaches of his balanced brain, the higher moral sentiments. This is why five years must elapse before he can act on his resolve.

In Washington's mental debate, as opposed to Mr. Listwell's, right thinking ultimately wins out over true feeling; but it is critical to Douglass's portrayal of a superior mind at work in a black man to show that Madison Washington is as capable of noble passion as of sustained intellection. The heroic slave's feelings are shown to be so strong, in fact, that they keep him as if chained to a rock long after his head has correctly instructed his clear conscience that revolt is the only reasonable course of moral action for a slave.

Like Mr. Listwell at the tavern perfidious, Douglass himself had trouble holding his tongue when white Americans patiently explained to him that he and his race fell behind them and theirs in reasoning capacity. (Douglass's great natural intelligence, according to William S. McFeely, probably came from his black mother's side of the family rather than his white father's.)[17] But Douglass smoldered all the more when he heard black people identified as emotionally backward, too. "My friends," he fumed from the lecture podium, "there are charges brought against coloured men not alone of intellectual inferiority, but of want of affection for each other." The imputation of emotional deficiency in "the Negro" troubled Douglass so much, in fact, that the historical Madison Washington's futile attempt to liberate his wife from slavery becomes as important to his narrative as the mutiny, "a glorious illustration of affection in the heart of a black man."[18]

In real life, Madison Washington had escaped alone to Canada; only after reflecting on the loss, apparently, did he return for his wife. Under the license of romance, Douglass makes this noble deed still more selfless. The fictional Washington is so reluctant to leave his wife in the first place that he hides for five years in the nearby woods where he can keep an eye on her safety, and even then he is permitted to flee only because fire destroys his hiding place. When, safe in Canada, Douglass's hero impulsively returns to the plantation, his wife must be killed off by her cruel master (and the romancer) before the black Washington can be free at last to lead his historic mutiny.

Meanwhile, alone in the forest, the devoted husband is "goaded almost to madness by the sense of the injustice done to him" (HS, 30). By contrast with "white history," which could only explain the revolts of Washington, Nat Turner, and other slaves as insanity, Douglass's "black" version of American history interprets the mental turmoil leading to Washington's declaration of independence as an alternative to it.

Since, in Douglass's romance, as in Stowe's and Clemens's, savagery lies within the white society of the plantation, the wilderness—emblematic of that "whole wilderness of thought" where "fantastic pictures" pass through "the subtle chambers of the mind"—becomes Washington's asylum. (This is why Huck Finn lights out for the Indian territory at the end of his adventures.) A psychologically neutral territory beyond the bounds of the plantation, the wild wood gives Douglass's recluse the latitude he needs "to give vent to his pent up feelings." Restored to emotional and intellectual balance, he can then commonsensically "debate with himself the feasibility of plans, plans of his own invention, for his own deliverance" (*HS*, 30). That "debate" is an internal one, as in Huck Finn's case, a sign that Madison Washington's rational faculties are still in good working order and, thus, a sign of mental health. Had Douglass's hero, who will maintain an even keel and a level head in the stormy seas of mutiny, been denied the right to express his countervailing feelings—he is "goaded" to the brink as it is—he might have lost *all* his faculties and been drawn over the edge into the black depths of total madness, as in a Poe tale.

Dementia: The Pit

"When not recovered from," said Dr. Skae in his taxonomy of mental diseases of the mid–nineteenth century, "the most frequent termination of mania or monomania" is "dementia." "In mania or monomania" (that is, mental derangement, whether general or partial), "there is an excessive activity of some feelings, or emotions, or faculties" resulting in "a disturbance of the equilibrium of the mind." The depths of madness, or "dementia," by contrast, are to be recognized by an "asthenia" (loss, impairment) of the faculties or, in extreme cases, by their total "obliteration" (*MD*, 534).

Instead of slumbering, that is, in some cave or dungeon on the borders of the mind under a species of enchantment worked by the conscious will, part or all of the demented mind goes to sleep and never wakes up again, a definition in keeping with older notions of madness as a loss of mind that turned men and women into beasts fit only to be tied and whipped—or buried alive.

In America of the 1840s, however, whips and chains and other forms of physical restraint were giving way, theoretically, to the noncorporeal treatment of mental disease. Under this new regime, the patient was responsible for keeping an eye on himself. Through the "judicious direction and encouragement" (in the asylum, the prison, the school) of the "moral feelings," as Samuel Tuke said, the patient was encouraged to develop "the power of self-restraint." Mr. Hyde was to become his own Dr. Jekyll, even if it meant letting him out of jail for good behavior.[19]

The new "moral" (as opposed to physical, if not immoral) treatment of mental disease recognized the potential for madness, as with Melville's Ahab, in "the whole race from Adam down." Foucault's "negative fact" had now taken on a "very positive" significance, not because it meant that, being sick, the man must be merely a beast, but because it meant that a degree of psychological hurt was to be considered natural to the condition of being human. A little madness was actually beginning to appear "wholesome," as Emily Dickinson said, "even for the king," a healthy antidote to pure reason, once the king or captain of the mind (#1333).

In Melville's fictional attack on the traditional conception of a mind "like a watch" as the distinguishing quality that puts man (and God) above the brutes, Captain Ahab's wounded body, emblem of his emotional hurt and rage, is the mark of his humanity—so long as he does not, in his pain, sacrifice the free will of others. Once Ahab resolves to chase the whale no matter what the cost, he loses his humanity and goes over the edge into total madness, a hole in the sea much like the white, foaming maelstrom that plagued Ulysses, or like the pits and graves and whirlpools in Poe.

The American Romantics, of course, like their counterparts in Europe, had long flirted with the idea that madness is akin to genius. But even those who shunned flights of fancy, as the narrator of "The Fall of the House of Usher" does, welcomed the new theories of insanity on the grounds that the partial nature of madness offered the best hope of curing it. For if it was possible, as Gall said, to "modify" a particular "moral quality" or "intellectual faculty" of the mind according to the development of a "particular cerebral part" of the brain, then modifying the physically diseased part or organ through "moral" treatment might cure the mental disease.

In the treatment of madness in the nineteenth century, therefore, moral means gradually replaced such physical ones as applying cold water to the head and other body parts, or immuring the patient within the confines of a crumbling institution, a domestic vault or the belly of a whale.

Before the Civil War, however, as the American conscience was coming to grips with the moral implications of a society built upon human slavery, but before the dilemma reached the crisis point, it tended to hide its guilty secrets even from itself, airing them, if at all, under the dark cover of metaphor and allegory, as in Poe's classic tale of impending dementia, "The Pit and the Pendulum." Like the rest of the master-slave literature based on faculty psychology that I have been discussing, Poe's tale assumes a pre-Freudian, master-slave model of "repression," both psychological and political.

The mental condition of the prisoner in "The Pit and the Pendulum" is more precarious even than that of the speaker in "The Raven," for if the prisoner falls into the abyss at the bottom of his cell, he will go completely (not just partially) mad. The pit in Poe's psychomyth represents not only the grave but also nepenthe—total forgetfulness, or loss, of the mental faculties, the lowest "level" of the mind—"unconsciousness" as faculty psychology understood it.

The upper reaches of cognition under the old model are represented in Poe's tale, where dementia is the wage of enslavement, by the shafts of light that enter the prisoner's cell through trapdoors in the ceiling. The onlookers who dispense this "skylight," token of the cosmic mind, like the whiteness of Ahab's whale, are merely the agents of a "grand" tribunal, the kangaroo court that, without benefit of habeas corpus, casts the condemned man, a victim of the Inquisition, into his pitch dark cell for (unspecified) crimes against the state— a condition not only roughly equivalent to that of the slave in pre–Civil War America but, under faculty psychology, to the shadow, or "black," side of the psyche that was supposed to be kept under perpetual lock and key by the rational, or "white," side. Even when he swoons, Poe's prisoner can still recall the flames of the candles that burned before him at the bar of this white "justice."

In a post-Freudian scheme, the grand inquisitors in Poe's tale, and the watchers overhead who enforce their regime, political and religious, would be allied with the superego; or they would be other panoptic social constructs, perhaps ones imposed by the arbitrary nature of language. In Poe's psychology, however, these figures, shadowed by white light and hooded like Pym's nemesis at the pole, represent judgment without mercy, the arbitrary will driven by an intellect unchecked by empathy for its victim—another unfeeling mind in the clouds (i.e., "whiteness").

Between the pit of psychic oblivion (the involuntary yielding of the light of the mind to total darkness) and the high court of absolute volition (where the will of the individual is usurped by a "superior" will) there lies in Poe's tale a middle ground of normal interplay among the powers of the mind. The prisoner in "The Pit and the Pendulum" swoons often, probably because he has been drugged. When conscious, however, he retains the presence of mind of Pym aboard the sinking *Ariel*, or of the clear-headed mariner in "The Descent into the Maelstrom" who uses his knowledge of physics to calculate his way out of the spinning vortex.

Incarcerated against his will, the prisoner, of course, desires to escape. Freedom for him, by contrast with those reclusive dreamers in Poe who take to their cells voluntarily, lies *outside* his mournful chamber; to reach it, he brings all of his cognitive faculties to bear, bending every ounce of his willpower to achieve the one desire upon which life and sanity depend.

Instructed by his intellect, the prisoner's mind moves rapidly but systematically from cognition to cognition, searching for a way out: the rats! At the same time, his will must hold in check the fears and anxieties that threaten to swamp it, as when the sharp pendulum descends slowly toward the prisoner's throat; *un*consciousness now would be fatal.

With his own blood, the desperate prisoner (unlike Clemens's Jim in the comic "evasion" that mars the ending of *Huck Finn* for some readers) entices the rats in his cell to gnaw his bonds and set him free. No sooner, however, does the prisoner overcome one great obstacle to free will in human existence—the pendulum, time itself—than he runs up against another, space, the pit. Which also seems to answer to the will of the Grand Inquisitor: all at once the sides of the prisoner's cell begin to close, forcing him into the abyss at the center. From this final precipice, there would seem to be no escape. At the last instant, however, the helpless victim, slave to a hostile physical universe and an alien will, is miraculously arrested in his fall by the long arm of General Lasalle, who liberates the city and throws open the dungeons. Against all logic, Poe has again wrenched around the ending of his tale to show that he, at least, still has free will and a sense of moral decency.

Which is what saves the teller of gothic tales from his own nefarious designs, at least theoretically. Much of the pleasure to be derived from a Poe tale, I think, comes from perversely submitting, as if pushed by an imp, to the "fierceness of the delight" of its horror. Fallen into the tale-teller's clutches for a time, we get carried away, the "victims" of an artful hallucination, like the typical heroines of gothic fiction (especially when written by men).

The descent lasts only "the hour of perusal," however, and our moral liberty is returned to us, perhaps enhanced by having explored forbidden horizons, at the end. The writer's rude assault upon the reader's mind is but a therapeutic game that releases our pent-up feelings—as the prisoner-thoughts of faculty psychology are released from their cells—by temporarily suspending the dictates of the will, as in Hawthorne's sketch of the slumbering (but not extinguished) consciousness.

If we read Poe's wild tale of 1843 not only as exercise in faculty psychology but also as a critique of slavery and the psychological pressures it placed on the American conscience before the Civil War, however, the outcome is far grimmer. "The Pit and the Pendulum" would seem to hint that the author already

suspected, correctly as it turned out, that the dark prisoners whom the abolitionists had failed to liberate by "moral" means would be freed from their dungeons and chains only by military force. The insanity of social upheaval, however, Poe insinuates here as in *Pym,* was not just a disease of the South, which
was not diagnosed as a "problem" region of darkness for the nation until the
1830s. By linking slavery with universal human psychology as he conceived it,
Poe could both assuage (and exploit) the guilt of his part of the dividing nation
and, at the same time, implicate the northern part in the breakup of the whole.[20]

EIGHT

Out of the Black Depths; Or the Transformation

Exaggerations will be revenged in human physiology. . . . Great genius and the people of these states must never be demeaned to romances. As soon as histories are properly told there is no more need of romances.

—*Walt Whitman*

In unconscious states . . . the mind is astonishingly fertile and inventive in its fiction-making, but in conscious states this is not so. The plots we choose to impose on our own lives are limited and limiting. And in no area are they so banal and sterile as in this of love and marriage. Nothing else being available to our imaginations, we will filter our experience through the romantic clichés with which popular culture bombards us.

—*Phyllis Rose*

 FREDERICK DOUGLASS'S white black man, Madison Washington, is the least exotic (in theory) of the composite creatures we have encountered so far. Douglass does not explain how or where his slave develops his heroic characteristics, only that he shares the same noble traits of the "forefathers" of the American Revolution and that he has always had them. (What *is* "revolutionary" here is Douglass's claim that the noble traits in question are not limited by biology to a single race or color.) Even Douglas, however, would seem to be offering no fundamental critique, in *The Heroic Slave*, of his age's received notions of the mechanisms of inheritance.

Nor could Harriet Beecher Stowe, despite her truly radical views on culturation and the genetics of race, entirely slough off the nineteenth century's most basic assumption, before Darwin, about human heredity: that character, whether innate or acquired, was heritable, "like every other faculty" (Galton). In the faculty psychology of Stowe's fiction, moreover, distinct traits of the parents (such as "Ideality" on the one side and "Firmness" on the other) would be passed along intact to the offspring of a Mary Scudder and a John Marvyn of *The Minister's Wooing*. Or those characteristics would reside, fully differentiated, in the minds even of twin brothers, such as the St. Clares. Evidently, in accordance with her age's model of mind, Stowe not only held (where Darwin did not) that all traits of human "character" (benevolence and combativeness equally with intelligence and feeble mindedness) could be inherited; she apparently believed that the mental limits or boundaries of those traits were heritable, too.

As the Twig Is Bent

Even at midcentury, the fundamental assumption behind the characterizations of human beings in most nineteenth-century fiction and science is that character is something the individual is born with. The "mind of the infant," wrote Sampson Reed in his essay "Genius"—a fertile source, along with Reed's *Observations on the Growth of the Mind* (1826), of the organic life-metaphors of Emerson, Thoreau, and the other Transcendentalists—"contains within itself the first rudiments of all that will be hereafter, and needs nothing but expansion; as the leaves and branches and fruit of a tree are said to exist in the seed from which it springs."[1] Thus Thoreau came to know only beans, never turnips or carrots, when he weeded his beanfield in a ritual of self-discipline. A romance disguised as a spiritual autobiography, *Walden* does not ask the reader to become a different person but a whole person, Emerson's great theme.

William James, who did more than any other American to upset it, called this idea of an inborn, essential self "animistic." It posited a ready-made mind to do its thinking, he said, an "ontological" view. For James in 1890, "the richer insight of modern days" would be "the growing conviction that mental life is primarily teleological; that is to say, that our various ways of feeling and thinking have grown to be what they are because of their utility in shaping our reactions to the outer world" (*PBC*, 4).

Thoroughly familiar with Herbert Spencer's *Principles of Psychology* (1855), James noted that "few recent formulas have done more service in psychology than the Spencerian one that the essence of mental life and bodily life are one, namely, 'the adjustment of inner to outer relations'" (*PBC*, 4).

Instead of grounding mind in the indivisible soul, or assigning spirits to trees (a still more "primitive" form of animism), phrenology located the mind of faculty psychology in multiple "organs" of the brain that could be exercised like muscles and other tissue. Thus the phrenologists seemed to agree with Spencer and James that "the essence of mental and bodily life are one." This early "functionalism" was phrenology's greatest legitimate contribution to the

science of mind: mental activity could be explained as a function of neural activity in the brain.

In the phrenologists' view, however, no degree of change in mental function
could bring about a change in kind—in the individual, race, or gender. Since
type, species, in these days before Darwin, had been fixed from creation, the
willow could never become an oak tree, nor the cabbage a cauliflower—not
even with a college education. (For hazarding the theory that "training is everything," Mark Twain's Pudd'nhead Wilson, as late as 1894, was given his unflattering nickname and run out of town; and even Clemens himself seems to have
trouble believing that the drop of "black blood" in Valet de Chambers's veins
did not account for his negritude.) The phrenologists, moreover, with their
rigid physiology of mind, were even greater mental segregationists than the
Scottish Common Sense philosophers, whom they regarded as mere "metaphy-
sicians."

Dugald Stewart, as George Combe noted with disdain, had reasoned that
"the capacities of the human mind have been, in all ages, the same; and that
the diversity of phenomena exhibited by our species is the result merely of the
different circumstances in which men are placed." To Stewart, a democracy of
mind seemed "one of the most obvious suggestions of common sense" (*SP*, 561).

To Combe and the other phrenologists, such a doctrine (that the "character"
of individuals and of nations "depends altogether on external circumstances")
was not only "speculatively erroneous," it also laid "the foundation of a great
deal of hurtful practice" (*SP*, 562). Especially erroneous to Combe were Stewart's views on memory and imagination, which Stewart had held to be "general
faculties" of all sound minds rather than specialized "activities" of the discrete
organs to which phrenology assigned them (*SP*, 469–70). At the foundation of
phrenology, consequently, lies the proposition, in Combe's words, that "there
is no mode of activity of the mind which is not the gift of nature" (i.e., inborn),
"however much it may be improved by judicious exercise" (*SP*, 481).

Believing the brain to be "the organ of mind," the phrenologists did not
wish to contend, since all functioning human beings manifestly possessed
brains, that any individual or class lacked a mind. However, by identifying a
"plurality" of organs, or "congeries" of faculties—as against the doctrine of
"the *whole* brain as one organ" (Stewart)—these early neurologists could assign, as Combe did, "great" quantities of one sort of gray matter to one person,
race or gender and "very little" to another (*SP*, 62).

Hence the common prejudice among whites, even in Britain, that the mental
and, more especially, the moral "advancement" of "the Saxon" would be held
back by "union" with "the Afric" (Mrs. Stowe and Frederic Douglass notwithstanding) because, in Combe's words, the history of Africa ("so far as Africa

can be said to have a history") presents "one unbroken scene of moral and intellectual desolation" (*SP*, 563).

Since the boundaries of their mental organs were thought to be physical, not just metaphysical—each faculty occupying its own "region" or "chamber" in a particular crease or fold or lobe of the brain—the compartments of the phrenologist's mind were watertight in the individual as in the nation, race, or gender.

This meant, in effect, that the mind was divided into ideologically separate regions with different systems of belief, or with beliefs based on fundamentally different motives. The "African" or "southern" region of the mind (where sensation predominated) could never altogether elude the guilty shadows of its fears and desires, no matter how wildly misplaced (in the sense of confusing an effect with a cause) upon "the Negro" or any other object of dark superstition. Like the effeminate Clifford in Hawthorne's *House of the Seven Gables*, or the besieged heroine of a gothic romance, it could run screaming from the house. But the more "primitive" faculties—a faculty was primitive, according to Combe, if it was inherently stronger in one gender than the other—of the "feminine" part of the mind could not escape from its prisoners, no matter how deeply they were buried away, just by desiring to: "If we wish to repress the activity" of a sentiment, said Combe, "we cannot do so merely by willing that the sentiment be quiet" (*SP*, 466).

At the same time, the divided view of mind implied that the "northern" or "European" region (that "masculine" part of the mind governed by cognition) had the duty of a moral watchdog to impose its rational beliefs upon the fetishism of the lower region, though it could never hope to carry out that duty without inciting rebellion and reprisal from below. (Poe, an unregenerate Southerner, whose work was marginalized as "merely regional" by an earlier generation of critics of the romance, was especially sensitive to the psychological pressures of his day because he was writing at precisely the time when the antislavery movement was building steam in the North by locating the national devil in the nether regions beneath the Mason-Dixon line.)

Memory: The Ebony Cabinet

It is the "African" or "feminine" side of Uncle Tom Shelby's mind, according to the segregationist view, that makes him long so for the humble home from which he has been displaced and that explains why, even in her title, Harriet Beecher Stowe identifies Uncle Tom's memory-haunted cabin as the focal spot of her narrative.

As the steamboat carrying Tom to market glides slowly down the river, Harriet Beecher Stowe says of him what Clemens was to say, in effect, of Jim in moments of reverie on the raft when he longs for his wife and family left behind on the shore: "His poor, foolish heart would be turning backward to the Kentucky farm, with its old shadowy beeches—to the master's house, with its wide, cool halls, and, near by, the little cabin, overgrown with the multiflora and bignonia. There he seemed to see familiar faces of comrades, who had grown up with him from infancy." In the haze of memory, Tom sees "his busy wife, bustling in her preparations for his evening meals"; he hears "the merry laugh of his boys at their play, and the chirrup of the baby at his knee" (*UCT,* 124–25).

And then memory fails him: "With a start, all faded, and he saw again the cane-brakes and cypresses and gliding plantations on the shore, and heard again the creaking and groaning of the machinery, all telling him too plainly that all that phase of life had gone by forever" (*UTC,* 125).[2] Actually, it is Tom who is moving here and not the "objects" of his vision; but we have entered, as Emerson did when contemplating apples from the field, the mental landscape of the psychological romance where distant cabins, piled cottonbales, and approaching canebrakes stand for ideas or places in the mind. In this region of gliding forms, Tom's mind, struggling to maintain its sanity, clings for stability and balance to vestiges of the familiar domestic scene, just as Hawthorne's persona in "The Haunted Mind" clings mentally to commonplace objects on the chair in his familiar room.

Or just as Hawthorne's Hester Prynne, exposed to public ridicule on the scaffold, vainly reaches back in memory for comforting images of her idyllic girlhood home: "Standing on that miserable eminence, she saw again her native village, . . . and her paternal home; a decayed house of gray stone, with a poverty-stricken aspect, but retaining a half-obliterated shield of arms over the portal, in token of antique gentility." Then memory fails Hester, too: "Could it be true?" All her fond memories but daydreams? Yes, the marketplace with its stern onlookers (including her old husband), the illegitimate child, and the letter on her breast—"these were her realities,—all else had vanished!" (*SL,* 58–59).

After Arthur Dimmesdale dies, Hester does in actuality what she only dreams of doing here. She returns for a time to England, the country of her reveries of childhood. Hester will not find a happy home in the land of memory, however, for Hawthorne's characters never do. Try as she might, Hester cannot dwell for long in fond recollection of "Our Old Home," as Hawthorne called the British Isles in a collection of essays from his consular years. Thus Hester on the scaffold finds outside her mind "the identical shapes" she finds inside it, a phrase that Hawthorne was to use again in the "American Claimant" manuscripts to designate the infinite regressiveness of memory (*ACM,* 56).

Though Hawthorne tried at least three times to compose a long narrative on the theme of an American "claimant" to an English estate, he was never able to complete a romance set in England. The reason, I think, was not the conventional one suggested by Kenyon and Hilda of *The Marble Faun*, who hasten back to America (as the Hawthornes themselves did in 1860) lest "between two countries we have none at all" (*ACM*, 461).

In one version of the abortive return-to-the-fatherland story, the claimant, called Middleton, enters an English farmhouse which he does not realize to be his ancestral home because, though an old mansion, it still seems too modest. "Is there nothing here that you ought to recognize?" asks his guide, Alice, whose father has cheated Middleton's out of the family inheritance, "—nothing that you kept the memory of, for long ages?" (*ACM*, 27).

Then, in one of the most revealing moments in the manuscripts, Middleton approaches an ebony cabinet, "one of those tall, stately, and elaborate pieces of furniture that are rather articles of architecture than upholstery." Throwing open the doors, Alice reveals the columned portal of a miniature palace with a mirror inside "that opened a long succession of mimic halls, reflection upon reflection, extending to an interminable nowhere." It is the grand seat of the family estate of Middleton's childhood memories, "a fairy reality, inches for yards": "And this then was that palace to which tradition, so false at once, and true, had given such magnitude and magnificence in the stories of the Middleton family, around their shifting firesides in America. Looming afar through the mists of time, the little fact had become a gigantic vision" (*ACM*, 27–28).

The obvious moral of the claimant's literal return to the land of memory, is, "Let the past alone; do not seek to renew it; press on to higher and better things—at all events to other things; ... the right way can never be that which leads you back to the identical shapes that you long ago left behind." Hawthorne then concludes with a refrain worthy of Bunyan urging his readers up the Hill of Difficulty in *The Pilgrim's Progress:* "Onward, onward, onward!" (*ACM*, 56).

Memory alone is always an insufficient faculty in Hawthorne's fiction because it can bring to present consciousness only the "identical shapes" of which the mind has been conscious before. To dwell in memory, Hawthorne had come to believe, was to revert to a perpetual childhood—of the self and the race. It was to languish in a mental Africa, source of the ebony in which Middleton, the quintessential Anglo-American, encases his false visions of property and wealth based on heredity.

In the long chapter of the *Elements* devoted to Memory, Dugald Stewart discovered the most basic function of this faculty to be identical with that of "Conception," a person's capacity to "represent to himself sensations of which he has been formerly conscious" (lust for wealth and property, say) as well as "external objects which he has formerly perceived" (for example, an ebony cabinet). When a conception referred to events, as distinct from objects and their relations, it necessarily carried the knowledge, in the healthy adult mind, that the event was past. When the re-presenting of past events to the mind was accompanied by a conscious act of will, according to Stewart, it was then called, "Recollection" (*WDS*, I, 298).[3]

This is where the memory of "the savage" differed from that of "civilized man." Like a man half-asleep, the primitive mind had no control over its recollections. The savage lived in the land of the past without ever knowing it, a nominative world of symbolic objects, charms and fetishes; and he could only wonder at the causes of such transitive events as an eclipse of the sun, or his sudden capture and transportation to America.

Even the "cultured" mind, when it dwelt too exclusively in the chambers of memory and reflection, said Stewart (and Hawthorne and Poe), was in danger of regressing to a more primitive state. For the faculty of memory, even in its most advanced operations, as Stewart defined it, served only as a repository of old ideas, not a source of new ones—a mirror rather than a lamp. Having collected its album of mental images, memory turned them over to other faculties for further processing, or else the memorialist reverted to a state of infancy or imbecility, much like that of Captain Delano's childish "good nature" in "Benito Cereno."

If Melville's representative man of the Old World, the Hispanic captain, can cease nevermore to reflect upon the raven shadows of the past, his representative man of the New World, the Yankee captain, does not even realize that he is living in a sort of fool's paradise for old boys. (The name of his ship, which has no women on it, is *The Bachelor's Delight*.)

As if parodying Hawthorne's view of history in the American claimant stories ("Onward, onward, onward!"), the New World captain blithely instructs the Old World captain, former master of a slave ship, to throw open his attic and let the fresh air circulate through the recesses of his mind: "'But the past is passed; why moralize upon it? Forget it. See, yon bright sun has forgotten it all, and the blue sea, and the blue sky; these have turned over new leaves.' 'Because they have no memory,' he [the Spanish captain] dejectedly replied; 'because they are not human.'"[4] To be fully human, says the romancer of darkness ("a blackness ten times black" in Hawthorne's case, according to Melville), the mind must recognize and embrace even its fugitive shadows.

Memory, however, is only a starting place. Memory, said Dugald Stewart, merely "regulates" future conduct; the one faculty of the intellect that could actually change it in these days before Darwin was the imagination: "The faculty of Imagination is the great spring of human activity, and the principal source of human improvement," Stewart believed. "Destroy this faculty, and the condition of man will become as stationary as that of the brutes" (*WDS*, vol. 1, 391).

The Hill of Difficulty and the Fall of Man

So long as the faculties were conceived as separate and distinct from one another, the individual parts of a mind or nation were thought to "preserve their individuality," as George Combe said, even in combination. This psychology of discrete faculties, I take it, is one source of the ambiguity in the early nation's doctrine of *e pluribus unum*, a whole out of or among many parts, an ideal that could justify states' rights as well as republicanism. Even chuckle-headed Huck Finn seems to recognize the "mixed up" but undissolved nature of the products of this fundamental American doctrine when he describes "the dreadful pluribus-unum mumps" to the Wilks girls: "'It's a new kind, Miss Mary Jane said.' 'How's it a new kind?' 'Because it's mixed up with other things.' 'What other things?' 'Well, measles, and whooping cough, and erysiplas, and consumpion, and yallerjanders, and brain fever, and I don't know what all.' 'My land! and they call it the *mumps*?'" (*HF*, 203–4).

As much as the notion that the different races had different brains, this idea of irreducible differences within the same brain may have slowed the process of racial integration in nineteenth-century America and helped to justify, in some minds at least, both the "secession" of the southern states from the union and the use of force by the North to hold it together. It also dictated, to a degree, the kinds of narratives that Americans of the nineteenth century constructed about themselves—particularly in their fictions, and particularly when the authors of those fictions were conservative in their racialism, as Hawthorne was.

As a serious model of mind, faculty psychology could not survive Darwinism. Reversing Spencer's adjustment of "inner to outer relations" by proposing that "primitive" mental functions are predetermined by physical form— women love children more than men do because they have more highly developed organs of "Philoprogenitiveness," as indicated by the shape of the head and other body parts—the phrenologists got evolution backward.[5]

The heroes and heroines of the great American literary "renaissance" of the 1850s represent, consequently, a final flowering (or last gasp) of the old psychology. Like Madison Washington or Topsy or Thoreau (the character) at the pond, they are essences, and essences do not fundamentally alter when they brush up against mere circumstance. Instead of adapting to the environment, they require the environment to adapt to them, the reverse of the Spencerian formula. (A chronicle of "inner adjustments" to "outer relations" could be a serviceable definition of the "realistic" psychological fiction that flourished in America in the 1880s and nineties.)

If characters in this literature "just grow," or if they shrivel instead of blossoming—even if they turn into a weed like Roger Chillingworth, or a plank like Claggart in Melville's *Billy Budd*, or a stone like Bartleby, the scrivener—it is not because they have failed to adapt to circumstances; for the congenitally weak or flawed characters of romance, like Hepzeba and Clifford Pyncheon, have never tried to adapt. They have merely reverted to type, gone to seed, either by refusing to cultivate some essential aspect of themselves, or by working one plot in their gardens to the exclusion of all others. (Though Bartleby's "I prefer not to" sounds at first like an Emersonian assertion of self-reliance, his "resolve" to do nothing leads to an atrophy of the will; in the end, Bartleby is just another monomaniac of the period.)

They have, in short, failed to take advantage of the greatest spiritual benefit that faculty psychology seemed to offer common sense. This elusive phantom, source of the old psychology's tremendous hold over the American mind in the nineteenth century, is summed up in the one-word motto that the phrenological Fowlers inscribed above the head of Franz Josef Gall in their advertisements: "Improvement." (Faculty psychology was to leave its most enduring mark upon the theory of mind in the educational bent—Sampson Reed's "expansion"—of much American psychology after 1900, particularly the work of John Dewey.)

Although the mental and moral character of the individual "at any given time" was "the result of his natural endowment of faculties," as George Combe said, those faculties could be "modified" (if not fundamentally changed) through "judicious exercise" in accord with "the circumstances in which he has been placed." Nature might "prescribe the limits to" (Combe) the faculties of the individual, but nurture could determine which inborn faculties were allowed to expand and which lay dormant, thus affecting the balance of the whole (*SP*, 561).

So while it may be true that characters in this earlier fiction do not "develop"— the word Howells and Henry James repeatedly used to describe how character is formed in the modern novel as distinct from what they, Hawthorne, Susanna Rowson, and other writers of the nineteenth century, called the "romance"—it is not true that the characters in classic American literature do not *change*.

Richard Chase was probably right when he wrote that "part of James's great program for improving the novel consisted of the reconstruction, on new grounds, of romance." However, one commonplace established by *The American Novel and Its Tradition* (1957)—and a generation of historical critics who somehow overlooked the importance of faculty psychology upon the characterizations of fiction—is long overdue for revision; and that is the idea that "character" is subservient to "plot" in nineteenth-century fiction (James himself refused to separate the two, of course) because characters in romances, as opposed to novels, "appear to be given quantities rather than emerging and changing organisms."[6]

Characters in the romance do change, I would argue; they just do not change in the same way we have come to expect characters to change in the novel. The reason, again, for these differences in fictional technique is that the psychology underpinning "classic" American literature is different from the psychology that became available to James and modernist fiction at the end of the century.

In American fiction before 1865, characters are types because they are based on a psychology of inborn capacity or faculty; in American fiction of the eighties and nineties, character is "situational" because based on a new, evolutionary, or "developmental" view of the self. Howells, the father of American literary realism, was contrasting the new, "realistic" fiction with the old, "idealistic"—in the sense of exemplary, typical—kind when one of his characters muses, "I suppose I should have to say that we didn't change at all. We develop. There's the making of several characters in each of us; we *are* each several characters, and sometimes this character has the lead in us, and sometimes that."[7]

If, then, in the novel, characters "develop," in the romance, they metamorphose. The heroes and heroines of romance, that is, like the villains and fools, may not be able to effect in themselves a change in kind. But like the acorn or butterfly, they can undergo a change of form, or "transformation."

The chief transformation in Hawthorne's *Marble Faun* (British title: *The Transformation*) is that of the Faun himself, the young "pagan" Donatello, a creature of prelapsarian innocence like the classical nymphs and fauns of his ancestral Italy.[8] Donatello has inherited his family's "deficiencies both of intellect and heart," and for him, as for Roderic Usher, they reach the crisis point amid crumbling walls, in his case the walls and towers of ancient Rome (*MF*, 235).

Walking through the oldest part of the city at night, Donatello and his friends come upon a precipice: "They all bent over, and saw that the cliff fell perpendicularly downward to about the depth, or rather more, at which the tall palace rose in height above their heads. Not that it was still the natural, shaggy front of the original precipice; for it appeared to be cased in ancient stonework, through which the primeval rock showed its face, here and there, grimly and doubtfully. Mosses grew on the slight projections, and little shrubs sprouted out of the crevices, but could not much soften the stern aspect of the cliff" (*MF*, 168). Soon after, at the apparent bidding of Miriam, the dark lady of Hawthorne's tale, Donatello heaves a mysterious monk over this steep edge to his death. The murder takes place as in a dream, and suddenly Donatello's innocence is lost: as with Adam after the fall, the "simple and joyous creature," says Hawthorne, "was gone forever" (*MF*, 172).

Donatello's fall has its fortunate side, however, for like a stone statue turned to life, it kindles him into "a man." "In the black depths," says Hawthorne, "the Faun had found a soul, and was struggling with it towards the light of Heaven" (*MF*, 268). Much later in the book, Miriam will even speculate that Donatello's crime may have been a blessing in disguise. "Was it a means of education," she wonders, "bringing a simple and imperfect nature to a point of feeling and intelligence, which it could have reached under no other discipline?" The other characters dare not follow into the "unfathomable abysses" where Miriam's perilous meditations lead. So she goes on fearlessly alone: "I delight to brood on the verge of this great mystery" (*MF*, 434).

Miriam's great mystery is one that Hawthorne himself brooded upon throughout his career as a romancer: "The story of the Fall of Man! Is it not repeated in our Romance of Monte Beni?" (subtitle of *The Marble Faun* in both British and American editions) (*MF*,434).

Though steeped in Calvinist theology, Hawthorne was fundamentally a psychologist rather than a theologian. By original "sin," therefore, he usually means guilt, the difference being, as Doris Lessing has said in a more recent tale of Italy, that sin can be atoned for but guilt must be borne. Yet if sin is just a birthmark of the race and an instrument, at that, "in the education of intellect and soul," as in Donatello's case, why does Hawthorne feel so guilty about it that even his most innocent characters, especially women, must suffer as if their hearts were black as murder? (*MF*, 435).

The fall (and subsequent "moral" rise) of Miriam suggests that Hawthorne may have had in mind a specific transgression—incest, the sin of the fathers that more than any other, he thought, threatened the very foundations of the New England home—beneath all the veiled references to secret sin in his fiction.

For the view from the foot of Donatello's shaggy parapet, we must look back from Hawthorne's last romance to his earliest, *Fanshawe*. Here is the same prospect translated to the wilderness of Maine: "They stood beneath a precipice, so high that the loftiest pine tops (and many of them seemed to soar to heaven) scarcely surmounted it. . . . yet steep as is the height, trees and bushes of various kinds have clung to the rock, wherever their roots could gain the slightest hold. . . . the cliff is indebted to them for much of the beauty that tempers its sublimity."[9]

The villain of Hawthorne's narrative, an "angler" of souls who has snared the young heroine, Ellen Langton, will die when he attempts to scale these rugged heights. So precarious is this slope, a landmark in all of Hawthorne's major works, that it might be called The Hill of Difficulty, which presents itself to Christian in John Bunyan's *The Pilgrim's Progress*.

With its doorways to hell in every hillside, *The Pilgrim's Progress* had long been required reading in New England, and Hawthorne knew Bunyan well. Just before Donatello commits the murder, Miriam and Hilda sound as if they have been studying Bunyan's allegories. Approaching the precipice of a moral crisis, Miriam leans toward fatalism. The "pit of blackness," she says, lies "beneath us, everywhere"; human happiness is but a "thin crust spread over it." Hilda protests that we alone are responsible for our moral condition: "there is no chasm," she urges, "nor any hideous emptiness under our feet, except what the evil within us digs" (*MF*, 161–62).

In Bunyan's Christian allegory, The Hill of Difficulty is a test of moral fortitude. When Christian, the weary pilgrim, comes upon this hill on the road of life, he is tempted to go around it, but at last he chooses "the narrow way," which lies straight up the hill. Fortifying himself with a drink from a spring— a spring likewise relieves the craggy landscape in *Fanshawe*—Christian sings this little verse as he begins to climb:

> The Hill, though high, I covet to ascend,
> The difficulty will not me offend:
> For I perceive the way to life lies here.
> Come, pluck up Heart, lets neither faint nor fear:
> Better, thou difficult, th' right way to go,
> Than wrong, though easie, where the end is wo.[10]

In the psychological landscape of the nineteenth-century American imagination, a steep hill, or precipice, signifies not only a moral challenge, as in Bunyan's narrative, but a test of mental balance, too, the way to sanity. It is this steep and narrow path that Miriam must tread, as Hester Prynne before her.

English and Christian on her mother's side, Miriam is Italian and Jewish on her father's. Bound by him to marry a close member of the family, Miriam runs away because she fears "the insanity which often developes itself in old, close-kept breeds of men, when long unmixed with newer blood" (*MF*, 430–31). At first, she is thought to have committed suicide, but Miriam is stronger in mind than Zenobia, the likewise darkly beautiful woman of complicated blood who (in the preferred fashion for females, according to Havelock Ellis later in the century) drowns herself for love in *The Blithedale Romance*. Miriam, says Hawthorne, is "not of the feeble nature" that resorts to such a "poor resource" (*MF,* 431). Miriam will throw herself over the brink for no man. Instead, says Hawthorne, she "flung herself upon the world and speedily created a new sphere," the common sense way of warding off the mental disorders to which the imaginative, artistic mind was thought to incline (*MF,* 435).

Madness follows Miriam like a shadow, however, when she perversely admits the Monk into her studio as a model. "Insanity must have been mixed up with his original composition," she will say of this dark figure, Donatello's victim, in her "confession" at the end of the romance. "He had me in his power" (*MF,* 432). The Monk's power over Miriam comes from his connection with her father. The successor, if not the original, of the man her father had consented to be her husband (a man "so evil, so treacherous, so wild, and yet so strangely subtle"), the Monk casts a visible shadow over Miriam's portraits of herself and other women.

Though a skilled artist, Miriam has trouble depicting women of passion. She begins with a "fiery conception" of "perfect womanhood" only to see her work turn upon her in "utter scorn" for the "feeling which at first took such powerful possession" of her mind and hand.[11] Against her will and to her dismay, the noble female figures upon Miriam's canvases turn into man haters whose own hands are "crimsoned" by the blood of their male victims. Again and again in her cloistered studio (the "outward type," says Hawthorne, of the "poet's haunted imagination"), Miriam "failed not to bring out the moral, that woman must strike through her own heart to reach a human life, whatever were the motive that impelled her" (*MF,* 44). (When Zenobia is dragged from the water in *The Blithedale Romance,* the grappling hook is lodged in her breast just above the heart.)

Miriam, apparently, has been poisoned against men by her father, whether for her protection, like Beatrice in "Rappaccini's Daughter," or to make her his own. Hawthorne himself grew up in a closely knit household dominated by women, and biographers have long wondered whether incest, or incestuous desires, might not have been the "great secret" that Hawthorne, according to his friend Herman Melville, "concealed" throughout his life, and "which would, were it known, explain all the mysteries of his career." (Miriam's illicit feelings are associated explicitly with a forbidden "brother," Brother Antonio, the monk who serves as a male model in her studio.)

When the jealous Donatello offers to toss the monk from the cliff, Miriam consents with a glance. Whatever Miriam's relation with her father has been in the past, she is now casting her father's shadow from her, and thus the shadow of both incest and madness, often linked in the nineteenth-century imagination, especially in New England, where class consciousness left only a few suitable old families for bluebloods to marry into. This is the subterranean "fall" (and consequent moral rise) of the dark woman in Hawthorne's story, masked by the more conventional musings of Kenyon and the Protestant vestal, Hilda, on the subject.

As with the prisoners that spring forth in "The Haunted Mind," a repressed or potential part of Donatello is also released by his feelings of remorse for the murder. "Here is Donatello," Miriam jibes long after the deed, "haunted with a strange remorse and an immitigable resolve to obtain what he deems justice upon himself." When Donatello confesses to the authorities out of guilt— birthmark of the human race, as opposed to such prehuman species as fauns and nymphs—this primordial child of instinct with "no head for argument" has acquired both a brain and a heart ("that intelligence which passion had developed in him") (*MF*, 173, 433). Miriam has had a brain all along, but her restless intellect has overshadowed her emotions. Miriam's fall is fortunate, too, at bottom, because it restores her faculties of feeling without miring her in the slough of sexual loathing on the one hand or the tarn of incestuous desire on the other (a dilemma Hawthorne himself may have faced as a young man before his marriage to Sophia Peabody).

Had America's chief romancer of the head and heart followed the stony inclination of his Puritan forebears and denied the light to the creatures of his brain because of their transgressions, his new Adam and Eve might have slipped backward through the abyss of sin into the "black depths" of total depravity— or madness. By awakening the slumbering moral faculties of his two principal characters, Hawthorne has transformed them into more complex versions of themselves and thereby "saved" them (or at least Donatello) from being slaves to the "base" or "animal" or "savage" aspects of their natures. As phantasmagoric products not only of Hawthorne's brain but also of the mind of his time, however, the marble faun and dark lady of Hawthorne's romance have not "evolved" (or "developed") into *different* creatures, as their successors in modern fiction will have the power to do. Not even the most morally advanced and socially successful heroes and heroines of Hawthorne's romances can do that. The best they can hope for, under the dispensation of faculty psychology, is to achieve a sane balance among their faculties, and among themselves.

The Marriage of Head and Heart

Besides studying Dugald Stewart's *Elements of the Philosophy of the Human Mind* in college, Nathaniel Hawthorne withdrew at least once from the Salem Library Stewart's *Philosophical Essays*. His program in that book, as Stewart summarized it, was to examine "how far . . . our moral feelings or emotions are entitled to consideration; checking, on the one hand, our speculative reasonings, when they lead to conclusions at which our nature revolts; and on the other, sanctioning those decisions of the understanding, in favor of which the head and the heart unite their suffrages." [12]

Stewart went on to determine (as Hawthorne did) that "our moral feelings or emotions" are entitled to as much consideration as "our speculative reasonings" in making ethical choices; and William James would soon give the emotions even greater suffrage in shaping humane social institutions.

To George Combe and the mental conservatives, however, an equal union of the mind's constituents seemed visionary, if not miscegenational. Even marriage, which could lead to hereditary insanity if the parties were too closely related, could only bring two healthy minds or two eligible houses (or genders or states) into alliance; it could not create "a new individual." This was the province, even for Stewart and Hawthorne, of Imagination alone. Memory and most of the other intellectual faculties were simply "combining" faculties, like marriage and the federal government.

Combe and the mental segregationists had their adversaries, of course. As early as 1840, Frederick Rauch, first president of Marshall College, attacked "the habit of representing mind as a compound of many faculties, as a whole made up of parts" in his *Psychology, or a View of the Human Soul, Including Anthropology,* the first book in English to use—a full fifteen years before Spencer's *Principles*—the new term for the study of mind in its title. The divided view "has been more or less relinquished," Rauch wrote, more hopefully than accurately; "and one directly opposed to it has been received. There is but *one* thinking power in man." [13] Rauch, however, was about fifty years ahead of his time. Though Orestes Brownson and others hailed it as a work of genius, his *Psychology* had little impact in schools dominated by the textbooks of Thomas Upham, Francis Wayland, and Joseph Haven. [14]

In America, the idea of a single integrated mind, or "state" of mind, would not replace that of separate and discrete faculties—"all related to each other, and yet all comparatively independent" (Upham)—until well after the Civil War. [15] Even most abolitionists, including the neo-Lamarckian Stowes and Whitmans, still held, in common with the most ardent advocates of states' rights, a pre-Darwinian notion of the composite nature of human identity. Thus the characters in their narratives, and particularly their mental organs, are stitched together out of whole pieces of the old mind and heart.

As long as American culture labored under the inherent segregationism of the old psychology, the most perfect of unions could not be conceived to effect the synthesis of inherited traits (resulting in a genuinely new species) posited by the post-Darwinian view of heredity—not even under one constitution. Rather, under the old eugenics of the faculties, any "union" of houses, races, or states represented, at best, a new (and potentially precarious) *balance* among the traits inherited from individuals. Thus even Frederick Rauch, when affirming that "the mind is neither a multitude of faculties, nor is it a simple, identical activity," fell back upon a familiar metaphor: "it is a *union*."[16]

Though Dugald Stewart disdained mechanistic explanations of remembering, he could not resist an analogy that had become a commonplace by his day: "The analogy between committing a thing to memory that we wish to remember, and engraving on a tablet a fact that we wish to record, is so striking as to present itself to the vulgar." (*WDS*, vol. 1, 304). To the vulgar mind, this analogy would also seem to apply strikingly well to Holgrave's daguerreotype plates in *The House of the Seven Gables* (1852), Hawthorne's most comprehensive meditation on history and the past.

The mysterious flashes of light in the house of the seven gables on the night Judge Pyncheon dies are explained the next morning when Holgrave, an infiltrating Maule in disguise, hands Phoebe Pyncheon a newly developed daguerreotype of the dead man. He took it, Holgrave explains, "as a memorial valuable to myself; for, Phoebe, there are hereditary reasons that connect me strangely with that man's fate" (*HSG*, 303). In Holgrave's skillful hands, the daguerreotype has become what Oliver Wendell Holmes would soon pronounce all of photography to be—a "mirror with a memory." Holgrave is applying the new science to make an accurate picture of the moment for future use, the proper function of memory as Hawthorne understood it from Stewart.[17]

At first, however, Holgrave's "sun-pictures," as daguerreotypes were once called, would seem to ally him with the unreflecting sun worship of Captains Delano and Ahab. Of all the personages in Hawthorne's tale, Holgrave, the "reformer" who sees the past as a "dead giant" clinging to the present, is the least likely to play the part of memorialist. What has changed Holgrave's mind, of course, is Phoebe, who uses sunlight in the proper way, bringing the sunshine of her disposition to every corner of the dark old house.[18]

When Holgrave, man of ideas and images, has been warmed by Phoebe's affections, he comes down from his isolated chamber among the gables to join her in the garden, much as Hawthorne remembered himself coming down from his ivory tower ten years before to marry Sophia Peabody. As an antidote to his violent brooding upon the past, Holgrave has written down a chapter of the family history in "the form of a legend." The therapeutic narrative tells the story of Alice Pyncheon, Phoebe's ancestor, who is made, under hypnosis, to do the will of the wizard Matthew Maule.

Holgrave's reading mesmerizes Phoebe: his newly found artistry of words invests him with a power that a merely photographic science, in Hawthorne's mind, could never achieve. Unlike his ancestor, the wizard Maule, however, Holgrave refuses to violate the sanctity of another human heart with the powerful tool that his skill as a romancer gives him. Having descended from the wizard's tower to the fringed garden, from attic to adytum, he will trespass no further without Phoebe's consent.

Thenceforth, the curse upon the house—brought about, like the madness that follows incest, by the sins of the fathers—is lifted, and the two families can intertwine safely and sanely in the new generation. The couple in the garden are transformed by moonlight, and a changed Holgrave can say: "Moonlight, and the sentiment in man's heart, responsive to it, are the greatest renovators and reformers" (*HSG*, 214).

Instead of madness, moonlight in Hawthorne's works is usually a metaphor for the transforming power of the imagination, the only faculty, according to Dugald Stewart, capable of generating "a new creation of its own" (*WDS*, vol. 1, 355). Not so critically disposed toward the imagination as he is sometimes made out to be, Stewart believed that the "operations of imagination serve to illustrate the intellectual processes, by which the mind deviates from the models presented to it by experience, and forms to itself new and untried objects of pursuit" (*WDS*, vol. 1, 359). Without an active imagination, in other words, Stewart believed, the human mind is condemned to dwell endlessly upon its own changeless reflections of the past, as in the mirrors of Middleton's ebony cabinet, devolving thereby in infinite regression to an "interminable nowhere." This was a condition Stewart found as odious as Hawthorne did.

As a faculty of the intellect, however, the imagination alone produced but pale images, idealized forms (to common sense) of real life. If they are to take on the color of reality, said Hawthorne, the shapes of dreams and moonshine must be touched with "the sentiment in men's hearts," usually figured in his work as a fire burning warmly on the hearth, as in the "Custom House" sketch. There thought and feeling, the chill moonlight from the night sky and the rich glow of the anthracite within, come together and imbue themselves each with the other, as in the "neutral territory" of the romance—or a healthy marriage.

To ensure a healthy grafting of the two families in *The House of the Seven Gables*, both branches must be uprooted from the house of memory, with its infinite regressions to the past, and transplanted to a new house in the country. It is Holgrave, the reformer turned romancer, who wishes at the end that the Pyncheon's country house were built of stone instead of wood, a far cry from the "radical" who earlier wished to purify the old house in town by fire. Then the family might alter the interior in each generation "to suit its own taste and convenience," he says, while the exterior, unchanging, might signify permanence through the years (*HSG*, 314). (We know that the new family line of Maule-Pyncheons will branch profusely into the future because Miss Hepzibah's hens start laying again the moment they alight at the new house.)

What Holgrave (and Hawthorne) have in mind for themselves and their descendants here, as Richard Harter Fogel has said, is not, however, a Hegelian "synthesis" but a balance between the two houses and their constituent faculties, a union of equals (but opposites) based on radically new views of marriage and the family that were taking hold in American culture before the Civil War but that had not yet been renovated by the new views of mind that were soon to come.

This is why Hester Prynne, though stronger than the girlish Phoebe, cannot be allowed to redeem the times in *The Scarlet Letter:* she is a dutiful single mother with a balanced mind, but her "marriage" has failed. The "angel" who one day atones for the evils engendered by the forefathers will be a woman, Hawthorne prophesies at the end of *The Scarlet Letter,* and she will be "wise" like Hester, as well as "pure and beautiful." But she will be made wise by joy, he says, rather than "dusky grief." If this revelation carries us back to the conventional notion of the angel in the household, Hawthorne's sympathetic portraits of dark ladies also draw this less predictable moral about the sexes: that before the new Eve can save her fallen Adam, "the whole relation between man and woman" must be reestablished "on a surer ground of mutual happiness" (*SL*, 263).

As a true record of the past, Holgrave's daguerreotypes, not to be confused with stereotypes, will protect both himself and the ex-convict Clifford, who has fled the scene of Judge Pyncheon's mysterious death in a mad panic. They will also prevent the faulty recollections of ebony cabinets for marble mansions that haunt the Pyncheons's parlor along with the Middletons' fireside in the American claimant manuscripts.

Besides taking true pictures of his own, the iconoclastic Holgrave, whose name, nonetheless, implies an old iconography of mind, reveals the debilitating illusion behind the Pyncheon family's most revered picture of the past. "That picture!" says Clifford of the great portrait of Colonel Pyncheon, founder of the line, on the wall: "'Whenever I look at it, there is an old, dreamy recollection haunting me, but keeping just beyond the grasp of my mind. Wealth, it seems to say!—boundless wealth! . . . What could this dream have been!' 'Perhaps I can recall it,' answers Holgrave. 'See! There are a hundred chances to one, that no person, unacquainted with the secret, would ever touch this spring'" (*HSG*, 315).

Memory has touched the spring, but only imagination and the moral sentiments can dispel the false dreams of enormous wealth and power that have long haunted the house of Pyncheon. The long-hidden Indian deed to vast lands that Holgrave finds behind the fond family portrait is now a worthless relic of hereditary succession to property and the ruthless exploitation of the "natives."

Incest, Cannibalism, and Other Improprieties in the New England Home: Fleeing the Coop of Heredity

Theft, mesmerism, attempted suicide, conspiracy to murder, and witchcraft: Hawthorne might have stopped with these as sufficiently indicating the decline of the Pyncheons and the Maules, the two New England families who have been feuding for two centuries in *The House of the Seven Gables*. For a full measure of degeneracy, however, he also heaps madness, incest, and worse upon both their houses. These uglier forms of depravity creep in by way of the henhouse in the Pyncheon's garden, where an "illustrious breed" of chickens has grown all but barren under the shadow of the grim old house.

Once as large as turkeys, Hepzibah Pyncheon's wizened hens have shrunk in the present generation to the size of pigeons. Of these "feathered people," says their amused chronicler, it was "evident that the race had degenerated, like many a noble race besides, in consequence of too strict a watchfulness to keep it pure" (*HSG*, 89). Many a close-kept New England breed would benefit, this play of fowls insinuates, if not from a fox in the henhouse, then by a bird of another feather from time to time. (Hawthorne's comic conceit can also be taken to insinuate that, in his conservative view, any intermingling of the races was best kept to the "feathered" kind.)

The only living offspring of these "speckled" (and thus miscegenational?) fowl, the Roderick Usher of the henhouse, bears all the "hereditary marks" of the family line: knobby knees, motley plumage, and a scanty crest atop its tiny head that resembles the scraggly turban with which old Miss Hepzibah covers her thinning gray hair. This is a tale, evidently, of heredity and family inbreeding (*HSG*, 152). (And, as usual, it has all the family resemblances engendered upon nineteenth-century fiction by faculty psychology, thus constituting "the romance" as a recognizable genre in the best Wittgensteinian fashion.)

Miss Hepzibah, of course, has never married, but she loves her brother, Clifford, who has returned at last to the family fold after thirty years in jail for a crime he did not commit and who, on the whole, prefers the company of his pretty young cousin Phoebe. No sin within her capabilities is so black that Hepzibah would not commit it to gratify her mentally wasted brother.

One day a "prodigious cackling and gratulation" emanates from the region of the chicken coop. Of Chanticleer's two "wives," the chickless one has at last produced an egg, and Hepzibah at once appropriates it for Clifford's breakfast. "Thus unscrupulously," says Hawthorne, "did the old gentlewoman sacrifice the continuance, perhaps, of an ancient feathered race, with no better end than to supply her brother with a dainty that hardly filled the bowl of a teaspoon!" (*HSG*, 153). (He might have said the same, in 1852, of another ancient race of dark plumage whom the American housewife and the Bristol merchant sacrificed almost as willingly for such dainties as cotton and sugar.)

Since the ancestral chickens represent the Pyncheon family in miniature, this act of "cannibalism" also borders upon genocide. Miss Hepzibah's "incestuous" tie to her brother has caused her to break the oldest of taboos, and this atavism brings madness, a comic frenzy in which Hawthorne shows both the evils of an unreflecting primitivism and the folly of trying to exorcise the shadows of the past by a half-baked program, as he saw it, of social reform. (Hawthorne's meliorative view of history called for genuine change, but at a rate that would have been far less acceptable to Frederick Douglass than to G. W. F. Hegel.)

In a bizarre closing chapter of *Seven Gables* entitled "The Flight of Two Owls," Hepzibah and Clifford, its ancient siblings, bolt from the old house like a couple on a long delayed honeymoon. Miss Hepzibah has hardly set foot outside for half a century, when, suddenly, she and her brother are thrust upon a train, the fire and brimstone conveyance upon which Hawthorne's Mr. Trancendentalist glides to hell in "The Celestial Railroad."

As his mind careens along, threatening to jump the track at every turn, Clifford, like Roderick Usher, attributes his mental troubles to the old house itself: "It is clear to me as sunshine—were there any in the sky—that the greatest possible stumbling-blocks in the path of human happiness and improvement are those heaps of bricks, and stones, consolidated with mortar, or hewn timber, fastened together with spike-nails, which men painfully contrive for their own torment, and call them house and home" (*HSG*, 261).

Clifford is looking for a mobile home, a perch or train (or raft), where his thoughts need not dwell for long. "Let us alight, as the birds do," he tells Hepzibah, "and perch ourselves on the nearest twig, and consult whither we shall fly next!" The flight of these two old birds, however, shows the folly, in Hawthorne's view, of the individual's trying to escape from the house of heredity through adaptation to new environments in a single generation. "They think you mad," Hepzibah tells her brother as he rants on in this vein, a feeble echo of Holgrave, the radical "reformer," who has earlier fulminated (in *his* madness) about how "the moss-grown and rotten Past is to be torn down, and lifeless institutions to be thrust out of the way" (*HSG*, 262–67, 179).

It is not the New England home and family as institutions that have driven Clifford temporarily madder than before; it is their decay under a greedy patriarchy, ever watchful of its hereditary power. For generations, the head men of the house of Pyncheon have cheated the descendents of the rival Maule family of their rightful inheritance, and what now "taints the whole house" for Clifford, who usually suffers from amnesia, is the "vision or image" in his "mind's eye" of the present (or immediately former) head of household presiding over the parlor in an obscene parody of the Victorian father (*HSG*, 261, 263). For evil Judge Pyncheon has recently died there of an apoplexy—or the family curse; and Clifford can not get the bloody image of the corpse out of his head. It is this vivid mental picture, the fixed idea of madness, that he is attempting to flee.

The wild thoughts of Clifford and his sister are arrested, however, when their train stops at a solitary way station, and they are presented with a trinity of architectural images: a dilapidated wooden church, "black with age"; a deserted farmhouse "as venerably black as the church"; and "the relics of a wood-pile" (*HSG*, 266). Like the disenchanted fairy reality of Middleton's ebony cabinet, these ebon relics of village life shadow forth the couple's only sane course of action: to return home and live with the "results" of their past experience, which memory holds intact, according to Dugald Stewart, "for the future regulation of our conduct" (*WDS*, vol. 1, 307–308).

This is their only healthy choice and, to Hawthorne's mind, where home and family rose high above the ruins of these other social edifices, especially the church, their best hope: for "sprouting up among the chips and scattered logs," green grass is replenishing the rotten woodpile at the farmhouse door (*HSG*, 266). Instead of purifying it by fire, as Holgrave would the house of the seven gables, this relic of the past may someday supply the old farmhouse's new inhabitants and winter visitors with the warm glow of a cozy hearth.

The Will to Believe

Haunted by the image of the patriarchal corpse in the parlor, Clifford may also be fleeing the old house to escape the town beadle, because, a ghost of the past, he thinks he is guilty of frightening Judge Pyncheon to death. If so, Clifford's diseased mind has confused "Conception" and "Imagination," a common failing of the aesthete in his ivory tower, according to the phrenologists, and of the mind of the savage.

Imagination, said George Combe, is to be conceived as "the power of representing things absent to one's self or others." In this "primitive and most correct sense," he observes, "there is scarcely a shade of difference" between imagining an idea and conceiving one (*SP,* 481–82).[19]

Since the powers of discerning cause and effect (causality) and other relations (comparison) are feeble in the mind of the savage, the phrenologist believed, it never moved beyond that "primitive" level of mental activity where the intellectual functions are undifferentiated. Moreover, the savage's acts of belief were governed by feeling (the "African" side of the mind) rather than intellection (the "European" side). Hence the "fetishism" that Combe as well as Hegel attributed to "the African tribes." A thing absent, a god or devil, say, is displaced upon a present object (such as Queequeg's little black idol, Ahab's white whale, or Poe's raven), which, though real, is actually unrelated except in the mind of the believer, who merely *feels* a connection between them, and thus believes without a conscious act of will. Not only is the savage, then, by definition, a madman, but the man of imagination in this philosophy is also a kind of savage to the extent that he believes in his own analogies and simulacra.

In the divided view of mind promulgated by the mental segregationists of the nineteenth century, "Perception", "Conception," "Memory," and "Imagination"—the mainstays of the fiction writer and essayist if not the poet—had nothing directly to do with emotion. They were "modes" of "the Knowing and Reflecting faculties," which, according to Combe, "are subject to the will, or rather constitute will themselves" (*SP,* 467). The "Propensities and Sentiments," by contrast, "have the attribute of Sensation alone." That is, they have no memory or imagination because they "only feel." Any belief based on emotion, said Combe, was merely "the *consequence* of the feelings having become overwhelming" and did not involve conscious choice (*SP,* 467, 463).

It was on this issue of belief that Combe found Dugald Stewart particularly "blameable." To Stewart as to Coleridge, belief was always preceded by cognition, even when the object of belief was known to be fictitious, as in the theater. And it was followed by an act of conscious choice. In short, Stewart believed in the will to believe.[20]

To Combe's mind, which assigned various mental functions to independent physical organs in the brain, Stewart's theory of belief was, again, merely "metaphysical." For Hawthorne (and later William James), however, it went to the heart of moral philosophy and the moral life because, in the mind's theater, Stewart gave the emotions a leading role in distinguishing virtue from vice.

Thus a recently wed Sophia Hawthorne wrote to her mother in 1843: "Waldo Emerson knows not much of love— He has never yet said any thing to show that he does— He is an isolation— He has never yet known what union meant with any soul——."[21] The sage of Concord, greatest philosopher of his time in America, Hawthorne was saying, in effect, was not to be considered a fully developed adult. He was incomplete—like Donatello, the prehuman creature that her husband would write about in *The Marble Faun*, who must learn to love (and hate) before he can be completely humanized, a view of human growth that no longer treated the passions as a mere obstacle in the path to mental health but as the pathway itself.

NINE

The Prisoner of Omelas

There was an exhibition at the Zoological Park, in the Bronx, yesterday which
had for many of the visitors something more than a provocation to laughter....
The exhibition was that of a human being in a monkey cage. The human
being happened to be a Bushman, one of a race that scientists do not rate high
in the human scale, but to the average non-scientific person in the crowd of
sight seers there was something about the display that was unpleasant.

—*New York Times* (1906)

Over an immense department of our thought we are still, all of us, in the
savage state. Similarity operates, but abstraction has not taken place.

—*William James*

 IF A MATURE black man, fully developed in every fac-
ulty (like Madison Washington when he takes command
of the slave ship in Frederick Douglass's *The Heroic Slave*),
had been put in charge of Huck Finn's adventures on the
river instead of "Nigger Jim" (the sometimes demeaning
stereotype, however well-intentioned, of a motherly black
man who must take orders from a white boy who is sometimes disguised as a
girl), then the raft would never have been hit by a steamboat. And all hands
would have made it safely up the Ohio to freedom, as planned (however infea-
sibly), instead of drifting deeper and deeper southward into bondage, like Poe's
Pym, in a fog of indecision and dreamlike suspension of the will.

The collision of raft and steamboat on the Mississippi of Samuel Clemens's
imagination suggests how little power the black genie of Huck's tale has over
his own destiny after emancipation. (At the end of Clemens's narrative, Jim,
emasculated, during the "evasion," by the conventions of aristocratic fiction, is
left to grovel in the pit of minstrel show darkeyism.) It also represents a historic
divide between "classic" and "modern" American literature, and between ways
of thinking about the mind. Though we can only recover the tip of the submerged vessel here, the remaining chapters in this book deal with the new psychology, its effect upon American literature and culture after the Civil War,

and, specifically, the reluctance (or inability) of the generation of Americans who fell between the "Romantics" and the "moderns" to give up, altogether, the old ways of thinking about themselves.

Old Times on the Raft

On the surface, the thinking processes of Huck and Jim as conceived in 1885 by Clemens—a borderline Southerner who went west to wait out the Civil War and then returned to live permanently in the East—may seem to be propelled along, still, by the mechanisms of faculty psychology that carry Uncle Tom's and Mr. Haley's thoughts forward on the wagon taking Tom to market. But Huck's thoughts are soon launched upon the *stream* that William James was to describe in *The Principles of Psychology* (1890) as "the stream of thought, of consciousness, or of subjective life."[1]

Huck's celebrated crisis of conscience begins as a parody, or comic reversal, of the traditional mental debate of faculty psychology at moments of moral crisis; but when Huck decides to go to hell, Clemens is carrying "blackness" to new latitudes in American culture. The instant Huck conceives the idea of writing a letter, he starts to rationalize: Jim would be better off back home if he's *got* to be a slave anyway, so Huck should send the letter; Miss Watson will be so mad she'll sell Jim down the river and he and Jim will be "disgraced," so Huck had better *not* send it. Torn between conflicting "rational" alternatives, Huck decides to compose the letter and see how he feels. Then he "set there thinking" and "thinking" and "went on thinking" (*HF*, 222).

It is neither Satan nor the impetus of a perverse idea, however, that precipitates Huck's socially "insane" choice to help a slave go free—his thinking faculties try manfully to make him send the letter—it is the boy's pent-up emotions. Before he can stop them, Huck's reflections, like Uncle Tom's on the steamboat to New Orleans, shade into a dream of the past, and his suppressed feelings break loose from their cells and come rushing back in a litany of love for Jim that brings the debate in Huck's mind to a screeching turnaround. When Huck destroys the incriminating letter, his dilemma is said to be resolved "forever" (*HF*, 223).

Huck does not realize that his conflict is an *internal* one, a battle going on inside his mind and heart; thus he assigns his thoughts and feelings to external agencies incarnated in parts of the body: "it hit me all of a sudden that here was the plain hand of Providence slapping me in the face and letting me know my wickedness was being watched all the time from up there in heaven, whilst I was stealing a poor old woman's nigger that hadn't ever done me no harm" (*HF*, 222).

Huck objectifies his guilt in the chastening hand of "Providence" because his mind is so simple and childlike that it does not recognize his gods and demons as reflections of his own fears and desires, especially his love for Jim. This is the "fetishism of the savage" who divides the universe into external precincts belonging to God and the Devil, North and South, white and black because (according to G. W. F. Hegel and more recent phenomenologists of the self) he is afraid to confront his own "evil" impulses. A marginalized white "boy" who talks "black," according to Shelley Fisher Fishkin, Huck would appear to have a "black mind" to go with his black tongue.

Within Huck's "troubled" breast, there would also seem to beat a "feminine" heart. Under the watchful eyeball of the great overseer, who "ain't agoing to allow no such miserable doings to go only just so fur and no further," Huck's blood curdles in his veins, and/or he is chilled to the very marrow of his bones: "I most dropped in my tracks I was so scared." Without Jim, his shadow, to turn to, Huck is preparing to swoon into the outstretched arms (or hand) of "One that's always on the lookout" (*HF*, 222).

After deciding to write the letter, which, when sent, will be irretrievable (without the assistance of Poe's Monsieur Dupin), Huck feels suddenly "light as a feather," then "glad and excited," then "good and all washed clean of sin" (*HF*, 222). Ready to get down on his knees and pray to his new lord and master now, Huck is "trembling," an appropriately "primitive," and therefore "female," response to authority, whether in submission or revolt, according to G. Stanley Hall's *Adolescence*, the first, otherwise sound, modern study of Huck's age-group in America.

"Woman's body and soul," wrote Hall in 1904, "is phyletically older and more primitive, while man is more modern, variable, and less conservative." Thus, he said, "Women are always inclined to preserve old customs and ways of thinking." Even when breaking with custom and the law, Hall determined, "Women prefer passive methods; to give themselves up to the power of elemental forces, as gravity, when they throw themselves from heights or take poison, in which methods of suicide they surpass man. Havelock Ellis thinks drowning is becoming more frequent, and that therein women are becoming more womanly." (Certainly, no one would deny the "elemental" role of gravity in this analysis.)[2]

Huck does not drown on the river—though he pretends to be a "drownded" boy in the "Raftsman episode"—but he is throwing himself from a moral height when he takes the plunge and tears up the letter. The role of the letter itself in Huck's conversion to "blackness" is interesting. It is the letter that brings Huck's moral dilemma to a crisis; and it is the destruction of the letter, upon which Huck has unknowingly displaced his fears and desires, that resolves it.

Letters, writs are the black-on-white tokens of a literate, "civilized" culture rather than an oral, "primitive" one; this letter is the letter of the law under the Fugitive Slave Act, and thus a scarlet letter or item of *black* mail. Son of the illiterate town drunk, Huck has learned his letters imperfectly from the likes of Miss Watson and the Widow Douglas; thus he views the letter with awe and dread, as he views the entire book he is writing so laboriously. "If I'd a knowed what a trouble it was to make a book I wouldn't a tackled it and ain't agoing to no more," Huck says with relief just before he heads for Indian territory at the end (*HF*, 295–96).

The letter, then is a "white" fetish, a totem of the reigning social order of the shore (as opposed to the raft) that, in Clemens's view, worships false gods, particularly mammon. An instrument of white magic and control, the letter is the token or talisman of a mysterious, autocratic power that Huck believes in, and rightfully fears, without a conscious act of will, the way Ahab believes in the whale, or Jim believes that a hair ball can tell fortunes. Or the way Stowe's Uncle Tom believes in the Bible.

That Huck's "Africanism" (and femininity) come out most darkly at the moment of his conversion to Protestantism is the plain hand of the satirist slapping religious and moral hypocrisy in the face. Had the infamous "moral sense" of "the damned human race" owned up to the wickedness it was perpetrating before 1861 under the odious pretense of philanthropy, Clemens insinuates, the war that destroyed the idyllic America of his boyhood dreams might never have been fought. Clemens was not kidding when he said that, to his way of thinking, Sir Walter Scottism "caused" the Civil War by promulgating, especially in the South, the "sham civilities" of a false chivalry, or moral code, that was too "refined" to recognize its own capacity for savagery. He might have said the same of the whole system of human psychology that Sir Walter (whose romances exemplify it) and the other Scots imported to a raw, half-formed country that had little more, in some regions, than the divisions of race, and the wealth extracted from racial exploitation, upon which to base its class distinctions.

In *Huck Finn*, consequently, the Mason-Dixon lines between black minds and white minds—and between thinking and feeling, masculine and feminine—are washed away. As Huck drifted further south into the traditional stronghold of whiteness, Clemens and his age were discovering all human minds to be "black," "primitive," "female" in the newly evolving sense of being inevitably bound by their own subjectivity.

The River of Consciousness

Critical of the old order and cast of mind, Clemens himself, of course, realized that Huck's moral debate takes place only in his head, which is so addled or feverish that Huck hears voices: "But something inside of me kept saying, 'There was the Sunday school, you could a gone to it; and if you'd a done it they'd a learnt you, there, that people that acts as I'd been acting about that nigger goes to everlasting fire'" (*HF*, 222). The slip in pronouns here from first person into second, indicating Huck's confusion between self and other, *me* and *you*, could make him a candidate for psychoanalysis in his later years. As the grammar of a new "primitivism" in the American consciousness, however, it is well nigh perfect.

Though Huck apes the saints-or-sinners mentality that Clemens was satirizing, Clemens himself had already run up against the "functional" model of mind that his generation was formulating in the wake of Darwin. "There has been nothing less than a revolution in the conception of psychology," said J. Mark Baldwin, professor of psychology at Princeton, in 1893. A great popularizer of the new views, whose *Story of the Mind* Clemens read with interest, Baldwin defined the chief differences between the old psychology and the new as follows: the earlier psychology held to "a 'ready-made' view of consciousness—technically, an 'intuition' view." "In opposition to these characters," said Baldwin, "current psychology is 'functional'—holding to mental 'functions' rather than to mental faculties; and finds this function to be 'genetic' rather than intuitive—the functions 'grow' instead of being 'ready-made.'"[3]

Besides replacing faculties (or capacities of the mind) with functions (uses of the mind), the new psychology also tore down the walls between the old divisions that separated one faculty in the house of the mind from another. "The old conception of 'faculties,'" wrote Baldwin, "made the different phases of mental process in large measure distinct from one another. Memory was a 'faculty,' a 'power,' of the mind; thought was another, imagination a third." Under the old scheme, one faculty was "held in reserve" while another was on stage. "The new functional conception," said Baldwin, "asks how the mind as a whole acts, and how this one form of activity shapes itself to the different elements of material which it finds available." To the mind's one form of mental activity, the new psychology gave the generic name *consciousness*; and, by contrast with the divided view of mind, said Baldwin, it held not only that "the process in consciousness is one" but that "it is a psycho-physical process as well."[4]

Just before he tears up the letter, Huck has begun to think, or rather feel, in the manner Balwin describes, with his "mind as a whole" operating more or less all at once:

> I see Jim before me, all the time, in the day, and in the night-time, sometimes moonlight, sometimes storms, and we a floating along, talking, and singing, and laughing. But somehow I couldn't seem to strike no places to harden me against him, but only the other kind. I'd see him standing my watch on top of his'n, stead of calling me—so I could go on sleeping; and see him how glad he was when I come back out of the fog; and when I come to him again in the swamp, up there where the feud was; and such-like times; and would always call me honey, and pet me, and do everything he could think of for me, and how good he always was; and at last I struck the time I saved him by telling the men we had small-pox aboard, and he was so grateful, and said I was the best friend old Jim ever had in the world, and the *only* one he's got now; and then I happened to look around, and see that paper. (*HF*, 223)

A reprise of Huck's adventures on the river with Jim, this sentimental passage would seem to be the traditional rehearsing of the past in visual form as it parades before the mind's eye. And so it is; but instead of presenting a procession of ideas passing *through* the mind as in Uncle Tom's reverie among the cotton bales, Clemens gives the illusion here of genuine subjectivity, of the mind itself moving in its own fluid element. "It is nothing jointed," as Williams James was soon to say of any personal consciousness; "it flows. A 'river' or a 'stream' are the metaphors by which it is most naturally described" (*PBC*, 159). (Huck's thoughts "strike" or don't strike "places" and "times" in his memory because they are flowing like a raft or boat that is navigating a difficult shore or islands in the stream.)

Huck's thoughts *are* "jointed," as the representation of thought on the printed page must inevitably be—by all those semicolons, which, however, do away with the either-or, if-then logic of debate and dialectic. There is no subordination of ideas in Huck's inner world because all of his memories of Jim are emotionally equal. And though Huck's thoughts present themselves in chronological order, his words are run together with little in the way of formal, grammatical coordination because Clemens is imitating the parataxis of consciousness as he was coming to understand it on the new "functional" model. (The intrusive, moralizing narrator of *Uncle Tom's Cabin* has entirely disappeared in this passage, which gives the impression that we are listening directly to the language of Huck's thoughts.)

Moreover, though Huck cannot get Jim out of his head, it is not because he is crazy or dreaming, or has an "inferior" subjectivity in some darkly Hegelian sense. In Huck's mind just before he happens to see "that paper" again—an alien object that would have bitten him had it been a snake, so unmindful has Huck become of the "objective" world—there are no hierarchies of thought and feeling, only successive "states of mind," as William James would say, where "thought may be equally rational in any sort of terms" (*PBC*, 167).[5]

Huck's remembrances of Jim are what save him from John Bunyan's heaven; they are presented as normal and, in the new order of consciousness, "rational," precisely because they are *not* warring, but are consistent with one another and with his state of mind. "If we feel in the terms, whatever they be, a fringe of affinity with each other and with the topic," says James in his chapter "The Stream of Consciousness," "and if we are conscious of approaching a conclusion, we feel that our thought is rational and right" (*PBC*, 168).

The abiding topic of thought in Huck's case is freeing Jim. And like Pym at the pole, he is rapidly approaching a conclusion to this line of thought; so even though Huck doesn't know where he is going yet, he has free will under the new model of consciousness—that is, his thoughts would be considered voluntary—because, even when Huck thinks he is going to hell, he feels "all right" about the terms in which his thoughts express themselves along the way. "Any thought the quality of whose fringe lets us feel ourselves 'all right,'" says James in the *Principles*, "may be considered a thought that furthers the topic. Provided we only feel its object to have a place in the scheme of relations in which the topic also lies, that is sufficient to make of it a relevant and appropriate portion of our train of ideas" (*PBC*, 167–68).

When thought and desire flow together in his recollections of the past, then, Huck may be both a disarmed savage, like Stowe's Uncle Tom, and (from the standpoint of the shore) a junior madman, like the alienated artists of Poe's and Hawthorne's tales. But he is also himself—*a* self, or personal consciousness as defined by the new psychology, where identity is closely linked to memory. ("No psychology, at any rate," William James wrote all too confidently in the days before the word became absolute master of the spirit, "can question the *existence* of personal selves" [*PBC*, 153].)

How does Peter, when he wakes up in the morning with Paul, know that he is Peter and not his companion? Peter knows who he is because "he makes connection with but *one* of the two streams of thought which were broken by the sleeping hours." He and Peter may have experienced the same events and touched the same objects during the day, but they cannot experience the same thoughts. ("A permanently existing 'Idea,'" said James—outmaneuvering "the Intellectualists" in one direction as he outmaneuvered "the Sensationalists," notably Hume, in the other—"which makes its appearance before the footlights of consciousness at periodical intervals is as mythological an entity as the Jack of Spades" [*PBC*, 158, 157].)

Peter may know Paul intimately, but not in the same way he knows his own personal consciousness: "He *remembers* his own states," said James, "whilst he only *conceives* Paul's." The difference, for James—who dismissed the contention of the phrenologists, such as the Combe, that "Memory" and "Conception" were activities of the intellectual faculties only, and who paid far more attention to the theory of emotion of another Scot, Alexander Bain—was one of intensity. "Remembrance" (as with Huck when he leaves the raft and goes ashore permanently to save Jim), said James, "is like direct feeling; its object is suffused with a warmth and intimacy to which no object of mere conception ever attains" (*PBC*, 158).[6]

Under the old conception of mind and character, mere warmth of feeling as the sole guide to conduct, no matter how intimately connected to the "topic" of cognition, was considered the mark of an inferior mind, that of a child, woman, savage, or madman. In his *Observations on Madness and Melancholy* (2d ed., 1809), Dr. John Haslam of Bethlem Hospital, London, defined insanity as "an incorrect association of familiar ideas, which is independent of the prejudices of education, and is always accompanied with implicit belief, and generally with either violent or depressing passions." This was, as Klaus Doerner notes, but an echoing of "the tradition of the intellectual insanity concept; passions are merely secondary symptoms."[7] By the 1840s in America, however, passions were becoming *primary* symptoms—both of mental disease, as in Ahab's case, and of mental health. By 1890 an exercise of emotion would be considered, by many, fundamental to "moral" adult behavior; and some psychologists, such as William James, would even argue that no "prejudices," however irrational, are ever "independent of . . . education."

A Specifical Emotion

Despite the many genuine reforms in the treatment of mentally ill persons that went along with the shift from "madhouses" to "asylums" in Britain and America in the first half of the nineteenth century, the old practice of putting the insane away in a dark pit or cell was still all too common before 1865. One of the terse entries in the journals of Dorothea Dix, pioneer in the "moral treatment" of mental illness in America in the first half of the nineteenth century, reads as follows: "*Concord.* A woman from the hospital in a cage in the almshouse."[8] The reference is to Concord, Massachusetts, home of Emerson, Thoreau, and the Alcotts. The center of plain living and high thinking that Concord has come to stand for in romanticized American history, however, was largely the construction of Transcendentalism and "the shot heard round the world."

The recently published letters and journals of Horace ("the Goat") Hosmer of nearby Acton, a former student of the Thoreaus, bring to light a different aspect of the region. Hosmer attributed the damaged minds of many of these benighted souls to the alcohol that flowed freely in their parents' day from the numerous taverns in the adjoining New England villages: "Within less than a mile of where I lived there were four fools who were tied in their chairs and fed like infants in one family. . . . Less than two miles south of this place there were three sons who knew barely enough to drive oxen. . . . There was a fool confined in a cage in a house on Main St. when I went to school to Henry & John Thoreau. . . . [T]here was a caged fool in the first house south of where I live, there was one in South Acton, one in Acton Center, a girl, whose brother is a Methodist minister and so on."[9] (Hosmer's list omits at least one other certified "idiot" of the region, as he was then officially classified, Waldo Emerson's impaired younger brother, Bulkeley.)[10] Except that the actual details of the case that Dorothea Dix uncovered (literally) were far more horrible than even Poe could have dreamed up, her worst specimen of a "caged fool" could have served as the inspiration for "The Pit and the Pendulum."

Fresh from convincing the state of Massachusetts to enlarge and modernize the Worcester State Hospital for the indigent insane—the very institution to which Mrs. E. P. W. Packard, the asylum reformer and activist, had been needlessly committed at age nineteen by her father—Dix placed this shameful case before the state legislature of Illinois in 1847:

> He was confined in a roofed pen, which enclosed an area of about 8 feet by 8. . . . The interstices between the unhewn logs freely admitted the scorching rays of the sun then, as they now afford admission to the frequent rains and driving snow, and the pinching frosts. He was, said a neighbor, 'fed no better than the hogs.' His feet had been frozen, and had perished; upon the shapeless stumps he could, aided by some motion of his shoulders, raise his body partially up the side of the pen. . . . Of course, no fire is here introduced in the cold winter weather; but a singular expedient has been adopted, as horrible as it is singular. Beneath the pen is excavated a pit about six feet deep and six on either side. This dreary, ghastly place is entered through a trap-door; neither light, heat, nor ventilation are there; but there is to be found a pining desolate, suffering maniac, whose piteous groans, and frantic cries, would move to pity the hardest heart.[11]

When Dix asked the sister of the patient-prisoner why the family did not send her brother to an institution, she replied: "We had rather take care of him, than leave him to strangers, because we are kinder, and treat him much better than they would."[12] Relics of Foucault's "classic period" in the treatment of mental disease, when dementia was sufficient proof that afflicted persons were no longer human, the methods of the "caring" sister in this grim, true-life fairy-tale of madness in the New England family, though criminal, were still not illegal in Illinois in the early decades of the nineteenth century.

As with Gall's "moral qualities" and Tuke's "moral feelings," however, the nineteenth century was elsewhere coming to define "morality" as a matter of emotion rather than intellect—in ordinary speech as in the technical lexicon of the mind doctor. It is this now obsolete sense of *moral* as "emotional" that the science fiction writer, Ursula K. Le Guin, resurrects for modern readers in "The Ones Who Walk Away from Omelas" (1973), a moral fable that might have been modeled on Dix's or Poe's tales of the pit but that actually takes its cue expressly from William James.

Set in the haunted realms of thought's dominion, Le Guin's psychomyth leads us to a Poesque chamber "in a basement under one of the beautiful public buildings of Omelas, or perhaps in the cellar of one of its spacious private homes." This subterranean room is little more than a pit or dungeon "about three paces long and two wide" with a dirt floor, "a little damp to the touch, as cellar dirt usually is." The room is inhabited by an androgynous child, a subhuman brute who lives in such squalor that a few of the good citizens who see "it," cowering in its own excrement, turn their backs forever on this privileged land where the many thrive because of the deliberate misery of the one.[13]

The child is feeble-minded: "Perhaps it was born defective or perhaps it has become imbecile through fear, malnutrition, and neglect. It picks its nose and occasionally fumbles vaguely with its toes or genitals, as it sits hunched in the corner farthest from the bucket and the two mops. It is afraid of the mops."[14]

The sacrifice of a single damaged mind would seem a small price to pay for the general good of society, and Le Guin is well aware that those who leave Omelas do so for emotional rather than strictly rational reasons. They are the "moral" ones, her parable of the scapegoat implies; like the hypersensual Roderick Usher, they hear the still, small voice of the "specificial and independent" faculty (not all that far removed from Poe's "Perversity," when stripped of his irony) that William James identified in a passage Le Guin quotes from "The Moral Philosopher and the Moral Life" (1891). James was speaking of the buried consciousness, of a sort of devil's bargain that predicated the happiness of an entire society upon the hidden torment of one "lost soul":

Or if the hypothesis were offered us of a world in which Messrs. Fourier's and Bellamy's and Morris's utopias should all be outdone, and millions kept permanently happy on the one simple condition that a certain lost soul on the far-off edge of things should lead a life of lonely torment, what except a specifical and independent sort of emotion can it be which would make us immediately feel, even though an impulse arose within us to clutch at the happiness so offered, how hideous a thing would be its enjoyment when deliberately accepted as the fruit of such a bargain?

Of this passage, says Le Guin, "The dilemma of the American conscience can hardly be better stated."[15]

Alas, Le Guin's modern utopia—"Omelas" is the mirror-image of "Salem, O," just the sort of serious word play in which Poe and the nineteenth century delighted—would seem to have no place for a Dorothea Dix or a Samuel Tuke, who actively sought to liberate those prisoners locked away in their cells by an older, more benighted sense of "conscience grim" (as Poe called it). No one comes to the child's aid in Le Guin's moral allegory; "it" is deemed a hopeless case, apparently, even by those who walk away from an "ideal" society flawed at its foundations by the exploitation of the weak and helpless. ("They" walk toward the distant mountains. What they do there, or whether they ever arrive, is not recorded.)

William James, however, was writing at a time when the American conscience still professed to believe that its worst ills, mental and social, could be healed, or at least addressed, through the good will of individuals as decent as himself. As late as the 1890s, the moral faculty as James conceived it—a highly evolved emotional sense that could not help taking pity on the weak and the oppressed—was still thought to distinguish the behavior of men and women from that of brutes. Thus the image of the caged idiot, or hunkering beast, lingered in the American moral consciousness as a frightening reminder of its identity—but for evolution, if not the grace of a supernatural power—with the ape: "*That shape*," said a distraught William James in *The Varieties of Religious Experience* (1902), "*am I.*"[16]

TEN

Mrs. Packard, Miss Dickinson, and the Purloined Regina

The Earth waits for her Queen.

—*Margaret Fuller Ossoli*

In respect to the powers and rights of married women, the law is by no means
abreast of the spirit of the age. Here are seen the old fossil footprints of
feudalism. The law relating to woman tends to make every family a barony or a
monarchy or a despotism, of which the husband is the baron, king, or despot,
and the wife the dependent, serf, or slave. That this is not always the fact, is
not due to the law, but to the enlarged humanity which spurns the narrow
limits of its rules. The progress of civilization has changed the family from a
barony to a republic; but the law has not kept pace with the advance
of ideas, manners, and customs.

—*Justice William Wetmore Story*

 IN THIS CHAPTER we examine the "case histories" of
two fascinating mid-nineteenth-century women: Mrs.
E. P. W. Packard, a now obscure victim of the black-white,
master-slave psychology I have been analyzing, who was
literally locked away in a dungeon for disagreeing with
her husband's religious doctrines, and Emily Dickinson,
whose claims of mastery over her own mind, as well as those of the "masculine"
gender, are grounded somewhere between the old geography of the faculties
and the new "functional" or "evolutionary" psychology that was taking shape
after the Civil War and that would find its definitive form in the 1890s. In both
cases, the dominant metaphors for the sovereign will, particularly as informed
by emotion, are those of queenship; in both cases the queenly authority of these
iron-willed women is vested in letters and other writs that are stolen, mutilated,
or otherwise mishandled or misappropriated so as, symbolically as well as actually, to jeopardize that authority and call their right reason into question; and
in both cases these soiled writs are stand-ins not only for the sovereign mind

but also for the queenly body. Finally, however, despite their contemporaneity, Packard and Dickinson belong, psychologically, to different eras, almost different centuries.

With a new understanding of the mind as uniting the suffrages of all the faculties in a uniquely subjective act of personal "consciousness," Dickinson looks forward to the functional psychology of William James and modernism. Mrs. Packard, for all her revolutionary zeal in the service of women's rights and asylum reform, clings to a divided view of mind in which intellect, the king of the faculties, lawfully but "unmanfully" imprisons emotion, the queen. Both believe in the will to believe, but Dickinson (like Bain and James) redefines the psychology of belief in such a way that believing and knowing, feeling and thinking, become virtually indistinguishable.

As is customary by now in these proceedings, we turn first to a fictional model of the cultural and psychological mechanisms in question before looking at the real-life examples. This fictional model is another barely veiled moral allegory in which the powers of affection, vested in a love letter, are wrongly usurped by a heartless but—in the political sphere—still more powerful intellect; only to be returned to their rightful place in order of precedence over the will—both of the individual and the state—by another, equally potent intellect acting in the service of the heart; in short, an exacting tale of suppression and reprisal conceived by a master of revenge.

Blackmail

An incriminating letter from a man (not her husband) has been purloined from the highest lady in the land, presumably the queen. The thief is the Minister D——, who has hidden the letter where the chief of police, despite repeated probings with a long needle, cannot find it. He retains C. Auguste Dupin, Poe's great detective, to secure the lady's secret property, lest the Minister, against her will, expose its contents to the king. The stakes are high, for he who holds the letter holds not only the key to the mystery but to the lady's good name and, therefore, to order or disorder in the kingdom. Will it be rudely turned by a brute, or returned to her intact by a gentleman?

The victims in Poe's detective stories are always women, and they are usually overpowered by brutish men or, in the case of "Murders in the Rue Morgue," an actual ape. There is no murder in "The Purloined Letter," and the criminal is a high-ranking court official. Yet among Poe's detective stories it is this one in which power and gender are most clearly at issue.

Dupin solves the mystery of the letter's hiding place by calling to mind, in Common Sense fashion, the "whole train of thought [that] would necessarily pass through the mind of the Minister" (*PPTE*, 693). Entering his opponent's thoughts and following them to their logical conclusion, Dupin reasons that the Minister is too intelligent to hide the letter in the "ordinary *nooks* of concealment," where the chief of police will surely look (*PPTE*, 693). A crafty man of letters, he figures, would resort "to *simplicity*" when hiding the letter and, sure enough, this is what Dupin sees when he enters the Minister's chamber: "At length my eyes, in going the circuit of the room, fell upon a trumpery filigree card-rack of pasteboard, that hung dangling by a dirty blue ribbon, from a little brass knob just beneath the middle of the mantel-piece. In this rack, which had three or four compartments, were five or six visiting cards and a solitary letter. This last was much soiled and crumpled" (*PPTE*, 695). Dupin recognizes the purloined letter at once. "It was clear to me," says the detective, "that the letter had been turned, as a glove, inside out, re-directed, and re-sealed" (*PPTE*, 696).

With its shallow compartments, where the purloined letter is now "buried," the Minister's card rack offers a clue to his shabby "interior," much as the trumpery filigree of the Grangerford's "mansion" in *Huck Finn* signifies the decadence of a code of honor that sets two houses feuding against each other with a love letter, and that requires even Huck, who can hardly read the code, to indite a formal letter betraying his companion (and his own "feminine" impulses) into bondage.

The Minister's skill with letters is almost as great as Dupin's, so when his "lynx eye" first falls upon the letter in the queen's boudoir, he "fathoms" her secret at once (*PPTE*, 682). Where the chivalrous Dupin reads in the letter an opportunity to serve the queen in matters of the heart, however, the Minister sees it only as the means of furthering his own political (and perhaps sexual) ambitions by taking advantage of the queen's indiscretion. An "unprincipled" man of genius whose hand soils every item it touches, the Minister proves to be the "*monstrum horrendum*," or horrible monster, of the tale (*PPTE*, 697).

The Minister has handled the queen's private property most rudely. Dirty and torn, the letter is "thrust carelessly, and even, as it seemed, contemptuously" into a "compartment" of the rack dangling from the mantle—as the body of the younger female victim is thrust into a compartment of the chimney in "Murders in the Rue Morgue" by the orangutan. Having torn the letter from its original hiding place and turned it inside out "as a glove," the Minister has transformed himself into the ravishing brute of Poe's other detective stories (*PPTE*, 695).

How does the lady feel about this gross invasion of privacy and breach of her queenly authority? Though Poe takes us into the minds of the men who protect or persecute her, we are never made privy to the lady's thoughts. For a woman's point of view on the politics of gender in Poe's America (and in the

Paris of C. Auguste Dupin, Paul Broca and Gustave LeBon), we must turn to the real-life story of a wife who lost not only her free will but also her physical liberty because of purloined love letters and a restless intellect.

Mrs. Packard's Rebellion

As a junior at Amherst College, Edward Dickinson, the poet's father, took an active part in the commencement exercises of 1822. They included a colloquy, "A Comparative View of the Native Genius of Males and Females" (*PWMP,* 31).[1] Which side of the issue he debated is not known, but we do know that his partner in the colloquy was Theophilus Packard Jr., son of a Congregationalist minister known as the Sage of Shelburne.

Whatever their respective positions in the debate, young Dickinson went on to father a female whose native genius would dispose her to question the male-centered orthodoxies of Calvinism, while young Packard went on to marry one. Here the similarity ends, however. For while Edward Dickinson merely ignored the intellectual boldness that is a hallmark of his daughter's poems, Packard in 1860 had his wife committed to an insane asylum in Illinois for exercising her intelligence in matters of religious doctrine.

Here are some of the views of Elizabeth Parsons Ware (or, as she became known, Mrs. E. P. W.) Packard on the differences between her husband's Calvinism and true Christianity, as presented to the Trustees of the Illinois State (Mental) Hospital at Jacksonville around September 1862:

> Calvinist marriage requires the subjection of woman. Christian marriage requires the protection of woman.
>
> Calvinism defends slavery. Christianity befriends liberty.
>
> Calvin taught that the greater part of God's family would transcend God's ability to discipline [them] into subjugation to his authority and obedience to his commands. . . .
>
> Christ taught that there were no limits to God's mercy, that . . . free-agency is an indispensable law of our moral nature, over which the death of our natural body has no influence.[2]

To these and more than thirty other points of doctrine, Mrs. Packard added her "reflections," including this one: "This impious, Calvinistic attempt to *chain my thoughts,* by calling me 'insane,' for opinion's sake, and imprisoning me on this account is a *crime* against the constitution of this free government, and also a crime against civilization and human progress." Her "rebellion" from her husband, she further reflected, was "the legitimate fruit of the Calvinistic law of marriage, which enslaves the wife."

Mrs. Packard had indeed been committed to a state mental institution "for opinion's sake": she had dared to contradict Theophilus, a conservative Presbyterian minister, on matters of church dogma, inspiring her adult Sunday school class to lively debate, in his absence, on doctrinal issues. Even worse, Mrs. Packard was thinking about going over to the Methodists. (Despite the prominent brow and forehead visible in a surviving photo, the Reverend Mr. Packard's intellectual faculties seem to have been recessive, compared to those of his wife. In turn, Mrs. Packard's organ of "Combativeness," a back-brained faculty located just behind the ear, according to phrenology, would have rated a "very large" on the Fowlers' scale.) Accordingly, after twenty-one years of marriage, Theophilus Packard appeared in his wife's bedchamber on June 18, 1860, accompanied by two local doctors and the sheriff.

Each doctor seized a wrist, and as they felt Mrs. Packard's elevated pulse they solemnly and in unison pronounced her "insane"—an obvious setup (PWMP, 70). Elizabeth Packard was then handed over to the sheriff and physically hauled off to Jacksonville, where Theophilus signed a document of admittance that included the following line: "Supposed cause is excessive application of body and mind." Mrs. Packard, in other words, had failed to wrap her convictions in dimity silence and refined inaction. Beneath her husband's signature in a different hand appears the notation, "June 1863, Dis[charged] order Trustees" (PWMP, 75). It was added three years later to the day.

Theophilus Packard did nothing illegal when he packed his wife off to the state mental hospital, which is the very aspect of the case that seems most preposterous today. Illinois state law in 1860 expressly permitted "married women and infants" to be institutionalized without a trial or hearing and "without the evidence of insanity required in other cases." All it took for commitment was "the request of the husband" (or guardian of the infant) and "the judgment of the medical superintendents of the state asylum at Jacksonville" that the woman was "evidently insane or distracted."[3] Mrs. Packard did not even rate the diagnosis of the chief superintendent at first. Since Dr. Andrew McFarland was out of town when Theophilus Packard knocked at the hospital door with his wife in tow, she had to be admitted by McFarland's assistant. Apparently, Theophilus's authority as a minister and male head of household sufficed.

Authority, at any rate, is a key term in Mrs. Packard's quarrel with her husband—the "Mrs." was to remain a part of her professional name as lobbyist, author, and publisher—and in the vocabulary of other women of the time who sought to rewrite the "personal liberty" laws in America. Pronounced insane

FIG. 11 Elizabeth Packard and her husband, Theophilus Packard Jr., before he had her committed to an Illinois asylum for disagreeing with his religious doctrines. To the phrenologist, the prominent foreheads of this couple would indicate mutually strong, if contrary, intellectual faculties.

on the sole authority of men, Mrs. Packard saw herself as "a martyr for the rights of opinion in women in the year 1860 in this boasted free America" (*PWMP*, 85). Claiming "equality" with her husband in her "individual right to my private opinion," Mrs. Packard did not, however, fundamentally question male authority as she might have a century later (*PWMP*, 85). She charged, rather, that Theophilus had abused his rightful authority as a husband, in much the same way that John Calvin abused his as a minister.

The Unholy Family

If Mrs. Packard saw her husband as an infidel (like Calvin), she also saw herself as a martyr. But this was only one of the metaphors by which a strict Protestant upbringing had taught her, and many of her contemporaries, to figure a woman's place in the home and state as well as in the church. Another was the conventional analogy she drew between divine rule and secular rule: "Christianity is loyalty to God's government." (*PWMP*, 200). And between the earthly family and the heavenly family: the ideal husband corresponded—Theophilus had obviously strayed from the ideal implied by his name—to God, the "Father of all the human family," who had "Omnipotent power" to accomplish "all the benevolent purposes of his paternal nature" (*PWMP*, 201). Just who the ideal wife might be in this scheme came out later in the records of the trial that Mrs. Packard demanded in order to establish her sanity.

Theophilus Packard broke none of the laws of the state when he locked his wife away in an asylum for three years; but when she was released at last into his custody, he nailed her bedroom window shut and refused to let her out. The involuntary physical confinement of a sane person *was* against Illinois law, and sympathetic neighbors got wind of it. They sought a writ of habeas corpus on Elizabeth's behalf from Judge Charles R. Starr of the twentieth judicial circuit court, and in January 1864 the trial of *Packard v. Packard* began in Kankakee City, Illinois, fifty miles south of Chicago.

Theophilus's first witness was Dr. Christopher Knott of Kankakee City, one of the physicians he had consulted in 1860 before taking his wife to Jacksonville, who certified that Elizabeth was "partially deranged on religious matters" (*PWMP*, 7). She was "perfectly rational" on other subjects, Dr. Knott testified (echoing the verdict of Thomas Gray in the Nat Turner case), but in matters of religion she was a "monomaniac," as he considered many religious people to be (*PWMP*, 7). "I would say she is insane," he explained, "as I would say Henry Ward Beecher, Spurgeon, Horace Greeley and like persons are insane" (*PWMP*, 7).

Even more self-incriminating than Dr. Knott's testimony was that of Dr. J. W. Brown, who had interrogated Mrs. Packard at her home under the guise of a sewing machine salesman. After discussing theology with Mrs. Packard, said Brown, he "had not the slightest difficulty in concluding that she was hopelessly insane" (*PWMP*, 7). This witness, nonetheless, made a potentially damaging point: he swore that Mrs. Packard told him she was "the personification of the Holy Ghost" (*PWMP*, 7).

Mrs. Packard countered with testimony from a Dr. Duncanson, who held both medical and theological degrees from Scottish universities. Duncanson reminded the court that Socinus, the sixteenth-century theologian, had espoused the belief that the Holy Ghost was female. Mrs. Packard was simply assigning to the Trinity the gender roles of its earthly equivalent, the holy family. Duncanson pronounced Mrs. Packard not only "sane," but also one of the most intelligent people, male or female, he had conversed with in years; he wished "we had a nation of such women" (*PWMP*, 15). The jury quickly agreed that Mrs. Packard was in full possession of her faculties, and Judge Starr ordered the defendant "to be relieved of all restraints incompatible with her condition as a sane woman" (*PWMP*, 16). Nonetheless, Elizabeth Packard's allusions to the Holy Ghost would come back to haunt her.

Calvin's interpretation of the Trinity as three separate but equal persons was anathema to Mrs. Packard, for whom it contradicted the basic Christian doctrine of a single, all-powerful God: "Christ taught there is but one God. Calvin taught there are three Gods" (*PWMP*, 200). No Unitarian like Emerson, however, Mrs. Packard solved the trinitarian puzzle for herself by subordinating God the son and God the mother to God the Father. Their subordinate power, Mrs. Packard believed, was merely "delegated," and when Christ accomplished his filial duty to save the world, "he should deliver up his delegated authority to his Father, and he himself be subject to him" (*PWMP*, 201).

Like Christ the heavenly son, the dutiful earthly son—Theophilus III in her case—did not claim equal authority with his father; nor did the ideal wife. She was but the "temple" of the Holy Ghost; her husband was the flame: so long, that is, as the paternal earthly authority did not, like a corrupt government, subjugate "the weaker vessel to the arbitrary will of the stronger" (*PWMP*, 85). Theophilus Jr. had abrogated the main responsibility of the post-Puritan gentleman and father in America: to be (in Mrs. Packard's words) "the protector of [the] true womanly rights of the weak" (*PWMP*, 85). In her experience, he was not the first.

A Kiss of Charity

While suffering from "brain fever," Elizabeth Parsons Ware, when she was nineteen, had been admitted as Case Number 404 to New England's first public mental institution, the Worcester State Hospital, billed as "a humane alternative for poor lunatics" (*PWMP,* 24–25). Elizabeth's family was not poor, but Worcester was close by, and its director, Samuel N. Woodward, a phrenologist like most of his counterparts at other mental hospitals, had made Worcester a model institution even before Dorothea Dix instigated her reforms by putting pressure on the Massachusetts state legislature.

Unlike Jacksonville even many years later, Worcester required a court order for admission. To obtain one, a standard form had to be filled out, no matter what the actual circumstances of the case. The boilerplate, in fact, demanded "a Lunatic so furiously mad as to render it manifestly dangerous to the peace and safety of the community that the said————should continue at large" (*PWMP,* 24). Young Elizabeth's name was duly entered in the blank, and on her admission form next to "occupation, teacher" was also entered "supposed cause, 'mental labor.'" The person who filled out and signed these "appallingly worded" documents, as Barbara Sapinsley has aptly called them, was Elizabeth's father (*PWMP,* 24–25).

Elizabeth remained at Worcester for six weeks, until March 18, 1836, when, according to the record, she "left the hospital this morning in a very favorable state, her mind free from insanity, her health restored, and all operations of the system going on favorably, her mind improved rapidly." Dr. Woodward further noted: "She is an interesting and intelligent girl" (*PWMP,* 26). Almost thirty years later, the equally distinguished Dr. Andrew McFarland, director of the Illinois State Hospital, would describe his patient as possessing "extraordinary mental capacity and power, great charm of manner, and taste in dress, and good judgment" (*PWMP,* 97). He would also give her a kiss in his office, strictly a "kiss of charity," Dr. McFarland maintained when under investigation by the Packard-Fuller committee in 1867 (*PWMP,* 83).

Dr. McFarland was speaking in July 1863, the month following Mrs. Packard's release from his care, at the annual meeting of the Association of Medical Superintendents of American Institutions for the Insane. In these early days of psychiatry before Freud and the terminology of psychoanalysis, McFarland diagnosed Mrs. Packard's case (without actually naming her) in the language of faculty psychology. The patient's behavior showed, he said, the "perversity of conduct" that his colleagues would normally attribute to a "moral insanity" stemming from emotional causes (*PWMP,* 98). Mrs. Packard's monomania seemed, however, to be clearly a notional (or intellectual) one. Her perverse behavior, he reasoned, must be caused by some "intellectual perversion" (*PWMP,* 98). But what was it? Mrs. Packard's intellect appeared to be perfectly sound. During "two years of the closest study," McFarland told the association, he could not seem to discover in her "any intellectual impairment at all" (*PWMP,* 97). So far, Mrs. Packard failed to meet the delusion test for insanity, whether emotional or intellectual.

McFarland's institution was required by charter to hold admitted patients under observation for a minimum of two years, which may explain why McFarland did not release Elizabeth Packard right away, when he still thought her a woman of intelligence, charm and good judgment. After three years of watching Mrs. Packard, he told the asylum association, McFarland asked the trustees of the hospital to discharge her "as the only way of getting rid of an intolerable and unendurable source of annoyance" (*PWMP,* 97). Among the "infinite" troubles she gave him was a sixteen-page letter entitled, "My Reproof to Dr. McFarland for his Abuse of his Patients," which Mrs. Packard published verbatim in her two-volume *Great Disclosure of Spiritual Wickedness in High Places* (1865).

Mrs. Packard had exposed McFarland as she had exposed Calvin—and her husband, Theophilus, whom she took to calling "Calvin" in her letters. In one of these letters, Mrs. Packard referred to a "love letter" she had written to Dr. McFarland. The "Mr. Baker" of this excerpt was Abner Baker of Mount Pleasant, Iowa, who had written similar letters to Mrs. Packard before Theophilus committed her to the asylum: "I don't think 'twould be best to let Calvin know I had sent you a love letter since I have been here and got an answer, too. For he might make it an occasion against us in the eyes of his clan. . . . Just put [it] between the folds of your shirts, in your private drawer and not in the family drawer between the folds of the fine table linen as I did Mr. Baker's letters. For my partner found mine and so may yours find yours, unless you are extra wise and discreet" (*PWMP,* 101).

There is no evidence that Mrs. Packard went any further than to bake hot biscuits for Abner Baker. Still, one wonders, did Theophilus lock his wife away for her opinions alone, or was he also persuaded by those purloined letters, the dirty laundry he thought he had found among the folds of her finest linen?

Patients could be released from the state hospital at Jacksonville only if they were cured or deemed "incurable" (and therefore to be moved out to make room for treatable patients). Dr. McFarland did not wish to pronounce Mrs. Packard sane—her "Disclosure" revealed, among other details, that he had kissed her. The doctor needed some other reason to discharge his patient, and in the pages of *The Great Drama* (final title of the book she began writing while still under his care), he found it—the Holy Ghost "delusion."

Even when they deduce that Mrs. Packard was "railroaded" into the asylum—each chapter of *The Great Drama* is named for a railroad car—historians of psychiatry, until recently, tended to accept McFarland's account of his patient's delusion as factually accurate. "It appears to be established," said Albert Deutsch, for example, in *The Mentally Ill in America*, "that she suffered from certain delusions ... that she was the third person in the Holy Trinity and the mother of Jesus Christ."[4] As Barbara Sapinsley established in 1991, however, Mrs. Packard was not speaking literally when she equated herself with the Holy Ghost and the queenly Virgin Mary. Unlike Nathaniel Turner or the mother of Nancy Farrer, Mrs. Packard probably never claimed to *be* a divine personage, only—as a woman and a mother—to be *like* one.

In *Packard v. Packard*, however, Theophilus argued that his wife had been discharged "without being cured and is incurably insane," and he entered into evidence a certificate to that effect signed by Dr. McFarland (*PWMP*, 4). First her father, then her husband, and now Andrew McFarland: once again Elizabeth had been betrayed by a man of authority in whom she had placed her trust. Her new protector had gone over to the side of Calvin.

Doctor in a Far Land

Even worse, Dr. McFarland had not followed her instructions about the incriminating letter. He was supposed to burn it, said the missive, since "any exposure of it might imperil my virtue in the estimation of *perverted* humanity" (*PWMP*, 209). Since it was not until after Mrs. Packard "got an answer," presumably from McFarland himself, that she admonished him to hide the letter in a secret place, McFarland's reply must have informed her that it was still intact; and now she understood why. Though McFarland did not purloin Mrs. Packard's letter, he had no intention of concealing it or protecting her intimate secrets from exposure. (To McFarland's mind, apparently, as in Poe's story, the letter was roughly synonymous with the physical lady.)

Instead of following her instructions to the letter, the doctor wrongfully appropriated (from Elizabeth's viewpoint) her words and feelings in order to protect himself—the next thing to blackmail. It was twenty years before Freud would coin the term *transference,* and Mrs. Packard, having no idea that she was projecting feelings upon McFarland that might not be altogether his own, was stunned when he turned over a private part of herself to the committee formed by the trustees to defend their hospital against the accusation that the superintendent they had appointed admitted patients improperly and then sexually abused them.

The committee found little evidence of abuse, and Dr. McFarland was retained. Though the Packard case is sometimes remembered as driving a de-

voted practitioner, who aided in the treatment of thousands of mentally disturbed persons, to hang himself, McFarland's suicide in 1891 was prompted by
his ill health and not, in all probability, by the events of thirty years before.
Instead of being ruined by the Packard case, McFarland went on to establish
Oak Lawn Retreat, a private sanitarium in Jacksonville, and to examine such
clients as Mary Todd Lincoln, the president's widow, who in 1872 had been
tried and found insane under the "Act for Protection of Personal Liberty in
Illinois" that Elizabeth Packard herself had convinced the state legislature to
pass five years earlier. (Dr. McFarland recommended against releasing Mrs.
Lincoln, and charged her son Robert a consultation fee of $100 [*PWMP*, 169].
Robert Lincoln took his mother out of the asylum anyway, as Elizabeth Packard's oldest had tried to do, sons of the nineteenth century being, apparently,
in Mrs. Packard's terms, more forgivingly Christ-like than their fathers toward
their "sainted" mothers, as Abe Lincoln called his.)

In direct response to Mrs. E. P. W. Packard's lobbying, the states of Iowa
and Massachusetts also enacted stricter commitment laws for mental institutions. And before Mrs. Packard's death in 1897, as Albert Deutsch has said, she
"indirectly influenced lunacy legislation in a number of other states"—not to
mention her efforts in Connecticut and elsewhere to abolish, as one of her bills
put it, "the legal nonentity of the wife" and thereby to curtail preferential treatment for husbands in the right to children and property under common law.[5]

In her crusade for asylum reform and greater personal liberty for women,
Mrs. Packard also sought to turn the tables, if not the key, on Dr. McFarland.
The Mystic Key: Or The Asylum Secret Unlocked (1866) is her "explanation" of the love
letter he so ungallantly used against her. It insisted upon a strictly allegorical
reading of the document. Her critics jeered at "symbolical" passages such as
this one from the actual letter: "To such an one alone can I entrust the key
with which to unlock the foundation of *conjugal love* within me, whose depths
no mortal has never yet sounded. This key I entrust to *you*, Dr. McFarland,
with all the trusting confidence of a *true woman*" (*PWMP*, 209). In the tradition
of nineteenth-century acrostics, Mrs. Packard also punned on her husband's
and her protector's names, wordplay that was not to be read as foreplay, she
later contended, but as an allusion to an unearthly, platonic state: "I have a right
to love a true man even if he is in a *far off land*, or a Farland. The only response
I ask of you, *now*, is to *help* me carry the heavy pack of lies before the public,
which *Pack-ard* has put upon me to bear so unjustly as a vindication of my as-
sailed character" (*PWMP*, 209).

Mrs. Packard underlined *now* because she had another condition in mind for
later. "If before I leave this institution," she wrote McFarland, he would "issue

the first edition" of the book she was writing, she would pay him back in less than three months and, in return, so long as he advanced her enough money to finance "not less than 25 copies," pledge the following: She would "regard the act, on my part, as an engagement sealed to be yours, alone, until death do us part!" (*PWMP*, 209). McFarland could continue "a husband in a *Farland*" until "*God's Providence*" brought him near enough "to recognize the relation with my bodily senses" (*PWMP*, 209). She must not love his "person," she told the doctor, so long as his own love was "justly claimed by another woman—your legal wife," but her heart had "never been wedded. It is whole and sound and unappreciated, except as you, the first *true man* I have ever met, accept it" (*PWMP*, 209).

When Elizabeth Parsons Ware's father had signed over his nineteen-year-old daughter as a "furious lunatic" to the authorities at Worcester, the deed marked, she said, the beginning of "his degeneracy as a man" (*PWMP*, 26). She would remember it in later years as the moment when "the father in him" was first overthrown by "Beezlebub," as she spelled this alternative name (meaning "lord of the flies") for the Devil (*PWMP*, 26). John Calvin also derived his authority from "Satan," according to Mrs. Packard. And if Theophilus—who seems, indeed, to have loved his theology more than his wife—took his ministry from Calvin, she reasoned, he must owe his authority, ultimately, to the Devil, too. Even Andrew McFarland, once Mrs. Packard's "prince of manliness," who pledged to "redeem" her name from that mark of the beast, "the brand of insanity," had transformed himself into a prince of darkness. (In Mrs. Packard's letters and books, the driest theological and parliamentary discourse is rendered in the language of melodrama and gothic romance.)

The scales had dropped from her eyes in the court room at Kankakee. This "revelation"—that the stigma of madness would not be lifted by McFarland's pen stroke but only inscribed the more deeply against her—showed the doctor in his true light, she said, as "the traitor instead of the man." He had but "assumed the mark of manliness for the malign purpose of betraying my innocence" and "to shield himself" (*PWMP*, 165). Clearly, as she saw it, McFarland was torturing her as Calvin's God tortured "his helpless victims," those members of his "family" whom he could not "discipline into subjugation to his authority and obedience to his commands" (*PWMP*, 201).

Her "Exposure of Calvinism" informed the trustees at Jacksonville that, failing to work his will upon some of his victims, Calvin's God "was determined to show his power over them by keeping them in endless, hopeless torment, and thus, fiend-like, manifest his despotic authority" (*PWMP*, 201). Was not Dr. McFarland, by his wanton disregard of her womanly authority, exhibiting the same fiend-like behavior? This once lordly man, as portrayed in *The Great Drama*, was now fit only to govern flies.

By turning McFarland into a black devil, however, and despite intentions as snow white as her finest linen, Mrs. Packard had sprung upon herself the trap set by her own protesting sort of religious enthusiasm. Her trinitarian idea of the family, earthly and divine, and of the female presence in it, had simply replaced Calvin's determinism of the head with a determinism of the heart. Instead of doing the inexorable will of God because of a reasoned understanding of his arbitrary power like a good Calvinist, Mrs. Packard's Christian did it out of love. "I love God," was the first principle by which she defended her letter to McFarland against the philistines. "This love," she said, "is spontaneous, free, independent of my own free will or choice" (*PWMP*, 164).

My Manly Protector

No earthly man, however, not even Dr. McFarland, Mrs. Packard professed to believe, was invested with absolute authority; any power he might wield came secondhand from God—or the Devil. As an independent woman and crusader for women's rights, Elizabeth Packard demanded for her gender "personal liberty" not only in matters of opinion but also in family finances, the rearing of children, and the balance of power between husband and wife. She would revere Theophilus or McFarland or any other man only insofar as he was true to his lordly "type—his origin—just in that proportion do I reverence and love him as my protector" (*PWMP*, 164). When Mrs. Packard said, "Man is made in God's image," however, she meant men alone; women were made in the image of the Virgin Mary and the Holy Ghost.

And herein lay the trap. Because (in Mrs. Packard's conception of the Christian family, human or divine) the greatest protection lay with the father, her womanly instinct told her to "fly to" the paternal arms. When McFarland "instinctively developed in my womanly nature, first the feeling of gratitude, then of reverence, then of love," said the author of the letter that gave him a despot's power over his helpless victim, "he became my manly protector" (*PWMP*, 165).

Even when Mrs. E. P. W. Packard became a formidable lobbyist, she still put herself under the protection of powerful men, such as Gen. Allen C. Fuller and Richard Oglesby, the governor of Illinois. Like many other women of her time, Mrs. Packard believed that the real strength of her "womanly nature" lay in its weakness. Against an old-fashioned paternalism that "kidnapp[ed] intelligent moral agents of their accountability," as Mrs. Packard said, the new maternalism offered only a religion of feeling (*PWMP*, 204). Opposing her husband when he usurped her intellectual powers, Mrs. Packard nonetheless let herself be guided by "woman's instinct," the feminine principle that (in the words of a magazine for women published just before she entered McFarland's asylum) "never hesitated in its decision, and is scarcely ever wrong where it has even chances with reason" (*PWMP*, 54).

Under the banner of the holy wife and mother, in other words, Mrs. Packard was still marching to the tune of the (all-male) Congregationalist clergy of Massachusetts, who summed up their official position on women's rights as follows: "the power of woman is in her dependence, flowing from the consciousness of that weakness which God has given her for her protection" (*PWMP*, 35).

That Mrs. Packard voluntarily subjugated her "womanly" self to the protection of powerful men would seem all the more to be the case, since her oldest son, Theophilus III, when he turned twenty-one requested and won from the trustees at Jacksonville his mother's release into his care. Elizabeth Packard, however, refused to go "home" with her son, ostensibly because she feared "Toffy" could not stand up to his father; actually, one suspects, because she did not want to leave McFarland, whom she still worshiped. This submission to her lordly master and keeper was an aspect of Congregationalism—and of gender relations—that Emily Dickinson, feverishly writing her own unanswered "letters" about the time of Mrs. Packard's trial, could no longer countenance, though the liberal Unitarianism of Emerson and Ellery Channing had done little to challenge it.

The Royal Seal

Suppose for a moment that the queenly personage of Poe's masterful tale of letters and the subjugation of women, in her relief and anger, fires back two letters of her own: one to her lover, whose identity remains secret, and the other to the police chief after he hands over the stolen goods. The queen's second "letter" might include lines like these:

> Mine—by the Right of the White Election!
> Mine—by the Royal Seal!
> Mine—by the Sign in the Scarlet prison—
>
> . . . .
>
> Mine—long as Ages steal! (#528)

The queen's first letter—to her (still) absent lover, who has been of little support during her ordeal—might seem deceptively yielding on the surface:

I am older tonight, Master—but the love is the same—so are the moon and
the crescent ... if I ... never forget that I am not with you—that sorrow and frost
are nearer than I—if I wish with a might I cannot repress—that mine were the
Queen's place—the love of the Plantagenet is my only apology—....

"Tell you of the want" [the queen's lover has apparently asked her to]—you
know what a leech is, don't you—and you have felt the horizon hav'nt you—and
did the sea—never come so close as to make you dance? ...

What would you do with me if I came "in white?" Have you the little chest to
put the Alive—in?[6]

One of the three surviving "Master" letters that Emily Dickinson wrote (but
may or may not have sent) to an unknown recipient around 1858, 1861, and 1862,
this excerpt from a queen's correspondence is partly a love letter and partly an
exercise of her royal prerogative. The mix is quintessential Dickinson, and it
implies an attitude toward men and authority that makes Mrs. E. P. W. Packard
at her most commanding look like a sniveling girl.

Much of Emily Dickinson's intellectual and emotional life before 1863 is
enacted in her writing as a struggle with a male authority figure. Sometimes
divine and sometimes divinely human, "He" resembles Mrs. Packard's ideal
father-husband when he conforms with the queenly will. When he doesn't, this
"distant, stately lover" becomes the faceless patriarch deified by Emerson and
Thoreau and vilified by Melville and Poe, as when Dickinson asks the "Master" what he would do with her if she "came 'in white.'" Would her lord and
master—Otis Phillips Lord, a Massachusetts superior court judge, has been
conjectured as one object of Dickinson's queenly favor—perhaps put her in a
box and close the lid, turning his face from her forever?

At the highest pitch of self-yielding and self-denial in Dickinson's letters
and poems, white recalls, as here, the color not only of the bridal veil but the
shroud. Dickinson was almost as obsessed with premature burial as Poe had
been; and in many of her proleptic poems, the female consciousness is buried
alive when a lordly man either rejects or abandons her. (Dickinson began to
dress habitually in white after her father died in 1874.)

In what is probably the best-known example, "I heard a Fly buzz—when I
died—" (#465), the mourners expect "the King" to claim his lady at the moment of her death, but she is received instead by a lowly fly (perhaps sent by
Mrs. Packard's Beelzebub). In "Because I could not stop for Death" (#712),
the master sends a carriage for the lady in white, only to leave her plodding
along endlessly toward immortality. Indeed, eternal separation seems to be the
true condition of lovers in Dickinson's work. The greatest of her love poems,
"I cannot live with You—" (#640), ends with this paradox:

So We must meet apart—
You there—I—here
With just the Door ajar
That Oceans are—and Prayer—
And that White Sustenance—
Despair—

Despair is the last supper upon which Dickinson's ever-divided lovers must feed, and like bread (as distinct from the wine implied earlier in this poem) it is white, not even whole wheat.

Thus Sam Bowles, another candidate for Dickinson's "Master," always found her "'Near, but remote.'" After one visit to the Dickinsons in Amherst, during which the poet remained upstairs, Bowles received a regal "apology" from her that read in part, "Perhaps you thought I didn't care—because I stayed out, yesterday, I *did* care, Mr. Bowles . . . but something troubled me . . . so I didn't come."[7] (Editor of the Springfield *Daily Republican*, Bowles published six of the eleven poems to appear during Dickinson's lifetime.)

Despite the deep sense of pain and loss in Dickinson's poetry, until her father died when she was forty-four, the only other known "event" painful enough to "trouble" seriously Dickinson's outwardly tranquil life was her failing eyesight. At the time she wrote this letter to Bowles, the poet was beginning to suffer from an eye condition, subsequently cured or arrested, that perhaps caused her to fear for a time that she was going blind. This circumstance may account for why 366 poems in the Dickinson canon appear in the handwriting of 1862. Had she actually written more than a poem a day in that year, or was she simply copying and consolidating perhaps a decade of close work in preparation for the worst? Eye troubles may also explain why Dickinson curtailed her social life in the early 1860s, confining her activities to her father's house in Amherst, often to a single room of her own on the second floor overlooking the garden.

A poet who faced blindness just as she was reaching maturity in her vocation might, understandably, retreat from the world to write furiously before the light went out. But Dickinson's isolation evidently grew upon her. Over the coming years, she was to spend less and less time even on the familiar ground next door at the Evergreens, home of her brother Austin and his wife, Sue, to whom some of Dickinson's early "love" poems are addressed. And long after her eyes had healed, Dickinson would remain aloof from visitors, especially male ones, such as Bowles or her "mentor," Thomas Wentworth Higginson, or even Judge Lord.

Whether or not they addressed Lord, married at the time—as were most of the other men in Dickinson's life—the "Master" letters carried an ambiguous message. Like Madeline Usher rising from the grave, Dickinson's queenly presence in the letters "upbraided" their recipient for discarding her even as she longed to embrace him. "Oh, did I offend it—," admonishes the final surviving letter (1862) in the series, another "apology" to the king who would set her aside in a dark place if she came to him "in white."[8]

Free to marry again after his wife died in 1877, "Phil" Lord was clearly in love with Dickinson, and she perhaps with him. Having lived husbandless for so long, however, and perhaps not overly fond of men in the first place, Dickinson preferred the estate of the lovers in "I cannot live with You—". One intimate (but still arms-length) letter she wrote during this period to Lord, who pressed for physical consummation and marriage, recalled the yeasty metaphor of that poem: "I hope it has no different guise when my fingers make it. It is Anguish I long conceal from you to let you leave me, hungry, but you ask the divine Crust and that would doom the Bread."[9] Though "hungry" for her Lord, Dickinson chose to put him off, feeding on the "white sustenance" of spirits separated in body (and blood)—until Judge Lord died in 1884.

The role of letters as stand-ins for Dickinson's queenly lady in her intercourse with persons at a distance (including the reading public) suggests, however, that Dickinson not only resisted the intimacy of physical contact but the loss of power it entailed as well, a power derived from "Anguish" but vested in words, especially terms of negation. "Don't you know you are happiest," she told Lord, "while I withhold and [do] not confer—dont you know that No is the wildest word we consign to Language?"[10] A frequent metaphor for poetry and the poetic use of language in Dickinson's lexicon of tropes is "Snow," a word, as Cynthia Griffin Wolff has pointed out, with "no" in the center.[11] White may be the color of maidenly submission and the wintry shroud, but it also the color of the nun's or saint's renunciation of the world; and "*this* implication of 'white,'" as Wolff has observed, "asserts not receptivity, but mastery and the will for self-determination" (*ED*, 409).

Letters come in white envelopes on white paper, and they bear the living sentiments ("the Alive") of the author. Besides the one containing his cold heart, the "chest" into which her distant master would fold the surrogate white sheets, stamped with the scarlet seal of Dickinson's amply restrained personal passions, would be, presumably, a letter chest, a more elegant version of Mrs. E. P. W. Packard's linen drawer or the filigree card holder in "The Purloined Letter." White in Dickinson's letters and poems betokens the power of the written word, instrument of *her* mastery. "Mine, says the queen, "by the Right of the White Election!" (#528). Since she, instead of the grim Father of Calvinism, exercises this right, "the White Election" must be the writing of poetry,

Dickinson's chosen vocation. By contrast with the blackmail occasioned by Poe's and Mrs. Packard's purloined letters, however, the power of the word for Dickinson lay not with the mere recipient but with the author of the letters. As attested by Dickinson's manuscript poems—"my letter to the World" (#441), resurrected from a bureau drawer after her death by her sister, Lavinia—letters, words do not lose their power to communicate the author's will even when locked in a dark casket or dungeon. They live on—potentially forever, surrogates "in white" of the buried but undying female consciousness. Like Mrs. Packard's, therefore, Dickinson's (also married?) lover in a far land will strive in vain to put the lid on her queenly authority.

"Mine—here—in Vision—and in Veto!" (#528). Notice the *here* in this proclamation. Unlike the saint, Dickinson's saintly queen does not postpone her royal gratification forever. In her wordplay, far more sophisticated than Mrs. Packard's, *No* (the Veto) is homonymous with *know* (the Vision), another word that contains it and that, like *snow*, also contains the word *now*. "Now" as well as "No" is the mixed message of much of Dickinson's poetry as of her "love letters." By dwelling upon feelings of pain and loss, the "white sustenance," instead of "the divine crust" of immediate gratification, Dickinson proposed, in a sense, to eat her white bread and have it, too.

Through the pain of "No-ing," of denying herself the immediate pleasures of marriage and the "common" life, the queenly poet expected to *know*. But she did not reserve this higher consciousness to some future estate; she wanted it "here" in the present, the *now* of *know*. Appropriating as the vestment of her knowledge the chill whiteness by which an earlier generation identified an exclusively male potency, the female consciousness in Dickinson's poems put on a regal power. And though her power grew out of pain, it gave her command of the word. Dickinson may have hesitated to marry Judge Lord, or anyone else, because the terms of her vocation required her to go "hungry," and marriage, she feared, would diminish the pain that earned her daily bread, "Anguish" being, in her psychology, the leavening of the poetic consciousness. (Again, I hasten to point out, the tropes in this last sentence are Dickinson's, not mine; and as usual she is turning convention on its head, even as she uses conventional imagery.)[12]

The White Exploit and the Notch Between

In Dickinson's poetry, as in Poe's allegory of the thwarted will, "The Pit and the Pendulum," the span of human existence from birth to death is often represented by a "crescent" or an "arc" or (in one poem, "A Clock stopped—," which funnels in and out of the word *Noon* at the center like an hour glass filled with white sand) by a "Pendulum of snow" (#287). As a schoolgirl, Dickinson had studied William Paley's *Natural Theology* (1802) with its classic example of "a watch upon the ground" as evidence of "design." Since we can say of nature as of the watch "that its several parts are framed and put together for a purpose," Paley inferred a grand designer from the orderly arrangement of the natural universe.[13] Dickinson concurred, but the fragments of clocks and watches scattered about in her poems give the "argument by design" a sinister twist. God's plan, or plot, for the universe, to her mind as to Poe's (in *Pym* and *Eureka*), would seem to involve disintegration, the "annihilation" of the individual consciousness.

Poe's model for a universe run on such a plan was a pair of interlocking cones that spin, not unlike the gyres that would intersect in the poetry of William Butler Yeats, signaling a "second coming" when "things fall apart" and "the center cannot hold." The phenomenon in nature that brought this model most vividly to Poe's mind was the whirlpool, or maelstrom; and one of Dickinson's poetic versions of "The Pit and the Pendulum" (there are others, such as "A Pit—but Heaven over it," #1712) turns on just this figure for the disintegrating universe run by a distant, watchmaker God:

> 'Twas like a Maelstrom, with a notch,
> That nearer, every Day,
> Kept narrowing its boiling Wheel
> Until the Agony
>
> Toyed coolly with the final inch
> Of your delirious Hem— (#414)

So close to mental dissolution that her agony is displaced to the hem of her dress, Dickinson's delirious lady is too far gone to resolve this crisis by the cool exercise of reason that saves Poe's prisoner from the sharp pendulum, or that enables his self-possessed mariner to calculate his way out of the whirlpool in "A Descent into the Maelstrom." The only way out for the lady in the damp gown would seem to be the mysterious "notch" in the perimeter of the maelstrom's "boiling Wheel."

Cynthia Griffin Wolff sees the notched whirlpool as "a cog in some strange cosmic machine."[14] Like Poe, Dickinson has placed us inside the watch that proves the existence of God even as it "ticks our lives" toward the grave. This reading is corroborated in the next stanza, which explicitly introduces a timepiece:

As if a Goblin with a Gauge—
Kept Measuring the Hours—
Until you felt your Second
Weigh, helpless, in his Paws—

Elsewhere in Dickinson's poetry, the "notch" is the narrow passage—the coffin, closed carriage, or grave—that separates this life from the next; it is the claustral void that the mind must confront once the pendulum of Poe's tale ceases to swing. Accordingly, nicked by time, Dickinson's prisoner in the maelstrom poem faces the pit:

As if your Sentence stood—pronounced—
And you were frozen led
From Dungeon's luxury of Doubt
To Gibbets, and the Dead—

Riddle: What is like drowning in a whirlpool, falling into the paws of a demon, and mounting the gallows to be hanged all three?

The answer can not be Death itself, because the speaker in Dickinson's gothic nightmare is suddenly snatched back to consciousness from each of these extremities. Instead of a literal death, "It" would seem to be a flirting with death, the temporary insanity of slumping into the void as if swooning into a lover's bed. Familiar with the common play upon sexual intercourse as "dying" in Elizabethan and seventeenth-century poetry, Dickinson found the mere sight of Death "So appalling—it exhilarates—" (Just "Looking at Death, is Dying," she said in another "'Tis" poem of the period, #281.)

Whereas Poe's characters often yield themselves willingly to the darkness, however, even Dickinson's most abandoned "inebriates" resist its erotic tug with their last ounce of consciousness. In the end, "'Twas like a Maelstrom, with a notch," offers a choice between "anguishes" similar to the dilemma of the lovers in "I cannot live with You—": "Which Anguish was the utterest—then— / To perish, or to live?" Though it may lead to paradise, death, like love, is to be feared in Dickinson's poetry because it swallows up the individual consciousness.

Yet if she found the grave so repulsive, why did Dickinson as a young poet flirt with death so ardently? If she feared and hated death, why was she, apparently, like young Walt Whitman, half in love with it?

Surely there was little to titillate the mentally healthy witness in the ghastly deaths that often attended childbirth in the nineteenth century before Dr.

Oliver Wendell Holmes, at great risk to his career from the medical establishment, linked puerperal fever to the physician's or midwife's dirty hands. Even the homely "mouse in the breast," tuberculosis, which could leave the victim a becomingly pale corpse in its early stages, could so disfigure the patient if it advanced too far before she died (as it did in the case of Dickinson's pretty cousin Mary Norcross) as to preclude an open casket. The fact is, until her father died in Dickinson's middle age, the poet's acquaintance with death was largely theoretical, despite the illusion of personal intimacy with death and dying in so much of her early poetry. Also, there were less morbid reasons for Dickinson's fascination with human extremity than a young woman's romancing the shadow of Mr. Death, as she romanticized the more fleshly, if not so eligible, gentlemen of her acquaintance (while likewise keeping them at a distance).

According to the personal legend that has grown up around her, no ghostlier recluse ever held herself more remote from the world than Dickinson. Yet, actually, in the privy chambers of her queenly ambition, no rival strove with greater fervor than she to speak as the "representative" American poet that Emerson, in "The Poet," so confidently predicted would be a man—"He is isolated among his contemporaries by truth and by his art, but with this consolation in his pursuits, that they will draw all men sooner or later"—and to whom Walt Whitman predictably assigned his own testosterone in the 1855 "Preface" to *Leaves of Grass* (*EEL*, 448).

A not so morbid reason for Dickinson's fascination with the grave, therefore, as for Whitman's, was precisely the democratic nature of death. In death as in sleep, said Dickinson, "All Hue" is "forgotten": "Color—Caste—Denomination— / These—are Time's Affair— / Death's diviner Classifying / Does not know they are—" (#970). The universe may be the menacing experiment or machine of a distant watchmaker god who, as in the maelstrom poem, "remembers" only at the last instant, if at all, to rescue the faint heroine from the more punctual "Fiend" with the time gauge (and scythe?). But death is also the great leveler: in death, whether the chrysalis be "Circassin," "Blonde," or "Umber," said Dickinson, from it emerges "Equal Butterfly." No matter that the newspapers branded Nat Turner as a savage fanatic, Madison Washington as a thief and murderer, and Mrs. E. P. W. Packard as a fool, "Death's large—Democratic fingers," like those of a soothing lover, "Rub away the Brand—" (#970).

Feet of the Bold

Another reason why "It" in "'Twas like a Maelstrom, with a notch," cannot be a literal death is that the words of the poem are ascribed to the anguished speaker, and death is the one journey from which no Ishmael returns to tell the tale. The "White Exploit," Dickinson called it, because death presented to her writer's consciousness not so much a snow-capped mountain waiting to be scaled as an eternally blank page waiting to be filled. Even for the poet, death was the one compelling subject that "Once to achieve, annuls the power / Once to communicate—" (#922). Helped along by the Trinitarian doctrine of a long wait between the moment of dying and the judgment day, Dickinson solved this technical problem—how to communicate the one experience from which no witness survives—by (almost) never allowing the deceased speaker in the proleptic poems to reach the end of her journey. "Foot of the bold did least attempt it—," says Dickinson of the great nonadventure of actually reaching the land of the dead, because the dead "perish from our Practice" (#922). The truly bold cling to life with the undying will of Poe's buried (but not entirely dead) Madelines and Lenores.

The boldest "feet" in Dickinson's constant punning allusions to her own work are the poet's, and the power to communicate in words is as much at issue in her nightmares of the buried consciousness as in Poe's. The mesmeric power over the minds of ordinary people that Poe ascribed to prose, however, Dickinson appropriated to poetry. In an America psychologically as well as politically leveled by the trauma of the Civil War, Dickinson could claim a "representative" status for the reclusive poet because she was redefining the "science" of human motives as the generation of Poe and Emerson had understood it.

When Dickinson attended Mount Holyoke Female Seminary in 1848, the curriculum included besides William Paley's "natural theology" the mental philosophy of Thomas Upham, Hawthorne's old teacher and perhaps America's most effective purveyor of the Scottish Realism of Reid and Stewart. Upham had published the first two-volume edition of his *Elements of Mental Philosophy* in 1831, leaving open the question into just how many classes the human faculties are properly to be divided. Having discovered Asa Burton in the meantime, he brought out in 1834 a new one-volume treatise on the will that opted for the tripartite system, but this innovation was not fully incorporated into his *Elements*, the Mount Holyoke text, until the new edition of 1869, more than twenty years after Emily Dickinson had left the classroom. All of which is to say that an important part of her curriculum was already outmoded when Dickinson was still a schoolgirl.[15]

Long after he adopted the three-part division of the mind into intellect, sensibilities, and will, Upham adamantly clung to a cherished tenet of the earlier intellectual philosophy: that in the mind's chain of command, the intellect always comes first. "As a general thing, there is, and can be no movement of the sensibilities, no such thing as an emotion, desire, or feeling of moral obligation, without an antecedent action of the intellect" (*UEMP*, vol. 2, 25–26).[16] That is, Upham still believed with Stewart and Reid that before the mind can truly fear or desire something, it must *know* who or what it fears or desires. Thus in the normal mind of man or woman, cognition (seen by many in Upham's day as the "masculine" part) had primary authority over emotion (the "feminine" part).

Having mapped the principalities of the three-part mind and having set the order of precedence among them, Upham felt he could say, as early as 1834, "The work is finished. The depths of the mind have been entered; the heights have been ascended; the boundaries have been set up."[17] Upham's imperialistic metaphor, celebrating the early psychologist's role as explorer and colonizer, assumes the geographic model (as in Poe's "mountain of Mind" and Sophia Hawthorne's "Chimborazo heights") characteristic of faculty psychology and most other nineteenth-century views of mind before Freud, whose early conceptions were likewise spatial.

The generation of Poe and Hawthorne had tested those boundaries, fringed as they were by gender and racial limitations. Dickinson and her generation pushed them even further. On her mountain of Mind (as on that of William James), not only do the old boundaries disappear, pure intellect—the ethereal region raised to the heights by the rationalists of the eighteenth and early nineteenth centuries—descends to the tableland, and emotion rises to the summit.

Besides being ill and homesick, Dickinson may have decided not to return to Mount Holyoke after only a year because, at eighteen, she realized that the new seminary, not yet a college, largely rehashed what she had already been taught. (As a secondary school student at the Amherst Academy, however, Dickinson's assigned text in mental philosophy had been Upham's still earlier work of 1831 on the "Intellectual Powers.") "We have a very fine school," she wrote her friend Abiah Root about the Amherst Academy. "There are Mental Philosophy, Geology, Latin, and Botany. How large they sound, don't they?"[18] But not large enough, the "Mental Philosophy" especially, for the mature Dickinson, whose poetry by 1862 already assumes a theory of mind and motive that lies closer to William James's conception of consciousness than to Thomas Upham's.

Whether It Be Rune

If Dugald Stewart's texts dominated American education about the mind in 1825 (as Thomas Jefferson said), and if Upham's held sway around 1855, by 1870 the field was overtaken by textbooks in which mental philosophy was giving way to a recognizably modern "psychology" of the mind, such as that exemplified by the work of Alexander Bain (1818–1903), another Scot, who built his system on the ruins of his countrymen's theory of Common Sense. "For a half-century," writes a modern editor of his two major works, "Bain's volumes *were* psychology in the English-speaking world."[19]

Earlier commentators had insisted, with Dugald Stewart in *Philosophy of the Active Powers*, that emotion and intellect "are very intimately, and indeed insepa-rably, connected in all our mental operations" (*EW*, 2). The titles alone of Bain's books—*The Senses and the Intellect* (1855) and *The Emotions and the Will* (1859)—sug-gest a fundamental change in Anglo-American thinking about the mind that would pave the way for the next text to dominate the schools in America, Wil-liam James's *Principles of Psychology* (1890). Bain still divided the mind into three parts; but by relegating intellect and emotion to different volumes of his psy-chology, he was no longer placing them in adjoining chambers of the mental structure it purported to elucidate. And though he did not fully discuss the emotions until his second volume, Bain put feeling first. That is, he asserted, we feel *before* we think—if we think at all.

Common Sense philosophy had always made thinking antecedent to feeling even in the deranged mind. Emotion may drive the will, but the intellect dic-tates its course of action: in the healthy mind, said Stewart, "our intellectual powers are the instruments by which we attain the ends recommended to us by our active propensities" (*EW*, 2). The instrument Stewart particularly had in mind was the compass. Stewart and his followers in the Scottish tradition ad-mitted that "passion is the gale" driving the ship, but "Reason," he iterated in *Philosophy of the Active Powers*, is "the card," the floating dial that indicates direc-tion (*EW*, 2).

Just as Emily Dickinson dismantled Paley's watch, removing herself from "the dial life" so disinterestedly set going by the watchmaker, Bain dismantled the mind's compass by severing the emotions from any necessary tie with a guiding intellect even in the normal mind. So much for Stewart's "cool exercise of reason," designed to impose "manly" restraint upon the passions; at a stroke, Bain had—in Stewart's (and Upham's and Hawthorne's) terms—radically "feminized" the mind.

Bain not only pulled apart the old idea of mind; he also redefined the main function of the instrument as precisely as Emily Dickinson was redefining it in the poems of the 1860s. "How adequate unto itself / Its properties shall be / Itself unto itself and none / Shall make discovery" (#822). The "It" in this poem is no riddle: it is "Consciousness," the "basis of the great superstructure known as Mind" in Bain's system and the chief property exercised by the mind in Dickinson's poems of separation and loss (*EW*, 3).

Occupied with mental phenomena, or "states of mind," Bain (and Dickin-son) accepted one great legacy of Common Sense realism—its reliance on the data of the senses as the starting point of knowledge and feeling—and rejected the other: that those data give all normal minds the same direct (or "real") perception of "material things." On the contrary, said Bain (as had David Hume, yet another Scot, before him): "There is no possible knowledge of the world except in reference to our minds. Knowledge means a state of mind; the notion of material things is a mental thing. We are incapable of discussing the existence of an independent material world; the very act is a contradiction."[20]

William James would give this aspect of the new view of mind its definitive statement in his *Principles*, published shortly after the first, posthumous collection of Emily Dickinson's poetry: "Every thought is part of a personal consciousness." But Dickinson had already written in 1864 that "This Consciousness that is aware, / Of Neighbors and the Sun," is "Attended by a single Hound / Its own identity" (#822).

Like Bain, America's first great poet of the private sensibility was not a "realist" but a phenomenalist (more precisely, an "epiphenomenalist," to the extent that she believed, with Bain, that mental processes depend upon physical ones for their expression). The mind in Dickinson's poetry has lost not only the Transcendentalist's intuitive contact with other minds, human and divine, but also the realist's direct knowledge of the material world. Informed by the senses, the private consciousness could still read the "book" of nature, but any significance it assigned to a natural phenomenon, for example a bird's song, was strictly subjective.

This had been true of Poe's recluse in "The Raven" when reading a supernatural meaning into the bird's croak. Poe's grieving lover, however, was a madman, whereas Dickinson denies even to the healthiest minds the power to apprehend "common" meanings in the most familiar natural objects. A tree may crash in the forest, or a bird may sing, and each will make a "real" noise, whether or not any human auditor is there to hear. The bird, says Dickinson in "To Hear an Oriole sing," "sings the same, unheard, / As unto Crowd—" (#526). But hearing (or seeing or feeling) an oriole (or loon or whale) lies in the ear or eye or touch—ultimately the mind—of the beholder: "The Fashion of the Ear / Attireth that it hear / In Dun, or fair—" (#526).

This is especially so when the beholder assigns human significance to a natural object: "So whether it be Rune, / Or whether it be none / Is of within" (#526). However cryptic, runes were letters of a human alphabet, taking their meaning from writer and reader. Any "Tune" (i.e., message or music) that the auditor perceives in the noise a bird makes, she and her language have encoded there: "The 'Tune is in the Tree—'" objects the "Skeptic," whether realist or idealist; to which Dickinson the phenomenalist retorts, "'No Sir! In Thee!'" Emerson might tear his bird from the cradling bough and declare, "Nothing is fair or good alone"; but this "fair" reading of nature, to Dickinson's mind, is no less imposed upon it than the "dun" reading of Poe's dark fowl by a madman. What we lose by a strictly "internal" view of nature is "The Object Absolute"; what we gain is the free exercise of a supremely human consciousness. Or as Dickinson herself put the matter: "Perception of an object costs / Precise the Object's loss— / Perception in itself a Gain / Replying to its Price" (#1071).

Bain on Pain

Before he defined *consciousness*, Alexander Bain ran through more than a dozen of the usual meanings of the term, including one from Dugald Stewart: "This word denotes the immediate knowledge which the mind has of its sensations and thoughts, and, in general, of all its present operations." Under such a definition, Bain objected, consciousness is simply one faculty among many—albeit an important one—and an intellectual faculty at that (*EW*, 603).

For Bain—and here is where the new consciousness psychology spoke most directly to Emily Dickinson—"the property named feeling, or consciousness" was "an ultimate, or irreducible, manifestation," not just of a single faculty at work, but of the whole of "mental life" (*EW*, 3). And it was roughly synonymous with emotion: "The three terms, Feeling, Emotion, and Consciousness, will, I think, be found in reality to express one and the same fact or attribute of mind."[21] And again: "Emotion is True Consciousness" (*EW*, 611).

If feelings or emotions stimulate the personal consciousness more than other states of mind, which feelings are the most exciting? Poe had recommended sad or mournful ones to the poet, particularly those elicited by "the death of a beautiful woman." In Dickinson's proleptic poems, the mournful feelings are those of the dying woman herself.

Locked in a dark bedchamber or coffin or grave, Dickinson's lady in white hardly enjoys a prospect ideally suited to mental health. "The prisoner in the black-hole has a much more rapid transition of ideas," said Bain, "than he that walks abroad in the light of day." As if speaking directly to Poe's prisoners or the faint lady in the maelstrom poem, Bain recommended "the observation of the outer world by the senses" as a means of calming and arresting "a morbid whirl of the brain." Unlike the earlier Scots, however, Bain conceded "that many of our studies that regard the outer world have precisely the same exciting and exhausting tendency as is now described" (*EW*, 607).

The new consciousness psychology saw no essential difference between the "studious life" of the poet or philosopher and the experiments of the scientist because, said Bain, "the mode of viewing the phenomena of mind and the mode of viewing the phenomena of matter" are the same, "the general fact of consciousness being equally indispensable to both." If anything, Bain found the introspective life more "exhausting" than the so-called active life precisely because it was, mentally, the more "exciting." This is basically the argument of Dickinson's "renunciation" poems (such as "Success is counted sweetest / By those who ne'er succeed" [#67]; "A *Wounded* Deer—leaps highest—" [#165] ; or "Renunciation—is a piercing Virtue" [#745]) where deprivation and loss constitute not only the subject of the poem but also its experience.

If "To comprehend a nectar / Requires sorest need" (#67), then the consciousness that sucks the marrow of life most deeply, by this logic, belongs to the person who severs herself most completely from life's immediate pleasures. (A good philologist, Dickinson surely knew that "nectar" in its root meaning refers to an "anti-death" drink, a "liquor never brewed.") As the logic of deprivation spilled over into Dickinson's personal life, she left behind the mental philosophy she had learned in school. In place of Upham's perpetual conflict between intellect and emotion for control of the will, mental life for Dickinson as for Bain came largely to consist of the struggle between two basic, contrary emotions: the consciousness of pleasure and the consciousness of pain. "According to the degree of either pain or pleasure," said Bain, "is the degree of consciousness, or feeling" (*EW,* 600). In this version of the psychomachy—where the inner struggle is not between virtue and vice, good and evil, but between classes of feeling—pain, moreover, had the edge. "In fact, we are so constituted," said Bain, "that the fountains of emotion are more completely stirred by certain kinds of pain than by the generality of pleasures" (*EW,* 33). Because the "excitement of the brain" is greatest "under irritation, or suffering," he concluded, "Pain is perhaps the most intense and decided manifestation of consciousness" (*EW,* 600).

One of Dickinson's most violent metaphors for the consciousness under "irritation, or suffering" was the forge of the blacksmith. In the following account of the psyche's trial by fire, she throws open the door of the forge and exposes us to a blinding white light:

> Dare you see a Soul *at the White Heat?*
> Then crouch within the door—
> Red—is the Fire's common tint—
> But when the vivid Ore
> Has vanquished Flame's conditions,
> It quivers from the Forge
> Without a color, but the light
> Of unanointed Blaze.

Least Village has its Blacksmith
Whose Anvil's even ring
Stands symbol for the finer Forge
That soundless tugs—within—
Refining these impatient Ores
With Hammer, and with Blaze
Until the Designated Light
Repudiate the Forge— (#365)

Before transferring its heat to the molten ore in this poem about consciousness at the melting point, the fire in Dickinson's forge is the color of the blood
that burns oxygen (one of "Flame's conditions") in the human heart. When
that flame goes out, the heart might be expected to die; and, indeed, "Dare you
see a Soul *at the White Heat?*" can be read as another proleptic poem in which the
whitened soul "quivers" into the "Degreeless Noon" of eternity as the internal
workings of the watch fly to pieces under the relentless hammering of the
blacksmith. The heart that "dies" in this extended sonnet, however, probably
does not cease to beat altogether. More likely, it is only tempered by the hammer and the heat, since the forge "tugs" on in the second octave, "soundless"
because metaphysical.

In "Holy Sonnet" number 14, John Donne, using the metaphor of a tin-
smith, had asked God to "batter" his heart until it mended and admitted Him,
even if the "ravishing" God applied for entry with the force of a rapist. Though
it is unlikely she read Donne, Dickinson's blacksmith is not exactly Longfellow's village smithy beneath the sheltering tree. Recalling the obscure master
who fumbles with the maiden soul in Dickinson's love poems, his lurid forge
would seem to be that of a sooty Vulcan, the rapist god. If we see its glare as
the light of faith, the forge pounds at the skeptic's heart until her doubts melt
away and the purified soul "repudiates" the turmoil of its earlier struggle to
take a lover, or a vocation, independently of the iron master's will. By this reading, "Dare you see a Soul *at the White Heat?*" rings upon the Calvinist tradition of
"election" as set forth, for example, in Jonathan Edwards's fire and brimstone
sermon, "Sinners in the Hands of An Angry God," where a chosen few are
plucked arbitrarily ("elected") to heaven while the rest slip helplessly through
God's fingers into the flames.

We draw closer to the heart of Dickinson's vision, however, if, crouching
inside its mysterious portal, we look upon the white glare of the "finer forge" as
the "Designated Light" of a personal consciousness refined by strong feelings,
whether of pleasure or pain. Besides alluding to a chosen one, *anointed*, in the
context of a blacksmith's shop, implies a blaze dampened with water to reduce

its heat. "*Unanointed*," the fire in Dickinson's internal forge flames so high that it burns itself out, yet the "impatient ores" in the heart's forge do not consume each other, leaving only the radiance of pure intellect devoid of passion. They flow together into a new compound whose intense light, though born of heat, is "Without a color."

This is what happens to the mind in most of Dickinson's poems on the aftermath of intense suffering, such as "After great pain, a formal feeling comes—" (#341). When the heart, the feeling part of the mind, grows "stiff" under constant pounding, the rest of consciousness, instead of losing its "impurities," as it would under the old psychology, glazes over, too. Brought to the highest pitch by emotion at the white heat, the overwrought "emotional consciousness" (Alexander Bain's term) blanks out the "intellectual consciousness" (*EW*, 610, 613). Ceasing for a time to feel, the battered psyche ceases to know. And ceasing to know, it ceases to believe: it loses what Bain called "volitional" consciousness. Dickinson's forge, in fact, recalls Bain's metaphor of the fort: "Sound belief," he writes, "instead of being a pacific and gentle growth, is in reality the battering of a series of strongholds, the conquering of a country in hostile occupation" (*EW*, 583).

Though they have a common basis—the perception of "difference" in hue or pitch, for example—intellect and emotion were "antithetical" modes of consciousness in Bain's scheme. Thus, he believed, when the mind is fully engrossed "under pleasure and pain," this "engrossment . . . extends so far as not to permit the full possible development of the intellectual modes of excitement" (*EW*, 622). This neutralizing, or numbing, effect upon "intellectual consciousness" of too much emotional "excitement" suggests why the color white, Melville's colorless all-color, blankets Emily Dickinson's poems so ambiguously.

What the "White Exploit" (death or dying) and the "White Election" (poetry or the poetic life) had in common for Dickinson was pain. Giving up pleasures of the moment, she chose to live intimately with present pain (or the idea of pain) because she considered painful emotions to be mentally more invigorating than pleasurable ones. Pain fed the poetic consciousness, in Dickinson's view, as no other sensation could. Carried to the white heat of "pure" emotional consciousness, however, pain burned itself out—and the other modes of consciousness along with it. At the melting point, as the deprivation poems attest, Dickinson found that "Pain—has an Element of Blank—."

To fill in that blank, like a lover inscribing her heartfelt words in scarlet letters upon white paper, was the great purpose of Dickinson's life. Consequently, she assigned tremendous power to the Word, a power, according to consciousness psychology, that resides in the mind of the individual user of language, not in nature or the Oversoul (as Emerson's ideal theory of language had alleged). Language gave human beings the power to detach their experience from its merely "local habitation" (Bain's phrase) in immediate sensation—as when we instinctively draw back from an open flame—and to relocate experience as meaning in the mind, thereby making possible such conceits as the forge of Dickinson's blacksmith.

By the "intervention of language, the coupling of the 'name' with the 'local habitation,'" said Bain, we give "a distinct existence" to mental phenomena, "and they become a subject of mental manipulation on their own account" (*EW*, 572). For the poet, especially, naming is as close as human beings get to creating. Dickinson was not taking us back to Emerson's and Whitman's idea of the poet as Adam in the garden, however, because her poet looks more like Eve, and because the displacing power of language enables the poet of private consciousness only to make propositions about things—light, for example— not things themselves. The poet's power to fill the notch or void in human knowledge with language, in other words, engendered belief rather than truth.

The Psychology of Belief

Belief, in its "primordial form," Bain defined as "the expectation of some contingent future about to follow on our action" (*EW*, 569). (He might almost have said that present actions, in William James's phrase, "present themselves far less in the guise of effects of past experience than in that of probable causes of future experience.") As such, belief may be either true or false. I refrain from touching the fire because I believe it will burn; or I light a fire before dawn to assure that the sun will rise. Both are genuine acts of belief, though one is based on superstition and the other on fact, for both meet Bain's two principle criteria by which belief, the third "mode" of consciousness, is to be distinguished from emotion and intellect.

However simple—that fire burns—or however complicated—Paley's argument by design, say—no proposition about life or death, according to Bain, "can be set forth as belief that does not implicate in some way or other the order, arrangements, or sequences of the universe" (*EW*, 570). Like a watch, in other words, belief speaks always of relations (as in William James's account of "The Will to Believe," where the whole of consciousness consists largely of the perception of relation).

The second criterion by which we identify belief, or the "volitional consciousness," is that it must be active. Belief, says Bain, "has no meaning, except in reference to our actions," particularly of the will (*EW*, 568). Besides presuming to know how the parts of the universe fit together, that is, belief also implies conscious choice. (God himself can appear as a rapist, as in Dickinson's more violent poems of religious conversion, when he denies the power of volition to the human consciousness.)

Just such a technical act of belief underlies Emily Dickinson's apparent rejection of the world: "Renunciation—is the Choosing / Against itself— / Itself to justify / Unto itself—" (#745). The poet makes a calculated choice to withdraw only "When larger function— / Make that appear— / Smaller—that Covered Vision—Here—". Or, less cryptically: "The abdication of Belief / Makes the Behavior small— / Better an ignis fatuus / Than no illume at all—" (#1551). Better the false light of faith—in God, an ideal lover, or some other "contingent future"—than to act blindly and to no great purpose "Here" and "Now."

Because they seemed "small" by comparison with "the Behavior" (including the writing of poetry) that she could imagine for herself in the future, Dickinson said "no" to the usual gratifications of the moment. She gave up or postponed marriage, children, a front pew in the Congregational Church, and other prizes that would normally befall the daughter of Amherst's leading citizen in the 1870s because she was "letting go / a Presence—for an Expectation—" (#745). This is close to Alexander Bain's definition of belief in its simplest form—"the expectation of some contingent future about to follow on our action"—except that Dickinson did not expect the hoped-for future to follow any time soon.

Assuming that we live in a "contingent" universe, Dickinson made her leaps of faith knowing that they were acts of will rather than acts of God, though she nonetheless believed in them, an attitude William James would soon call "pragmatic." Still it was hope, I would argue, rather than the white sustenance, despair, that moved Dickinson to take up the ascetic life.

In the higher forms of belief, such as "Faith, in the religious sense," said Bain, "we dwell in the prospective." Moreover, he argued, the extent of "our future happiness" is just "in proportion" as we do so (*EW*, 573). When Dickinson proclaimed, "I dwell in Possibility," she distanced herself as far as possible from Bain's man who "thinks merely of his present, or of the work that is under his hand," therefore narrowing his "sphere of belief ... to the utmost limits, having reference only to the instrumentality of actual operations" (*EW*, 573). Courting the possible at the expense of the actual, Dickinson knew that she was taking future happiness on blind faith, since "The Future—never spoke— / Nor will He—like the Dumb— / Reveal by sign—a syllable / Of His Profound To Come—" (#672). But she was not merely giving up pleasure for pain (however theoretical) in the prospect of future good; she was seeking a present condition of belief in which, according to Bain, "Ideal emotion is consummated in its happiest phase" (*EW,* 573).

Besides a satisfying future, that is, Dickinson was also expecting an immediate psychological benefit. Here is where Dickinson's psychology seems to intersect most sharply with Bain's and where twentieth-century readers who see her as a chronic depressive most require his prosy gloss. "As beings . . . that look before and after," said Bain, we give "the state of belief . . . an incessant control over the temper for happiness or misery. . . . In all that regards our future happiness, therefore, and the future of all those interests that engage our sympathy, belief, when the assurance of *good* in the distance, is the name for a serene, satisfying, and happy tone of mind. Through it, as has long been said, we have already the realizing of what we long for" (*EW,* 573).

By detaching both pain and pleasure from mere circumstance through the language of poetry, Dickinson seems to have willed herself into a profound state of belief. Her belief in belief gave her bold feet the sure-footedness, in the melodramatic language of gothic fiction, to stare unfaintingly into the pit and record what she saw in that darkness made visible. ("The believing and decided temper," said Bain, "is ever and anon arresting us on the brink of some abyss of distraction and terror, and thereby conserving in their purity our times of enjoyment, and interfering to save us from new depths of despondency" [*EW,* 575].) From the more Poesque elements in her poetry, however, we can infer that while Dickinson's faith in *some* future beyond the grave never faltered, she was not always secure in "the assurance of *good* in the distance" and, therefore, of a "happy tone of mind" in the moment.

Though God, especially in her early work, may play the gallant lover in one poem and the chill villain in the next, Dickinson, in matters of religion, probably never entirely disbelieved; but she did have her doubts. (When Dickinson pretended to let Colonel Higginson become her "mentor," she was beyond the bourne of his old-fashioned notions of the ideal master.) Logically, "the opposite of belief," as Bain noted, "is disbelief." Psychologically speaking, however, to Bain's way of thinking "these two states are identical" (*EW,* 573). The traveler's journey advances to a fork in the road, said Bain: "I believe that the one will conduct me to my home, and disbelieve the same affirmation respecting the other. In either view," proposes Bain, "my mind is in the condition of certainty, conviction, or faith, and I derive both the means of reaching my dwelling, and the cheering tone that a conviction gives to one who is looking forward to a wished-for end" (*EW,* 573–74).

What really disturbs the psyche as it approaches the brink—marriage, eternity, or any other "odd fork in being's road" that occupies the mind in

Dickinson's poetry—is not the prospect of good suddenly turning into evil (so long as both remain prospective), it is the present uncertainty about which one to expect in the contingent future. "The real opposite of belief as a state of mind is not disbelief," Bain affirms, "but doubt, uncertainty; and the close alliance between this and the emotion of fear is stamped on every language" (*EW*, 574). Hence, at the extremes in Emily Dickinson's poetry, the "volitional consciousness" alternates between belief and its contrary, or inverse, "Terror," leaving the will wildly free on the one hand ("Mine—By the Right of the White Election!" [#528]) and innervated, or frozen, on the other ("A Quartz Contentment—Like a Stone" [#341]).

Between these psychological extremes, balancing on the dot of snow where elation and depression shade into each other, Dickinson gave the following order of priority to the choices afforded her by the new psychology:

> The Heart asks Pleasure—first—
> And then—Excuse from Pain—
> And then—those little Anodynes
> That deaden suffering—
> And then—to go to sleep—
> And then—if it should be
> The will of its Inquisitor
> The privilege to die— (#536)

Back to Africa

And the will therein lieth, which dieth not. Who knoweth the mysteries
of the will, with its vigor?

—Edgar Allan Poe

Kilimanjaro is a snow covered mountain 19,710 feet high, and is said
to be the highest mountain in Africa. Its western summit is called by the
Masai "Nga'je Nga'i," the House of God. Close to the western summit there
is the dried and frozen carcass of a leopard. No one has explained what the
leopard was seeking at that altitude.

—Ernest Hemingway

Nothing in the world more dangerous than a white schoolteacher.

—Toni Morrison

FOR EMILY DICKINSON in the 1860s and seventies, belief—whether in love and an earthly master, or in the afterlife and a heavenly master—still entailed the conscious will to believe. Thus even in such proleptic poems as "I heard a Fly buzz—when I died—" and "I Felt a Funeral, in my Brain," the mind clings to consciousness even as the body fails it and the physical senses go out one by one. This "gothic" strain in Dickinson's poetic imagination was a holdover from (or critique of) faculty psychology's full faith and credit in the sovereignty of the will.

If intellect was king of the will and emotion the queen, Emily Dickinson (like William James) merged the sovereignty of the two in the unitary offspring of a new mind: "this consciousness that is aware." Older faculty psychology, however, had assumed a sort of master-slave relationship between the cognitive faculties and the appetitive faculties, as between the mind and the physical body. Even one's "repressed" thoughts, the ghostly train that escaped at night when the will was sleeping, had to be whipped back to their dungeons at daybreak and made to stay under lock and key in a kind of perpetual servitude by the moral sense. Otherwise, the age feared, its darkest emotions and animal desires might burst from their cages as in a Poe tale (or a slave uprising) and pull the insufficiently watchful victim down into the abyss. Or the mire.

If I were to illustrate with yet another Poe text the perpetually vigilant aspect of volition under the old psychology, it would not be with his masterful story of blackmail in which the queenly powers of affection are temporarily purloined by the usurping master intellect of the heartless minister. I would choose, instead, Poe's own favorite among his tales, "Ligeia," wherein the dark heroine—betrayed, perhaps even murdered, by her mentally unbalanced husband—comes back to life (or seems to) in the physical body of the pale heroine, the lady Rowena, by dint of a deathless will. (Since the will was swayed more by emotion than intellect, and since savage, dark women were thought to have stronger emotions than their pale sisters or husbands in Poe's day, the pasty Rowena hasn't a ghost of a chance to retain even the use of her own body when Ligeia needs it to upbraid her amnesiac husband for his haste in burying her—and marrying again.)

Faculty psychology's faith in the absolute power of willpower was permanently crippled at the close of the nineteenth century by the "discovery" of the unconscious, a region of the mind that was always beyond the control of the waking will. The appeal of a lordly consciousness ever wielding its sovereignty through absolute command over its volitions died slowly, however. As late as William Dean Howells's *The Shadow of a Dream*, published in 1890, the same year as William James's *Principles of Psychology*, the morally conservative Isabel March, for example, still will not allow her long suffering husband, Basil, to advance the heretical notion that "our feelings are not at our bidding, and that there is no sin where there has been no sinning."[1]

Under faculty psychology, the will, in its capacity as the moral sense (or "executive" of the moral faculties), had been a harsh taskmaster, demanding total obedience from all other departments of the mind, as from the body and its wayward parts. While it conveyed the supreme gift of free will upon the mentally and morally healthy individual, therefore, faculty psychology also imposed upon the psyche what Howells, in another context, would call "a fearful responsibility." This is the burden of his own tale of a raven beauty of strong will, *An Imperative Duty* (1891).

Howells's Dr. Olney, who is modeled on S. Weir Mitchell, makes light of the scruples, but not the other dark charms, of the ravishing Rhoda Aldgate, who, having discovered "the remote taint of her servile and savage origin"— that she has a black ancestor—thinks she is duty-bound to go down South and become a field-worker (*ID*, 223).

Miss Aldgate is a youthful member of the old school. Finding her blackness "repulsive ... in all its shades," Rhoda goes into a "frenzy of abhorence" that brings on a temporary insanity caused not by her newly discovered blackness but by her white heritage: the "hypochondria of the soul," in Dr. Olney's diagnosis (as in Nathaniel Hawthorne's), "into which the Puritanism of her [white] father's race had sickened . . . her, and which so often seems to satisfy its crazy claim upon conscience by enforcing some aimless act of self-sacrifice." Thus the aristocratic Rhoda conceives it to be her "imperative duty" to throw over Olney and "go and live among them and own it [her blackness]. Then perhaps I can learn to bear it, and not hate them so" (ID, 197, 233, 230).

For Howells, Rhoda's self-sacrifice is "aimless" (because improperly directed by her addled will) and thus just as "crazy" as her hate. An advocate of psychological "realism" in fiction, Howells is here satirizing the hyper-refined moral sense or "taste" of Emerson and the philosophical idealists, with its "disgust toward the real business of life" (Stewart). Thus he brings his couple together in the end, as Mrs. Stowe could not, and lets their healthy emotions perform "the effect of common sense" (ID, 231).

Under the new psychology, as Howells and Dr. Olney already knew, the moral sense was necessarily set free from the responsibility of monitoring every waking thought and desire in the rest of the mind and body. ("There's a whole region of experience—half the map of our life—that they tell us must always remain a wilderness, with all its extraordinary phenomena irredeemably savage and senseless," Howells wrote in the The Shadow of a Dream.)[2]

The moral sense was emancipated from this imperative duty, that is, in those minds that could give up the old fetishism of an absolutely free will and accept their kinship with the brute. William James wittily captured the difficulty of doing so for sensibilities brought up on Victorian standards of decorum and self-control when he retold the story, borrowed from Charles Renouvier, of "Dr. Livingstone's argument with the negro conjurer": "The missionary was trying to dissuade the savage from his fetishistic ways of invoking rain. You see, said he, that, after all your operations, sometimes it rains and sometimes it doesn't, exactly as when you have not operated at all. But, replied the sorcerer, it is just the same with you doctors; you give your remedies, and sometimes the patient gets well and sometimes he dies, just as when you do nothing at all" (WJW, 943).

So compelling is this "logic" that the pious missionary is thrown back upon a fetishism of his own. Dr. Livingstone replies that "the doctor does his duty, after which God performs the cure if it pleases Him. Well, rejoined the savage, it is just so with me. I do what is necessary to procure rain, after which God sends it or withholds it according to His pleasure" (WJW, 944).[3]

Not even Dr. Livingstone had a greater sense of "duty" than William James, who, like Emily Dickinson, had come by 1891 to define "moral" as "emotional," and thus the moral sense as just the sort of instinctive fetishism to which the missionary reverts when his fondest beliefs are challenged by the African sorcerer. As he and his age reluctantly (on the whole) gave up mental and moral philosophy for "psychology," therefore, James was not giving up all claims to moral responsibility in human conduct. Rather, what he and his colleagues in the new field of mind had to tell their contemporaries at the end of the nineteenth century was that the old notion of absolute freedom of the will based on a dispassionate, innate power to judge and rationally control human motives was a myth.

Though he applauded Herbert Spencer's ideas of adaptation in the individual, James had little use for the Spencerian theory (at odds with the older "segregationist" school of faculty psychology) "that what was acquired habit in the ancestor may become congenital tendency in the offspring." A "vast superstructure," he noted, "is raised upon that principle" (*WJW*, 947).

The hereditarian view of mind rested, James pointed out, upon a few examples of inherited instincts in animals. "In the human race, where our opportunities for observation are the most complete," he wrote in "Brute and Human Intellect," "we seem to have no evidence whatever which would support the [hereditarian] hypothesis" (*WJW*, 947). Thus James challenged such "Hegelisms," as he called them, as the notion that the genders and the races give the world different shapes because they are born with different minds. The entire human race, James came to believe, is born into the "fetishistic" or primitive subjectivity of Hegel's Africa; and those individual minds that achieve a "higher" subjectivity do so only because successful adaptation to their environment—the Spencerian "adjustment of inner to outer relations"—requires it.

The full story of how the evolutionary (or functional) view "freed" the Anglo-American mind from the hereditarian (or segregationist) view at the end of the nineteenth century would require another volume, and it might well begin with an account of the neuroses, as they were coming to be called, of the James family. For not only the youngest daughter, Alice, whose unrelenting sense of moral responsibility for curbing the slightest insurrection of mind or body kept her bedridden most of her adult life, but all of the male members of the James clan clung like men overboard to many of the most "primitive" moral fetishes of their time and tribe. This was especially true of William James before he lost his faith in the will to believe.

Freeing the Prisoner of Omelas: William James

Because all associations are learned—Man "is *par excellence*," James epigrammatized, "the *educable* animal"—the human race's habitual ways of thinking were not inherited, in James's mature view, but socialized—by the family, the tribe, the nation. The order of associations in the individual human mind, however, he believed early in his professional career, will vary according to the degree to which it learns to be "analytical" or remains merely "intuitive." Both are forms of "reasoning" that distinguish the intellect of all human beings from that of the lower animals; but of the two, James said, analytic reasoning represents a "higher stage" of adaptation (*WJW*, 943).

Since, however, all environments were not equal—not everyone could grow up in the elite James family, for instance—not even all trained minds, James argued, are trained alike. Moreover, not all minds react to the same environment in the same way. A brother and a sister might grow up in the same household and yet develop different minds because her brain was more "instinctive at the outset" while his displayed a "mere absence . . . of definite innate tendencies" (*WJW*, 948).

"We observe an identical difference," James wrote in 1878, the year he married Alice Gibbens, "between men as a whole, and women as a whole" (*WJW*, 948). (Having delivered ten lectures on "The Brain and the Mind" at Johns Hopkins in February of that year, James signed a contract in June for what would eventually become *The Principles of Psychology*. During his honeymoon in July, his friends were amused to learn, he worked on the book.)

Young Professor James's explanation for the intellectual differences between men and women (as between nations) was as complicated as his explanation for why one type of reasoning is "higher" than another; but it had to do with how "the masculine brain"—in 1878 James was also teaching comparative vertebrate anatomy and physiology at Harvard—reaches maturity later than the "feminine" brain. "A young woman of twenty reacts with intuitive promptitude and security in all the usual circumstances in which she may be placed," he began. "Her likes and dislikes are formed; her opinions, to a great extent, the same that they will be through life. Her character is, in fact, finished in its essentials. How inferior to her is a boy of twenty in all these respects" (*WJW*, 948–49).

Warming to his task, James blundered on: "Feeling his power, yet ignorant of the manner in which he shall express it, he is," said the learned philosopher of his youth of twenty (revealing far more than he probably intended), "when compared with his sister, a being of no definite contour." And then, struggling to recover the advantage: "But this absence of prompt tendency in his brain to set into particular modes is the very condition which insures that it shall ultimately become so much more efficient than the woman's" (*WJW*, 949).

When, at age sixty, William James recalled the mental breakdown he suffered while he himself was still in his twenties, he remembered it as a loss of personal contour or form, a metamorphosis in reverse. The "shape" that took possession of his will at this remembered turning point in James's life was that of an autistic youth, the piteous form that Ursula K. Le Guin would borrow from him to fit out the cellars of Omelas: "There arose in my mind the image of an epileptic patient whom I had seen in the asylum, a black-haired youth with greenish skin, entirely idiotic, who used to sit all day on one of the benches, or rather shelves against the wall, with his knees drawn up against his chin, and the coarse gray undershirt, which was his only garment, drawn over them inclosing his entire figure. He sat there ... looking absolutely non-human."[4]

In *The Varieties of Religious Experience* (1902), James attributes this harrowing memory to a "nervous" Frenchman, but his biographers agree that the Frenchman, whose language he had spoken fluently since childhood, was a thin disguise for William James himself. James was tracing his demon to the moment of its inception as the unwanted offspring of fear and memory, still a fertile source of specters, both sexual and racial, in the late nineteenth-century mind: "This image and my fear," said James, "entered into a species of combination with each other."[5]

Though "greenish" instead of black or brown or red, the "non-human species" that issued from this unnatural union—represented in James's mind by an impotent male youth and the androgynous "quivering" mass to which the prospect of becoming like "it" reduced him—was just the sort of "effeminate progeny" that Louis Agassiz had shuddered to think of in 1863 as the "mixed" offspring that would flow from an intermingling of the races in America.[6] It was to this queasy mentor that young William James would apply, two years later, for moral and vocational guidance.

Before dividing minds by sex, young James had addressed the differences he saw in the national minds of more or less equally developed European countries. Basically, what he concluded was that women are born with Italian brains while men develop German ones. The "untutored" German, James said, was apt to be more "loutish" than his counterpart in Italy who exhibited "instinctive perceptions, tendencies to behavior, reactions, in a word, upon his environment" (*WJW*, 948).

James's Anglo-Teutonic prejudices told him that if "drilled" (i.e., disciplined), however, the more speculative German, because of the "mere absence in his brain of definite innate tendencies," could graduate, like the young man who, at twenty, had fallen behind his sister, to "complex regions of consciousness" that the instinctual Italian could never hope to attain (*WJW*, 948). (Not surprisingly, when Professor James helped to establish America's first graduate school at Johns Hopkins, it was based on the model of the German universities.

His novelist brother, however, seemed always to prefer the "feminine" culture of the Italians to the "masculine" culture of the Germans.)

Willy James probably encountered the epileptic youth of his adult night-mares around 1863 when, searching for a vocation, he first visited an asylum in Northampton, Massachusetts, run by William Henry Prince, husband of the Jameses' mentally disturbed cousin Kitty Prince, whose mother had also gone mad. Two years later, in 1865, still seeking to test his masculinity (as he said) and to develop his German brain, James embarked with Louis Agassiz, the Harvard biologist who was so disgusted by miscegenation, on a specimen-hunting expe-dition to Brazil. The twenty-three-year-old William James had barely arrived in Rio, however, when he came down with a high fever and an infection that blinded him temporarily in both eyes and sprinkled his face with eruptions resembling those of smallpox. During the weeks of quarantine, he had time to reflect: "I am now certain that my forte is not to go on exploring expeditions," he wrote Henry Sr. from the hospital. "I am convinced now that I am cut out for a speculative rather than an active life."[7]

Though William James's eyes would trouble him for years to come, he re-covered his sight sufficiently to proceed up the Amazon with Agassiz, and the eruptions on his face eventually went away. The impression left on his mind by the epileptic boy, however, did not. James's delayed reaction to this catatonic figure, lodged in deep memory, suggests why, many years later, the moral phi-losopher would lose a kingdom rather than condone the torment of a single lost soul on the edge of the universe.

In retrospect, the epileptic boy of color became to James's mind a horrifying image of what he himself might have been under different circumstances, a hid-den but always "potential" self hunched and waiting for him to assume its form: "*That shape am I,* I felt, potentially," James wrote in 1902. "Nothing that I possess can defend me against that fate, if the hour for it should strike for me as it struck for him."[8] So horrible was the memory of this emasculating shadow self—it had reduced his manhood to a quivering mass—that young James, in 1870, suffered a "dorsal collapse," the effects of which lingered until he married Alice Gibbens in 1878, and she, as James said, "cured" him.[9]

After *his* mental collapse, Henry James Sr. had turned for comfort to the writings of the Swedish mystic, Emanuel Swedenborg. His eldest son, by con-trast, before he married, looked to the mental and moral philosophy of the mid–nineteenth century. (The elder James was a one-legged man whose miss-ing member, though made of cork rather than whalebone, stood tall in the fam-ily memory as a token of its spiritual and bodily vulnerability—to each other.)

Besides the neo-Kantian essays of Renouvier that he had been reading, Wil-liam James's diary for April 29, 1870, cites Alexander Bain, the faculty psycholo-

gist whose theory of emotion may have informed Emily Dickinson's philosophy of pain. Noting that the day before "was a crisis in my life," James went
on to write, "To-day has furnished the exceptionally passionate initiative which
Bain posits as needful for the acquisition of [healthy] habits. I will see to the
sequel."[10]

This was an early Jamesian affirmation of the will to believe—"My first act
of free will shall be to believe in free will," the diarist resolved—and in the
narrative that he was to make of his remembered life (the "sequel"), it started
the psychically (and physically) maimed hero on the road to recovery.[11] Having
found his place and vocation, like Ben Franklin arriving in Philadelphia and,
in retrospect, mapping out his future, young James had entered the period of
his life and career that would culminate in *The Principles of Psychology*, an inspired
adaptation (or is it a defense?) of old-fashioned mental and moral philosophy
to the new functional psychology.[12]

Almost as reluctant as his sister to posit a part or region of mind utterly
beyond the control of the moral sense, William James, in the *Principles*, grafted
the "moral" aspect of the old psychology onto the new "functional" kind by
focusing upon the mental habits—particularly those formed under strong
emotion, Bain's theme—that the self must develop if it is to be a free-thinking
agent. No one made the connection between habit (the old "attention" of the
associationists) and free will better than Howells in his review of the *Principles*:
"In fact, the will of the weak man is *not* free," Howells interpreted James to
mean; "but the will of the strong man, the man who has *got the habit* of preferring
sense to nonsense and 'virtue' to 'vice,' is a *freed* will."[13]

By 1892, the year of Alice's death, William James's life—as highly wrought
in his memory of its crisis points as Alice's diary or Henry's fiction—had entered a new phase, one more in keeping with other turn-of-the century lives,
such as that of Henry Adams, one of America's first modern autobiographers
to speak of multiple selves, than with Ben Franklin's earlier life of the applied
will. Even as *The Principles of Psychology* issued from press, William James's faith
in the power of the will to serve, unfailingly, as the mind's moral watchdog had
begun to slip. About this time, during another mental crisis similar to the one
he had journalized about twenty years before, James wrote his increasingly in-
valid sister that he had tried the will to believe again but "it is no go. The Will
to Believe won't work." James's lapse of faith in the will to believe coincided
with his field's discovery of the unconscious, "the most important step forward that has occurred in psychology since I have been a student of that science," he avowed in 1901 while lecturing in Edinburgh, seat of the old, faculty
psychology.[14]

Return of the Native: From Eliot to Morrison

By the turn of the century, a touch of "mixed blood" was more likely to inspire admiration than revulsion in the minds of some Europeanized American males, especially when it flowed in the veins of a beautiful woman. Howells's Dr. Olney of *An Imperative Duty* does not fall in love with Rhoda Aldgate until "the thing that had been lurking in a dark corner of Olney's mind, intangible if not wholly invisible [namely, his suspicion that Rhoda has a black ancestor] came out sensitive to touch and sight" (*ID*, 199). (Howells's language here sounds remarkably like that of *Dr. Jekyll and Mr. Hyde*, another tale of the beast within, by Henry James Jr.'s good friend Robert Louis Stevenson.)

Once Rhoda's racial identity has come to light, Olney is far from put off: as he "followed some turn of her head, some movement of her person," writes Howells, "a wave of the profoundest passion surged up in his heart." Even Howells, however, struggling like the rest of his generation to adapt his long-held conceptions of self and civilization to the new discovery of an "irredeemably savage" wilderness within, was enough the child of his race's "Puritanism" to assure (or warn) the reader that this mood in his doctor "was of his emotional nature alone; it sought and could have won no justification from his moral sense, which indeed it simply submerged and blotted out for the time" (*ID*, 223).

When Rhoda and Olney marry, therefore, they must be sent off—permanently, unlike Hawthorne's Hilda and Kenyon of *The Marble Faun*—to live in Rome rather than America, where the olive-skinned Rhoda is taken for an Italian and where Olney "represents to her that it would not be the ancestral color, which is much the same in other races, but the ancestral condition which their American friends would despise if they knew of it" (*ID*, 234). In effect, Howells was saying, the American mind in 1890 was still too Teutonic (and "masculine") to admit even the mildly mixed offspring of Rhoda and Olney to its bosom without rationalizing its ancestral fears of miscegenation and "moral" degeneration.

By 1920, however, the "lost" generation of Ernest Hemingway and Isak Dinesen—the first to be reared on the new Freudian psychology—would not only delve into the depths of the "hidden self" (James) for reassuring traces of their instinctual, emotional (and, therefore, moral and civilized) nature; they also would return, literally, to the geographical origins of the human race to uncover and nourish the life-giving "primitivism" that many felt after the turn of the new century lay unhappily buried in the dry sands of materialism (and modernism).

After Dr. Livingston's "argument with the negro conjurer," as reported by William James, we still have no assurance that it is going to rain. Nor does it rain at the end of T. S. Eliot's "The Waste Land" (1922), a landmark, we are often reminded, in the making of the modernist sensibility. A few heavy drops fall and the thunder speaks, but Eliot's poem ends in dryness and desuetude, no longer limited to the male consciousness in its basic ignorance of what Alice James called the "succulent science" of life.

This dry spell in the American mind's conception of itself lasts, in fact, for almost three more decades, until, beginning in the 1950s, rain returns to the wasteland in a sprinkling of narratives and films from Bernard Malamud's *The Natural* (film version, 1984, by Barry Levinson, who also directed *Rain Man*, 1988) and Saul Bellow's *Henderson the Rain King* (1959), to John Gardner's *Nickel Mountain* (1979) and Terry Gilliam's *The Fisher King* (1991), where the rainmaker is a Robin Williams. What does this omen portend for the future of Western civilization, the "postmodern" sensibility, and race and gender relations in America, to say nothing of climatology and the greenhouse effect?

The particular science of life that inspired "The Waste Land" was physical anthropology, as represented for Eliot by the work of Sir James Frazer, the Scottish anthropologist whose *Golden Bough* (1890–1915) is cited in the footnotes of Eliot's poem. The study of human evolutionary biology, racial variation and classification, this branch of anthropology was the same one from which the polygenisists of "the American school" had hanged themselves in the nineteenth century.

Where they erected "a vast superstructure" of racial prejudice upon the remnants of a few skulls and bones that found their way to Edinburgh and Philadelphia, however, Frazer went back in time and geography to the "cradle of civilization" to study the remains of "primitive" cultures in their homeland, Africa. This was the direction (and general direction is all I am trying to indicate here) that "Africanism" of all forms was to take in the "white" consciousness for the next half century, particularly in America.

Frazer did not actually follow Dr. Livingston, his fellow Scot, into the bush and desert. He used mostly secondary sources, and most of the human remains he unearthed consisted of written narratives. Thus his status as a founder of modern anthropology is now suspect, much as Alex Haley's reputation as a genealogist tracing his "roots" back to Kunta Kinte in 1976 has been clouded. (In both cases, the place where fact shades into "faction," Haley's term, is the *griot* or storyteller.) Nevertheless, Sir James pointed the way for a new generation of anthropologists after the turn of the century who would return to the origins of the human race to see how it had evolved, in much the same way that the Freudians were returning to the childhood of individuals.

And like the work of Carl Jung in psychology, Frazer's volumes appealed greatly to the mythologizing Anglo-American imagination (the subject of this book), particularly as represented by Eliot, D. H. Lawrence, and Ezra Pound. Not to mention Faulkner. Where Frazer saw progress through the ages from magical to religious to scientific thought, however, many writers saw regression "in our time."

The part of Frazer's thesis that most fascinated Eliot was the idea that the rites and rituals of the proto-agricultural peoples he studied, no matter how widely separated by geography, enacted essentially the same drama of periodic rejuvenation. The chief or king, embodying the male principle, united at monthly, yearly, or other regular intervals with his queen(s), who embodied the female principle. By virtue of sympathetic magic, a "totemism" that takes the part for the whole much as the Transcendentalism of Concord did—another of Frazer's many compilations was *Totemism and Exogamy* (1910)—the fruitful joining of the royal pair, often in a public ceremony, insured fertility through-out the land and thus the perpetuation of the tribe.[15]

In the modern wasteland of Eliot's poem, as in the "ash heaps" of *The Great Gatsby* (1925) and other bleak landscapes of the postwar imagination modeled on it, God is dead and the female principle has been channeled into the likes of Fitzgerald's Daisy Faye Buchanan and Nicole Diver, or the Mrs. Macombers of Hemingway's fiction, or Eliot's "lovely woman" who "stoops to folly" and then turns to put another record on the gramophone instead of being hauled off to the pillory to join Hester Prynne.

This is why, in *The Great Gatsby*, Myrtle Wilson, who is unfruitfully married to pale George of the ash heaps, Fitzgerald's fisher king, must lose a breast along with her other vital signs in the "accident": once Daisy's main rival, Myrtle is now no longer fertile. For Eliot's generation depicted what they saw as the moral collapse of civilization after World War I as a retreat from life-giving "primitivism." Thus they went back, for their metaphors of sexual and social vitality, beyond the dark ages of Mark Twain's Joan of Arc and Connecti-cut Yankee in King Arthur's court, to an emotionally (and otherwise) fertile Africa of the imagination.

This was, more or less, where Marcus Garvey and other "black nationalists" of the 1930s thought they were going with the "Back to Africa" movement, which envisioned a return to the homeland and the founding there of a new civilization purged of the evils of whiteness—a "black" version of the myth of eternal return. (For his "un-American" agitations, Garvey, a Jamaican by birth, was duly deported.)

This same cultural mythology, based on a return to Africa or Africanism, was still flourishing in America in the 1950s. Joyce and Eliot had used the "mythic method" primarily for purposes of irony, to show how far short their times fell by comparison with the age of heroes. Ralph Ellison's enactment of the fisher king ritual in *Invisible Man*, 1952, is much like Eliot's in that his hibernating hero is still waiting for spring at the end. (The "flower-studded wasteland" of the college where Ellison's "boy" learns to do what's expected of him is run by a black headmaster drawn from Melville.)

But many of Ellison's contemporaries used the myth of Africa without irony to irrigate the wasteland of the American consciousness in the waning decades of modernism. Jewish writers of the period, in particular, perhaps because the Holocaust had given savagery a new meaning, emerged from the desert to ask, "Where do we go from here?" Often their answer, too, was back to Africa, as in Bellow's *Henderson the Rain King*.

A portly white knight—"Your highness, I am really kind of on a quest"— as well an American millionaire with a purple heart, Henderson returns to the heart of Africa to become the Sungo, a fertility god who makes the sun go away and the rains come. His mentor is Prince Dahfu, prospective king of the Wariri tribe now that he has returned from his medical studies at Oxford. Fascinated with "the relation between body and brain," Dahfu is well read in many fields, especially psychology. "He would say for instance," says Henderson, "'James, *Psychology*, a very attractive book'" (*HRK*, 65, 236).

The urbane "native" of Bellow's romance would seem to be the truly civilized man; and the physically gross Henderson, a Connecticut Yankee driven to Africa by his nameless appetites—"I *want*, I *want*"—would seem to be the true primitive (*HRK*, 28). For all his learning, however, Dahfu hopes to be reincarnated as a lion. Bellow's African prince still believes in "the transformation of human material" (as he calls it) or metamorphosis, the basis of ancient myth and "primitive" religion, and a corollary of faculty psychology in the nineteenth century, particularly in Henderson's native New England (*HRK*, 236).

Assuming with Emerson and Thoreau that outer form is but the spire of imperishable inner being, Dahfu practices physiognomy upon his proto-Jewish friend. (Unlike most of Bellow's aging heroes, Henderson is not, technically, Jewish; but he shares many of their "Jewish" characteristics, such as a moral distaste for swine and a deep reverence for his ancestors.) Dahfu is especially taken with Henderson's nose: "I have never seen a face, a nose, like yours. To me that feature alone, from a conversion point of view, is totally a discovery" (*HRK*, 238).

Besides William James's *Principles of Psychology*, Dahfu, during his sojourn in the West, has apparently come upon such treatises on the mind-body relation as A. Bue's *Le Nez: L'Etre Devoile Par Sa Forme* (The nose: One's being revealed by its form). Published in Angiers and Paris in 1872, it bears on the title page the

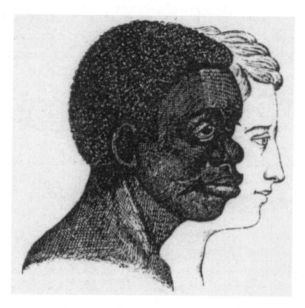

FIG. 12 An example of neoteny in the service of racialism. Illustration from A. Bue,
Le Nez: L'Etre Devoile Par Sa Forme (1872).

plainly racist image of a rounded "African" profile superimposed on an el-
egantly elongated "caucasian" one. Henderson himself has long since given
up such Slawkenbergian notions of race, ethnicity, and gender. An admirable
modern—*Henderson* was published soon after *Brown v. Board of Education*—Bellow's wandering proto-Jew from North America protests vehemently when the
African reads his heredity in his nose and then holds him personally account-
able for it: "Why should I be responsible any more than a tree? If I was a willow
you wouldn't say such things to me" (*HRK*, 238).

What Henderson has learned by going even further back to "Our Old
Home" is the same hard truth that Hawthorne's claimant learns from staring
at his reflection in the ebony cabinet: he cannot return to the past and start
history over again, as the American Adam of *Walden* and Whitman's poems
thought he could do in the nineteenth century. Nor is it his responsibility to
try. (The "virtuoso" of Hawthorne's sketch, incidentally, when identified at
last, turns out to be "the Wandering Jew," whose richest and most burdensome
treasure is his immortality.)

Seeking the pinnacle of whiteness—deification by the simple, awestruck natives of Africa—Henderson barely escapes with his life, having become the
bone-headed tool of crafty politicians and priests who, scheming to keep the
people in the dark, recognize all along what a juicy scapegoat he would make.

Henderson cannot turn back the clock with his lance, and so he boards a prop-driven plane and heads home to his wife and family in the suburbs. Unlike the aging Huck Finns who light out for Africa in Ernest Hemingway's fiction, Henderson is brought back alive to dwell *in* his time and to deal with the burden of history as best he can.

All but carrying a banner with the inscription, "Seize the Day," the usual motto of Bellow's questing heroes, Henderson takes along a lion cub, the spirit of Africa but in infant form so that it will not lick its master's blood on the return trip. When the plane stops to refuel in Newfoundland (no less), polar land of snow and whiteness, Henderson deplanes with the cub and a small boy of "Persian" extraction. No chasm opens to receive them, however. Anticipating a fruitful reunion with his wife, Lilly, a gardener, Henderson takes over from the "beautiful" propellers and spins exuberantly around the plane, holding the boy and the cub aloft in the brisk northern air. "I'm dying to breathe some of this cold stuff . . . [a]fter so many months in the Torrid Zone," he tells the stewardess. "You get what I mean?" (*HRK*, 340).[16]

Bellow's tale of a rejuvenating Africanism in the American consciousness remains essentially comic, not just because it has a happy ending but because his hero is a sort of African prince in whiteface (like Huck's Jim at the end of *their* journey). For a tragic study from the back-to-Africa lode, we must turn to Toni Morrison's *Beloved*, one of the most powerful modern romances of American Africanism since *Uncle Tom's Cabin*. It is a throwback of a different order.

Morrison has at her command techniques of narration that simply were not available even to the most brilliant novelists in England and America before the generation of Joyce, Wolfe, and Faulkner. There is nothing like this, for example, in the work of Hawthorne or Melville or even Henry James:

> We are not crouching now   we are standing but my legs are like my dead man's eyes   I cannot fall because there is no room to   the men without skin are making loud noises   I am not dead   the bread is sea-colored   I am too hungry to eat it   the sun closes my eyes   those able to die are in a pile . . . if I had the teeth of the man who died on my face I would bite the circle around her neck   bite it away   I know she does not like it   now there is room to crouch and to watch the crouching others   it is the crouching that is now always now inside   the woman with my face is in the sea   a hot thing. (*B*, 211–12)

With its pile of bodies and mad fixation on a dead person's teeth (as in Poe's "Bernice"), this is American gothic fiction of the grimmest sort. The psychology behind Morrison's "stream of consciousness" technique, however, is necessarily post-Jamesian (not to mention postmodern) because it takes us into a region of the mind where there is no distinction between past and present, where it is "now always now." (Of this primitive jungle far beyond the "fringes" of William James's orderly mind, William Faulkner writes in *Go Down, Moses*, "there is no was, only is.") To take us into this dark region is essentially what Morrison's book as a whole seeks to do in its capacity as a memorial to the "Sixty Million and more" (she estimates) Africans subjected to the atrocities of the middle passage, relived here in the aching consciousness of Morrison's title character.

Memory, or "re-memory" as her Sethe calls it, is thus a key element in Morrison's fiction as in Hawthorne's and Poe's:

> "Can other people see it?" asked Denver.
> "Oh, yes. O, yes, yes, yes. Someday you be walking down the road and you hear something or see something going on. So clear. And you think it's you thinking it up. A thought picture. But no. It's when you bump into a rememory that belongs to somebody else." (*B*, 36)

Here—in the nineteenth-century concept of "thought pictures" suspended in the chamber of memory—is the psychological basis for Sethe's belief in ghosts. Sethe is Morrison's Ligeia, and her will to live and morally justify herself overshadows her fears of the ghosts with which her white masters have cursed the past.

Like great ghost stories of the nineteenth century—"The Turn of the Screw" (1898) comes to mind—*Beloved*, however, leaves open the possibility of a "rational" explanation for the supernatural phenomena that haunt Sethe's house at 124 Bluestone Road: Sethe is bordering on madness. (Numerologists, please note: each of the numbers in Sethe's Cincinnati address doubles the other, and together they add up to the mystical 7, the number of letters in the name on Beloved's tombstone. "Ten minutes for seven letters. With another ten could she have gotten 'Dearly' too?" [(*B*, 5].)

The interior of the gray and white house at 124 is said to be haunted by a spiteful baby ghost, the restless spirit of the daughter Sethe has willfully murdered to keep her out of slavery; but the house clearly stands, like so many grander structures in older American fiction, in "thought's dominion." As Roderic Usher does, Sethe and the other inhabitants of 124 think the house is alive and out to get them. Even the dog, Here Boy, is convinced—when the ghost slams him into a wall, breaking two of his legs and dislocating an eye— that the place is haunted by evil things in robes of sorrow.

But Beloved, the grown "daughter" who shows up on Sethe's doorstep, is arguably no ghost. (I say "arguably" because, of course, it is possible to see the "real" ghosts of slavery in Morrison's narrative, just as it is possible to see "The Turn of the Screw" as a story that asks the reader to believe in ghosts. My contention, however, is that Morrison's narrative, like James's, takes on a haunting new dimension if we read it as a psychological tale, too.)[17] By this reading, one purpose of the stream-of-consciousness sections in the novel is to reveal to us that Beloved's biological mother died at sea in the middle passage ("the woman with my face is in the sea") (B, 211). Beloved, however, is unable to die, and thus join the pile of black bodies on the deck, including that of the man with the white teeth, who died beneath her in the random pile of bodies on the slave ship.

Not even Poe can match such real-life horrors, though the tale of young Pym buried in the hold of the *Grampus* comes close to capturing the claustro-phobic terror that turns Beloved's mind, as Halle's is turned by watching the two white boys steal milk from Sethe's breasts while he crouches in the hayloft, helpless, like the bound husband in Higginson's parable of the enslaved will.

Whereas Pym fixates on Augustus, his twin "brother"—as Roderic Usher is obsessed with his twin sister, Madeline, who is also buried alive, whether in reality or imagination—young Beloved, maddened, fixates upon her lost mother: "Sethe's is the face that left me" (B, 213).

Sethe's need is equally great. The memory of her bloody deed haunts even her waking thoughts. So when Beloved, fresh from the water, where the girl is still trying to find her drowned mother, presents herself at 124 in a black dress and "new skin, lineless and smooth," Sethe latches on to her with a Dickinson-ian will to believe that is born of endless pain (B, 50). Taking in this black wraith, Sethe has, in effect bumped into somebody's else's "rememory" and accepted it as her own.

So has Morrison. In the fashion of the nineteenth-century American ro-mance, in which she is thoroughly steeped and upon which she theorizes so lucidly in *Playing in the Dark*, Morrison's modern romance recalls a host of "mind pictures" to memory's cabinet; but this time they capture the point of view of the black consciousness rather than the white. This is what the shadow knows and, especially in its female incarnation, feels. Not just 124, but all of the interi-ors in Sethe's region of Cincinnati are haunted: "Not a house in the country ain't packed to its rafters," says Sethe's mother-in-law, Baby Suggs, "with some dead Negro's grief" (B, 5).

What has cast such a shadow upon Sethe and her race? The plain answer (in Morrison's mind, apparently, as well as Sethe's) is the white man—the *muzungu* or "men without skin." (In this romancing of history, no mention is made of the fact that slave catchers, if not slave traders, were often black.)[18] And chief

among these white demons is "schoolteacher" (whose name is not to be dignified with a capital), Morrison's Simon Legree, the overseer who takes control
of *Sweet Home* when Mr. Garner dies. Schoolteacher is the most brutal (and
brutish) reversion to nineteenth-century type in the book. He is the Haw-
thornian man of the head who commits the unpardonable sin of violating the
sanctity of the human heart out of a cold intellectual curiosity to see what
makes it tick.

Schoolteacher is a writer of sorts, and "letters" are one means by which he
(like the man who carves Beloved's tombstone) exercises his power. "He liked
the ink I made," Sethe tells Denver, "and it was important to him because at
night he sat down to write in his book" (*B*, 37). A master of schoolchildren
before he became a master of slaves, this *monstrum horrendum* is not only the lineal
descendent of Faulkner's McEachern in *Light in August* but also of Poe's evil minister in "The Purloined Letter"—and of the polygenisists of the nineteenth
century.

The book schoolteacher is writing, with the emotional detachment of Samuel Morton examining one of his skulls, Sethe tells Denver, is "about us but we
didn't know that right away" (*B*, 37). Constantly questioning the slaves about
their behaviors, schoolteacher takes to carrying a notebook; he is still avidly
taking notes as his oafish (read "savage") nephews steal Sethe's milk.

It is schoolteacher's ghastly appearance at the head of the posse that casts
Sethe, a fugitive from the dominion of whiteness, over the edge in the dark
shed where she slits her baby's throat, leaving her, if not totally demented, in
the moral pit of having to justify that "what she had done was right because it
came from true love." These mad acts—Sethe tries to kill Denver, too—
simply confirm the white schoolteacher's cherished theories about the savagery
of blacks. "They are all testimony," he tells his overgrown white boys, "to the
results of a little so-called freedom imposed on people who needed every care
and guidance in the world to keep them from the cannibal life they preferred"
(*B*, 151).

A firm disciplinarian, schoolteacher does not fail to reason with the boys
for driving Sethe "wild," especially the nephew who had the poor judgment to
"overbeat" a "creature" who makes fine ink and has ten good years of breeding
left. "Schoolteacher had chastised that nephew, telling him to think—just
think—what would his own horse do if you beat it beyond the point of education." Or a dog: he'd be feeding it, schoolteacher explains patiently, "and the
animal would revert—bite your hand clean off" (*B*, 150).

When Sethe reverts to her original "savagery" at the end of the novel, it is
because she thinks schoolteacher has come back to haunt her: "And no one,

nobody on this earth, would list her daughter's characteristics on the animal side of the paper" (*B*, 251). The white apparition, whom Sethe goes after with an ice pick until the women of the neighborhood collectively wrest it from her, is actually the harmless Mr. Bodwin, an old abolitionist of Scottish descent who has kept Sethe from hanging and has given her and what's left of her family a place to live at 124, his homeplace.

In Morrison's modern horror story of the black consciousness beseiged by a malevolent whiteness, however, the blacks and whites of earlier gothic fiction do not meet; the poles are simply reversed: the blacks (particularly black women) are humane and civilized because they have feelings, and the whites (almost to a man) are savage and brutish because they do not. Thus even Mr. Bodwin, who has come back to the haunted house to search for his old toy soldiers and who can only gape at Beloved's naked form on the porch, is presented, without irony, as a sort of lawn fetish, like Flannery O'Connor's "artificial nigger": an aging, artificial whiteboy, Mr. Bodwin is left with no more dignity or humanity than the effigy of a "blackboy" that sits in his kitchen over the motto, "At Yo Service" (*B*, 255).

Mr. Bodwin has actually been at the service of Sethe and the abolitionist movement for a lifetime; but Sethe (and Morrison) give him and his kind no quarter. Sethe tries to kill him because she is partially mad, a monomaniac of the emotional rather than the notional kind. Morrison herself turns him into an uncomprehending caricature, for Mr. Bodwin is white and male and, therefore, by definition, lies on the "animal side" of the ledger. Thus Mr. Bodwin (like Mr. Norton in the prologue to *Invisible Man*) is left to dwell in the Africa of perpetual childhood, without so much as a glimmer of understanding that a spiteful black ghost has come within an ace of slitting his throat.

Not 124, then, but *Sweet Home* is Morrison's equivalent of the Shelby plantation that Stowe's Uncle Tom so longs to return to as the steamboat carries him down river to New Orleans. Morrison's Eliza Harris, however, has no love for the place; yet she can't get it out of her mind. ("But it's where we were," said Sethe. "All together. Comes back whether we want it to or not.") It is this old Kentucky home of slavery that Sethe is thinking about when she warns Denver about the psychological realities of the haunted mind: "Where I was before I came here, that place is real. It's never going away. Even if the whole farm— every tree and grass blade of it dies. The picture is still there" (*B*, 36).

The picture is still there, that is, in the cabinet of memory. Sethe thinks that painful memories, when inscribed deeply enough, like letters on a tombstone, cannot fade; and she is afraid to revisit them. Don't go there, she tells her surviving daughter:

"Never. Because even though it's all over—over and done with—it's going to always be there waiting for you. That's how come I had to get all my children out. No matter what."

Denver picked at her fingernails. "If it's still there, waiting, that must mean that nothing ever dies."

Sethe looked right in Denver's face. "Nothing ever does," she said. (B, 36).

Though Sethe believes in ghosts, Morrison herself is not so sure they can be relied upon to keep the horrors of slavery alive in the national consciousness. After all, that black time is "over and done with," and history soon forgets, as Beloved is all but forgotten in the final chapter. Thus Morrison's book is ultimately a plea for remembrance: "This is not a story to pass on" (B, 275). (The stress, I take it, should be on *pass*.)

Whether or not we see Beloved as a real ghost, Morrison's story bears witness to the horrors of slavery and thus may be read as another case of "haunting back," like Harriet Jacobs's *Incidents in the Life of a Slave Girl*.[19] Jacobs's Linda Brent does not go mad, neither does she swoon into silence. In the bosom of her black woman in the attic, Jacobs insinuates, as in that of Poe's dark heroine, Ligeia, "the will therein lieth, which dieth not." Toni Morrison updates this master plot of the American slave narrative in *Beloved* with her haunted (and haunting) portrait of Sethe, confined to 124 by the demons of slavery that inhabit the raven chambers of her memory, yet pulled back from the edge of madness by Paul D and Denver, the one true daughter who has escaped the grave with all her faculties intact.

Abbreviations

Frequently cited sources are identified parenthetically in the text and in the notes by the following abbreviations:

ACM   Nathaniel Hawthorne, *The American Claimant Manuscripts.* Volume 12 in *The Centenary Edition of the Works of Nathaniel Hawthorne.* Edited by Edward H. Davidson, Claude M. Simpson, and L. Neal Smith. Columbus: Ohio State University Press, 1977.

AMP   Charles Colbert, *A Measure of Perfection: Phrenology and the Fine Arts in America.* Chapel Hill: University of North Carolina Press, 1997.

AR   *Anatomy of Racism.* Edited by David Theo Goldberg. Minneapolis: University of Minnesota Press, 1990.

B   Toni Morrison, *Beloved* (1987). New York: Penguin, 1988.

CNT   *William Styron's Nat Turner: Ten Black Writers Respond.* Edited by John Henrik Clarke. Boston: Beacon Press, 1968. Contains the complete text of *The Confessions of Nat Turner, The Leader of the Late Insurrection in Southampton, Va., As Fully and Voluntarily Made to Thomas R. Gray.*

ECPT   *Ralph Waldo Emerson: Collected Poems and Translations.* Edited by Harold Bloom and Paul Kane. New York: Library of America, 1994.

EEL   *Ralph Waldo Emerson: Essays and Lectures.* Edited by Joel Porte. New York: Library of America, 1983.

EW   Alexander Bain, *The Emotions and the Will.* Volume 5 of *Significant Contributions to the History of Psychology, 1750–1920.* Edited by Daniel N. Robinson. Washington: University Publications of America, 1977. A photographic reprint of the British first edition (London: John W. Parker and Son, 1859).

HF   Mark Twain, *Adventures of Huckleberry Finn* (1884). Edited by Thomas Cooley. New York: Norton, 1999. Reprints the text of the Iowa-California edition, edited by Walter Blair and Victor Fischer with the assistance of Dahlia Armon and Harriet Elinor Smith.

HRK   Saul Bellow, *Henderson The Rain King* (1959). New York: Penguin, 1976.

HS   Frederick Douglass, *The Heroic Slave* (1853) in *Three Classic African-American Novels*.
           Edited by William L. Andrews. New York: Penguin, 1990.

HSG   Nathaniel Hawthorne, *The House of the Seven Gables* (1851). Volume 2 in *The Cente-
           nary Edition of the Works of Nathaniel Hawthorne*. Edited by William Charvat et al.
           Columbus: Ohio State University Press, 1965.

ID   William Dean Howells, *An Imperative Duty* (1892). Edited by Edwin H. Cady.
           New Haven: College and University Press, 1962. Bound with *The Shadow of a
           Dream*.

IS-I   O. S. and L. N. Fowler, *The Illustrated Self-Instructor in Phrenology and Physiology*
           (1849). New York: Fowler and Wells, 1854.

MD   David Skae, "Mental Diseases" in *The Encyclopaedia Britannica or Dictionary of Arts,
           Sciences, and General Literature*, 8th. ed., vol. 14, 526–39. Boston: Little, Brown, 1857.

M-D   Herman Melville, *Moby-Dick, Or The Whale* (1851). Edited by G. Thomas
           Tanselle. New York: Library of America, 1983. A reprint of the Northwestern-
           Newberry Edition.

MF   Nathaniel Hawthorne, *The Marble Faun* (1860). Volume 4 in *The Centenary Edition
           of the Works of Nathaniel Hawthorne*. Edited by Roy Harvey Pearce et al. Columbus:
           Ohio State University Press, 1968.

MM   Steven Jay Gould, *The Mismeasure of Man*. New York: Norton, 1981.

MOM   Nathaniel Hawthorne, *Mosses from an Old Manse*. Volume 10 in *The Centenary Edi-
           tion of the Works of Nathaniel Hawthorne*. Edited by J. Donald Crowley et al. Colum-
           bus: Ohio State University Press, 1974.

OTA   Phillips Verner Bradford and Harvey Blume, *Ota: The Pygmy in the Zoo*. New
           York: St. Martin's, 1992.

PBC   William James, *The Principles of Psychology: Briefer Course*. New York: Holt, 1892.

PER   *Edgar Allan Poe: Essays and Reviews*. Edited by G. R. Thompson. New York: Li-
           brary of America, 1984.

PD   Toni Morrison, *Playing in the Dark: Whiteness and the Literary Imagination*. Cambridge,
           Mass.: Harvard University Press, 1992.

PH   G. W. F. Hegel, *Vorlesungen uber Die Philosophie Der Geschichte*. Translated by John
           Sibree as *The Philosophy of History*. New York: Collier, 1900.

PPTE   *Edgar Allan Poe: Poetry, Tales, and Selected Essays*. Edited by Patrick F. Quinn and
           G. R. Thompson. New York: Library of America, 1996.

PWMP   Barbara Sapinsley, *The Private War of Mrs. Packard*. New York: Paragon House,
           1991. Contains "My Exposure of Calvinism."

SL   Nathaniel Hawthorne, *The Scarlet Letter* (1850). Volume 1 in *The Centenary Edition
           of the Works of Nathaniel Hawthorne*. Edited by William Charvat et al. Columbus:
           The Ohio State University Press, 1962.

SP   George Combe, *A System of Phrenology* (1834). Boston: Benjamin Mussey, 1851.

TO   Thomas Wentworth Higginson, *Travellers and Outlaws* (1889) in *Black Rebellion: A
           Selection From* Travellers and Outlaws. New York: Arno Press, 1969.

T-TT   Nathaniel Hawthorne, *Twice-Told Tales*. Volume 9 in *The Centenary Edition of the
           Works of Nathaniel Hawthorne*. Edited by J. Donald Crowley et al. Columbus: Ohio
           State University Press, 1974. Contains "The Haunted Mind."

UEMP   Thomas C. Upham, *Elements of Mental Philosophy* (1831). 2 vols. New York: Harper & Brothers, 1869.

UTC   Harriet Beecher Stowe, *Uncle Tom's Cabin* (1852). Edited by Elizabeth Ammons. New York: Norton, 1994. A reprint of the original book edition (Boston: John P. Jewett). *Uncle Tom's Cabin* first appeared serially in 1851–52 in the antislavery newspaper, *The National Era*.

WAL   Henry David Thoreau, *Walden* (1854) in *The Writings of Henry David Thoreau*. Edited by Lyndon Shanley. Princeton: Princeton University Press, 1971.

WDS   *Works of Dugald Stewart*. Cambridge, Mass.: Hillard and Brown, 1829. Contains *The Elements of the Philosophy of the Human Mind* in two volumes bound as one.

WJW   *William James: Writings, 1878–1899*. Edited by Gerald E. Myers. New York: Library of America, 1992.

Notes

Preface

1. Full titles for frequently cited sources are given in the list of abbreviations preceding the notes.

2. Henry Adams, *The Education of Henry Adams: An Autobiography* (Boston: Houghton Mifflin, 1918), 489.

3. Carrying the argument of their earlier collaboration, *Metaphors We Live By* (Chicago: University of Chicago Press, 1980), to its logical extreme, George Lakoff and Mark Johnson go so far, in *Philosophy in the Flesh: The Embodied Mind and Its Challenge to Western Thought* (New York: Basic Books, 1999), as to assert that there is no truth beyond that created by metaphor and that the only reality in which metaphor is grounded is the human body. Thus, they argue, Western philosophy's notions of detached reason and a disembodied mind have no real basis in fact and are actually at odds with the findings of the cognitive sciences. My argument has to do with metaphor as well; but instead of contending that the metaphors of mind and body to be examined here are at odds with the cognitive sciences of today, my intent is to show that metaphor, no matter how obviously inaccurate the "truths" it purported to embody, was what passed for the "science" of cognition (and of race) in the nineteenth century. Thus even the most rationalistic explanations of mind to be encountered in the following pages advance, typically, by analogy with parts of the human body.

4. When Melville's one-legged Captain Ahab meets one-armed Captain Boomer in a chapter of *Moby-Dick* entitled "Arm and Leg," the two join in a sort of grotesque dance: "With his ivory arm frankly thrust forth in welcome, the other captain advanced, and Ahab, putting out his ivory leg, and crossing the ivory arm . . . cried out . . . let us shake bones together!" (*M-D*, 1260). Whatever else they say about Melville's sensibility, such lost limbs in his fiction bespeak a complicated theory of human perception that suggests Melville already understood what was to become a central proposition in later theories: namely, in the words of William James in "The Consciousness of Lost Limbs" (1887), that "in all

perception, indeed, but half of the object comes from without. The larger half usually comes out of our own head" (*Essays in Psychology: William James*, ed. Frederick H. Burkhardt [Cambridge: Harvard University Press, 1983], 212).

5. Thomas Cooley, *Educated Lives: The Rise of Modern Autobiography in America* (Columbus: Ohio State University Press, 1976); Terence Martin, *Instructed Vision* (Bloomington: Indiana University Press, 1961), and *Parables of Possibility: The American Need for Beginnings* (New York: Columbia University Press, 1995); William Charvat, *The Origins of American Critical Thought, 1810–1835* (New York: A. S. Barnes, 1936).

6. Jenney Bourne Taylor and Sally Shuttleworth, *Embodied Selves* (Oxford: Clarendon Press, 1998).

7. Eric Sundquist, *To Wake the Nations: Race in the Making of American Literature* (Cambridge: Harvard University Press, 1993). Other critics who are especially enlightening on "whiteness" as a racial category include bell hooks, "Representing Whiteness in the Black Imagination" in *Cultural Studies*, ed. Lawrence Grossberg, Cary Nelson, and Paula A. Treichler (New York: Routledge, 1992); Dana Nelson, *The Word in Black and White: Reading "Race" in American Literature, 1638–1867* (New York: Oxford, 1992); Ruth Frankenberg, *White Women, Race Matters: The Social Construction of Whiteness* (Minneapolis: University of Minnesota Press, 1993); and David Roediger, *The Wages of Whiteness* (London: Verso, 1991).

8. Shelley Fisher Fishkin, *Was Huck Black?* (New York: Oxford University Press, 1993). Fishkin surveys the scholarly writing on "blackness" and "whiteness" in "Interrogating 'Whiteness,' Complicating 'Blackness': Remapping American Culture" in *Criticism and the Color Line: Desegregating American Literary Studies*, ed. Henry B. Wonham (New Brunswick: Rutgers University Press, 1996), 251–90.

9. West's essay is collected in his *Keeping Faith: Philosophy and Race in America* (New York: Routledge, 1993), 33–43.

10. Jared Gardner, *Master Plots: Race and the Founding of an American Literature, 1787–1845* (Baltimore: Johns Hopkins University Press, 1998), xii.

11. Sander L. Gilman, *Difference and Pathology: Stereotypes of Sexuality, Race, and Madness* (Ithaca: Cornell University Press, 1985).

12. Dana Nelson and Joan Dayan, *Fables of Mind: An Inquiry into Poe's Fiction* (New York: Oxford University Press, 1987). Dayan also talks about Poe and disguised forms of slavery in "Amorous Bondage: Poe, Ladies, and Slaves," *American Literature* 66 (1994): 239–73.

13. Teresa Goddu, *Gothic America: Narrative, History, and Nation* (New York: Columbia University Press, 1997), 10. Goddu's claims for "the gothic" are similar to mine for "the romance" insofar as she takes to task the "many readings of the female gothic [that] continue to imprison it within the private sphere, viewing it either in psychological terms or solely in terms of domestic ideology" (94). However "psychological," the romance, like the gothic, I would argue, is also fundamentally political because the faculty psychology on which the romance (as well as much of gothic literature) is based assumes a master slave economy and is thus related directly to the marketplace. (Goddu's most revealing, for me, chapter is entitled "(Un)Veiling the Marketplace: Nathaniel Hawthorne, Lousia May Alcott, and the Female Gothic.") Other critics who have, nonetheless, found gothicism "a useful site for feminist revisions of female identity and resistance to patriarchal power" (Goddu, 94) include Lynette Carpenter and Wendy K. Kolmar, eds., *Haunting the House of*

Fiction: Feminist Perspectives on Ghost Stories by American Women (Knoxville: University of Tennessee Press, 1991); Eugenia DeLamotte, *Perils of the Night: A Feminist Study of Nineteenth-Century Gothic* (New York: Oxford University Press, 1990); Kate Ferguson Ellis, *The Contested Castle: Gothic Novels and the Subversion of Domestic Ideology* (Urbana: University of Illinois Press, 1989); Michelle Massé, *In the Name of Love: Women, Masochism, and the Gothic* (Ithaca: Cornell University Press, 1992); Tamar Heller, *Dead Secrets: Wilkie Collins and the Female Gothic* (New Haven: Yale University Press, 1992); Elaine Showalter, *Sister's Choice: Tradition and Change in American Women's Writing* (Oxford: Clarendon Press, 1991); Kari J. Winter, *Subjects of Slavery, Agents of Change: Women and Power in Gothic Novels and Slave Narratives, 1790–1865* (Athens: University of Georgia Press, 1992); Susan Wolstenholm, *Gothic (Re)Visions: Writing Women as Readers* (Albany: State University of New York Press, 1993); and, of course, Sandra Gilbert and Susan Gubar, *The Madwoman in the Attic: The Woman Writer and the Nineteenth-Century Imagination* (New Haven: Yale University Press, 1979).

14. Dennis Berthold, "On Teresa Goddu's *Gothic America*," in *Romantic Circles*, ed. Stephen E. Jones et al. (7 July 1998; updated 1 December 1998), www.otal.umd.edu/rc/reviews/goddu.html. Even Goddu herself perpetuates the myth of American exceptionalism, according to Berthold, because she treats "slavery, racialism, and capitalism as strictly American phenomena, an exclusionary practice that implicitly argues for a 'gothic' that develops independently of British (or other) generic and social practices." The faculty psychology by which I will be linking a variety of American texts with "slavery, racialism, and capitalism" is, indeed, I hope to show, as much British and Continental in origin as American.

15. Edgar A. Dryden, *The Form of American Romance* (Baltimore: Johns Hopkins University Press, 1988).

16. Nathaniel Hawthorne, "The Virtuoso's Collection" (*MOM*, 484).

Introduction. Vestiges: Little Shop of Race and Gender

1. This passion for measuring parts of the human body in the service of racism is the subject of John S. Haller's *Outcasts from Evolution: Scientific Attitudes of Racial Inferiority, 1859–1900* (New York: McGraw-Hill, 1975). For a general history of the age of measurement and machines, see Howard Mumford Jones, *The Age of Energy: Varieties of American Experience, 1865–1915* (New York: Viking, 1971).

2. Jack the Ripper, who murdered and sexually mutilated somewhere between four and twenty young women, most of them prostitutes, in London in the 1880s, was first presumed by police to be (or be close to, perhaps a relative of) someone who had contracted syphilis from a prostitute, a simple case of like "curing" like, as Sander L. Gilman has observed. ("'I'm Down on Whores': Race and Gender in Victorian London" [*AR*, 146–70].) As the number of his victims increased, however, "the Ripper's" case became one of the most sensational examples of mutilation as social pathology in the nineteenth century, and a new theory of Jack's identity was advanced, one based on race, though still tied to the Victorian obsession with mutilation and dismemberment as signifiers of "moral" disease. The "vague contours of Jack the 'victim,'" says Gilman, "gave way to a very specific visual image of Jack." Jack the Ripper (who was never actually identified or caught) was now presumed to

be a Polish Jew with (judging from the sketches in the *Illustrated Police News*) a grotesquely hooked nose, swarthy complexion, black beard, and black felt hat who wore a "dark jacket and trousers" and "spoke with a foreign accent" (*AR*, 156).

3. For a full, grisly analysis of the topos of the broken body in American culture, see Robyn Wiegman, *American Anatomies: Theorizing Race and Gender* (Durham, N.C.: Duke University Press, 1995).

4. T. S. Eliot, "The Metaphysical Poets," in *Selected Essays* (New York: Harcourt Brace, 1950), 247.

5. In *Gender Trouble: Feminism and the Subversion of Identity* (New York: Routledge, 1990), Judith Butler, speaking primarily of sex and gender roles, brings together, in the idea of "performativity," a booming tradition of scholarship on these and other aspects of self as social constructions. It is not my intention here to verify (or contest) Butler's thesis about how they might be formed; but the constructions of madness, race, and gender I am describing might well be used to support any project that seeks to show that categories of identity once considered normative and fundamental were temporally constituted and falsely naturalized. Surely, to cling to them would be, as Butler says, nostalgic and parochial—if not evidence of brain fever. However, those who criticize Butler's theory on the grounds that it disenfranchises, as totally imaginary or fictive, the "real" identities historical persons have based on "authentic" articles of faith and belief might find support for their views in the intensity with which the constructs I describe were once held to be factual and true. The best argument I know *against* theorizing such categories as race and gender into insignificance (or mere signification), however, is that of Henry Louis Gates Jr. in his "Critical Remarks" (*AR*, 319–29). It may be possible to treat race and racism as matters of pure "symbolics" (as Julia Kristeva does so brilliantly in an essay on Céline's anti-Semitism that Gates cites); but to do so denies the historical possibility of agency. "And since self-identification proves a condition for agency," writes Gates, "the imperatives of social change require us to construct ourselves just as *all* the furniture in the social universe was." Thus Gates speaks of a "utopian" aspect of "the theory project" that implies "we can now divest ourselves of our social identities" without proposing "another one to take its place." At the other extreme, however, as Gates observes, "the imperative to historicize" can be "equally incapacitating" because it can take all social constructions to be products of particular historical moments now gone. "If a term exhaustively derives its meaning from the social totality at any historical moment," Gates argues, "then for the purposes of analysis . . . yesterday is too long ago" (*AR*, 324).

6. F. O. Vaille and H. A. Clark, *The Harvard Book*, vol. 1 (Cambridge: Harvard University Press, 1875), 247.

7. "The Living Temple" (originally titled "The Anatomist's Hymn"), in *The Poetical Works of Oliver Wendell Holmes* (Boston: Houghton Mifflin, 1908), 143–44.

8. Thomas Francis Harrington, *The Harvard Medical School*, ed. J. G. Mumford, vol. 2 (Boston, 1905), 640; quoted in Eleanor M. Tilton, *Amiable Autocrat: A Biography of Dr. Oliver Wendell Holmes* (New York: Henry Schuman, 1947), 201.

9. *The Poetical Works of Oliver Wendell Holmes*, 143.

10. Holmes's letter (Dec. 12, 1849) is quoted in Tilton, *Amiable Autocrat*, 414, n. 23.

11. Sophia Hawthorne to Mrs. Elizabeth Peabody, September 29, 1850, Berg Collection, New York Public Library.

12. Oliver Wendell Holmes quoted in Tilton, *Amiable Autocrat*, 196.

13. Anne Moive and David Jessel, *Brain Sex: The Real Difference between Men and Women* (New York: Dell, 1991), 9.

14. Nobert Bennett Bean, "Some Racial Peculiarities of the Negro Brain," *American Journal of Anatomy* 5 (1906): 353–432.

15. Franklin P. Mall, "On Several Anatomical Characters of the Human Brain, Said to Vary According to Race and Sex, With Especial Reference to the Weight of the Frontal Lobe," *American Journal of Anatomy* 9 (1909): 1–32.

16. Paul Broca, "Sur le Volume et la Forme du Cerveau suivant les Individus et suivant les Races," *Bulletin Société d'Anthropologie Paris* 2 (1862): 152; quoted in *MM*, 104.

17. Gustave LeBon, "Recherches Anatomiques et Mathématiques sur les Lois des Variations du Volume du Cerveau et sur leurs Relations avec l' Intelligence," *Revue d'Anthropologie*, 2nd series, vol. 2 (1879): 60–61; quoted in *MM*, 105. LeBon also said that women "excel in fickleness, inconstancy, absence of thought and logic, and incapacity to reason." Mark Twain, whose fiction attributes a higher form of intelligence to women, children, and "savages," once attributed the same back-brained propensities that LeBon regards as typically female to a steamboat captain: The man, he said, "had more selfish organs than any seven men in the world.... They weighed down the back of his head so that it made his nose tilt up in the air" (*Life on the Mississippi* [Boston, 1883], 270).

18. "I'd like immensely to read your autobiography," Howells wrote to his friend Mark Twain in Febuary 1904. "You always rather bewildered me by your veracity, and I fancy you may tell the truth about yourself. But *all* of it? The black truth, which we all know of ourselves in our hearts, or only the whity-brown truth of the pericardium, or the nice, whitened truth of the shirtfront? Even you wont tell the black heart's-truth" (Henry Nash Smith and William M. Gibson, eds., *Mark Twain–Howells Letters*, vol. 2 [Cambridge: Harvard University Press, 1960], 781.) Howells's letter of 1904 provides the epigraph for John Crowley's definitive *The Black Heart's Truth: The Early Career of W. D. Howells* (Chapel Hill: University of North Carolina Press, 1985).

19. The Transcendentalist studied nature and the visible universe because it revealed, by analogy, an invisible world of universal ideas. Thus in 1843 when William Cooper Howells, an Ohio printer and father of the novelist William Dean Howells, established a Swedenborgian newspaper called *The Retina*, he gave it the following subtitle: *The Tablet Whereon Truth's Rays Impress the Images of Thought* (Edwin H. Cady, *The Road to Realism* [Syracuse: Syracuse University Press, 1956], 17.) For William Cooper Howells as for Emerson, intuition or insight was always a higher power than mere physical sight. "It is thus we wish to use our RETINA," said the senior Howells, "to impress upon it the forms of things within the soul's vision" (Cady, 18). The American Trancendentalists, however, came to their philosophical idealism by way of a national tradition of commonsense realism; so even Howells's newspaper had to function as an organ of worldly observation, as in Emerson's account of the mechanical process of seeing, before it peered into the sublime. "*The Retina*," he announced, speaking both of the printed organ and its anatomical counterpart, "is the expression of the optic nerve ... and its use is to convey to the mind the images of objects in the material world" (Cady, 18). Natural facts might symbolize spiritual facts ("things within the soul's vision") as Emerson said; but even in the transcendental order of perception from lower to higher, "objects in the material world" had first to register in the mind as "images"—

direct and accurate ones, according to the philosophy of Thomas Reid—of the external reality they pictured to the mind's eye.

20. A wonderful comic rendering of the virtuoso in his cabinet is the morose taxidermist of Dickens's *Our Mutual Friend*, whose shop contains a store of "human warious." Mr. Venus's joy in his "science" is tempered by his otherwise not so fastidious lady's distaste for it, a conflict of intellect and feeling that is typical of narratives grounded in faculty psychology.

21. Barnum as the premier American exhibitionist is the subject of numerous studies; see, especially, Neil Harris, *Humbug: The Art of P. T. Barnum* (Boston: Little, Brown, 1973) and A. H. Saxon, *P. T. Barnum: The Legend and the Man* (New York: Columbia University Press, 1989).

22. Richard D. Altick, *The Shows of London* (Cambridge: Harvard University Press, 1978), 269. Sartje Bartmann or Sartjie Baartmann or Sarah Bartmann (the name under which she was reportedly baptized in England) came to London in 1810, where she was exhibited, according to Altick, "under the most degrading circumstances imaginable" as an "imported savage." According to a contemporary observer, Bartmann was "surrounded by many persons.... One pinched her, another walked round her; one gentleman *poked* her with his cane; and one *lady* employed her parasol to ascertain that all was, as she called it, '*nattral*.'" A caricature from the popular press of the day even represents a portly, well-dressed politician as approaching the undraped subject with a pair of widely spread calipers. Since she was sometimes displayed in chains, a British court looked behind the curtains of this shabby show and determined that the Hottentot Venus willingly displayed herself for profit, thereby upholding a cherished principle, both of British common law and nineteenth-century psychology, as celebrated in a bawdy London street ballad: "That in this land of libertie / Where freedom groweth still, / No one can show another's tail / Against the owner's will." The Hottentot Venus was soon replaced in the public gaze by the "Venus of South Africa," Tono Maria, who was actually from Brazil. In Maria's case it was not only the exposed "African" body that fascinated but also her (approximately) one hundred scars, one for each act of adultery, the gullible spectator was told, in which she had been caught by her husbands (Altick, 268–72).

23. Georges Cuvier, "Extrait d'Observations Faites sur le Cadavre d'une Femme Connue à Paris et à Londres sous le Nom de Vénus Hottentotte," *Mémoires du Muséum d'Histoire Naturelle* 3 (1817): 259–74; quoted in Stephen Jay Gould, *The Flamingo's Smile* (New York: Norton, 1985), 298–99.

24. My concern with people and their parts on display is primarily political and psychological; for a sociological perspective, see Robert Bogdan, *Freak Show: Presenting Human Oddities for Amusement and Profit* (Chicago: University of Chicago Press, 1988).

25. The brain weights in the rest of this paragraph are gleaned from Gould, who draws heavily on the essays of Paul Broca published in the *Bulletin Société d'Anthropologie Paris*.

26. For a succinct account of Whitman and phrenology, see Justin Kaplan, *Walt Whitman: A Life* (New York: Simon and Schuster, 1980), 148–56. The first scholar to discuss Whitman's fascination with phrenology in any depth was Edward Hungerford in "Walt Whitman and His Chart of Bumps," *American Literature* 2, no. 4 (January 1931): 350–84. See also, Arthur Wrobel, "Whitman and the Phrenologists," *PMLA*, 89, no. 1 (January 1974): 17–23.

27. Flannery O'Connor, *The Complete Stories* (New York: Farrar, Straus and Giroux, 1974), 245–46.

28. O'Connor, *Complete Stories*, 268–69.

1. A Geography of the Mind

1. Sophia Hawthorne to Elizabeth Palmer Peabody, February 16, 1851, Berg Collection, New York Public Library.

2. The term *phrenology* was coined by Thomas Forster in his "Observations on a New System of Phrenology, or the Anatomy and Physiology of the Brain, of Dr. Gall and Spurzheim," *Philosophical Magazine and Journal*, 45 (1815): 44–50. For general accounts of phrenology, see John D. Davies, *Phrenology: Fad and Science* (New Haven: Yale University Press, 1955) and Madeline B. Stern, *Heads and Headlines: The Phrenological Fowlers* (Norman: University of Oklahoma Press, 1971.)

3. Quoted in Kaplan, *Walt Whitman*, 148.

4. Bruce A. Rhonda, *Letters of Elizabeth Palmer Peabody, American Renaissance Woman* (Middletown, Conn.: Wesleyan University Press, 1984), 105; Kaplan, *Walt Whitman*, 149.

5. Cited in the appendix to George Combe, *The Constitution of Man* (1828; Boston: Allen and Ticknor, 1834).

6. A. O'Leary, *Delineation of Character, As Determined by the Teachings of Phrenology, Physiology, and Physiognomy* (Boston: Bradley, Dayton, 1860). George H. Crosby's copy is in the collection of the Ohio State University libraries.

7. Kaplan, *Walt Whitman*, 153.

8. The traits by which O'Leary read Crosby's head appear as a chart in *Delineation of Character*, 4–5.

9. Kaplan, *Walt Whitman*, 149.

10. Orson Squire Fowler, *Practical Phrenology* (New York: Nafis & Cornish, 1846), 56. The faculties marked for study in both cases are numbers 13 (self-esteem), 14 (firmness), 18 (veneration), 19 (benevolence), and 37 (comparison), though most of Washington's lumps appear to be in his throat and jowls. The greatest prominence in Washington's face comes just above the nose, indicating a highly developed "organ" of "Individuality." Franklin's profile bulges in the same spot, but it is not marked. Marked differences between the two men show up in the faculties of Amativeness (Washington) and Inhabitiveness (Franklin). In other words, Franklin, according to Fowler, was less lusty than Washington and more likely to stay at home, traits that do not square with Franklin's own charts of his personality in the *Autobiography*.

11. The color of Queequeg's skin is ambiguous, but there is no doubt that he is a man of color: Queequeg's face, says Melville, "was of a dark, purplish, yellow color, here and there stuck over with large, blackish looking squares" (*M-D*, 815).

12. Terence Martin, *The Instructed Vision: Scottish Common Sense Philosophy and the Origins of American Fiction* (Bloomington: Indiana University Press, 1961), 8.

13. *The Collected Works of Dugald Stewart*, vol. 2 (Edinburgh: T. & T. Clark, 1877), vii.

14. Asa Burton, *Essays on Some of the First Principles of Metaphysicks, Ethicks, and Theology* (Portland: Mirror Office, 1824), 53–61, 253–54.

15. Nathaniel Hawthorne, "Preface" to *The Blithedale Romance*, in *The Centenary Edition of the Works of Nathaniel Hawthorne*, vol. 3 (Columbus: Ohio State University Press, 1964), 1; and "Preface" to *HSG*, 1.

16. Burton, *Essays on Some of the First Principles*, 91.

17. Edwards quoted in Jay Wharton Fay, *American Psychology before William James* (New Brunswick: Rutgers University Press, 1939), 45. Edwards's innovation in the eighteenth century was to link the emotions and passions with volition instead of cognition, but he still clung to scholasticism's ancient two-part division of mind. Jeremiah Day, in *Examination of President Edwards's Inquiry on the Freedom of the Will* (New Haven: Durrie and Peck, 1841), explained both where Edwards departed from tradition and where, in Day's opinion in 1841, he failed to depart far enough: "Though President Edwards agrees with many European writers, in dividing the powers of the mind between the understanding and the will; yet he differs from most of them, in the wide extent which he gives to the latter faculty. They commonly confine it to *imperative acts*; leaving the emotions and passions, if any definite place is allowed them, to fall under the head of the understanding." Edwards's arrangement, "which considers the emotions and passions as belonging to the will," said Day, "is quite as rational as theirs." However, Day maintained, writing almost a hundred years later, "the fact is, that each of these methods of classifying our faculties, is found to be defective." What is "greatly needed," he felt in 1841, is "a *threefold* division of our mental powers" (11–12). As with most of his contemporaries in the first half of the nineteenth century, however, it did not occur to Day to question the dividing, *per se*, of the mind into distinct faculties or powers.

18. F. H. Foster, *A Genetic History of the New England Theology* (Chicago: University of Chicago Press, 1907), 251–52.

19. Burton, *Essays on Some of the First Principles*, 21–22. Burton's remark about "free-moral-agency" is quoted in Fay, *American Psychology before William James*, 192.

20. Burton, *Essays on Some of the First Principles*, 22.

21. Johann Daniel Gros, *Natural Principles of Rectitude* (New York: T. & J. Swords, 1795), 19.

22. John Witherspoon, *Lectures on Moral Philosophy*, *Works*, vol. 3 (1800; rpt. Princeton: Princeton University Press, 1912), 278.

23. Samuel Stanhope Smith, *Lectures on Moral and Political Philosophy*, vol. 1 (Trenton: Fenton, 1812), 23; Levi Hedge, *Elements of Logic* (1819; reprint, New York: Armstrong, 1849), 15–16.

2. *The House of Madness*

1. Quoted in Edward H. Davidson, *Selected Writings of Edgar Allan Poe* (Cambridge: Riverside Press, 1956), 494–95, n. 32.

2. In chapter 21 of *Incidents*, all other avenues of escape from the horrors of slavery being closed to her, the pseudonymous Linda Brent retreats, by means of a cleverly fashioned trapdoor, into her grandmother's tiny (9′ × 7′) garret. There she stays for years, we are told, in this unlighted, unheated space with only a "loophole" in the claustral walls to connect her (by dint of preternatural far-sightedness) to her children and the outside world. Though Jacobs may invert, or skirt, the "passive victim" convention of the seduction novel by taking responsibility for her actions, as Jean Fagan Yellin has said, she is not

overturning so much as using other conventions of nineteenth-century fiction (foreword to *Incidents in the Life of a Slave Girl* [rpt. Cambridge: Harvard University Press, 1987], xxx). *Incidents* combines elements not only of the gothic tale and the captivity narrative but also of the desert-island adventure and the detached-observer fantasy that Hawthorne exemplifies in such sketches as "Sights from a Steeple" and "Sunday at Home." *Robinson Crusoe* is specifically alluded to in the providential appearance of the gimlet that allows Linda Brent to bore her lifesaving "loophole." And her—or could it be the choice of her editor, Lydia Maria Child?—chapter title itself, "The Loophole of Retreat," is a direct echo of William Cowper's "The Task": "'Tis pleasant, through the loopholes of retreat, / To peep at such a world,—to see the stir / Of the great Babel, and not feel the crowd." (Carolyn Karcher gives an account of Lydia Maria Child's editing of *Incidents* in *The First Woman in the Republic: A Cultural Biography of Lydia Maria Child* [Durham: Duke University Press, 1994].)

3. Jared Gardner, *Master Plots: Race and the Founding of an American Literature 1787–1845* (Baltimore: Johns Hopkins University Press, 1998), 128.

4. The *Encyclopaedia* containing Dr. Skae's taxonomy of mental diseases was a printed version of the "cabinet" of natural science (and other fields). The *Britannica* did not originate in London or Oxford, however, but was first compiled "upon a new plan," according to the title page of 1771, "By a Society of Gentlemen in Scotland."

5. Among other causes, Usher's mania stems from a "distempered ideality" (*PPTE*, 324). "It is this faculty," says George Combe, "that gives *inspiration* to the poet" (*SP*, 306). The "organ" of ideality, according to Combe and Gall, is to be found "in the anterior lateral parts of the head, above the temples" (*SP*, 304). A prominence there would indicate a poet, and an overprominence, a mad poet of the sort Dr. Skae diagnosed Poe himself to be. True to form, Usher's head exhibits "an inordinate expansion above the regions of the temple" (*PPTE*, 321).

6. One apparent problem with this reading is that we have a witness, the matter-of-fact narrator, Usher's old chum. He is the voice of reason and common sense in the tale, and, I would say, the principal means by which Poe shows their limitations. The dense narrator will not admit the power of the irrational even when it comes crashing down upon him. Shut up in Usher's old house, particularly his host's opium-filled chamber of dreams, the narrator, however, has inhaled the fumes of madness. Only half aware of his condition, he pronounces a mutual hallucination, the fantastic vision of Madeline Usher, to be a stark reality before he runs raving into the moonlight, the great house collapsing (or appearing to collapse) behind him.

7. Whereas Hawthorne's physician represents the emotional monomaniac, his minister, Arthur Dimmesdale—whose hand at the guilty breast refers constantly to Dr. Skae's "one object," the *A*-shaped stigmata that he emblazons there and across the dome of heaven— would be a case of "notional" (or intellectual) monomania. In 1899, however, James Edgar Smith interpreted the symptoms, if not the causes, of Dimmesdale's mental disease to be more passional than intellectual. In a drama based upon Hawthorne's earlier romance and entitled *The Scarlet Stigma* (Washington: J. J. Chapman), Smith depicted "stigmatization" as "a rare incident of ecstasy." Noting, cogently, that "not many well authenticated cases have been reported by competent medical authorities," he nonetheless maintained that "there can be no doubt of its occasional occurrence." The Satan of Smith's play, therefore, was "an hallucination," and the letter on the minister's chest, "merely the culmination of his

auto-hypnotic ecstasy, or trance," essentially the same diagnosis that Thomas Gray came to in the "case" of Nathaniel Turner.

8. Willis's response to Burke is recalled in *The Life and Times of F. Reynolds, Written by Himself*, vol. 2 (London: Colburn, 1826), 23–24.

9. Anonymous, *Some Particulars of the Royal Indisposition of 1788 to 1789, and of Its Effects upon Illustrious Personages and Opposite Parties Interested by It* (London: R. Taylor, 1804), 31–32.

10. Quoted in William F. Bynum, "Rationales for Therapy in British Psychiatry, 1780–1835," *Madhouses, Mad-doctors, and Madmen*, ed. Andrew Scull (Philadelphia: University of Pennsylvania Press, 1981), 35–57.

11. Benjamin Rush to James Rush, June 8, 1810, in L. H. Butterfield, ed., *Letters of Benjamin Rush*, vol. 2 (Princeton: Princeton University Press, 1951), 1052.

12. Albert Deutsch, *The Mentally Ill in America: A History of Their Care and Treatment from Colonial Times*, 2d ed. (New York: Columbia University Press, 1949), 167.

13. Rev. Andrew Snape, "Sermon Preached before the Lord Mayor . . ." (London: Bowyer, 1718), 15.

14. E. D. Cope, "Two Perils of the European," *The Open Court* 3 (1890): 2054.

15. Michel Foucault, *Madness and Civilization* (New York: Pantheon, 1965), 66–69.

16. Samuel Tuke, *Description of the Retreat* (York: Alexander, 1813), 141. Samuel Tuke was William's grandson.

17. Skultans discusses the lingering authoritarianism of the asylum keeper and the "mad-doctor" in *English Madness: Ideas on Insanity, 1580–1890* (London: Routledge & Kegan Paul, 1979).

18. Jay Grossman links Hester's plight with Hawthorne's conservative position on slavery in "'A' is for Abolition?: Race, Authorship, *The Scarlet Letter*," *Textual Practice* 7 (1993): 13–30.

19. Under the mesmerizing gaze of the masculine eye, Hester is overcome with a "leaden affliction" and grows so drowsy that she must fight to stay conscious, a sure sign that her willpower is being drained away by the masculine consciousness. On the scaffold where Hester's will almost goes to sleep, we are back, psychologically, in the cave in the hillside of Hawthorne's first romance, *Fanshawe*, in which the villain, a dark "Angler," keeps Ellen Langton "as if chained to the rock"—and thus under the sway of his rod—by "a species of fascination." If she lapses into "dreamless slumber," this drowsy maiden will be his helpless slave (*Fanshawe* in *The Centenary Edition of the Works of Nathaniel Hawthorne*, vol. 3 [Columbus: Ohio State University Press, 1964], 439–40).

20. "Such is frequently the fate, and such the stern development, of the feminine character and person," Hawthorne theorized in the gender psychology of his day, "when the woman has encountered, and lived through, an experience of peculiar severity. If she be all tenderness, she will die. If she survive, the tenderness will either be crushed out of her, or—and the outward semblance is the same—crushed so deeply into her heart it can never show itself more. The latter is perhaps the truest theory" (*SL*, 163–64). Thus Hester, unable or unwilling to express her true feelings, must wander "without a clew in the dark labyrinth of mind; now turned aside by an insurmountable precipice; now starting back from a deep chasm." Meanwhile, the Reverend Mr. Dimmesdale, similarly bewildered by his emotionally "repressive" tendencies, "stood on the verge of lunacy, if he had not already stepped across it" (*SL*, 166).

21. Cooter quotes Rumball approvingly in "Phrenology and British Alienists, ca. 1825–1845," collected in *Madhouses, Mad-doctors, and Madmen*, 60–61.

22. F. J. Gall, *On the Functions of the Brain and of Each of Its Parts*, trans. Winslow Lewis Jr., ed. Nahum Capen, vol. 2 (Boston: Phrenological Library, 1835), 224.

23. Foucault, *Madness and Civilization*, 69.

24. Sydney Smith, "Account of the York Retreat," *Edinburgh Review* 23 (1814): 189–98; quoted in Scull, *Madhouses, Mad-doctors, and Madmen*, 110.

25. John Haslam, *Observations on Madness and Melancholy*, 2d ed. (London: J. Callow, 1809), 10.

3. American Africanism

1. Georges Cuvier quoted in Paul Topinard, *Anthropology* (London, Chapman and Hall, 1878), 493–94.

2. Omitted in published editions of Agassiz's letters, these lines from the manuscript (December 1846) in the Houghton Library, Harvard University are restored by Gould in *MM*, 45.

3. In his studies of pathology and the representation of human difference, Sander L. Gilman has noted a similar "ethnic eczema" as a marker of race in anti-Semitic literature ("I'm Down on Whores," *AR*, 164). What if, as in the case of Queequeg's tattoos or Hester Prynne's scarlet letter, which she tarts up with gold thread, the stigmata are self-inflicted or self-altered? Then, perhaps, following Sander Gilman's logic, these bodily markers of difference or disease can be seen to call into question the health not of the "victim" but of the larger body (racial, sexual, social, political) from which they set the individual apart. For example, the scarlet letter is supposed to set Hester apart from the Puritan (read "Victorian") community as a fallen woman. To the community of Hawthorne's day, Hester's moral fall represents the threat of more than moral disease and must be treated by isolating her—the function of the stigmatizing letter—from the social body. In the paradigm of social pathology that Hawthorne covertly alludes to, the next step in Hester's decline should be prostitution, followed by suicide, usually by drowning. (The wages of sin are literally death to the prostitute of the Victorian imagination, according to Gilman, because she was typically perceived as the carrier of deadly "social" disease, usually syphilis ["I'm Down on Whores," *AR*, 150–153]). Hester, however, is not the prostitute she is "supposed" to be. Overturning the expectations of the magistrates, she retains not only her virtue but also her physical and mental health, throwing the charge of disease back on the community—signified by her altering of the letter—which must then reinterpret the differences marked by the letter before it (the ailing community) can be whole again. On disease and other bodily disfigurements as markers of race and gender, see also Gilman's *Difference and Pathology: Stereotypes of Sexuality, Race, and Madness* (Ithaca: Cornell University Press, 1985).

4. Race as an articulated category of human difference begins in European languages in the fifteenth century (David Theo Goldberg, "The Social Formation of Racist Discourse" in *AR*, 295). But the analogy between race and gender is, by and large, a nineteenth-century phenomenon. Nancy Leys Stepan documents this root metaphor in *The Idea of Race in Science: Great Britain, 1800–1950* (London: Macmillan, 1982) and in "Race and Gender: The Role of Analogy in Science," *Isis* 77 (1986): 261–77; rpt. *AR*, 38–57. Stepan's aim, however, unlike

mine, is not to explain how and why race science and other constructions of human difference in the nineteenth century came to identify women with the "lower" races but "to use
the race-gender analogy to analyze the nature of analogical reasoning in science" (*AR*, 41).
Her conclusion is that "the metaphors functioned as the science itself—that without them
the science did not exist" (*AR*, 44). A theory of metaphor, therefore, is as central to the
study of science, Stepan argues, as to literary studies. Nor is such theorizing merely "academic." We need "to expose the metaphors by which we learn to view the world" in any
age, says Stepan, "not because these metaphors are necessarily 'wrong,' but because they
are so powerful" (*AR*, 54). This is an argument, it seems to me, that can only take on greater
force, when, as in most of this book, the metaphors in question *are* wrong or, rather, lead
to views of the world that are wrong.

5. Ralph Waldo Emerson, *Miscellanies*, ed. Edward W. Emerson (Boston: Houghton,
Mifflin, 1904), 407.

6. Henry Wadsworth Longfellow, Review of *Twice-Told Tales*, *North American Review*,
April 1842.

7. Emerson, *Miscellanies*, 406, 628.

8. Louis Agassiz, "The Diversity of Origin of the Human Races," *Christian Examiner* 49
(1850): 144.

9. Ibid.

10. Robert E. Beider, *Science Encounters the Indian, 1820–1880: The Early Years of American Eth-
nology* (Norman: University of Oklahoma Press, 1986), 67. Morton tells how he was overtaken by the collecting impulse in his "Account of a Craniological Collection; with Remarks on the Classification of Some Families of the Human Race," *Transactions of the
American Ethnological Society* 2 (1848): 217.

11. George Combe, "Review of *Crania Americana*" (with B. H. Coates) in *American Journal
of Science* 38 (1840): 352.

12. Samuel George Morton, *Crania Americana* (Philadelphia: John Pennington, 1839), 81.
In *Crania Aegyptiaca* (1844), Morton turned his attention from "red" skulls to "black" ones,
as the racial debate of the 1830s and forties came to center on the enslavement of African
Americans. Jared Gardner describes Morton's method and findings in the new book:
"Morton gives himself a twofold project: first, to determine which race had originally inhabited ancient Egypt, 'the parent of civilization'; and, second, to figure out what role
blacks played in that ancient civilization. He again presents the skulls with great care, but
here the immediate problems of racial classification become even more dizzying. Stripped
of their flesh, the mummified skulls offer few signs by which race is traditionally determined; thus Morton must turn to the tool racial theorists had long relied on: intuition.
Those skulls that seem to Morton to be Caucasian in feature are placed in one group; those
that appear "Negroid" are placed in another. Not surprisingly, when he then measures the
skulls he has so divided, Caucasians once again come out on top" (*Master Plots*, 137).

13. Like Poe's Ligeia, the presumption that bigger is better refuses to die even in modern
craniometry. Applying computerized imaging technology to the brain of Albert Einstein,
preserved since his death in 1955, Sandra Witelson and her colleagues at McMaster University in Hamilton, Ontario, determined in 1999 that "Einstein's brain weight was not
different from controls, clearly indicating that a large (heavy) brain is not a necessary condition for exceptional intellect." The researchers, whose findings were reported in the

McMaster *Lancet*, determined, however, that in the inferior parietal region, which is related to mathematical thinking, Einstein's brain was 15 percent wider than normal and that he lacked the normal "sulcus," or groove, in the same region, thereby creating an "extraordinarily large expanse of highly integrated cortex within a functional network." In other words, as Sarah Boseley reported for the Scripps Howard News Service, "Einstein's Brain Larger in All the Right Places" (*Columbus Dispatch*, June 18, 1999, 1A).

14. "Corrected values" for Morton's calculations are plotted in Gould, *MM*, 66.

15. Thomas A. Bailey, *The American Pageant: A History of the Republic* (Boston: Heath, 1956), 369–70, 100–103. When Charles V. Hamilton, coauthor of *Black Power*, taught at "a southern Negro college," he once asked a colleague in the history department, himself an African American, what textbook he used. "Oh, I always use Bailey's *American Pageant*," said the colleague. "It is simple and clear and my students like it and find it easy to read" (*CNT*, 75).

16. Richard Hofstadter, William Miller, and Daniel Aaron, *The American Republic*, vol. 1 (Englewood Cliffs: Prentice-Hall, 1959), 514–15.

17. The opening of the slave trade in remote regions of Africa is documented in Leda Farrant, *Tippu-Tip and the East African Slave Trade* (New York: St. Martin's, 1975) and Alfred Swann, *Fighting the Slave-Hunters in Central Africa* (Chicago: AFRO-AM Press, 1969).

18. William Henry Sheppard's early missionary work is recounted in his *Pioneers in the Congo* (Louisville: Pentecostal Publishing, 1902) and in his articles on the early Congo mission, including "An African's Work for Africa," *Missionary Review of the World* 19 (October 1906): 770–74 and "Light in Darkest Africa," *Southern Workman* (March 1905): 218–27.

19. Sophia Hawthorne to Nathaniel Hawthorne (August 14, 1862), Morgan Library, New York; italics added.

20. Ibid.

21. William S. McFeely, *Frederick Douglass* (New York: Norton, 1991), 218.

22. Jacobs, *Incidents in the Life of a Slave Girl*, 92.

23. In "Nat Turner's Insurrection" (1866), Thomas Wentworth Higginson also notes that Turner has "strongly marked African features," a verbal echo of Gray's account. (The confession itself had been widely reprinted, even though Higginson had never seen a copy of the rare "original pamphlet" published by Gray in Baltimore in 1831. Instead, Higginson worked mainly from newspaper accounts and from "another small pamphlet" published that same year in New York and "containing the main features of the outbreak.") Higginson, however, adds a detail that is not in Gray and that sounds more like Frederick Douglass's fictional accounts of heroic, rebellious slaves: "a face full of expression and resolution." Gray says that Turner's expression is "deliberate" but goes on to give him the horrifying, preternatural composure of a madman. Higginson, on the other hand, implies that Turner's mental resolve follows a rational weighing of alternative behaviors, the mark of the truly masculine will in faculty psychology. And, incidentally, where Gray saw "excrescences" on Turner's skin, Higginson reported "peculiar marks on his person, which, joined to his mental precocity" (outer being a sure sign of inner to the physiognomist) all but guaranteed on the part of his younger followers "a superstitious faith in his gifts and destiny" (*TO*, 278–279).

24. Paul Broca, *Dictionnaire encyclopédique des sciences médicales*, ed. A. Dechambre (Paris: Masson, 1866), 295–96.

25. In James Fenimore Cooper's romance of 1826, the noble Uncas, last of his tribe, is

permitted to court Cora Munro (but not her fairer skinned half-sister, Alice) because she has black ancestry. When Natty Bumppo shoots Magua, who claims Cora as his property and tries to breach her father's stronghold by stealth, the treacherous Indian of Cooper's tale falls to his death from a craggy precipice.

26. In America, the myth of a superior order of courage in white men was shattered by the Civil War. Thus Henry Fleming, the young white soldier of Stephen Crane's *The Red Badge of Courage* (1898), fights as savagely as Cooper's braves when his "battle sleep" descends upon him; but when the desire for self-preservation prevails, he runs as blindly as he fights. Marking the regions of both his animal propensities and his reflecting faculties, the blood-stained bandage around Henry Fleming's temples and forehead is a false badge of "Caucasian" courage, for Crane's typical soldier acts solely on instinct, reflecting upon his deeds only afterward, whether he runs or stands.

27. In *A History of New York* (1809), Washington Irving parodied this sort of white man's reasoning: "It is true, the savages might plead that they drew all the benefits from the land which their simple wants required. . . . But this only proves how undeserving they were of the blessings around them—they were so much the more savages, for not having more wants; for knowledge is in some degree an increase of desires, and it is this superiority both in the number and magnitude of his desires, that distinguishes the man from the beast. Therefore the Indians, in not having more wants, were very unreasonable animals; and it was but just that they should make way for the Europeans, who had a thousand wants to their one" (quoted in Michael L. Black and Nancy B. Black, eds., *A History of New York* [Boston: Twayne, 1984], 44).

28. In America at the end of the century that mind was particularly fixed upon "manifest destiny." For a study of how this obsession and racist attitudes toward native Americans fed off of each other, see Richard Drinnon's *Facing West: The Metaphysics of Indian-Hating and Empire Building* (Minneapolis: University of Minnesota Press, 1980).

29. Withholding their knives and forks, anthropologists at the 1904 exhibition nonetheless bombarded the Pygmies with dynamometers, pulse controllers, cephalometers, aesthesiometers, pantographs, sphygmographs, and tape measures. The general public used less "scientific" devices. One of the pygmies under study, Ota Benga, who was soon to appear in a monkey cage at the Bronx Zoo, recalled dodging the occasional lighted cigar thrust from the crowd to test his reflexes (*OTA*, 121). All the instruments, *including* the newly devised I-Q test, pointed to the usual conclusions by "civilized man" about the pygmy mind of the African: "African Pygmies" who took the tests, reported the anthropologists, "behaved a good deal in the same way as the mentally deficient person, making many stupid errors and taking an enormous amount of time." One visitor to the 1904 exhibition, Henry Adams, remembered it as a species of madness in the "Arabesque" style favored by Charles Brockden Brown and Poe: "The world had never witnessed so marvellous a phantasm; by night Arabia's crimson sands had never returned a glow half so astonishing, as one wandered among long lines of white palaces, exquisitely lighted by thousands on thousands of electric candles, soft, rich, shadowy, palpable in their sensuous depths . . . listening for a voice or a foot-fall or the plash of an oar" (*The Education of Henry Adams*, 467).

30. Quoted in William Dean Howells, *Life and Character of Rutherford B. Hayes* (Cambridge, Mass.: Houghton, 1876), 39.

31. Harry Barnard, *Rutherford B. Hayes and His America* (Indianapolis: Bobbs-Merrill, 1954), 175.

32. Ibid, 175.

33. Howells, *Life and Character of Rutherford B. Hayes,* 38–39.

34. Ibid., 39.

35. Ibid.

36. Ibid., 40.

37. Soon after he won the Farrer case, young Rutherford B. Hayes was to successfully defend a number of fugitive slaves from his law office in Ohio. Years later, it was Hayes who appointed Frederick Douglass marshal of the District of Columbia, the first appointment of an African American to any office in this country that required the approval of the Senate. Hayes, however, had gotten elected, in part, by making concessions to white supremacists in the South. Thus Hayes's inauguration in 1877, writes William S. McFeeley, "spelled the end of federal responsibility for the rights of black people in the South" (*Frederick Douglass,* 289). The name, incidentally, of the president's and former soldier's trusty war horse, to whom is dedicated a small sheaf of papers in the archives of the Ohio Historical Society: Old Whitey.

38. Higginson attributes the gruesome "story" of Antonio to Lydia Maria Child, who got it from Charity Bowery, "an old colored woman, once well known in New York" (*TO,* 301). Such executions, says Robyn Wiegman, portray their victims as "monstrocities of excess whose limp and hanging bodies function as the specular assurance that the racial threat has not simply been averted, but rendered incapable of return." Thus they "operate according to a logic of borders—racial, sexual, national, psychological, and biological as well as gendered" (*American Anatomies,* 81). Among the murders attributed to the "understandable wave of hysteria" (Thomas Bailey's *American Pageant*) and frenzy of retaliation that followed the Turner rebellion, at least one other, besides Antionio's at the fork in the road, enacted the symbolic enforcement of arbitrary boundary lines: "A party of horsemen started from Richmond with the intention of killing every colored person they saw in Southampton County. They stopped opposite the cabin of a free colored man, who was hoeing in his little field. They called out, 'Is this Southampton County?' He replied, 'Yes, sir, you have just crossed the line, by yonder tree.' They shot him dead, and rode on" (*TO,* 300).

39. Herman Melville, "Benito Cereno," in *The Piazza Tales,* ed. Harrison Hayford (New York: Library of America, 1984), 755.

40. But if the black head on a pike was clearly a sign of retribution, whose retribution was it? Sundquist argues convincingly that "Blackhead signpost was an instance of suppressive terror, but it was also an instance of admission that such terror was inadequate—that it was always . . . *counterterror.*" In the case of Antonio and the Turner revolt, the severed head was not Nat Turner's but, says Sundquist, "in standing for Turner and the defeat of his revolt, it also perforce stood for the 'silent satisfaction' with which he (and presumably many other slaves) had witnessed the like dismemberment of the masters." In Sundquist's view, the *Confessions of Nat Turner,* with its inherently ambiguous authorship, is therefore not just a piece of white propaganda but "a written simulacrum of Turner's violent rising and a jeremiad of the most extreme kind" whereby Turner continues even now to terrorize (and purify?) the white consciousness (*To Wake the Nations,* 71–72).

41. The official legal function of such "tableaux" of horror must be disguised, however. "In the circuit of relations that governs lynching in the United States," says Wiegman, "the law as legal discourse and disciplinary practice subtends the Symbolic arena, marking out a topos of bodies and identities than not only defines and circumscribes social and political behavior but also punishes trangression, from its wildest possibility to its most benign threat" (*American Anatomies*, 81).

42. Sundquist *To Wake the Nations*, 43.

4. Romancing the Shadow

1. Herman Melville, *Piazza Tales*, 754.

2. Ibid.

3. Ralph Ellison, *Shadow and Act* (1964; New York: New American Library, 1966), 177–78.

4. One of the most exhaustive accounts of slave uprisings in America, and the one of perhaps greatest inspiration to the "black militants" of the 1960s, was Herbert Aptheker's *American Negro Slave Revolts* (New York: Columbia University Press, 1943). "History's potency is mighty," Aptheker later wrote in a review of Styron's novel. "The oppressed need it for identity and inspiration; oppressors for justification, rationalization and legitimacy. Nothing illustrates this more clearly than the history writing on the American Negro people" (*CNT*, vii). Aptheker's own "history writing," manifestly Marxist in its pursuit of rebellious masses rising up against the capitalist system that oppresses them, has been criticized by James M. McPherson, a Princeton historian, for magnifying "rumors into conspiracies" and elevating "vague, half-formed plots into full-scale revolts" (*CNT*, iii–iv). On the thorny issue of the magnitude of slave rebellions in North America, McPherson maintains that "most scholars agree that major revolts were less frequent in the United States than among slaves of Latin America and the West Indies." In *American Negro Slavery* (Gloucester, Mass.: P. Smith, 1918), Ulrich B. Phillips makes the classic "white" argument that this was because slavery in the United States was less harsh than elsewhere and the slaves were, therefore, happier with it. At the other pole of white theorizing about the black experience, Stanley Elkins—in *Slavery: A Problem in American Institutional and Intellectual Life* (Chicago: University of Chicago Press, 1959)—argues that slaves in the United States were less rebellious than in Latin America and elsewhere because the North American system was *more* repressive, reducing the slave (in McPherson's words) "to the psychologically dependent status of a child" (*CNT*, iii). As examples of history writing, it seems to me, both of these narratives simply carry forward, in their different ways—the "child" is happy in one, in the other he is not—devices of characterization implicit in faculty psychology and universally employed in nineteenth-century fiction. A more modern strain, in its psychology at least, of "history writing on the American Negro people" is the scholarly genre, concurrent with Elkins's, that identifies the North American slave not as rebel or victim but as a trickster who (again in James McPherson's words) "deliberately broke or mishandled tools, stole the master's property, engaged in work slow-downs, and in other ways quietly sabotaged the efficient operation of plantation slavery." Kenneth Stampp's *The Peculiar Institution* (New York: Knopf, 1956) is, according to McPherson, the "best statement of this interpretation" (*CNT*, ii). Thomas Wentworth Higginson's own interpretation of

slave rebellions is ambiguous on this matter of whether greater psychological freedom bred political revolt or submission. On the one hand, Higginson points out in *Travellers and Out-laws* that the leaders of the rebellions he chronicles were generally better treated than their fellow slaves; but so, on the other hand, in most of the cases he cites, were the slaves who betrayed the rebels to the white authorities.

5. Ashraf H. A. Rushdy has even suggested that Styron's *Nat Turner* and the controversy it provoked "formed part of a crucial transformation in the intellectual study of slavery—a transformation which has led to a renaissance of African-American literary representations of slavery." Rushdy points out that before 1968, there were "only two notable twentieth-century African-American novels about slavery in the United States, Arna Bontemps's *Black Thunder* (1936) and Margaret Walker's *Jubilee* (1966). Since then there have been dozens, including the works of John Oliver Killens, Ernest J. Gaines, Charles Johnson, Toni Morrison, and Barbara Chase-Riboud. "These novels are not direct results of the conflict over Styron's novel," Rushdy admits, "nor are they in any meaningful sense 'responses' to his novel. Rather, these contemporary narratives of slavery emerged from a set of intellectual, institutional, and social conditions which the debate over Styron's novel and the Clarke collection crystallized and helped bring about." "Reading Black, White, and Gray in 1968" in *Criticism and the Color Line*, 66.

6. "History takes still more from those who have lost everything," Bennett further quotes Merleau-Ponty as saying, "and gives yet more to those who have taken everything. For its sweeping judgments acquit the unjust and dismiss the pleas of their victims" (*CNT*, 3).

7. My synthesizing account of "the romance" and other cultural forms is not intended to promote the notion of an "integrated American literature," as David Bradley and Shelley Fisher Fishkin have defined it. (*Was Huck Black?* 143.) Admirable as that multicultural project might be, I am sensitive to the pitfalls of canon formation cited by Cornel West, who argues that "ideologies of pluralism" may, even with the best of intentions, conceal "irresoluable conflict." The "white" narratives that I discuss are so fraught with "conflict, struggle, and contestation" (West), in fact, that to somehow integrate them with the struggles depicted in "black" narratives is to deny, or at least diminish, the boiling tensions that necessitate the disguises of romance and romanticized history in the first place. Cornel West, "Black Critics and the Pitfalls of Canon Formation," in *Keeping Faith: Philosophy and Race in America*, 33–43.

8. As Franny Nudelman has pointed out, even abolitionist rhetoric commonly depicted scenes of slaves in chains as "tales of suffering witnessed rather than suffering endured" ("Harriet Jacobs and the Sentimental Politics of Female Suffering," *English Literary History* 59 [1992]: 948). Thomas Gray's chief function, avowedly, in the *Confessions of Nat Turner* is to bear witness—not to the captive's suffering so much as to that of the witness himself (who is a stand-in for the reader). Parodoxically, abolitionist discourse, though politically antithetical to Gray's proslavery discourse, often resembled proslavery rhetoric when it depicted whippings or lynchings that were horrible to behold, for it thereby "appropriated the victim's position," as Teresa Goddu has observed, thereby "denying the slave agency or resistence" (*Gothic America*, 185 n. 8).

9. The narrator of "The Imp of the Perverse" is trying to explain, rationally, his obsession with such topics as cliff-hanging and circumlocution. It is not just with the acts them-

selves that he is obsessed, however, but with the telling of them. For such out-of-control speech or writing, however, there is no rational explanation, according to faculty psychology. Of this verbal species of "enthusiasm," Emerson, for example, observed: "How wearisome, the grammarian, the phrenologist, the political or religious fanatic, or indeed any possessed mortal whose balance is lost by the exaggeration of a single topic. It is incipient insanity" (*PER*, 424). For an analysis of the audience's role as a consumer of "horror" fiction, see Terry Heller, *The Delights of Terror: An Aesthetics of the Tale of Terror* (Urbana: University of Illinois Press, 1987).

10. Morrison never says that whiteness is not frightening; but the burden of her critique is that whiteness can be historicized as a racial category just as blackness has been. In this she is joined by a number of recent critics, among them Dana Nelson (*The Word in Black and White*), Ruth Frankenberg (*White Women, Race Matters*), and David Roediger (*The Wages of Whiteness*).

11. Poe's "perfect whiteness," as Teresa A. Goddu notes in "The Ghost of Race: Edgar Allan Poe and the Southern Gothic," is profoundly ambiguous. *Pym* "would seem to be reinstituting the color line by exorcising blackness in order to embrace whiteness. However, it is also possible to read the ending in precisely the opposite way: whiteness can only be embraced through blackness." I would like to suggest, with Goddu, "that *Pym's* obsession with 'whiteness' has less to do with a simple message of white supremacy than with a complex and even at times contradictory claim that, while white might be 'right,' it is neither perfect nor pure" (*Criticism and the Color Line*, 246).

12. *The Letters of Herman Melville*, ed. Merrell R. Davis and William H. Gilman (New Haven: Yale University Press, 1960), 129.

13. In the "Extracts" at the beginning of *Moby-Dick*, Melville quotes the passage in Isaiah that identifies the whale as a serpent: "In that day, the Lord with his sore, and great, and strong sword, shall punish Leviathan the piercing serpent, even Leviathan that crooked serpent; and he shall slay the dragon that is in the sea." (*M-D*, 783).

14. In the works of Melville, men often take the part of women, but they are not unmanned by doing so. It is his "marriage" to Queequeg at the beginning of *Moby-Dick* that saves Ishmael at the end when he floats to the surface of the sea on Queequeg's coffin, his mate's last bed. It is the bond (physical and figurative) between the two men in "The Monkey Rope" chapter that "weds" them "for better or for worse" as Queequeg dangles among sharks. His "free will had received a mortal wound," says Ishmael of this tie that makes them Siamese twin brothers. And it is more than "the very milk and sperm of kindness" that the crewmen of the *Pequod* wring from each other in the great masturbatory vision of "A Squeeze of the Hand": "Such an abounding, affectionate, friendly, loving feeling did this avocation beget," says Ishmael, that he was continually squeezing his shipmates' hands "and looking up into their eyes sentimentally; as much as to say,—Oh! my dear fellow beings . . . let us all squeeze ourselves into each other . . . Would that I could keep squeezing that sperm for ever!" (*M-D*, 1135, 1239.)

15. Leslie Fiedler, *Love and Death in the American Novel* (New York: Stein and Day), 1966.

16. *M-D*, 1152. Nathaniel Hawthorne, *The Letters, 1857–1864*, volume 17 in *The Centenary Edition of the Works of Nathaniel Hawthorne* (Columbus: Ohio State University Press, 1987), 434.

17. Whether regarded as male or female, the whale's most highly developed organs

show him to be equally "primitive." Ishmael's most protracted phrenological disquisition on the whale's head in *Moby-Dick* occurs in the chapter entitled "The Nut." If, "physiognomically" speaking, the whale is "a Sphinx," says Ishmael, "to the phrenologist his brain seems that geometrical circle which it is impossible to square." In other words, the whale's brain is a hard nut to crack. The creature's high, massive forehead, indicating prodigious cognitive powers, says Ishmael, is "phrenologically . . . an entire delusion." The outside of his head offers "no indications" of "his true brain." How, then, the narrator asks, can "unlettered Ishmael hope to read the awful Chaldee of the Sperm Whale's brow? I put that brow before you. Read it if you can." Ishmael plunges ahead with a reading anyway. Examined from behind, the whale's skull looks like a giant human skull; and if scaled down and placed on a plate of men's skulls, the depressions on the summit are such, explains Ishmael, that "in phrenological phrase you would say—This man has no self-esteem, and no veneration." What the whale's "most exalted potency" is, "you can best form to yourself the truest, though not the most exhilarating conception of," says the amateur phrenologist, by considering "his prodigious bulk." In other words, the whale is bluntly (and blindly) phallic. This reading of his "character" is further confirmed by Ishmael's extraordinary application of a "spinal branch of phrenology" to the whale's backbone, the vertebrae of which, he claims, resemble "a strung necklace of dwarfed skulls." (This is a "German conceit," but Ishmael has encountered it among cannibals, too.) Over the largest of these "undeveloped skulls" rises the whale's hump, and Ishmael is led by this furious trope to a reading of the whale's brain and spinal cord that affirms his primitive masculinity: "I should call this high hump the organ of firmness" (*M-D*, 1166–68).

18. Ishmael's little treatise on phenomenology was written before Edmund Husserl proposed, about 1905, that any such inquiry into "appearances" leave out of account, at least temporarily, all considerations of objective reality as well as purely subjective response, the very phenomena that Emerson weds in his Transcendental philosophy.

19. Holding that the mind knows only its own percepts and concepts and can never understand how they came about or grasp the "objects" of perception outside, Hume forever placed shadows, phantoms, figments of the brain between the mind and external "reality." Such a doctrine was anathema to the Common Sense realism that emerged, in part, from Thomas Reid's attack on Hume.

20. Chandler Robbins, *Remarks on the Disorders of Literary Men* (Boston: Cummings, Hilliard, 1825). The subject of Robbins's inquiry as quoted here is part of his extended title.

5. Bachelor's Bower: The Fearful Female

1. Orson Fowler quoted in Kaplan, *Walt Whitman*, 153.
2. Whitman quoted in Kaplan, *Walt Whitman*, 153.
3. Emerson was also aware of the role of the will in determining the order of thoughts in the normal mind of faculty psychology: "The thought of genius is spontaneous," he wrote in "Intellect," "but the power of picture or expression, in the most and enriched and flowing nature, implies a mixture of will, a certain control over the spontaneous states, without which no production is possible. It is a conversion of all nature into the rhetoric of thought, under the eye of judgment, with a strenuous exercise of choice" (*EEL*, 423).

4. *The Poetical Works of Oliver Wendell Holmes*, 143–144.

5. Harold Bloom and Paul Kane eds., *Ralph Waldo Emerson: Collected Poems and Translations* (New York: Library of America, 1994), 9.

6. O'Leary, *Delineation of Character*, 127.

7. Lorenz Oken, *Elements of Physiophilosophy*, trans. A. Tulk (London: Ray Society, 1847), aphorisims 3067–69. Oken and Agassiz are quoted in Stephen Jay Gould, *The Flamingo's Smile: Reflections in Natural History* (New York: Norton, 1985), 200–205.

8. The great Darwinian principle of biological "propinquity" (*On the Origin of Species*, 1859) is credited for his rearrangement of natural history in Gould, *The Flamingo's Smile*, 211. For the full flourishing of "the most damaging productions of 'race' in American culture," according to Robyn Wiegman, natural history had to yield the field to biology and the race "science" that accompanied it (*American Anatomies*, 43–78). The line of descent from natural history to biology, as Nancy Stepan has said, was anything but simple and direct, however (*The Idea of Race in Science*, 4); it required a "radical reorganization of knowledge" (*American Anatomies*, 29), and the new science proposed formidable obstacles to antiracist theories. See Nancy Stepan and Sander L. Gilman, "Appropriating the Idioms of Science: The Rejection of Scientific Racism" in *The Bounds of Race: Perspectives on Hegemony and Resistance*, ed. Dominick LaCapra (Ithaca: Cornell University Press, 1991), 72–103.

9. Emerson, *Collected Poems and Translations*, 9–10; this is the source of all quotations from "Each and All" in the following paragraphs.

10. O'Leary, *Delineation of Character*, 127.

11. Emerson, *Miscellanies*, 411.

12. *The Complete Poems of Emily Dickinson*, ed. Thomas H. Johnson (Boston: Little, Brown, 1960), #1551; all quotations from Emily Dickinson's poems are cited by reference to their numbers in this edition.

13. Quoted in James R. Mellow, *Nathaniel Hawthorne in His Times* (Boston: Houghton Mifflin, 1980), 191. Later, on another walking trip with Hawthorne, Emerson used a familiar metaphor for sharing his thoughts with his companion: "We were both old collectors who had never had the opportunity before to show each other our cabinets, so that we could have filled with matter much longer days" (Mellow, 191).

14. Emerson, *Miscellanies*, 419, 407.

15. Common Sense philosophy's distrust of the merely contemplative life is usually seen to reside in a deep distrust of the imagination and its products, such as fiction. Thus most writing in America before the Revolution was done, so this argument goes, in nonfiction forms: sermons, diaries, letters, autobiographies, didactic poems. (There are still consumers of print in this country, especially male consumers, who will not read a novel but who must have their morning newspaper or, in the evening, a good biography or work of history.) I have no doubt that Common Sense realism distrusted the imagination, which Dugald Stewart defined as the power of the intellect "to make a selection of qualities and of circumstances from a variety of different objects, and by combining and disposing these, to form a new creation of its own" (*WDS*, vol. 1, 355). Stewart's Realism differed most profoundly from his mentor's, Thomas Reid's, on just this issue. Reid held works of the imagination to be mere vapors in the mind of their author; Stewart maintained that they were real, "a new creation." I believe, however, that Realism's quarrel with the imagination stems not so much from epistemological doubts about the reality of works of the imagina-

tion, such as the romance, as from a fear of the passions, which Common Sense associated with the "feminine" side of human nature.

16. Thomas Jefferson to Nathaniel Burwell, March 14, 1818; *The Writings of Thomas Jefferson*, ed. Albert Ellery Bergh, vol. 15 (Washington, D.C., 1907), 166.

17. Emerson, *Miscellanies*, 425, 426.

18. Margaret Fuller, *Woman in the Nineteenth Century* (New York: Greeley & McElrath, 1845), 155, 156.

19. In his study of the influence of moral philosophy upon Unitarinism (*The Unitarian Conscience: Harvard Moral Philosophy, 1805–1861* [Cambridge: Harvard University Press, 1970]), Daniel Walker Howe noted the "dualism" of Common Sense philosophy. Though the Scottish philosophers emphasized the "reality" to be apprehended by the senses, they never said that heaven and spirit were not real; for them, as for the Transcendentalists, the immaterial could be just as real as the material. This balancing act, as Gregg Camfield has noted, "required not metaphysical hair-splitting, but rope-splicing between the essentially idealist, a priori and deductive Christian religion and the essentially materialistic [as in Emerson's accounts of the mechanics of visual perception and memory], a posteriori and inductive system of science" (*Sentimental Twain: Samuel Clemens in the Maze of Moral Philosophy* [Philadelphia: University of Pennsylvania Press, 1994], 24).

20. Life back in town could seem even more animalistic to Thoreau than life in the woods, however; Steven Fink gives an authoritative account of Thoreau's struggle with the commercialism of literary production in *Prophet in the Marketplace: Thoreau's Development as a Professional Writer* (Princeton: Princeton University Press, 1992).

21. Gordon Taylor, *The Passages of Thought: Psychological Representation in the American Novel, 1870–1900* (New York: Oxford, 1969), is the only book I know of that focuses upon how an "author's premises concerning the nature of the mind" shape the thought patterns of the characters. Taylor realized that "roughly between 1870 and 1900" those premises changed in basic ways, resulting in "a fundamental shift" in the "fictive psychology" of the American novel. Taylor describes that shift as follows: "The basic view of the mind underlying the representation of consciousness in fiction moves away from a notion of static, discrete mental states requiring representational emphasis on the conventional nature of particular states, toward a concept of organically linked mental states requiring representational emphasis on the nature of the sequential process itself" (*Passages*, 5–6). While I would agree that such a shift occurred, I would describe it as a shift in the understanding of consciousness itself and would argue that, before 1870, the "discrete mental states" Taylor writes about might be seen as stages or steps in a "process" of thinking that was even more strictly "sequential" than the flow of the stream or river that consciousness was becoming in the 1880s. It is a *winding* passage of thought that sweeps Huck Finn along through the debris of the older model, to which Huck still clings, even as Clemens's technique eats away at its foundations.

22. For basic primary documents on the principles of mental association as understood by John Abercrombie, William Hamilton, George Henry Lewes, Herbert Spencer, and others, see Jenny Bourne Taylor and Sally Shuttleworth, *Embodied Selves*, 73–101.

6. Mrs. Stowe's Fantasy of the White Black Man

1. Stowe's Simon Legree is another of the half-man, half-animal throwbacks of faculty psychology, with its inherently devolutionary notion of mental difference in kind by race and sex: "He was evidently, though short, of gigantic strength. His round, bullet head [presumably rounding to a point and, therefore, shorn of moral sentiments, like the head of "the Indian" in Fowler's crude cuts], large, light-grey eyes, with their shaggy, sandy eyebrows, and stiff, wiry, sun-burned hair, were rather unprepossing items . . . ; his large, coarse mouth was distended with tobacco, the juice of which, from time to time, he ejected from him with great decision and explosive force; his hands were immensely large, hairy, sunburned, freckled, and very dirty, and garnished with long nails, in a very foul condition" (*UTC*, 289). To the student of phrenology, physiognomy, and sarcognomy, Simon Legree's "rather unprepossessing" physical body held the key to deciphering his mental capacities or lack thereof. The cardinal rule of phrenology, as explained by Thomas Sewall, M.D., to the medical class of Columbian College in 1826, is that "every faculty desires gratification, with a degree of energy, proportionate to the size of its organ; and those faculties will be habitually indulged, the organs of which are largest in the individual" (*An Examination of Phrenology* [Washington, D.C.: B. Homans, 1837], 32). Because Simon Legree's animal organs are large and his moral and intellectual organs are small, he will always be, in Dr. Sewall's words, "naturally prone to animal indulgence in the highest degree" (*An Examination*, 32). Stowe's Uncle Tom, however, never behaves like a beast despite the animal powers suggested by his muscular physique because he has developed the moral organs that Stowe's animalistic characters lack and because he is subject to the second cardinal rule of phrenology, which pertains to mental and moral balance. If, as explained by Dr. Sewall, several of the animal organs and several of those of the moral sentiments are equally large in the same individual, "the rule then is, that the lower propensities will take their direction from the higher powers" (*An Examination*, 32–33). A professor of anatomy and physiology, Thomas Sewall was a proto–Oliver Wendell Holmes in his skepticism toward "bump reading" and his scientific use of anatomy to disprove it. His *Examination of Phrenology* is thus a point-by-point refutation of the "science"; but Sewall was lecturing and writing at a time when the unscientific basis of phrenology and physiognomy was still to be established, even among medical men. Sewall's own position was the one Darwin would reach several decades later: "I admit that there is a difference in the natural capacities of men. I am equally clear that this difference is utterly insignificant, compared with what is impressed upon the mind by circumstances" (*An Examination*, 56). The phrenologists, however, begged to differ. In addition to faculty psychology's idea of mental and moral balance as the fundamental constituent of sanity, the phrenologists appropriated, for their theory of temperament, the combining principles of the ancient psychology of the four "humours"—"Lymphatic," "Sanguine," "Bilious," and "Nervous" (George Combe's names)—from which faculty psychology itself may derive. Since they "rarely occur simple in any individual," as Combe notes, Simon Legree would appear to be a composite of the bilious and the nervous types, "a common combination, which gives strength and activity," according to Combe. Like Poe's Dirk Peters, Simon Legree is accompanied, though not counterbalanced, in Stowe's narrative by an "Augustus" type. Stowe's Augustine St. Clare, it would appear, combines the lymphatic and the nervous temperaments, "which is also common," says Combe, "and

produces sensitive delicacy of mental constitution, conjoined with indolence" (*SP*, 29, 93–94).

2. Richard Yarborough places Stowe's characterization of Tom in a different tradition in "Strategies of Black Characterization in *Uncle Tom's Cabin* and the Early Afro-American Novel," in Eric J. Sundquist, ed., *New Essays on Uncle Tom's Cabin* (New York: Cambridge University Press, 1986). Other particularly useful essays in this collection include Jean Fagan Yellin, "Doing It Herself: *Uncle Tom's Cabin* and Woman's Role in the Slavery Crisis"; Karen Halttunen, "Gothic Imagination and Social Reform: The Haunted Houses of Lyman Beecher, Henry Ward Beecher, and Harriet Beecher Stowe"; Robert B. Stepto, "Sharing the Thunder: The Literary Exchanges of Harriet Beecher Stowe, Henry Bibb, and Frederick Douglass"; and Elizabeth Ammons, "Stowe's Dream of the Mother-Savior: *Uncle Tom's Cabin* and American Women Writers before the 1920s."

3. On their honeymoon in England in 1840, Elizabeth Cady Stanton and her husband had attended the World Anti-Slavery Convention. When, on the first day, it was decided not to seat women delegates, Stanton and Lucretia Mott vowed to hold their own convention in America. Though eight years elapsed before they did so, the Seneca Falls gathering of 1848 was soon followed by others in Ohio, Indiana, Massachusetts, Pennsylvania, and New York. It was one of the Massachusetts meetings, attended by William Lloyd Garrison, Wendell Phillips, William Henry Channing, Theodore Parker, and Emerson, as Stanton recalled in her *Reminiscences*, that "first attracted the attention of Mrs. John Stuart Mill, and drew from her pen that able article on 'The Enfranchisement of Woman,' in the *Westminster Review* of October, 1852." In his *Autobiography* (1873), Mill himself, author of the influential *Subjection of Women* (1869), attributed "all that is most striking and profound" in that earlier book to his wife, the former Harriet Taylor. A young Sigmund Freud, in turn, came in contact with the Mills' ideas by reading the *Autobiography* (for which the Scottish philosopher Alexander Bain, whose work I cite in chapter 10, read proof, begging Mill's executor to let him remove passages that "outraged all reasonable credibility" in describing the "matchless genius" of Mrs. Mill). "This is altogether a topic on which one does not find Mill quite human," said young Freud. "His autobiography is so prudish or so unearthy that one would never learn from it that humanity is divided between men and women, and that this difference is the most important one. . . . For example he finds an analogy for the oppression of women in that of the Negro. Any girl," he assured his fiancée, "even without a vote and legal rights, whose hand is kissed by a man willing to risk his all for her love, could have put him right on this. . . . The position of woman cannot be other than what it is," Freud added in his best "Victorian" vein: "to be an adored sweetheart in youth, and a beloved wife in maturity." Freud's letter is quoted in Phyllis Rose, *Parallel Lives: Five Victorian Marriages* (New York: Vintage, 1984), 125.

4. *The Complete Works of Thomas Paine*, ed. Philip S. Foner, vol. 2 (New York: Citadel Press, 1945), 36.

5. *The Heath Anthology of American Literature*, ed. Paul Lauter et al., vol. 1 (Boston: Houghton Mifflin, 1998), 2036.

6. Elizabeth Cady Stanton, *Eighty Years and More: Reminiscences, 1815–1897* (New York: European Publishing, 1898), 32.

7. Ibid., 32.

8. Nancy F. Cott, *The Bonds of Womanhood* (New Haven: Yale University Press, 1977), 1–2.

9. Ibid., 2.

10. "We may discover in time," writes Nina Baym in *American Women Writers and the Work of History, 1790–1860* (New Brunswick: Rutgers University Press, 1995), that representations of women as "privatized and domesticated beings are actually minority stands in nineteenth-century American women's literature, owing their [apparent] prominence to present-day preoccupations" (4). Even now, Baym would reconfigure "the overall picture of women's writing" before 1860, pointing out that far more women of the period studied, taught, and wrote "history" than fiction (4). Moreover, Baym demonstrates, those women thought of themselves not only as observing the grand course of history but also as changing it. Supremely aware of the power of mass circulation and the printed word, and of themselves as disseminators of a "master narrative of world history," these women fervently believed, says Baym, that to tell that narrative was actively to take part in the plot. Hence Baym's quarrel with the political theory of Jürgen Habermas and his followers (7). Whereas the nineteenth century is often seen to oppose the public to the private (or domestic or female) sphere, says Baym, Habermas "opposes the public to the *official sphere*," both of which, in his discourse, are overwhelmingly "male." Pointing out that feminist critics of Habermas have often descried a "total absence" of women in Habermas's theory of public life, Baym offers her reading of the self-consciously "historical" writings of nineteenth-century American women as a counterargument: "Yet . . . for Habermas (like all students of modernity) print is a fundamental force in forming and disseminating public opinion, and since it is precisely print that American women were claiming in the nineteenth century, the absence of women is not mandated by the theory so much as it is a typical artifact of male myopia. . . . If print formulates and consolidates public opinion, and women are printed, then they are part of the public sphere as Habermas defines it" (5–6).

11. Sophia Peabody Hawthorne to Mrs. Elizabeth Peabody, September 3, 1843, Berg Collection, New York Public Library.

12. Poe's madman addresses the organ of "Combativeness" in "The Imp of the Perverse." He is aware, he says, that this commonly recognized mental organ is in charge when "we persist in acts because we feel we should *not* persist in them." "The phrenological combativeness," he goes on to say, "has for its essence, the necessity of self-defense. It is our safeguard against injury." The "Perverseness" that he proposes as a newly discovered region of the mind, however, is different: "in the case of that something which I term *perverseness*, the desire to be well is not only not aroused, but a strongly antagonistical sentiment exists" (*PPTE*, 827–828). Again, these are the ravings of a madman; but he could not split phrenological hairs with such precision if Poe himself were not steeped in that "science" and in faculty psychology.

13. Timothy Flint, *Recollections of Ten Years' Residence and Journeyings in the Valley of the Mississippi*; quoted in *SP*, 577.

14. The "moral sentiments" of Haley and Simon Legree are as crude as their grammar, yet another external marker of inner "characters" in this literature. Uncle Tom, by contrast, often speaks the King's English, an indication that the traits elevating his character are, indeed, essentially "white" ones.

15. For Stowe's conception of woman's place in the marketplace, see Gillian Brown, *Domestic Individualism: Imagining Self in Nineteenth-Century America* (Berkeley: University of Cali-

fornia Press, 1990) and Joan D. Hedrick, *Harriet Beecher Stowe: A Life* (New York: Oxford University Press, 1994).

16. Hegel's analysis of the psychology of the master-slave relation is worked out in *The Phenomenology of Mind* (1807) where the slave's "having and being 'a mind of his own'" is said to begin with his recognition "in the master" that self is "something external." Huck Finn would be a happy savage, to Hegel's way of thinking, because he has not yet reached this divided level of troubling self-consciousness.

17. Eva's face has a "dreamy earnestness" by which, says Stowe, "the dullest and most literal were impressed, without exactly knowing why." Not only her physiognomy and the shape of her head, but also "the turn of her neck and bust was peculiarly noble, and the long golden-brown hair . . . floated like a cloud" out of which shown "the deep spiritual of her violet blue eyes, shaded by heavy fringes of golden brown" (*UTC*, 127).

18. *Household Papers and Stories* (New York: AMS Press, 1967), 321. The comparison is Charles Colbert's (*AMP*, 280). "Faculty," writes Mrs. Stowe, "is Yankee for *savoir faire*, and the opposite virtue to shiftlessness. Faculty is the greatest virtue, and shiftlessness the greatest vice, of Yankee man and woman" (*The Minister's Wooing* [New York: Derby and Jackson,1859; rpt. Hartford, Conn.: Stowe-Day Foundation, 1978], 2).

19. Harold Aspiz, *Walt Whitman and the Body Beautiful* (Urbana: University of Illinois Press, 1980), 193–202.

20. Stowe, *The Minister's Wooing*, 10–11, 6.

21. Ibid., 32, 72, 92.

22. Stowe had little firsthand knowledge of the real situation of slaves in the South. Thus, as Charles Colbert points out (AMP, 241), she fell back on the usual ploy of the romancer for whom thoughts were pictures and character was, thus, to be rendered "realistically" by presenting habitual states or "scenes" of mind: she compared herself to a pictorial artist. Her "vocation" in *Uncle Tom's Cabin*, she told Gamaliel Bailey in a letter of 1851, "is simply that of a painter. . . . There is no arguing with pictures, and everybody is impressed by them, whether they mean to be or not." (Cited in *New Essays on Uncle Tom's Cabin*, ed. Eric J. Sundquist [London: Cambridge University Press, 1986], 9.) Before the advent of the modern short story, nineteenth-century writers of tales—I think because their theory of characterization was based on a psychology that demarcated states of mind in terms of physical line and space—often wrote "sketches" that were "realistic" in surface detail but that "idealized" the actual, as Hawthorne chided himself for doing in the "Custom House" sketch at the beginning of *The Scarlet Letter*. Lydia Maria Child's "Slavery's Pleasant Homes—A Faithful Sketch," for example, with its tragic mulatto, saintly black knight, brutish "pure" African, and other "black" types from the white fiction of the period, might more accurately be called "Slavery's Fanciful House of Horrors—Northern Elevation."

23. Issa Desh Breckinridge and Mary Desh, *A Memorial to Joel T. Hart* (Cincinnati: Robert Clarke, 1885), 19–20; quoted in *AMP*, 317.

24. Fowler, *Practical Phrenology*, frontispiece.

25. Walt Whitman, *Leaves of Grass*, ed. Harold W. Blodgett and Sculley Bradley (New York: Norton, 1965), 722.

26. Buchanan's theory of "Sarcognomy" (the "science" of interpreting mentality in the physical body as a whole) was set forth in his *Outlines of Lectures on the Neurological System of Anthropology* (Cincinnati: Buchanan's Journal of Man, 1854). Using an engraving of Hiram

Powers's *The Greek Slave* as a template, Buchanan laid out his "system" of anthropology in regions running from head to toe on the slave's marble body (the equivalent of North to South on a map). The "Region of Insanity" describes a horizontal band across the Venus mound; the region of "Hate" comprises the buttocks, or at least the left one. Both would appear to fall within the "Combative and Destructive Region."

27. The influence that Colbert attributes to phrenology I would trace to the faculty psychology behind it. Phrenology was simply one of the more outward and visible signs— and especially so, I would imagine, to painters and sculptors used to studying and rendering human heads—of the ubiquity of this psychological scheme.

28. Whitman, *Leaves of Grass*, 722.

29. Fowler, *Practical Phrenology*, 34–41.

30. Ibid., frontispiece.

31. Taylor and Shuttleworth offer a cornucopia of early primary documents on heredity and degeneration in *Embodied Selves*, 285–388.

7. Frederick Douglass and the Whiteness of Blackness

1. The theory of natural selection, as opposed to the fact of evolution, says, in effect, as I understand it, that if leopards born with light spots are more likely to escape the hunter's eye because they blend into their natural surroundings better than do leopards born with dark spots, then the light-spotted leopards, in general, have a better chance of surviving to pass on all their genes, including the trait for light spots. The differentation in spots, all other factors being equal, in other words, would make light-spotted leopards fitter than dark-spotted leopards in the survival of the fittest. Where modern evolutionists have extended Darwin's notion of fitness to include such components as fecundity, survival rate, and generation time, the Lamarckians, in a sense, defined fitness too narrowly. They said not only that the individual dark-spotted leopard whose spots got bleached by the sun, say, might live longer with the aid of her altered spots, but that she could pass on to her cubs the useful trait that she had "acquired." (If this were so, rats whose tails are cut off in the laboratory would produce short-tailed offspring.) The evolutionary theory of Herbert Spencer simply substituted acquired "habits" for acquired "traits."

2. Francis Galton, *Memories of My Life* (London: Methuen, 1909), 290.

3. *The Heroic Slave* was published in March 1853 in Frederick Douglass's anti-slavery newspaper and, according to William L. Andrews, is "recognized today as the first work of fiction in African-American literature" (*HS*, 11). In November of that same year, William Wells Brown published *Clotel; or, The President's Daughter: A Narrative of Slave Life in the United States*. This book, says Andrews, who has also edited a modern edition of *Clotel*, is thus, by a few months, "the second work of African-American fiction" (*HS*, 14). Henry Louis Gates Jr., would reserve the distinction of being "probably the first Afro-American to publish a novel in the United States" to Harriet Wilson, author of *Our Nig; or, Sketches from the Life of a Free Black* (1859). Gates's introduction to his Vintage edition (New York: Random House, 1983), where this claim is made, acknowledges, however, that Wilson is "the fifth Afro-American to publish fiction in English (after Frederick Douglass, William Wells Brown, Frank J. Webb, and Martin R. Delany)" (xiii). What is important here is not who came first (or whether Douglass wrote only a "novella," whereas Wilson produced a "novel")

but the fact that, as William L. Andrews says, "African-American fiction emerged in the crisis atmosphere of the 1850s when the prospects for the abolition of slavery and the reform of institutionalized racism in the American political life seemed bleaker than ever before in United States history" (*HS,* 7).

4. For Douglass's own nonfictional version of nineteenth-century race science, see his *Claims of the Negro, Ethnologically Considered. An Address Before the Literary Societies of Western Reserve College* (Rochester, N.Y.: Lee, Mann, 1854).

5. On November 26, 1841, the *Creole* had sailed from Hampton Roads, Virginia, with a load of tobacco and human cargo bound for the New Orleans market. Eleven days out, nineteen of the slaves, led by a man with the euphonious name Madison Washington, slipped their irons and took over the ship, wounding the captain and killing one white man. (In Douglass's romance, the captain and the owner of most of the slaves are killed.) The mutineers diverted the *Creole* to Nassau in the Bahamas, where British authorities soon freed them. The incident strained Anglo-American diplomatic relations for years, however, threatening the settlement of boundary disputes over territory separating the U.S. and Canada and hampering negotiations to suppress the slave trade in the Atlantic. In 1855, the year of Melville's "Benito Cereno," an Anglo-American commission paid $110,330 (approximately $823 per person) in claims to the American slave "owners." (The figure of 134 "fugitives" is given by William L. Andrews in *HS,* 11.)

6. Herman Beavers pairs these two narratives in "The Blind Leading the Blind: The Racial Gaze as Plot Dilemma in 'Benito Cereno' and 'The Heroic Slave'" (*Criticism and the Color Line,* 205–29). "Their literary kinship," says Beavers, "is manifest in their respective subversions of the racial gaze [and of the great "white" eye in the sky, I would say], which denote the inadequacy of anti-slavery rhetoric: so dependent on the visual sphere, so unwilling to redress voicelessness or acts of erasure" (*Criticism and the Color Line,* 226).

7. *The Frederick Douglass Papers: Series One: Speeches, Debates, and Interviews,* ed. John W. Blassingame, vol. 1: 1841–46, ed. John W. Blassingame (New Haven: Yale University Press, 1979), 68, n. 18.

8. Ibid., 67.

9. *The Selected Work of Tom Paine,* ed. Howard Fast (New York: Random House, 1945), 23, 30.

10. Ibid., 18.

11. *Frederick Douglass Papers,* vol. 1, 60, 61.

12. Ibid., 60.

13. James Beattie, *Dissertations Moral and Critical,* vol. 1 (Dublin, 1783), 113.

14. Ibid.

15. The dualism of faculty psychology and Common Sense philosophy did not disappear entirely after 1865; as Gregg Camfield has shown, it "provided the foundations on which both the various forms of idealism and materialism were built" (*Sentimental Twain,* 24). In his chapter "The Real and the Ideal in Sentimental Fiction," Camfield explains how "realists" and "materialists" like Mark Twain (and Huck) could be, at the same time, "sentimentalists" and "idealists."

16. Henry Nash Smith implies that Huck is a case of mental dissociation in "A Sound Heart and a Deformed Conscience," a chapter in his classic study, *Mark Twain: The Development of A Writer* (Cambridge: Belknap Press of Harvard University Press, 1962), 113–37. But

even Smith did not fully explain that Huck's "conscience" is an authentic, early nineteenth-century organ, one that has been taught to determine what is and is not proper moral behavior on the basis of rational thought—sense rather than sensibility. More recently, Gregg Camfield has analyzed Huck's famous crisis of conscience as an attack on "the absolute authority and accuracy of conscience implied in all of the nineteenth-century models." In particular, Camfield demonstrates, Clemens sought a new, "utilitarian model" of conscience (which he nonetheless distrusted) because the old models did not sufficiently accommodate the feelings: "Huck cannot feel his attachment to other human beings without his conscience 'stirring him up,' and he cannot act until he chooses the morality implied by one of the confused and confusing models of conscience he has internalized. But in spite of his need to act through conscience in order to find community, Huck cannot actually find within his conscience a social code that doesn't betray the very social feelings it is supposed to facilitate. Thus Clemens describes conscience as the enemy of humankind, a chimera that promises absolute morality and social connection but delivers a painful fraud" (*Sentimental Twain*, 149–150). Using the "cabinet" metaphor of faculty psychology, Clemens defined the old view of human conscience as "man's moral medicine chest" in *What Is Man? And Other Philosophical Writings*, ed. Paul Baender (Berkeley: University of California Press, 1973), 61.

17. *Frederick Douglass*, 18.

18. *Frederick Douglass Papers*, vol. 1, 67.

19. Tuke, *Description of the Retreat*, 159–60.

20. Though they do not concur on when the South first became a "problem" for the rest of the nation, most historians agree, according to Teresa Goddu, that "during the 1830s the South's problematic status became solidified" (*Gothic America*, 178 n. 5). On the making of the problematic South, see also Ronald Walters, *The Antislavery Appeal: American Abolitionism After 1830* (Baltimore: Johns Hopkins Press, 1976); Richard Gray, *Writing the South: Ideas of an American Region* (New York: Cambridge University Press, 1986); and Larry J. Griffin and Don H. Doyle, eds., *The South as an American Problem* (Athens: University of Georgia Press, 1995).

8. Out of the Black Depths; Or the Transformation

1. Elizabeth Palmer Peabody, ed., *Aesthetic Papers* (Boston: The Editor, 1849), 58–59. The entire text of Reed's essay, "Genius," appears on 58–64.

2. Tom, with his strong arms and chest, is about to be turned into a machine, an idea of the human body (as machine) that, according to Michel Foucault, emerged in the seventeenth century and made possible a "political anatomy" that was also a "mechanics of power" and that was different from slavery because it did not require that the body be owned by the authority directing its economies. "Indeed, the elegance of the discipline lay," says Foucault, "in the fact that it could dispense with this costly and violent relation by obtaining effects of utility at least as great" (*Discipline and Punish*, trans. Alan Sheridan [New York: Vintage, 1979], 137–38). If not a necessary component of slavery, such a "discourse" of the human body, according to David Theo Goldberg, was, however, a condition of "racist discourse" (*AR*, 295–318).

3. George Combe agreed with Stewart that memory "implies a new conception of im-

pressions previously received, attended with the idea of past time, and consciousness of their former existence." (*SP*, 484.) What he could not countenance (and what young Hawthorne found liberating) was his fellow Scot's heretical notion that the extent to which memory, imagination, and the other intellectual faculties vary from mind to mind depended more upon education than heredity. "What we call the power of Imagination, is *not the gift of nature*," Stewart observed in the *Elements*, "but the result of acquired habits, aided by favorable circumstances" (*SP*, 35). These powers, moreover, said the *Outlines*, "are gradually formed by particular habits of study, or of business" (*SP*, 35). Thus it is easy to see why William James, with his interest in "habit" and "attention" would be drawn to Stewart's ideas, especially concerning the psychology of belief. "Next to Association," said Combe, "Habit makes the most conspicuous figure in the philosophy of Mr. Stewart" (*SP*, 519).

4. Hawthorne, *Piazza Tales*, 754.

5. Poe says as much in "The Imp of the Perverse": "In the matter of phrenology, for example, we first determined, naturally enough, that it was the design of the Deity that man should eat. We then assigned to man an organ of alimentiveness, and this organ is the scourge with which the Deity compels man, will-I, nill-I into eating. Secondly, having settled it to be God's will that man should continue his species, we discovered an organ of amativeness, forthwith. And so with combativeness, with ideality, with causality, with constructiveness,—so, in short, with every organ, whether representing a propensity, a moral sentiment, or a faculty of the pure intellect. And in these arrangements of the *principia* of human action, the Spurzheimites, whether right or wrong, in part, or upon the whole, have but followed, in principle, the footsteps of their predecessors; deducing and establishing everything from the preconceived destiny of man, and upon the ground of the objects of his Creator" (*PPTE*, 826–27).

6. Richard Chase, *The American Novel and Its Tradition* (New York: Doubleday, 1957), 12–13, 22.

7. William Dean Howells, *A Hazard of New Fortunes*, ed. George Warren Arms (New York: Dutton, 1952), 540.

8. Nancy Bentley makes the connection between Hawthorne's faun and his ideas on slavery and savagery in "Slaves and Fauns: Hawthorne and the Uses of Primitivism," *ELH* 57 (1990): 901–37.

9. Hawthorne, *Fanshawe*, 437–38.

10. John Bunyan, *The Pilgrim's Progress*, ed. N. H. Keeble (New York: Oxford University Press, 1984), 34.

11. Like Clifford and, to a lesser degree, Holgrave in *Seven Gables*, Miriam is one of the many "dysfunctional" artists in Hawthorne's late fiction. Richard Brodhead argues in *The School of Hawthorne* (New York: Oxford University Press, 1986) that Hawthorne himself became dysfunctional as a writer late in his career by virtue of his becoming a national treasure.

12. *The Collected Works of Dugald Stewart*, ed. Sir William Hamilton, vol. 5 (Edinburgh: T. Constable, 1855), i. The references to Stewart's *Philosophical Essays* in the next paragraph are from the same source.

13. Frederick Rauch, *Psychology, or a View of the Human Soul, including Anthropology*, 2d ed. (New York: Dodd, 1841), 192.

14. Fay, *American Psychology before William James*, 202.

15. *UEMP,* vol. 1, 449.

16. Rauch, *Psychology,* 197.

17. And of most of the other intellectual faculties: "The great object of philosophy, as I have already remarked more than once," said Stewart, the most influential of the Scots from an American perspective, "is to ascertain the laws which regulate the succession of events, both in the physical and moral worlds, in order that, when called upon to act in any particular combination of circumstances, we may be enabled to anticipate the probable course of nature from our past experience, and to regulate our conduct accordingly." The essence of Common Sense philosophy, these ideas were to inform American thought in all its branches, from metaphysics and psychology to the theory of government. William James, for example, whose pragmatism derives in part from Stewart's realism, was probably alluding to the "revolutionary ideals" of Stewart when he wrote in 1891: they "present themselves far less in the guise of effects of past experience than in that of probable causes of future experience, factors to which the environment and the lessons it has so far taught us must learn to bend." "Ideals as 'the probable causes of future experience'—that," Ursula Le Guin, architect of Omelas, was to write in 1975 of James's apparent paraphrase of Stewart, "is a subtle and an exhilarating remark!"

18. For a reading of Holgrave's art as the work of a con man, see Michael T. Gilmore's chapter on *Seven Gables* in *American Romanticism and the Marketplace* (Chicago: University of Chicago Press, 1985). T. Walter Herbert finds deceptive even the domestic sunshine that Phoebe brings into the old house and that turns Holgrave into a romancer (*Dearest Beloved: The Hawthornes and the Making of the Middle-Class Family* [Berkeley: University of California Press, 1993], 106). In Walter Benn Michaels's reading, the property theme of *Seven Gables* is directly related to the economics of slavery ("Romance and Real Estate" in *The American Renaissance Reconsidered,* ed. Michaels and Donald E. Pease [Baltimore: Johns Hopkins University Press, 1985]); and Teresa Goddu has noted that "the voracious consumption of the marketplace is figured through Ned Higgins's devouring the gingerbread Jim Crow" as well as the performing monkey outside Clifford's window (*Gothic America,* 181 n. 12).

19. Among the "higher" activities of these intellectual faculties, Combe insisted, "there is a difference": Conception "is the cool and methodical representation of things absent, as they exist in nature. . . . Imagination is the *impassioned representation* of the same things, and not merely in the forms and arrangements of nature, but in new combinations formed by the mind itself." By "impassioned," however, Combe does not mean imbued with feeling, only vividly conceived: "Imagination is just intense, glowing, forcible, conceptions, proceeding from great activity of the intellectual faculties" (*SP,* 481–82).

20. Stewart, said Combe disparagingly, "states it as his theory that we, for an instant, believe the distress [of the actor or character] to be real; and under this belief feel the compassion which would naturally start up in our bosoms, if the sufferings represented were actually endured." (Hence Stewart's quarrel with the romance when it evoked sentiments too refined to be endured in the actual world outside of fiction.) By a "subsequent act of judgment," the will restrains the mind, in Stewart's more unified view, "from *acting* under the emotion; which, if the belief of reality continued," said Combe, "it would certainly do, by running to the relief of the oppressed hero or heroine" (*SP,* 461).

21. Sophia Hawthorne to Mrs. Elizabeth Peabody, September 3, 1843, Berg Collection, New York Public Library.

9. *The Prisoner of Omelas*

1. In the 1890 edition of the *Principles*, James had called his big chapter on consciousness, "The Stream of Thought." When he revised the book two years later for classroom use, he changed chapters around and rechristened the old chapter on the flow of mind "The Stream of Consciousness." The phrase that thereby entered the language as a term in pre-Freudian psychology is now invoked more often, however, to describe the representation of *unconscious* sequences of thought in fiction. James perhaps invited the appropriation when he wrote, in connection with that chapter, "Permanently recurring ideas are a fiction" and "Thought may be rational in any sort of imagery" (*PBC*, ix).

2. G. Stanley Hall, *Adolescence* (New York: Appleton, 1904), 194. The full title of Hall's landmark study (1904) is almost as comprehensive as those of the phrenological Fowlers: *Adolescence: Its Psychology and Its Relations to Physiology, Anthropology, Sociology, Sex, Crime, Religion, and Education.*

3. J. Mark Baldwin, "Psychology Past and Present," *Psychological Review* 1 (1894): 368.

4. Ibid.

5. Samuel Clemens and William James first met in Florence, Italy, in 1892. Clemens came away from their meeting with a copy of James's newly published *Principles*, in which he later made marginal notations; see Jason Gray Horn, *Mark Twain and William James: Crafting a Free Self* (Columbia: University of Missouri Press, 1996), 4–5. In his notebook for 1896, Clemens included a direct quotation from James's chapter on "Habit," the chapter that has so impressed Clemens's friend William Dean Howells when he reviewed James's book in 1891.

6. Huck, with feelings running high, leaves the raft for the last time in a canoe, which he then "buries," temporarily, as he thinks, as if it were one of the much distressed maidens of a Poe tale: "I landed below where I judged was Phelp's place, and hid my bundle in the woods, and then filled up the canoe with water, and loaded rocks into her and sunk her where I could find her again when I wanted her … " (*HF*, 224).

7. Klaus Doerner, *Madmen and the Bourgeoisie: A Social History of Insanity and Psychiatry*, trans. Joachim Neugroschel and Jean Steinberg (Oxford: Blackwell, 1981), 312.

8. Dix's journal is quoted in Deutsch, *The Mentally Ill in America*, 166.

9. George Hendrick, ed., *Remembrances of Concord and the Thoreaus: Letters of Horace Hosmer to Dr. S. A. Jones* (Urbana: University of Illinois Press, 1977).

10. Resulting from a "congenital weakness" of the brain, "idiocy" or "idiotism," according to Dr. Skae, "varies in degree from slight impairment or imbecility" to "total absence of intelligence" (MD, 538). The household "idiot" was a familiar presence in nineteenth-century families, which tended to be large, partly in anticipation of this hazard.

11. Deutsch, *The Mentally Ill in America*, 167–68.

12. Ibid., 167.

13. Ursula Le Guin, "The Ones Who Walk Away from Omelas: Variations on a Theme by William James," in *The Wind's Twelve Quarters* (New York: Harper and Row, 1975), 281.

14. Ibid., 281.

15. Ibid., 275.

16. William James, *Varieties of Religious Experience* (New York: Longmans, Green, 1925), 161.

10. Mrs. Packard, Miss Dickinson, and the Purloined Regina

1. A popular debating topic of the day, "the comparative mental capacity of the sexes" is weighed as follows by the president of the Montechute Lyceum in Caroline Kirkland's satiric, *A New Home—Who'll Follow?* (New York: C. S. Francis, 1839): "He gave it as his decided opinion, that if the natural and social disadvantages under which woman laboured and must ever continue to labour, could be removed; if their education could be entirely different, and their position in society the reverse of what it is at present, they would be very nearly, if not quite, equal to the nobler sex, in all but strength of mind, in which very useful quality it was his opinion that man would still have the advantage, especially in those communities whose energies were developed by the aid of debating societies." The topic for the next debate: "which is the more useful animal the ox or the ass?" (176–77).

2. The following propositions, along with Mrs. Packard's "reflections" upon them, are quoted from "My Exposure of Calvinism and Defence of Christianity, As Presented to the Trustees," appendix 1, 200–204, in *PWMP.*

3. Deutsch, *The Mentally Ill in America,* 424. Deutsch quotes the Illinois Statute.

4. Ibid., 424–25.

5. Ibid., 425.

6. *Letters of Emily Dickinson,* ed. Thomas Johnson and Theodora Ward, vol. 2 (Cambridge: Harvard University Press, 1958), 373–75. This is the second of the three "Master" letters; the other two are on pages 333 and 391–92, respectively.

7. Ibid., 382.

8. Ibid., 391.

9. Ibid., vol. 3, 617.

10. Ibid., 617.

11. Cynthia Griffin Wolff, *Emily Dickinson* (1986; rpt. Reading, Mass.: Addison-Wesley, 1988), 193.

12. Thus Thomas Johnson and an older generation of critics were beguiled into taking Dickinson's "Master" letters as evidence of a frustration born of her failure to marry. Over the last decade or so, however, many feminist and "queer" critics, among them Susan Howe and Martha Nell Smith, have questioned whether Dickinson even liked men very much, a conclusion that might be supported by my "queenly" reading of the poems and letters. Though I believe, with Cynthia Griffin Wolff, that Dickinson had more than a theoretically emotional interest in "her" Judge Lord, I think she took emotional and intellectual control of their relationship as surely as she took command of her relationship with Thomas Wentworth Higginson, who was Dickinson's "mentor" to about the same (negative) extent that Lord (or whoever else it might have been) was her "master." Indeed, my reason for pairing Dickinson with Mrs. Packard in this chapter is to show just how far the poet departed—even by comparison with a politically "radical feminist" of her day—from the strictures of the psychological models they (and every other woman of their generation) had been taught in the standard textbooks in the schools and often in the models of gendered behavior they encountered at home. Particularly helpful for Dickinson's obliquely formative relationship with her father is Antonina Clarke Mossberg, *Emily Dickinson: When a Writer Is a Daughter* (Bloomington: Indiana University Press, 1982). On Dickinson's sexual preferences, see especially Susan Howe, *My Emily Dickinson* (Berkeley: North

Atlantic Books, 1985); Martha Nell Smith, *Rowing in Eden: Rereading Emily Dickinson* (Austin: University of Texas Press, 1992); Martha Nell Smith and Ellen Louise Hart, *Open Me Carefully: Emily Dickinson's Intimate Letters to Susan Huntington Dickinson* (Ashfield, Mass.: Paris Press, 1998); and Judith Farr, *The Passion of Emily Dickinson* (Cambridge: Harvard University Press, 1992).

13. William Paley, *Works*, vol. 2 (London: Henry Fisher, Son, and P. Jackson, 1828), 1, 3–7.

14. Wolff, *Emily Dickinson*, 356.

15. The Mount Holyoke curriculum as listed in the twelfth annual catalogue (1848–49) is recorded by Edward Hitchcock in *The Power of Christian Benevolence, Illustrated in the Life and Labors of Mary Lyon* (Northampton, Mass.: Hopkins, Bridgman, 1852; New York, 1852); cited in *Emily Dickinson*, 567. A popular textbook in American schools and colleges, Upham's *Elements* went through many reprints and editions; however, his *Philosophical and Practical Treatise on the Will* (Portland, Me.: Hyde, 1834) was not fully incorporated into the material of the two original volumes (on the intellect and the sensibilities) until the edition of 1869. Separating the sensibilities from the "active powers" of the mind and placing them under the command of the intellect is a division of the faculties that a youthful Emily Dickinson was not likely to have found congenial at midcentury.

16. Or, as Upham put it in the 1840 edition, presumably the Mount Holyoke text: "we cannot be pleased or displeased without some antecedent perception or knowledge of the thing which we are pleased or displeased with" (*UEMP*, vol. 2, 26).

17. Upham, *A Philosophical and Practical Treatise*, 20.

18. *Letters of Emily Dickinson*, vol. 1, 13.

19. Daniel N. Robinson, *EW*, xxxvii.

20. Alexander Bain, *The Senses and the Intellect*, vol. 4 of *Significant Contributions to the History of Psychology, 1750–1920*, ed. Daniel N. Robinson (Washington, D.C.: University Publications of America, 1977), 370–71. This is a photographic reprint of the British first edition (London: John W. Parker and Son, 1855).

21. Ibid., 1.

Epilogue: Back to Africa

1. William Dean Howells, *The Shadow of a Dream*, ed. Martha Banta et al. (Bloomington: Indiana University Press, 1970), 115.

2. Ibid., 31.

3. James is quoting Charles Renouvier, "De la ressemblance mentale de l'homme et des autres animaux selon Darwin," *Critique Philosophique*, October 19, 1876, 191.

4. William James, *Varieties of Religious Experience* (1902; New York: Longmans, Green, 1925), 160–61.

5. Ibid.

6. Ibid.

7. Quoted in R. W. B. Lewis, *The Jameses* (New York: Farrar, Straus and Giroux, 1991), 174.

8. James, *Varieties of Religious Experience*, 160.

9. Jean Strouse, *Alice James: A Biography* (Boston: Houghton Mifflin, 1980), 180.

10. Lewis, *The Jameses*, 204–5.

11. Ibid., 204.

12. Whether, among the experts, William James's book was to be seen primarily as a treatise in psychology or in moral philosophy depended on which school the expert belonged to. Thus, when Wilhelm Wunt, the father of modern "experimental" psychology, returned a borrowed copy of the *Principles* to the journalist, Lincoln Steffens, he is supposed to have said: "It is literature, it is beautiful . . . but it is not psychology" (quoted in *The Autobiography of Lincoln Steffens* [New York: Harcourt, Brace, 1931], 150).

13. "Editor's Study," *Harper's Magazine* 83 (July 1891): 315.

14. Lewis, *The Jameses*, 511.

15. For Eliot, the missing link between modern "civilization" and the ancient fertility rituals by which "primitive" cultures (as reported in *The Golden Bough*) evoked rain or the flooding of the Nile for their crops—and thus the renewal of life in the yearly cycle—was King Arthur, as chronicled in Jessie L. Weston's *From Ritual to Romance*, which, as Eliot noted, provided "not only the title, but the plan and a good deal of the incidental symbolism" of his poem. A pioneering application of the methods of literary criticism to other branches of human culture, Weston's book assumed, as Frazer's did, that narrative has an element of ritual or public drama; thus her study lends support to Toni Morrison's argument that the romance, instead of evading "history," actually embroils us in it, history being a conjuration of exemplary event into story by the historian or *griot*.

As indicated by her title, Weston's own thesis, informed by Frazer's study, was that the holy grail and other paraphernalia of Arthur's knights and the Table Round could be traced back to the fertility rituals of ancient cultures. The mythic hero who Christianized Britain was only a metal sword point away from "paganism" and the age-old "savagery" of Africa. (It was not until 1995, incidentally, that sophisticated bone tools uncovered in Africa proved old enough to disprove, finally, the retrograde theory that the human race, while born there, did not achieve the trappings of "civilization" until they reached Europe.)

Reconstructing a symbology so ancient that its original meanings have been severed from the objects that once carried them, Weston interpreted the grail itself as an emblem of female sexuality, or the "female principle"; the lance for her (as for Captain Ahab), of course, represented the "male principle," a symbolism, Weston said, that survives into the present day in the pips on a pack of cards. (By this token, William James's knave of spades would be male, while the jack of hearts, with its concavities, would be female.)

Whether it belonged to Attis, Osiris, Arthur or "the Fisher King" of Eliot's poem, once the lance could no longer rain into the cup, it had to be replaced—as Lancelot takes over from the aging Arthur—either in effigy, or by the physical dismemberment of the hero, or by the sacrifice of a scapegoat. (The latter is the traditional method in the New England village of Shirley Jackson's "The Lottery," where the annual "winner" is stoned to death: "Lottery in June, corn be heavy soon.") Otherwise, if the lance withered, and the gods could not be appeased, the crops would die and the land would be laid waste.

16. In Africa, Henderson has witnessed the dance of life-and-death in which Prince Dahfu and his chief consort, spinning around each other at a dizzying rate, toss back and forth the empty skulls of his predecessors. (When the prince can no longer keep up in this duel of the sexes, his usefulness will be spent, and the chief consort will inform the priests

that it is time for another to take his part, which explains why Dahfu is always resting, and why he is so glad to see Henderson, who seems to want to be some kind of god.) "Leaping, leaping, pounding, and tingling over the pure white lining of the gray Arctic silence," Henderson, however, in his white "Newfoundland," is reenacting a ritual that he grudgingly performed as a youth in "the high latitudes" of Canada, Bellow's homeland, a ceremony that falls short of immortality but that does not require the immediate sacrifice of the old lion king so that a fresh king may reign. Now more of an old bear himself than a lion, Henderson once worked in an amusement park where he rode the roller coaster in the company of an ancient ("green with time") bear named Smolak: "This poor broken ruined creature and I, alone, took the high rides twice a day. And while we climbed and dipped and swooped and swerved and rose again higher than the Ferris wheels and fell, we held on to each other. By a common bond of despair we embraced, cheek to cheek, as all support seemed to leave us and we started down the perpendicular drop." "We're two of a kind,' Henderson says to the carnival master. "'Smolak was cast off and I am an Ishmael, too'" (*HRK*, 298–299). This is Bellow's (and Melville's) idea of community: thrown together for their moment in time, the passengers on his great roller coaster cling to each other—even across species boundaries—as it makes its dizzying circuit because they have nothing else to hold on to, a fragile basis for "civilization," surely, even in the green years, when the Civil Rights movement appeared to blossom and before Vietnam. But then "common despair" is a primitive bond even among the most advanced tribes.

17. Joan Dayan's work on the supernatural in the fiction of the Americas, which she traces to natural histories of slavery, would support a "real ghosts" reading of *Beloved* (*Haiti, History, and the Gods* [Berkeley: University of California Press, 1995].

18. Though slave owners were usually white, of course, a surprising number were not. "In Louisiana, Maryland, South Carolina and Virginia," says Larry Koger, "free blacks owned more than 10,000 slaves, according to the federal census of 1830" (*Black Slaveholders: Free Black Slave Masters in South Carolina, 1790–1860* [Jefferson, N.C.: McFarland, 1985], 1).

19. According to Teresa Goddu, "Jacobs cannot completely exorcise the demons of slavery; yet in bearing witness to them she haunts back" (*Gothic America*, 152).

Index

Beattie, James, 144–45, 147

Beavers, Herman, 273n. 6

"Because I could not stop for Death" (Dickinson), 204

"Bedlam," 41

Beecher, Henry Ward, 195

Beider, Robert E., 53

Belief: Bain on, 219–21; Stewart on, 176; willing of, 176, 190, 219–23, 230

Bell, Luther V., 65

Bellamy, Edward, 187

Bellow, Saul, 76, 232, 234–36, 281n. 16

Beloved (Morrison), xxi, 30, 236–41

Benga, Ota, 66, 260n. 29

"Benito Cereno" (Melville), 68–69, 71–72, 138, 161, 273n. 6

Bennett, Lerone, 73–75, 78

Bentley, Nancy, 275n. 8

Bercovitch, Sacvan, xxiii

Berkeley, George, 24

Berlin Act (1885), 55

"Bernice" (Poe), 236

Berthold, Dennis, xxv

Bethlem Royal Hospital (London), 41, 185

Billy Budd (Melville), 77, 163

Bingham, Caleb, 143

Birthmarks and skin marks, 48, 86, 257n. 3, 259n. 23

"Blackhead signposts," 69

Blackness: association of, with "savagery," 47, 51, 53, 68, 72–78, 87; as attribute of "civilization," xxi; emotions linked to femininity and, under faculty psychology, xvi–xx, 11, 35–37, 51, 53, 54, 57–59, 63–64, 69, 81, 87, 96, 100, 103–14, 119–22, 126, 158–59, 175–76, 179–81, 185, 212, 213, 228, 267n. 15; evolution of, against "whiteness," xxiii, 45–47, 72–78, 85; of feeling-driven will, 29; whites' embracing of forbidden, 71–93

Blacksmith metaphors, 216–19

Black Thunder (Bontemps), 263n. 5

The Blithedale Romance (Hawthorne), 28, 80, 166, 167

Boat (pirate) imagery: and Declaration of Independence, 142; Douglass's use of, 114; Emerson's use of, 42, 51–52, 76–77, 106; and pirate metaphor, 74–77; in Poe's "Arthur Gordon Pym," 84–85

Body parts: collecting of, by Native Americans, 119; collecting of, by whites, 1, 13, 53, 62, 64, 258n. 12; Emerson's imagery of, 97; emphasis on, in nineteenth-century literature, xvi, xxii, 1, 2, 41–43, 120–22; missing, 1, 2, 229, 247nn.3, 4; as outward sign of inward faculties, 41, 42, 86, 234, 247nn. 3, 4; in Parkman murder, 5. *See also* Birthmarks and skin marks; Brain; Cadavers; Eye imagery; Head; Mutilation

The Bonds of Womanhood (Cott), 117

Bontemps, Arna, 263n. 5

Boring, Edwin, xxii

Boseley, Sarah, 259n. 13

Bowdoin College, 21, 92

Bowery, Charity, 261n. 38

Bowles, Sam, 205

Bradley, David, 263n. 6

Bradstreet, Anne, xxi

Brain: Hawthorne's, 90; measurement of, 8, 13, 18, 53–54, 258n. 13; of white males, 64. *See also* Faculty psychology; Mind; Phrenologists

Brantley, Etheldred T., 49

Brazil, 229, 252n. 22

Broca, Paul: on blacks, 60–61; brain of, 1, 13; research of, 8–9, 54, 64, 96

Brodhead, Richard, 275n.11

Brown, Charles Brockden, xxiv, 28, 80, 135

Brown, J. W., 196

Brown, William Wells, 272n. 3

Brownson, Orestes, 169

Buchanan, Joseph Rhodes, 130, 131

Buck, Carrie, 7

Buck v. Bell, 7

Bue, A., 234–35

Bunyan, John, 125, 160, 166, 184

Dissociation. *See* Association

Dix, Dorothea, 33, 185–88, 197

Dr. Jekyll and Mr. Hyde (Stevenson), 231

Doerner, Klaus, 185

Donne, John, 217

Double standard, 116–17

Douglass, Frederick, 26n. 37; faculty psychology's impact on works of, xvi, xviii–xix, 138–50; as women's rights supporter, 117. *See also Heroic Slave*

Dryden, Edgar, xxv

Dunbar, Archibald, 46

Dunbar, William, 21, 46–47, 50, 64, 148

Duncanson (doctor), 196

Dungeons. *See* Burial; House metaphors

"Each and All" (Emerson), 98–103

Ebony magazine, 73

Edinburgh (Scotland), 21, 30, 53. *See also* Phrenological Society of Edinburgh

Educated Lives (Cooley), xxii

Edwards, Jonathan, 24, 217

Eighty Years and More (Stanton), 117

Einstein, Albert, 258n. 13

Elements of Mental Philosophy (Upham), 21, 23, 24, 211

Elements of the Philosophy of the Human Mind (Stewart), 160–61, 168–69

Eliot, T. S., xxi, 2, 232–34

Elkins, Stanley, 262n. 4

Ellis, Havelock, 166, 180

Ellison, Ralph, 71, 72, 76, 234

Emancipation Proclamation, 122

Embodied Selves (Taylor and Shuttleworth), xxii

Emerson, Bulkeley, 65

Emerson, Edward, 65

Emerson, Ralph Waldo, 58, 92, 210, 219, 265n. 18; as believer in intellect's control over emotions, xviii, 10, 59, 96, 97–104, 111, 122, 176–77; boat imagery of, 42, 51–52, 76–77, 106; and essay genre, 79; faculty psychology's impact on works of, xvi, 30, 96, 99, 234, 265n. 3; as narrator of whiteness, xxiv, 104; on real-

ism, 26; as Unitarian, 102, 203. *See also Specific works by*

Emotions (affections; animal propensities; appetitions; feelings; passions): appeals to, 116; domination of, over other parts of brain, xx, 141–42, 147, 168–69, 212–13, 240; as "feminine" or "black" faculty, xvii–xx, 11, 35–37, 51, 53, 54, 57–59, 63–64, 69, 81, 87, 96, 100, 103–14, 119–22, 126, 158–59, 175–76, 179–81, 185, 212, 213, 228, 267n. 15; as linked to intellect, 213, 215–19; monomania as excess of, 150, 263n. 9; need to control, 104–7, 119; as one part of mind's domain, xvi, 9, 21–22; and poetry, 79; as queen of the moral self, xx, 122–23, 176–77, 185, 187, 188, 223; in romance, 84. *See also* Pain; Remorse; Repression

The Emotions and the Will (Stewart), 213

Encyclopaedia Britannica, 255n. 4

"The Enfranchisement of Women" (Mill), 269n. 3

England, 55; Hawthorne on, 159–60; use of cadavers in, 3. *See also* Scotland

Enthusiasm. *See* Emotions; Madness: partial

E pluribus unum, xvii, 162

Esquirol, Jean Étienne Dominique, 40

Essay on Human Understanding (Locke), 90

Essays (as genre), 79

Eugenics, 136

Eve (Powers), 129

Examination of Phrenology (Sewall), 268n. 1

Examination of President Edwards's Inquiry on the Freedom of the Will (Day), 254n. 17

Eye imagery, 273n. 6; Emerson's "transparent," 86, 98–99, 101–2, 108; in Hawthorne's works, 37, 38, 91–93; in *Moby-Dick*, 89; phrenological associations with, 96, 112, 251n. 19; and physicians, 32–33, 36; Thoreau's use of, 107–9; and white penal code, 69; and whites, 100

Faculty psychology: anti-evolutionary bent of, xix, 155–77; conception of